A Memoir of My Former Self

A Memoir of My Former Self

A Life in Writing

SELECTED AND EDITED
BY NICHOLAS PEARSON

HILARY MANTEL

JOHN MURRAY

First published in Great Britain in 2023 by John Murray (Publishers)

1

A CIP catalogue record for this title
is available from the British Library

Hardback ISBN 9781399813884
Trade Paperback ISBN 9781399813891
ebook ISBN 9781399813914

Typeset in Minion Pro by
Palimpsest Book Production Ltd, Falkirk, Stirlingshire

Printed and bound in Great Britain by Clays Ltd, Elcograf S.p.A.

John Murray policy is to use papers that are natural, renewable and
recyclable products and made from wood grown in sustainable forests.
The logging and manufacturing processes are expected to conform
to the environmental regulations of the country of origin.

Carmelite House
50 Victoria Embankment
London EC4Y 0DZ

www.johnmurraypress.co.uk

John Murray Press, part of Hodder & Stoughton Limited
An Hachette UK company

Contents

CONTENTS

CONTENTS

Editor's Note

When Hilary Mantel died, unexpectedly, in Budleigh Salterton, Devon, in September 2022, she was a week away from moving to Kinsale, Ireland, a reconnection with her Irish Catholic roots. She and her husband Gerald McEwen had bought a house with views over the surrounding countryside. At the heart of this collection is a piece about the writer John McGahern, the great chronicler of Irish rural life in the shadow of the Roman Catholic Church. Their move to Ireland was also, in part, an attempt to re-establish European citizenship in the wake of Brexit. Here too can be found an essay about nationalism and identity, a theme that fed into Hilary's fiction, in particular her pinnacle achievement, the Wolf Hall Trilogy. Also in these pages is an essay about Jane Austen, a lifelong passion of hers. She had recently embarked on a novel, 'Provocation', that centred on the middle sister in *Pride and Prejudice*, Mary Bennett. At the time of her death, Hilary was a writer at the peak of her powers, one for whom fresh creative vistas were just opening up.

Reading the entirety of Hilary's writing for newspapers and periodicals in order to make this selection has been a revelation. Despite being her book editor for the last twenty years, much of what I read was new to me. Her wicked sense of humour, which was a mark of her in person, comes shining through many of these pieces. In fiction, writers tuck themselves away to various degrees, sometimes telling stories to escape themselves, even if they are hiding in plain sight. The story of Hilary Mantel is scattered throughout her novels. But in her journalism and essays a full and exhilarating self-portrait emerges: she isn't afraid to lay herself bare. This book is organised with that in mind – a patchwork of a life revealing itself.

Hilary loved newspapers. She talked about drenching herself in them. 'I can make any paper last two hours, and when I've finished, it's not fit for another hand; it looks as if a drunk has been making paper hats with it.' As she explained in her introduction to *Mantel Pieces*, a selection of writing from the *London Review of Books*, her early life as a novelist was not an income. The advance for her first novel was £2,000. She needed work to subsidise the slow process of writing fiction and it was to the periodicals she turned. She didn't feel qualified to do anything else. Auberon Waugh offered her a piece a month for the *Literary Review* for £40 a time. She wrote for Alan Ross at the *London Magazine*, but he paid her even less.

In 1986, Hilary submitted an essay to the Shiva Naipaul Prize, awarded to 'the writer best able to describe a visit to a foreign place or people. It is not for travel writing in the conventional sense, but for the most acute and profound observation of cultures and/or scenes evidently alien to the writer.' The judges included Martin Amis and the then editor of *The Spectator*, Charles Moore. Hilary's entry, 'Last Morning in Al Hamra', which describes her years living in Saudi Arabia, won the prize and was published in *The Spectator* in January 1987.

In 'Last Morning in Al Hamra', Hilary sets out her ambition. Expatriates tend to play out their lives in 'a plastic bubble of their own culture', protected from the world which is filtered through their own prejudices. But Hilary was an expatriate apart: she committed herself to look more closely, and this led her to get beyond the barriers that interfered with her strange surroundings and to a deeper understanding of herself: 'It needs only a pinprick of event, a chance germ, and the outside world has breached the defences. You know what you have avoided knowing; it is not the country that is foreign, it is not the climate or the people, it is you.'

On the back of this essay, Charles Moore offered Hilary the *Spectator* film column. She quickly learned to make notes in the cinema gloom and, over the next four years, would go on to write more than 160 reviews. Mickey Rourke was in his prime; suffice to say he didn't impress Hilary. Other actors did, and some extremely astute and often very funny reviews of films that have stood the test of time are included here. Hilary's first piece for the *New York*

Review of Books was published in 1989, and she continued to contribute there for the next twenty-five years. Also here are Hilary's BBC Reith Lectures, first broadcast in 2017, her meditations on how we interpret the past. 'Is there a firm divide between myth and history, fiction and fact, or do we move back and forth on a line between, our position indeterminate and always shifting?' she posited. As others have commented, the Reith Lectures are perhaps the finest distillation we have of the art of the historical novelist.

The majority of this collection comprises occasional pieces from various publications and in particular journalism published in the *Guardian*, for whom Hilary wrote for many years. Often, the starting point for these pieces is a fragment from her own life, continuing the story she began in her memoir, *Giving Up the Ghost*. The page was where she invented herself: from her unusual childhood to the years completing the Wolf Hall Trilogy, it was the place where she processed who she was and how she fitted into the world. What emerges is a portrait of Hilary Mantel's life in her own words, 'messages from people I used to be'.

Nicholas Pearson
July 2023

PART I

Once Upon a Life

On the One Hand

2007

Which hand do you write with? I asked myself this seemingly simple question when a diary column quoted Martin Amis, who was pondering the balance that writers seek between journalism and fiction. 'I think of writing journalism and criticism as writing left-handed,' Amis said, 'where the connection isn't to the part of me that novels come from.'

I've heard other writers use similar words and, being contrary and literal-minded, my reaction was to grab a pen in my left, my under-used hand, and see what came out. This is what my left hand wrote in the watches of last night:

> It's so slow, so uncontrolled . . . the least flourish skids all over the paper . . . 'W' I find is the very devil . . . tension transmits to your whole body, as if you were trying to write with your legs. No wonder it was so tiring to be at infant school. Noon, and you were done for.

If you persist – and 'each page', I wrote, 'is like a wall to be painted' – what comes out is a kind of irritable, condensed poetry. Your hand moves so slowly that you can keep changing your mind about what you are going to say, and sentences can end up anywhere at all. My stabs at the paper reminded me of Julius Caesar. As I was compelled to think one letter at a time, I found myself speculating on whether Shakespeare, who gave the Romans cloaks, also gave them clocks, and whether Caesar died with 'his mantle muffling up his face' or his mantel. I could have checked, but it was four in the morning, and the vexed small child I'd become couldn't reach the shelf with the *Complete Works*.

You can safely try this at home. You might get a message from your psyche – something strange, like the automatic writing supposed to be dictated by the dead. Thinking back over my career as a columnist, I know that my pieces came from my right hand – trained, clear, biddable and capable of keeping count. I wrote on the computer screen, but my dominant hemisphere was in charge, my right hand steering the topic. I could trust myself not to do anything wild. For four years in the 1980s, I wrote a film column for *The Spectator*. Eight hundred words were requested, and though from time to time I turned in 799, I was seldom expansive to the tune of 801. After a while I didn't even have to use a word count function. All my views – on anything – fitted into 800 words. 'Should we be in Iraq?' Eight hundred words. 'Is it cold out?' Eight hundred words.

Then, for a while, I wrote an opinion column, successfully concealing the fact that I had no opinions – or at least, not of the sort broadsheet editors want. If I were to be granted a coat of arms – an unlikely scenario, I admit – my motto would be 'It's not that simple'. Being a novelist has taught me, if I didn't know before, that almost all human situations are complex, ambiguous and shifting. There is always more information, and more emerging information, than you can process, but the crudities of public debate require oppositional postures, the drawing of lines in the dust. I wouldn't trust my left hand, even in what seemed a clear-cut controversy. My right hand, which is conventional, is, I hope, impeccably liberal, but what if my left hand turned out to be Ann Widdecombe, or to be a lyrical terrorist, seething with underdog's discontent?

Novelists, it seems to me, are the very last people who should be asked to comment on the news of the day, and sooner or later, when they have been pilloried for their views, most of them recognise this. It was senseless to ask them, as the media did, for their views on 9/11, or to ask them to take a line on any public catastrophe; why is their opinion, because it is dressed in fancy words, more valid than any other? I am not suggesting that artists should have no political engagement. Far from it: I can't imagine writing at all unless I were driven by political concerns, in the widest sense. But, while the columnist is retained to turn over clichés as fast as the stock at Topshop, the novelist should produce a couture response – lovingly tailored, personal, an unmistakable one-off.

Martin Amis recognised this, going on to say that novels and commentary come from different places within the writer. He quoted Norman Mailer on the creeping pace of fiction: 'you must let it weave and trickle through you'.

There's one good reason for novelists to write for the papers, and that's to subsidise, financially, the slow process of art. For sure, there are other benefits besides money – there's the publicity, the contacts. For many imaginative writers, working for the press is a fact of their life. But it's best not to like it too much. The desire to be a pundit must be suspect. If you have stamina and persistence, and your publisher sticks by you, you might, after forty years or so, frame a response to life that's worth the paper it's written on. You won't do it with the same hand, the same tools, that you use to produce journalism, criticism or reportage.

Fiction isn't made by scraping the bones of topicality for the last shreds and sinews, to be processed into mechanically recovered prose. Like journalism, it deals in ideas as well as facts, but also in metaphors, symbols and myths. It multiplies ambiguity. It's about the particular, which suggests the general: about inner meaning, seen with the inner eye, always glimpsed, always vanishing, always more or less baffling, and scuffled on to the page hesitantly, furtively, transgressively, by night and with the wrong hand.

I Once Stole a Book

2009

I once stole a book. It was really just the once, and at the time I called it borrowing. It was 1970, and the book, I could see by its lack of date stamps, had been lying unappreciated on the shelves of my convent school library since its publication in 1945. It was called *Moral Questions*. I was prepared at any time to give it back to a pupil who could show she needed it more than me.

Published in Dublin, it was a spin-off from a Catholic problem page in a weekly paper. Perplexed readers from all over Ireland would write in, and the author, the Very Rev. Michael O'Donnell, would set them straight. It was revealing, from the pagan redoubt of England, to see what troubled the Irish conscience. Whole novels seemed to lie between the lines. Must a man obey his parents all his life? Is it a sin to be hypnotised? 'Is it considered unlucky for two members of a family to get married inside the same year?' O'Donnell sees nothing against it; but when asked 'Should a woman get married if she dislikes children?' he reminds the questioner that she'd better get over herself before she trips down the aisle, as 'babies are essentially entailed in marriage'. He's surprisingly lenient to brides with a reason to blush; even if you've got a bit of a past, it's okay to wear 'a wreath and veil', provided your loss of virginity was managed discreetly and the whole congregation doesn't know; if, however, you're the parish bike, it would be a bit ridiculous. It's a yearning, melancholy, rural and lonely world, the world of *Moral Questions*: 'There is a certain Catholic boy I have longed to go with and marry. I have prayed night after night for this favour . . . Have I committed sin?'

I enjoyed the sex problems: 'Is it possible to get medical aid to prevent involuntary nocturnal happenings?' But my favourite section concerned the rules on fasting and abstinence. 'Is it permissible to

6

eat beans or other food, flavoured with meat, on Friday?' Absolutely not, snaps O'Donnell. 'Is turtle soup permitted?' Surprisingly, the answer is yes. Gelatine is allowed on Fridays, despite its animal origin. Beef dripping? Yes. Gravy? No. It's a minefield. Eight ounces of bread is advised during the Lenten fast; can you, begs one hungry man, toast the bread, make it weigh less, and so eat extra? This slacker's hopes are soon blighted. Yet the rules are inconsistent: 'throughout Ireland generally, butter is not allowed by custom at the evening meal; in Dublin, however, it is'. There's a general feeling that the sybarites in Dublin do themselves proud, and are always looking for a way to bend the rules. In fact, there is a prevailing weasel tone: just what can you get away with? Is it in order, on a fast day, to skip over diocesan boundaries to a more lax jurisdiction? 'A case might be made out in your favour,' O'Donnell smirks.

That the body of Mother Ireland, famished through the years thanks to potato blight and English wiles, was now persecuted with voluntary hunger . . . the idea brought tears to my eyes, though they were tears of laughter. I learned more about the land of my fore-fathers from *Moral Questions* than from any other source, if I except the novels of John McGahern. The sections on relations between the state and individuals were the most enlightening of all. 'What are the obligations of a judge who has received a bribe?' The English answer to this is shock: The what?! The what who has received a what? The Irish answer is, let's say, more circumstantial – though to be fair to the author, he doesn't recommend routine corruption of the bench, and he's not in favour of fiddling your income tax. What's striking is the efforts of his correspondents to get him on their side and obtain absolution in advance of the sin. County coun-cillors, it seems, are born to be bribed, and the general standard of civic conduct is that encapsulated by the popular electoral slogan, 'vote early, vote often'. As for misdemeanours such as peddling illicit liquor, poteen is sinful 'in certain localities', but not others – a baffling answer which suggests O'Donnell runs a still himself. But he's not a man who haunts the dog track; he seems surprised when asked if it's a sin 'to have two dogs known by the same name, and have one of them run when the other is expected'.

Who, I wondered, was Michael O'Donnell DD? A genius,

according to the book's introduction. Not only did he discourse in 'vivid, ironic and devastatingly accurate . . . Latin', but he knew canon law so well that if all the texts were burned, he could reconstruct them out of his own head. Born in Donegal in 1881, he must have cut a fine figure. 'He was, as his appearance bore evidence, of the princely line of the O'Donnells.' Poignant, that touch of snobbery. The rag-tag working-class Catholics among whom I grew up, crammed into black, English terraces and fodder for the textile mills, could go on pretending that we were all princes and princesses, in the never-never land where justice is done. The nuns who taught my generation made a sharp and early distinction, in the schoolroom, between nice, clean children from small families, and those raga-muffins who were number six or seven, and who turned up late and dirty-faced, wearing the hand-me-downs of their tribe. Father O'Donnell was firm on the matter, like any priest of his era: 'the Church recommends continence or abstinence, not contraception'.

Those were the days, before feminism, before Aids, before the sex abuse scandals, when I could laugh at what enrages me now: the hypocrisy, the waste, the damage. During my A-level year I had such pleasure from *Moral Questions* that, being the school librarian, I issued it to myself on lifelong loan. But later I lent it to a friend; and somehow it found its way back to a bookshelf congenial to it, by the pious Catholic hearthside of her in-laws. Many years later I needed it, to help me write my novel *Fludd*. I wanted to quote it verbatim; it was beyond me to make this stuff up. Drawing on the network of influence that spreads outwards from a master criminal such as myself, I activated a daughter of the house to travel from her home in Liverpool, divert the attention of her parents, and slip the book into her travelling bag. In this way it came home to the woman who appreciates it most, and who keeps it to hand in case of sudden difficulty. After all, suppose I had to carry out an emer-gency baptism, and no water was to hand? 'In a crisis we are allowed to use any liquid that, even probably, reaches the standard. Milk must be excluded; beer and tea are doubtful . . .' Use your discretion, the priest urges; no doubt there's many a sickly infant, born around 1945, whose papist life began with a sign of the cross and a splash of stout.

Exam Fever

2009

Nostalgia takes some perverse forms. I saw a book for sale the other week called *The Eleven-Plus Book: Genuine Exam Questions from Yesteryear*. Are there really people who would buy this and chortle over it as they recalled the torments of their childhood? Did they enjoy it so much that they want to relive it? Those clammy nightmares, where an illegible test paper and a broken pencil are set before you, and the clock is set ticking – do these people wake up next day and say, 'I had such a happy dream!'

I remember a good deal about the day I took my 11-plus. Subject to a special playtime, let out briefly between papers while the rest of the school was shut away, we careered around the asphalt, boys and girls together in one febrile whirlwind, crazed with adrenaline and caught up in a riot of chase and capture where everyone was chasing and no one was caught; and the dour nun who was in charge of us, I remember, stood goggle-eyed on the steps, wondering if we were going to trample her, or set fire to the school. It was everything to me, whether I passed or failed, and I remember being ill with nerves when the day for the results came – actually feverish, so that I had to be kept at home, and the result brought by a friend. Some orange squash, my mother said, should be given to the messenger who brought the good news; I remember how, when I tried to pour it, my hands shook and the fat neck of the bottle went chink, chink on the rim of the glass.

I don't, in fact, recall any of the questions. And nothing would induce me to relive those days by buying a book of them. As it turned out, I was good at passing exams, but I always wondered how much this meant. Once they became a matter of writing essays, my blinding verbal facility – no credit to me at all, I had done nothing to acquire it – meant that I sounded as if I knew what I was talking about, even when I didn't. You would have thought examiners would have seen right through me. At O-level we got a strange religious knowledge paper with questions that actually required thinking for oneself, an activity in which we had never been encouraged. Prepared only to regurgitate the trite little facts we had been taught, we were startled, and an impulse of bewilderment – I could feel it in my fingertips – ran right around the exam room; but I came out confident, because I reckoned that any fifteen-year-old who could, like me, wield the word 'parthenogenesis', was bound to get to the top of the heap. Regrettably, I was right. It didn't seem fair that words could do so much. At maths, of course, I was an abject failure. The simplest equation had me stumped.

In the sixth form, freed from numbers, my flannelling capacity only increased. If there had been an A-level in bullshit, I'd have got some sort of national award. My teachers' only anxiety, in the run up to exams, seemed to be that I might never stop writing – that I might simply refuse, and use up all the spare paper in the exam hall, and sit scribbling till darkness fell and they had to call the fire brigade to remove me, like someone who needed to be cut out of the wreckage of a car. Did I know, they asked me, that I would have only forty minutes for each answer? Yes, I knew, and I knew precisely how much persiflage I could pack on to each side of paper. In an attempt to slow me down, perhaps, they found an extra exam that no one else was sitting, in spoken English, and sent me off on the train with my bag of words to deploy them on some examiners whom I would, given the nature of the thing, meet face to face. I was not afraid, but by the time I left, it's possible that they were.

When I look back, it seems as if between the ages of twelve and twenty-one I was a trembling voyager on a sea of black ink, living in a permanent state of dread, because the consequences of failure, as they were represented to me, were unbearable. I was familiar, then as now, with every trick for procrastination, constantly guilty, constantly fretting that what I had crammed into my head would not be enough, and waking myself up at 3 a.m. to get in some extra hours of study. Once I had graduated from university I could have changed – other people managed it – but after a year freed from the desk and the library lamp I felt so useless, so futile and distressed, that I bought some more ink and paper and started writing a very big book. I know that, despite my bluffing abilities, I did work hard at school, much harder than I needed to, and I know that when the results came, I always felt as if I might be an imposter.

Do other people feel this? Is it a girl thing? These days I'm always glad when autumn comes, when the exam season is over, and the poor teenagers have had their results ridiculed, and everyone is bedded down, or not, in their university or college. In the lead-up, while the discussion of declining standards is going on, I'm subject to flares of retrospective panic. In recent years, I've found a new reason for it. I've asked myself whether going into school to collect A-level results in June was better or worse than waiting till this month to know if I've found favour with the Man Booker judges. In schooldays, there was a friend to share the crawling apprehension, and go to the pub with afterwards. Until recently, the Booker business was simple enough to handle. The committee's workings were private – leaks apart – until they issued a shortlist. Your publisher called you, sounding like an undertaker, to say that you weren't on it. You swallowed hard, and got on with your next book. Only once has my routine varied; when Adam Thorpe's *Ulverton* was omitted in 1992, I cried, because if *Ulverton* wasn't good enough, I couldn't think what you'd have to do.

But now, with the issue of an official longlist in July, the waiting consumes the summer, and by the time the shortlist is released you simply don't know what to do with yourself. You realise that, in effect, by becoming a writer you have agreed to sit exams all your life. There was a party on the evening of the shortlist announcement this week, one of those occasions where authors show their public faces; at previous prize ceremonies, where they didn't win, they have perfected fixed expressions of sickly sanctity or amused indifference. Inside (unless they are very unlike me) they feel like mad axemen. They would be glad to have the chance to trample a nun or set fire to a school. The more public the process is, the more cruel. Perhaps it's better, though, than sitting alone, tapping your fingers and shuffling your feet, waiting to know whether words have failed you.

Where Do Stories Come From?

2009

I once mentioned Charles Lamb's dictum that no one ever put down a newspaper without a feeling of disappointment. I didn't admit, at that point, that I am the exception; that the paper has never been printed that didn't make me happy. I understand the despondency and lassitude that overtake the reader at the repetitious parade of human folly, and the evidence, reinforced on a daily basis, of nature's malignity and the indifference of the gods; but me, I just like the small ads. I pick up the freesheets in towns I'm passing through, to find out about their local version of a good time, and what they buy and sell to each other, what rows have broken out in the council chamber, which luxury sauna has got some all-new blondes, and who wants planning permission for a conservatory roughly the size of their house. I like reading the 'In Memoriam' verses for people I've never known, and feeling sorry they're dead, if only because their relicts have such a woolly idea of scansion.

It was in the small ads of a local paper in Norfolk that I saw for sale three bridesmaid's dresses, identical, to fit sizes 24, 26 and 10; ever since, I have been imagining the photographs from the original wedding, and wondering if such bridesmaids ever occurred for a second time, or if the dresses are still hanging in a closet. When we lived in Sunningdale, a respectable parish, we had a dodgy car dealer in the area; he would add, to his description of every clocked and clapped-out vehicle he was trying to flog, the claim 'drives superb'. This term long ago entered our family lexicon. 'How's my new chapter?' I might ask my husband nervously. 'Drives superb,' he'll say. If next day I realise that it's broken down on the hard shoulder, emitting sparks and stenches, I blame myself for expecting a bargain in the first place; smooth engines and smooth writing don't come easy or cheap.

When it comes to the national press, I can make any paper last two hours, and when I've finished it's not fit for another hand; it looks as if a drunk has been making paper hats with it. I read all those parts of a newspaper that aren't news and aren't features and aren't really anything else but listings of one type or another: church services and engagements and wills, encapsulated yearnings for love and offspring, and traces of lives well spent. If the *Guardian* has a fault, it's that it doesn't offer enough of this peculiar entertainment and I have to supplement it with other papers if I want to know, for instance, the Princess Royal's daily engagements, or keep up with the Duchess of Kent through the efficient track-and-trace system provided by the Court Circular; not a Lord Lieutenant in any county shakes hands with her, but I know about it. Through close study of the 'Birthdays', I am aware, as others may not be, that Charles Moore and Jimmy Savile share a natal day, though not a year. I know of all the latest Crispins, Chloes and Clementines born into the chattering classes. I am particularly fond of the column called 'Appointments in The Clergy'; one week recently, I actually knew one of the clergymen mentioned, a coincidence which caused me to feel airy and full of grace, as if I'd just been baptised and got a second chance.

So I need not explain why I was reading a list of school reunions, when my eye fell on what follows: the address of a girls' school in Llandudno, and the notification that it was the 'Final Old Girls' Reunion'. Next April it will occur; the information tolled in my ears: why is it the last, how can anyone know? It may be that the organiser has just got tired of doing all the work: that fewer and fewer old girls are turning up, that some of them are shrill and grubby and have vodka bottles in their bags, and piercings, and toyboys in tow: or that Llandudno is just too hard to get to. But sadder explanations suggest themselves. Are there only two old girls left, and has one of them been given a bad prognosis? I can't help thinking what it would be like, two sassy old dames crumbling a final scone together, replacing in its saucer the teacup drained of Darjeeling, polishing their noses with a crumpled tissue: 'Well, Blinky, old thing . . .' 'Well, Nodders, old girl . . .'; brushing crumbs from their laps, laying down the final butter knife, stepping into separate taxis to go their final ways. Surely there's a short story in it. But it's not mine, is it? It's one for Jane Gardam.

Who owns stories and where do they come from? The last part of the question is one that readers ask all the time; writers are very poor at giving the answer. We don't like to say 'from the personal columns', or 'from the small ads', even if it's true. It sounds too obvious, too much like the way people assume authors operate. For years my family has supposed that in restaurants and pubs I eavesdrop on other tables, and so pick up ideas.

Only recently I've found the courage to say that in fact I don't hear well, and that my expression of rapt attention is my effort to prepare for a hard question, such as 'Still or sparkling?' Stories must be happening all the time and I simply don't hear them. I am not a ready writer of short fiction and I have almost to trip over a story before I recognise it. I tend to assume that whatever strikes me belongs somewhere inside a novel, and will have to hang about in my notebook for that novel to come along: which makes, I can tell you, for a prodigiously slow rate of progress at turning life into ink.

I can sometimes see a poem, but I don't have the craft and skill to make it work. Requests to 'write a fairy story' strike me dumb; aren't fairy stories just there? Yet I did once manage it, because I did it without thinking. I didn't recognise the result as belonging to me; it seemed like a stone kicked, or flicked off from my heel, into an underground stream. I have imagined whole novels (and sometimes written them) while wondering if they belonged to someone else: Beryl Bainbridge, mostly. BB gave me courage when I was a beginning writer; I used to think well, if she can get away with this outrageous stuff, maybe I can sneak in more of the same kind? The question about 'your influences', so often posed to writers, is hard to answer, however great the desire to give an honest reply. You'd like to know, yourself, why you do things the way you do. It hardly seems graceful to admit that, if you take your ambition from Shakespeare, you take your inspiration from 'Flats to Let'.

Persons from Porlock

2009

Last week I had a surreal conversation with my hairdresser, a welcome variation on the usual 'Have you got a holiday planned?' She was telling me of her love of Exmoor and how she'd like to move to the nearby coast. 'Porlock's perfect,' she said. 'And I don't think it's got a hairdresser. So, I could be in there.' She frowned. 'Have you ever heard of Porlock?'

Into my mind flitted a file of Persons, dropping by to have highlights. I suppose most readers (though perhaps not most hairdressers) know how Coleridge, waking from what we take to be an opium-induced slumber, scribbled down some lines of the poem he'd been composing in his sleep, but was interrupted 'by a person on business from Porlock'; when he returned to work, 'Kubla Khan' had evaporated, he said, except for 'some eight or ten scattered lines and images'. Ever since this mishap in 1797, writers have grumbled about the crass interrupters who wreck their inspiration; they probably grumbled before, but they didn't have a name for the phenomenon. No one has ever identified the nature of the Person's business. Some believe it was Coleridge's dealer dropping by with his narcotics supplies, in which case it was doubly ungrateful of him to complain. Thomas de Quincey is said to have originated this theory, which I like very much; I came across it on the internet, which is the same as saying 'I read it in the *Beano*.'

Stevie Smith had Coleridge bang to rights:

> Coleridge received the Person from Porlock
> And ever after called him a curse,
> Then why did he hurry to let him in?
> He could have hid in the house.*

---

* Stevie Smith, 'Thoughts About the Person from Porlock', *New Selected Poems* (New Directions Publishing, 1988).

She echoes my own idea of the matter. We all want interrupting, saving from ourselves, from the sentence, the paragraph, the chapter that's going nowhere: at least, going nowhere on that particular day. 'Oh Person from Porlock come quickly / And bring my thoughts to an end.' If Coleridge were alive now, he'd have rubbed his eyes and sprung to his desk to check his emails; having chucked out his spam, chortled over the ejokes sent on by old Wordsworth, and bashed out the replies to several footling enquiries about his availability to review the latest odes, he'd be well and truly free of that pesky poem going around in his head. If the problem is a whole novel that won't work but won't go away, the modern writer can take on a Project from Porlock. A film script is a good way of diverting yourself. You will have endless meetings with screeching optimists; they make such a change from publishers, who are always depressed. It's almost guaranteed to come to nothing, so you won't need another Project from Porlock to save you from having to deliver the first draft; besides, while the film industry lawyers are poring over the small print of the contracts, you may well have solved your initial problem, or just grown old and died.

Why does a writer have to divert herself, pray for interruptions or devise them herself? Sometimes because you have promised a novel before it's ready to be written – which is to say, you're not ready to write it, though when you sign the contract, you honestly think you are. You may know the characters, have the plot all worked out; you just don't know what it's about. There may be something else you have to do before you can push through the enterprise. It may be just a good deal of thinking. Or it may be that you need to write another, different book, which bridges the gap between where you are now and the self who is ready to keep her initial promise. That said, why is the act of writing, the moment-by-moment compression of the keys, so dreaded by so many writers? Why do they have to interpose opium, or alcohol, or some other stimulant or sedative, before they can perform their trade's basic function? You don't hear of accountants who can't open a spreadsheet, or farmers who take against fields.

The experienced writer says to the anguished novice: just do it; get something, anything, onto the screen or page, just establish a flow of words, and criticise them later. You give this advice but can't always take it. You dread setting off down any one narrative path, because you know your choice will make most of the others impossible. Select one, write it, and it begins to seem in some sense preordained, natural, correct; the other options fade from memory. Fear of commitment lies behind the fear of writing. Writers, as generations of jealous spouses have learnt to their cost, are not naturally monogamous. We don't want to choose; we want to keep open all the possibilities, fill a lifetime with fresh and less-than-final versions.

What is worst, what is most wretched, is being almost ready to write. A horrible day dawns when the prospect of writing hangs over you like a cloud from which you are afraid you might never emerge. You know you will do it, you know you will commit. You know that by the end of the day you will be wrung out, speechless, barely human. Recently I can't go into the dull walled garden of the flats where I live, because I've haunted it – I can see the spectre of myself walking round and round in the rain, last summer, trying to write the last pages of my novel: following my ghostly characters, Tudor lawyers walking arm in arm in the drizzle, talking about the trial of Thomas More. Like a dogged clerk I came after them with my notebook; when it started to rain hard, they went inside, and so did I, they brushing the raindrops from their velvet caps and I making my sick way back to the keyboard, conscious that these are the last pages, this is the last chance, if it's not right now it probably never will be. I admit that, by that stage, if a person had come between me and the last page, I'd simply have cut his head off.

The real puzzle about Coleridge's story is that 'Kubla Khan' lacks nothing as it stands. So why did he need an excuse? We're all geniuses in our dreams, though it happened that Coleridge was one in waking life too. The reader can't see where the lost lines would fit, or what they would add. Was Samuel T. paid by the word? Was he knuckling his forehead: fifty-four lines, call that a poem? There's a possibility always worth considering in cases of 'writer's block': could it be that you've said all you have to say? It would be cruel to suggest this to a practitioner in the grip of the condition. But, unfortunately for writers, there's no intellectual equivalent of the sexual climax; they don't always know when they've finished.

Which Bits of English History Are My History?

2009

'You were an answer,' my husband said, earlier this summer, as I came in one evening. I glowed. Who would not want to be an answer? 'Although,' he said, 'it was wrong.'

It turned out he'd been watching a book quiz in which the panel had to identify the voice of a woman author. 'Oh, a northern accent!' someone said. 'That will be Hilary Mantel.' In fact, it was Pat Barker. I sniggered at this story. Northerners all sound the same to those from the south, though they wouldn't confuse Essex with Somerset. It's more than thirty years since I've lived in the north, and people are still asking me where I come from. I don't worry about having a regional accent. I accept that to an RP speaker my broad slow vowels are evidence of stupidity. What bothers me is that nowadays, to a northern ear, I sound southern: that is to say, insufferably posh and affected. I don't belong anywhere. And this gives me a problem: which bits of English history are my history?

This summer we – that is, we in the south – have been celebrating with a flourish of exhibitions and talks the 500th anniversary of the accession of Henry VIII. All over the region, slightly shame-faced actors have been impersonating the golden boy, cavorting on horseback amid hamburger-gnawing crowds, while indoors in some vaulted hall another unconvincing costume party bobs around in their twentieth Tudor dance of the afternoon. They are impersonating our ancestors having fun; even if it's embarrassingly contrived, we understand the intention. But if you come from the north, what's to celebrate? What's Henry's legacy? Just a set of smashed-up abbeys, which look like the last traces of a vanished civilisation. You can't even say 'He came, he saw, he knocked things flat', because he left the demolition to other people; he'd been king for more than thirty years before he went up the country on progress, to see how the other half lived. And even then, like southern tourists today, he went to York.

When I grew up, an uneasy mix of Derbyshire and Irish, it seemed to me that whoever owned 'our island story', it wasn't me. It was Wasp history, it was southern, and of course it was masculine, though I don't think that aspect of it worried me till the 1970s came and I had my consciousness raised. When I began to write historical fiction, it was as natural to me to set my story in France as to write about any part of the English past. The French Revolution seemed to me so central to the modern world that I was surprised, when my book was published, to find that it was marginal to the perception of most readers. I knew that English people on the whole didn't know much about the revolution, being stuck in the Scarlet Pimpernel stage, but I didn't know they regarded it as essentially foreign; I thought we all owned it. I assumed that in future I would romp about the world, appropriating other people's revolutions for my books. But recently, after many years of hesitation, I made a move on to the centre ground and wrote about Henry VIII's court and its politics. How did this inner revolution occur? It's probably the result of age. When I started writing *Wolf Hall*, Tony Blair was still in office, and when the prime minister is younger than you, you feel wearily experienced, trodden-in rather than trodden down, and entitled to identify with the ruling elite.

When I say England, in this context, I'm not indulging in that smug slip of the pen that stretches 'England' to mean Britain. I am conscious of how parochial my novel is. I have learnt rather a lot about Tudor Wales, but Ireland is just a distant clamour, a clash of arms, an off-stage calamity. Henry's military commander Thomas Howard, when invited to go over yet again and pacify Hibernia, said he'd only do it if they built a bridge so he could come home for weekends without getting his feet wet. As for Scotland, I barely give it a mention in my book, so I'll have some apologising to do at the Edinburgh book festival; my excuse is that the Scottish politics of the era are so violently interesting that if I once began on them, they would monopolise the plot. As for the north of England, in my novel we only hear about it; you go there under protest and get out quick; it's where rebels and traitors live. In my next book, the sequel to my first Tudor effort, I have to persuade my readers that the broken stones of the abbeys can lie, that their pathos is unearned, and that dissolving the monasteries was a reasonable thing to do.

When the process is shown in period drama, brutes gallop in mob-handed, smiting shaven pates, slashing and looting; Thomas Cromwell and Oliver Cromwell are thoroughly confused. People may be surprised to learn that the dissolution of the monasteries began before the Reformation, that it was an intricate legal process, that in each case it took months and sometimes years of negotiation: that the monks got either parishes or pensions, and that many of them shed their habits and shot out of the cloister with the alacrity of men who no longer had skirts to trip them up. I might be able to persuade my southern readers of this. But I can feel, even now, the stony resistance of the reader north of the Trent.

Just now my imagination can only take in Tudor things: pictures, buildings, poems. So I'm not clear why, a couple of weeks ago, a gorgeous English summer day found me tramping over the site of the battle of Hastings. As a child, I would have taken only a polite interest in the fate of those broad, blithe acres of East Sussex. I wouldn't have felt any involvement, any sense of danger, any emotional identification with those waiting for the invader. And as for Harold's earlier engagement with the Vikings at Stamford Bridge, that was in Yorkshire, and on my side of the Pennines Yorkshire existed only as the butt of jokes. I wondered that day, looking from Battle Abbey down the tea-shoppe-lined street, whether we are still two nations, unable to imagine each other historically. It seems absurd, in such a tiny country. I accept that trans-Pennine animosity is not what is was, but perhaps school-children should be sent on north–south exchanges. I know many people who have travelled the world, but hardly know the north. They may have been to the Highlands. They have visited Edinburgh, the Lakes, York, and other spots you find pictured on fudge tins. They haven't been to Manchester, because they don't think it would be interesting. A new art gallery might magnetise them, or some quayside development that, frankly, could be anywhere. But the industrial legacy means only ugliness and deprivation, other people's misfortune and other people's foul weather. It's not long since the national forecasters used to say: 'Looking at tomorrow, you can see this band of rain coming in – but don't worry, it's moving north.'

Blot, Erase, Delete

2016

I have been trying to think back to what it was like when I was seen and not heard: when I was too young to talk; when nothing was transmitted but everything received; when I had the luxury of listening without a reply needed; when I could judge without responsibility; when I simply existed, with no further action required. When you are dumb, the world puts on a show. No one knows what you are thinking, or even if you are thinking, before you are old enough to speak.

It's said I prolonged this situation, to the point of enquiry: 'Doesn't she talk, what's wrong with her?' But parents are unreliable witnesses. They make up stories about your infancy to suit what they have decided is your character. Also – though they would never admit this – they mix up siblings, and misreport their early words and deeds. I could flatter myself by claiming I waited to speak till I had something to say. But I guess our first words are stupid ones. And throughout childhood I felt the attraction of sliding back into muteness. If they asked a silly question at school – what I thought was a silly question – I just didn't answer. I kept up this recalcitrance till I was eleven. There was a schoolroom crime called 'dumb insolence', but I don't think anyone mistook my silence for that offence. I looked so sorry about it, I suppose.

In those days I was groaning under a burden of truth. In my family, as in so many, an active censorship bore on both past and present. There were things you could say in the house, but not out of the house; perhaps there was a third category of things you could say in the garden. It is hard for a child to learn where the boundaries are, and also difficult not to be in the wrong place when adults utter what they regret. Aged eight or so, I seemed to lose my hearing for a year. Anything you said, I asked in a tone of hard incredulity to have repeated: 'What?' I must have developed a protective filter, because in time I could hear again. The voice continued to say 'What?' but it spoke inside. There were things you knew but must study to unknow, and things that could only be said allegorically. By way of allegory, a child might have a symptom. My brother couldn't catch his breath. No chance of saying the wrong thing, when you couldn't even breathe.

The time comes when you take up the pen. It is mightier than the sword, you hear. In my memoir *Giving Up the Ghost*, I wrote about the child's toy called the 'magic slate', which enabled you to write with a stylus on a sheet of transparent film, and have your writing appear – grey and faint, easily erased by pulling up a tab. I entered into a paradise of free expression, but: 'One day the light caught the surface at a certain angle, and when I held the slate away from me and turned it I saw that the pen left marks in the plastic sheet, like the tracks of writing on water. It would have been possible, with some labour and diligence, to discover the words even after they had been erased. After that I left aside the magic slate . . .'

At my primary school we wrote with nib pens. Ink was poured into wells which were silted, muddy at the bottom; only the top, to the depth of a fingertip, remained liquid, and if you plunged your pen further in, the nib emerged fuzzy and clogged by the accretions of the generations: the shavings of cedar pencils formed the grit at the bottom of the sump, together with hair torn from the exasperated head, dust motes that had floated in the sunlight before the Great War, compacted paper balls soaked by our grandparents some idle afternoon. Maybe this was why, when I began to write, I wrote like an Edwardian. Some children – some girls – had blotting paper and applied it every three or four words, so that their lines appeared deliberately antiqued, ready-faded, half-expunged. Their process drove me into a frenzy of irritation and dislike: the slow, painful scratch of metal as it snagged rough paper; the goggle-eyed stare at the result, as if the writer had insulted herself; the slow reaching for the pink sheet, the emphatic, vengeful pressure on the page.

I never trusted the blotters. Now they remind me of those people who jump up and wash straight after sex. Ink is a generative fluid.

If you don't mean your words to breed consequences, don't write at all; the only tip you can give to a prospective writer is 'try to mean what you say'. We feel protected when we write on a screen, but (as with the magic slate) we can be fooled. Erasure seems simple – blink and it's gone, overwrite the line. But nothing ever really goes away. The internet keeps regurgitating you. You can't bury or burn your traces. They won't be nibbled by rats, who used to love vellum, or munched by tropical ants, or consumed in the small fires that afflicted archives every few years, leaving scorched and partial truths for historians to frown over. You could get nostalgic about holes in the ground, graves for data – about the old days when they buried bad news. It seems you can't hide, repent or change your mind. As soon as you sit before the screen you start haunting yourself.

There was a time, early in my high-school life, when crossing-out was forbidden. No tearing out of pages either. You must show your workings. The painful steps towards error must be clear to all. I think it was a rule made so that our exercise books wouldn't fall apart, but at the time it seemed like a particularly peevish form of persecution and control. When my enemies raided my desk, they attacked my exercise books, but it was the blank sheets they tore out; my enemies were not very bright. At some stage I must have made a commitment to commitment, and to stand by my mistakes, because I noticed that only bubbleheads used washable, bright blue ink, and took to Permanent Black. Accidents will happen, of course. Probably people now won't have breathed it in or seen it: the bitter, metallic, ineradicable spill.

In the early 1980s I went to live in Saudi Arabia, which was then the Empire of Deletion, the world capital of crossing-out. Pre-internet, there was only print to be censored, though certain public sculptures had been removed. There was a street informally known as Thumb Street, though the thumb had been taken down long before we came; it was in case people had the idea of worshipping it, I suppose, for it was irreligious to represent the human form. In those days if you bought an imported newspaper or magazine, the censors had worked through it carefully. They crayoned black drapery across the welling breasts of starlets. They hampered the muscled legs of women athletes by giving them skirts, rudely triangular and sloping at the hem, their brio and haste and hatred and lust all skidding across the picture in big black lines from a permanent marker.

The effort was touching: the meticulous thoroughness. The authorities could have banned the newspaper. But that would attract comment. Besides, an army of highly trained human erasers must have work. I imagined grey hangars on the desert's fringe, where the contaminated material was carried in and out by men in protective suits, moving silently across the roads of the kingdom in unmarked vans. Probably it wasn't like that; but there was no way of finding out how it was. Some of the erasers were charged with reading the back of food packets for recipes, and eradicating the word 'pork' wherever it occurred, so removing from the world the very idea of pig. Keep the dietary laws, by all means, but what is forbidden goes trit-trot through your dreams; pigs came to them by night, I think, pink or piebald, hairy or smooth, huffing in their ears and rolling in their duvets. Yet the effort of deletion persisted. The existence of women was tackled by placing them under black curtains. The existence of Israel was tackled by simply leaving it off the maps.

This army of erasers came back to my mind at the time of the EU referendum, when the urban legend spread that votes for 'Leave' would be rubbed out by an army of secret service personnel, and Brexiteers began to take their own pens into the polling booth. How we laughed! But then as soon as the result was in, millions signed a petition to rub it out and do it again. The *bien pensant* suggested the result was not binding, but advisory – an opinion they would hardly have offered had the vote gone the other way. For a long time, people have suspected that voting was futile; that politicians did not mean their promises even at the time they made them; that even though they were printed, recorded, filmed, painted on vans and driven about the streets, they could be blinked away, vanished at will. Sometimes people speak allegorically, through folk-panics: we make our mark, but they just rub us out. I thought it was odd, when the MP Jo Cox was murdered in the street, that campaigning in the referendum was suspended. She was a politician – and so they stopped politics? If a poet died, would you say, 'Out of respect, ease off the verse?' If a historian died, would you try to stop events?

A better tribute to her would have been to continue the campaign, interposing a day in which all parties spoke the truth. But the world is not ready for that kind of memorial. It might violate some untested physical law, so we end in mass drownings or a ball of fire.

It has always been axiomatic that when the dying speak, they cannot lie. I knew a man whose mother told him, as she lay dying, who his real father was: like a woman in a Victorian melodrama. She might as well have climbed out of bed and kicked his feet from under him. The truth was far too late to do him any good, and just in time to plunge him into misery and confusion and the complex grief of a double loss. Some truths have a sell-by date. Some should not be uttered even by the dying. Some cannot be uttered. When a victim of Henry VIII faced the headsman, the standard scaffold speech praised the king: his justice, his mercy. You didn't mean this, but you had to think about the people left behind: some flattery might help them. Oppressors don't just want to do their deed, they want to take a bow: they want their victims to sing their praises. This doesn't change, and it seems there are no new thoughts, no new struggles with censorship and self-censorship, only the old struggles repeating: half-animated corpses of forbidden childhood thoughts crawling out of the psychic trenches we have dug for them, and recurring denials by the great of the truths written on the bodies of the small.

I have ninety-seven notebooks in a wooden box. I do not count them as suppressed volumes. I work on the principle that there is no failed work, only work pending: that there is nothing I won't say, only what I haven't said yet. In my novel in progress I have written, 'If you cannot speak truth at a beheading, when can you speak it?' A notebook written eight years ago says, 'I am searching for a place where the truth can be uttered: a place, I mean, that is not an execution ground.'

Last Morning in Al Hamra

1987

There are children, frail and moribund, who live inside plastic bubbles; their immune systems have not developed, and so they have to be protected from the outside world, their air specially filtered, and their nourishment – you cannot call it food – passed to them through special ducts, by gloved and sterile hands.

Professional expatriates live like that. Real travellers are vulnerable creatures, at once attracted and repelled by the cultures they move amongst, but expatriates are hard to reach, hard to impress; they carry about with them the plastic bubble of their own culture, and nothing touches them until it has been filtered through the protective membrane of prejudice, the life-support system that forms their invisible excess baggage when they move on, from one contract to the next, to another country and another set of complaints.

Still, expats do travel sometimes. Their journeys can be very small; a chance word, a look. It needs only a pinprick of event, a chance germ, and the outside world has breached the defences. You know what you have avoided knowing; it is not the country that is foreign, it is not the climate or the people, it is you.

When I went to Saudi Arabia, three years ago, I was driven from King Abdul Aziz International Airport to an apartment block off Jeddah's Medina Road; it was night, and I could not make sense of the city, and the next day produced no enlightenment. When you arrive in Saudi Arabia you cease to travel, in the ordinary sense. To move between cities you need letters from a higher authority, a sort of internal passport, and these are not granted without good reason; women, also, need written permission from their husbands if they want to make a journey. Within the city the situation is not much easier. Women may not drive, and they don't walk in the streets

26

either, if they know what's good for them. Nor do men, except under the pressure of extreme poverty; these streets are not made for walking. They are made for the car, and the cars eat up the people. Someone told me that every year more people are killed on the roads of the Kingdom than are born there; it seems a dubious statistic, but it may have poetic truth.

The city is cut up into its ghettos; palaces for the rich Hejazi merchant families, and for the princelings of the House of Saud; compounds behind walls for the *khawajas*, the light-haired ones, the managers and experts; prefab work camps for the Asiatics, the labour force, the people the Saudi newspapers call Third Country Nationals. It is not easy to move between these ghettos. Still, there are the small, telling, journeys that no regime can prohibit; I went upstairs to meet my neighbour.

Our first flat was uptown, spacious, none too salubrious. It was what people called 'very Saudi'; there was frosted glass in all the windows, to preserve the privacy of the inhabitants and the modesty of their women. Downstairs was a noisy Sudanese family, whose visitors rang our gatebell at all hours. Their dinner, a goat, was often tethered below my window, and I could see it if I went out on to the balcony; different dinners, some perhaps more succulent than others, but with the same way of twisting about at the end of the ropes, like people already hanged. Sometimes I thought of sneaking downstairs and cutting the dinner free, but where would it run? Only to death on the adjacent six-lane highway.

The cities of Arabia are all alike today; skyscrapers, fast roads, municipal greenery nourished at vast expense; a seafront called the Corniche, Al Kournaich, the Cornish Road. The joyless, oily sea is lined by vast amusement parks, where grave sheikhs and their male offspring test their nerve on the roller coasters; the women, in chaperoned parties, shop for furs and diamonds in vast glittering malls, in the Schönbrunns and Winter Palaces of the consumer's art. There is a pervading smell of sewage, a burning, used-up wind. Petrol is paid for out of small change. At the sliproad by the Marriott Hotel, Black children dash into the traffic and trail rags across your windscreen, tapping on the glass and holding out their hands for money. Sometimes you might see an old man sitting on the sidewalk, his thobe dirty, his knees pulled up to his ears, staring out at the stream of traffic. The pace of life is murderous. Each intersection has its little massacre.

The frosted glass seemed to be cutting me off from real life; one day drifted into the next. If I went out on to the balcony, men congregated in the street to stare at me and make easy-to-understand gestures, multicultural invitations, monoglot expressions of contempt. We moved downtown then, to another flat in Al Hamra; this is the city's best district, where the embassies congregate. It was a newish block of four flats; some Sri Lankan Christians, a well-connected Pakistani couple, and a Saudi accountant, his wife, his baby. The last occupant of our flat had been moved out forcibly; a lonely and garrulous American bachelor, an innocent sort of man, not young, he had got himself into trouble because he had spoken to the Saudi lady; he had met her on the stairs, she in her veil, going out to a waiting car, and he hanging around, hoping for company; he had harassed her by passing the time of day. His company had moved him into a hotel now, waiting to see if he would be deported; it seemed likely.

So we had to go very carefully, approach our neighbours with caution. We had our expatriate bubble-world to live in. We would eat hamburgers with friends, sit around talking, and watch illicit videos. We would buy *The Times* at £1.50 a copy, and read the bits that the censors had left for us. At the weekend you could drive along the coast looking for beaches; the Saudis have most of their sand in less than useful places, but they have come to like the seaside life, and have imported some from Bahrain. What else is there to do? There is a choral society. Home-brewing occupies many hours. The Brits play cricket against the Pakistanis, though matches may be regarded as unlawful assemblies, and broken up by the police. Ladies hold coffee mornings, where they sell craftwork to each other; and dinner parties, too, are a competitive sport.

All this time I was conscious that there was another sort of life going on, just above my head. I hardly ever saw my neighbour. We shared a communal hallway with a marble floor; it was no one's particular territory, no one hung around there. Sometimes – suitably garbed, long-sleeved, perhaps ankles showing – I would be taking

out the trash, or sweeping out the grey dust that banked up inces-
santly on the hall floor; my neighbour's husband would come striding
down the stairs. A hesitant half-smile would be met with an opaque
look, nothing that could be construed as acknowledgement from
one human being to another. He might have been looking straight
through me, to the paintwork and the brick wall.

The woman herself was just a shape, glimpsed sometimes in the
early evenings, bundled into her concealing black *abaya* and the
Saudi version of the veil – which covers the face completely, even
the eyes. Clutching her small baby, she swayed from the front door
to the car, and into the back seat. Family cars in the Kingdom are
furnished not only with fringed mats, and boxes of Kleenex, and
dangle-dollies, but with curtains; so that once she is safely in the back
seat, the woman can lift her veil. She cannot be seen then, she
cannot see; but what does she want with the view?

The girl upstairs was nineteen, my Pakistani neighbour told me.
And she wanted to meet me. My Pakistani neighbour was a good
Muslim, who concealed her limbs, and always covered her head, but
she had a wardrobe of Western clothes for trips abroad, and she
had, she said, lived for eighteen months in Hampstead. She explained
to me that our neighbours were a more than averagely traditional
family, more than averagely religious, and she hinted, but she did
not say, that the accountant might frown on his wife making the
acquaintance of a Westerner. It might be true. None of the women
I knew had any Saudi friends.

The newspapers, especially the Friday religious columns, would
spell the situation out. They would quote the Holy Koran, and especially the favourite surah, 'An-Nisa', verse 34: 'Men are in charge of
women, for Allah hath made one of them to excel the other . . .'
Such notions are not to be corrupted. 'Why can't they accept the
fact,' the letter-writers grumble, 'that the male has been created
superior to the female? God meant it to be this way.' There was a
day when my Pakistani neighbour called unexpectedly, and found
my husband ironing a shirt. The meeting was set back a little, I felt.
Meanwhile she went between us, like a good marriage-broker, whet-
ting our appetites, and talking about one to the other.

*

Then one day when I was hanging out some washing in the high-walled enclosure by my back door, I heard voices above my head. Jamila, my Saudi neighbour, had opened a balcony door; hidden, she was gossiping with a woman in the next block. Wrapped in their curtains, they called to each other. Her voice surprised me, up there in the air; harsh, guttural, uninhibited. For a moment she stepped out on to the balcony, holding a wisp of cloth over her nose and mouth; her neighbour, then, must have drawn her attention to my presence, and she glanced down. Both of them laughed. I did a servant's jobs about the place; this, I thought, was what caused the merriment.

In the end I went upstairs because Jamila wanted help in reading poetry. She was taking an English literature course at the Women's University, attending evening lectures, and she couldn't understand her set books. I was afraid that I wouldn't understand them either, but I sent a message that perhaps I could help. So on that first visit she ordered Pepsi-Cola for us; the accountant had just gone out to work. A huge black-and-white photograph of him, ten times life size and framed in gilt, dominated the living-room; the individual features were a blur of dots, the definition gone. On the empty bookshelves was a model clipper ship, which lit up and cast a soft reddish glow into the room. Daylight came uncertainly, greenish-grey, filtered through the broad dusty leaves of the tree outside the window. I had been watching this tree; it never budded, never lost a leaf. It might have been made of plastic. Jamila's living-room, higher than mine, looked out over the same vacant lot; commanded a wider view of desolation, where mosquitoes bred in standing pools.

Jamila set out her textbooks. She was a vigorous, square-jawed woman, who looked strong; her long hair had a rippling wave, and a coarse black sheen. Her face, unveiled, was very white, unnaturally so, slightly pitted from recently cleared acne; I thought of women in Europe, not too long ago, whitening and poisoning their skins with lead. Later she told me that one's marital fortunes could depend on the colour of the skin, although the man must take it on trust, because it is still not the custom in good families for the veil to be lifted before the ceremony. She had been lucky; her small daughter, however, had an unforgivably flat nose, and hair like wire. It doesn't, she told the accountant, come from my side of the family.

At the Women's University they do have male lecturers, but only on closed-circuit televisions. *Absalom and Achitophel* was what she had to read. 'I don't know anything about Dryden,' I said. I read the notes at the back of the book. It said the poem was all about political manoeuvres in the reign of James II. I thought we might get on with it, on that basis. Jamila was charmingly inattentive. She played with the gold bracelets which ran up her arm. 'Where did you meet your husband?' she said. 'Was it arranged by your family? Did you meet him in a discotheque?'

It's good for a girl to be educated, but not to be educated too much. After marriage, she may do courses as a hobby. If her family are very liberal, she may work, perhaps in a primary school, just for a year or two; or in a women's hospital. She may work anywhere, really, where she knows that she will not, on her daily journey, or in the course of events, come across a man. There's a whole sealed-off floor at the Ministry of Planning, where women economists sit at their desks, and communicate with their male colleagues by telephone. They send each other, not *billets-doux*, but computer disks.

It is apartheid: stringent, absolute. The cafés are segregated, the buses. Allah has laid a duty on both men and women to seek knowledge, but, says one of the letter-writers crossly, 'they can read books and do researches at home'. Education is an ornament. It makes one a better mother. The girls have a chilling saying: 'We will hang our certificates in the kitchen.'

Now her voice, rasping, confident, would be on the phone in the mornings. 'We are going to Mecca. Do you want anything?' When the coast was clear she would come downstairs, veiled for the minute's journey, and drink coffee with me. She would throw off her *abaya* inside the front door, and reveal her Levis and tight T-shirt underneath. 'You ought to get one of these,' she would say, dropping the black cloak on the sofa. 'Lots of English women wear them. You can just throw them on over any old things that you're wearing.' But she wanted to know, very much she wanted to know: what is it like to sit and talk to your husband's friends? What is it like to drink alcohol? What is it like to sit and drink alcohol and talk to your husband's friends?

We did not seem to progress with the Dryden. Her teachers wanted her to know about metre, they didn't care about the meaning. We sat at the dining table, polished by her maid with some lavender wax spray, the smell of which seemed to scour the inside of my nose; I would turn my head away, sniffing, counting for her the stresses on my fingers. Jamila reeked delicately of Joy. She would push across the table to me one delicate counter, of envy; and then on top of it place, with her shaped polished nails, another counter, of pity. Saudi women believe that their sisters in the West have been the victims of a confidence trick. They believe that men have lured them, with promises of freedom, from the security of their homes, and made them slaves in offices and factories. Their proper domain has been taken away from them, and with it the respect and protection to which their sex entitles them. Their honour has been sold; their bodies are common property. Liberation, say the Saudi women, is a creed for fools.

Her friend S'na came. It seemed that I might as well teach two people, and S'na was taking the course, but she was not married. This made a difference. She was twenty perhaps, but she seemed younger than Jamila. Marriage had given status to my neighbour, maternity had given her command. Within her limits she was free. S'na dressed more soberly, ankle-length dresses even beneath her *abaya*. She had a pretty lemon-coloured face, and because she was so pliant, by training and disposition, her tall thin body seemed to bend and sway in all sorts of unexpected places, as if she had no proper joints. When she took off her veil, unwinding the cloth, it seemed that her arms became water. It was some days before her voice rose above a whisper. When we sat side by side over our texts her eyes would slide away, and her little mouse hands would flurry and contract with fear, and if I asked her a question she would tremble. She had other burdens, beside the Dryden. She had to read *Huckleberry Finn*. 'Last year,' she mouthed, 'we did *The Nigger of the Nurses*, by Joseph Conrad. I didn't understand it.'

There was a second living room in Jamila's flat, a stuffy chaotic room, with big comfortable cushions on the floor, and the baby's toys strewn around. Jamila spent her mornings there, entertaining any acquaintances who might be conveyed there by their drivers; but if I was the one who turned up I would see her scrambling up hastily as the maid let me in, ready to show me into the grand salon with the proper chairs. I wanted to say, I would rather sit in there with you; I hinted it, but she only smiled. She didn't get dressed till eleven o'clock, perhaps noon; she had a repertoire of flimsy nightdresses, of silky housecoats that swirled out behind her as she brought in our coffee. A good deal of the morning she spent on the phone, laughing with her friends; the rest, watching television.

Television in the Kingdom is mostly *Prayer Call from Mecca, Islam in Perspective* and *A Reading from the Holy Koran*; then in the late afternoon there are cartoons for the children and for the men returning from their offices. But during the morning there are Egyptian soap operas. Large-bosomed women fill the screen, rolling their eyes, wringing their hands: each mater dolorosa in a dozen domestic dilemmas familiar to the viewer. Sometimes Jamila pretended to study. I saw her anthology of English poetry tossed aside on one of the cushions, the thin pages fanning over in the draught from the air-conditioner: 'The Burial of Sir John Moore', 'Sea Fever', 'Sailing to Byzantium'. Jamila said, 'What do you and your husband talk about, when you are alone?'

While we were chatting and construing our verse, Jamila's Malaysian servant crept about the house. The export of female servants is a big industry for the world's poorer Muslim populations. Sometimes Jamila would break off the Dryden for a tirade on the girl's shortcomings. She didn't come when she was called, didn't seem to understand any Arabic or the simplest word of English. Her name was hard to pronounce, and she had resisted Jamila's efforts to rename her something simpler. 'She's just an internal servant,' Jamila said, 'I want her just for the house. Just for the washing and ironing, for the cleaning and looking after the baby and helping me with the cooking. I don't want her going out gossiping and bringing gangs of thieves to the house.' Housemaids are regarded as fair game by Saudi husbands. Sometimes they run away, or commit suicide. The authorities in Sri Lanka (or so the *Saudi Gazette* reports) have made it compulsory for maids to undertake martial arts courses before taking posts in the Middle East.

'I hope you are not studying Shelley,' my Pakistani neighbour said. 'Shelley was an immoralist.'

'You can come to my house,' S'na said, in her usual whisper. 'Not to teach me. Just to talk.' Her eyes travelled to my legs, dubiously. 'Do you ever wear long skirts? That would be better.'

But I never went. I was resisting them. 'You should put on more make-up,' Jamila advised me. 'It makes you nice.' She gave me a blue opal on a thin gold chain. They could make me feel callow, unloved, a drudge. I saw Jamila dress for an evening party, in a modest gown of grey chiffon, pearls in her hair. When the oil price fell, my husband's job was under threat; there were cutbacks. Jamila telephoned. 'I'm sure,' she added, 'that we can do something about this. Tell us. My husband will fix it.' I was constrained and polite. Tears – of humiliation? – stood in my eyes. I felt I was becoming a worse human being; a recipient of favours.

There is no crime in Saudi Arabia, the newspapers say. There is no corruption. All women are chaste. All families are happy. The Indian clerks at the office tell a different story. In a shabby block of flats by the waterfront, a Third Country National is found raped and strangled on her bed; her infants, decapitated, are in the kitchen. The system is cracking up from the inside. Jamila tells me how it cracks, her voice low and thrilled. 'Some bad types of women go to the Jeddah International Market to buy jewellery. They let these men touch them. They put out their hands from their *abaya*, with their nails painted red, and the men try bracelets on them.'

Patrols walk the shopping malls, vigilantes armed with canes; they are the delegates of the Committee for the Propagation of Virtue and the Elimination of Vice. 'Some girls,' says Jamila, 'go to the shops with their telephone numbers on a paper, and give it to any man they meet. Then they ring up and have a relationship, they plan to deceive their parents and to marry.'

There are no crimes, but there are punishments. A woman is stoned to death. Amputations are carried out, after Friday prayers. We could never talk about these things. I felt, by the end of that interesting year, an increasing sense of oppression. I no longer wanted to spend the mornings with my two Muslim friends. We took a villa on an expatriate compound, and then a few months later we moved out of the city altogether, to one of the company 'villages' which resembled an English housing estate. It was only in the narrowest sense that you were abroad; only the heat told you, and your own tetchy bouts of homesickness. I knew that the journey upstairs to my neighbour's flat had been, for me, a significant one. I had been offered a friendship I could not accept. It was a chance to build a bridge; but I thought, no, you swim to my side. My values were changing. When I travelled at first I used to ask what I could get out of it, and what I could give back. What could I teach, and what could I learn? I saw the world as some sort of exchange scheme for my ideals, but the world deserves better than this. When you come across an alien culture you must not automatically respect it. You must sometimes pay it the compliment of hating it.

During my last months in Al Hamra I used to feel stifled, desperate for the open air. Sometimes I would continue my journey upstairs, past Jamila's apartment, and up to the flat roof. Hot winds, as if from convection ducts, pulled at my clothes, and plastic bags from Al Safeway Supermarket would blow past my head and tangle in the television aerials. The city lay below its dust haze, its grid plan scarred by construction sites, derricks and cranes spiking the sky. To the left was a strip of grey, the coast road, where miles of street lamps arched, like the bare ribs of some giant animal whose time has come. Beyond that was another grey strip, without lights, and I used to watch it hopefully, thinking of the months crossed off on the calendar, and knowing that it was the open sea.

Night Visions

2008

A few nights ago, I dreamed that I was going to be hanged. It was a public occasion, and there was a small crowd, but the hangman didn't turn up. The crowd were impatient – there was no rabid baying, but they expressed disappointment, in an eye-rolling, I-blame-Gordon-Brown way. I thought one of them might step forward to do the job. But no one had a rope.

I don't know whether the dreams of writers are better or worse than the dreams of other people, but I think perhaps they are different. I sometimes go by night to a foreign city, a place I cannot identify and have never been in waking life; I sit in a cobbled square sipping coffee, while I decide which of the city's two well-stocked bookshops to visit. Sometimes, when I am asleep, I read in a heroic, domed library, where I get a book in my hand, a huge dusty volume that contains the secrets of the obscure early lives of famous historical figures. The library dream is full of emotion; my heart leaps as I turn the pages – get nearer and nearer to the facts I desperately want. But when I wake up, they've gone, and all that is left is the maddening certainty that I used to know, but don't know now; the gulf between night and day has opened like the gap between youth and senility. Sometimes, by way of a change, I dream in verse. The lines fade away as I wake, and leave the rhythm behind, and that rhythm governs all my thoughts for the next few hours.

I am sure it is every writer's ambition to make dreams work for her, but when they do, it can be an eerie experience. I once dreamed a whole short story. Wrapped in its peculiar atmosphere, as if draped in clouds, I walked entranced to my desk at about 4 a.m. and typed it on to the screen. The story was called 'Nadine at Forty'. In its subject matter, in its tone, its setting, it bore no relation to anything

36

I have ever written before or since. It extended itself easily into paragraphs, requiring little correction and not really admitting any; how could my waking self revise what my sleeping self had imagined? By 6 a.m. I had finished. I was shaking with fatigue. A voice inside me said: 'Print it out.' I had saved the work, I trusted my back-up systems, and I could hardly make the effort to hit the keys, but I did print it, and just as well, because when I crawled back to my desk at 10 a.m. there was, apart from the printed copy, no trace of the story in my files. There were two computer geeks in the house at the time, and they made it their business to search the system. If it had been there, they would have found it. It had vanished with daylight, like an imp in a fairy tale – leaving, handily, a saleable piece behind, like the straw spun into gold by Rumpelstiltskin.

Years have gone by, but I have not lost a sense of the strangeness of the story behind the story. If there had been no printed version, it would have been hopeless to try to reconstruct it in the prosaic light of day. As most dreams do, it had wiped itself from my memory, as it had wiped itself from the computer's memory. Life being so short, and the possible books to write so many, it's good to function by night as well as by day; but would anybody become a writer, if they realised at the outset what the working hours were? There are no hiding places either; there's nowhere to hang out, figuratively speaking, and sneak a crafty cigarette. You are never safe from the marauding idea, and no matter how dull or drained you feel, your book has eyes everywhere. Sometimes, I daren't go out of the house in case I see something that starts off a chain of those damned sentences. They have me fettered in their service, and I suspect I would be their servant even if they paid no wages. There are plenty of books that tell you how to become a writer, but not one that suggests how, if you want a normal life, you might reverse the process.

Not all writers agree that fiction is a hazardous and unpredictable process. It is cooler and smarter to suggest that it is the product of cerebration. Writers do not want to think they are less rational than other people, and at the mercy of compulsions, but in their hearts they know they are like those people who are taken for walks by their dogs, towed through hedges and ditches by an untrained subhuman energy. That said, the forced and relentless nature of the business is not a legitimate cause for complaint. Writing is not breaking stones. It is not picking peas for a gangmaster, or fighting in a war. You can do it without going out in the rain, or undertaking the struggle – increasingly futile, in my case – to maintain a respectable appearance. It has more status than many jobs; as one of Ivy Compton-Burnett's characters says, 'It does not involve anything manual . . . not to the point of soiling the hands.'

But all the same, it imposes a strange requirement to live in different realities. One part of you deals with the day-to-day; it goes to Tesco. The other part goes down by night – or in sessions of thought as dark as night – into the subterranean passages between the lines, where your accumulated experience and technical expertise shed no more light than a birthday cake candle; where you hope to find not words, but images, hobgoblins, chimeras, piles of Medusa heads. You have to keep shocking your psyche, or nothing happens in your writing – nothing charged, nothing enduring. It's imaginary encounters with death that generate life on the page.

One day someone will ask me to unwrap that sentence and I'll be unable. I won't completely understand it until I'm back exactly where I am now, writing the last few thousand words of a novel and therefore on duty round the clock. This will not always be my condition. There will be a few dreamless nights and aimless days, just not yet. By the end of summer, I'll have finished the book, or the book will have finished me.

The Palace Revolutionary

2008

In 1752, when the future Duke of Orléans was five years old, he was taken from his nurses to begin his education. Dressed as a miniature courtier, his hair powdered, the child was inducted into a protocol intended to squeeze out of him any vestige of warmth or humanity. Idleness was the gateway to vice; there should be no downtime, and no daydreaming. Day and night, three attendants watched him. Every casual word was reported to his tutors. All signs of emotion, in his presence, were to be erased; he should neither express feeling, nor see it expressed. Above all, the child who would grow up to own a tenth of France was to be protected from his fellow countrymen; he should never glimpse a common, hungry Frenchman, a grubby Frenchman with an ardent heart. His world was to be as remote as if he inhabited another planet, with rarefied air.

Alas for systems. Louis Philippe Joseph grew up to be a revolutionary, and not a drawing-room revolutionary either. He'd begun, it's true, as a dispenser of charity, a funder of liberal causes, a strong candidate to be France's first constitutional monarch. But the revolution swept him into its great machine and chopped him up with the blades of its radical logic. Sitting in the National Convention as a deputy for Paris, he rubbed shoulders on the Jacobin benches with Danton, Robespierre and the unsavoury Marat – with whom nobody rubbed shoulders if they could help it. When Louis XVI was put on trial, the man who had taken the name 'Philippe Égalité' found himself dragged by the tide of history. Without a smile and without a sigh, he voted to send his royal cousin to the guillotine.

What brought him from the shining palaces of his childhood to the shabby, dangerous streets of revolutionary Paris? Readers are used to biographers making claims for their subjects, but when, in

Godfather of the Revolution: The Life of Philippe Égalité Duc D'Orléans, Tom Ambrose describes the duke as 'one of the most extraordinary figures in European history', it almost seems an understatement. There is little written about him in English. More famous by far is his serpentine secretary Pierre Choderlos de Laclos, author of *Les Liaisons Dangereuses*. The world of that brilliant and poisonous novel is the world in which Philippe grew up. When he was fifteen, his family became alarmed that the emotionless youth was showing no interest in women. Accordingly, they set him up with 'one of the most alluring young courtesans in Paris' – though one might find other, less cloying words for a little prostitute who, just fifteen herself, was regarded as tried and tested. Rosalie Duthé, who was a dancer at the Paris Opéra, left Philippe enthusiastic but deficient in technique. A subsequent lover thought his bedroom behaviour 'more appropriate to a common coachman than a Prince of the Blood'. Every seminal emission became the subject of a police report. Louis XV watched his nobility intently for challenges to his authority; only while they were copulating were they not conspiring. Reports on the young Philippe gave him all the pleasure a sniggering old voyeur could ask for.

Philippe married Marie Adélaïde de Bourbon, fresh from the convent and the greatest heiress in Europe. Her rococo apartments in the couple's Paris home, the Palais-Royal, were more extravagant than anything that awaited the new dauphiness, who was expected at Versailles. Philippe and his duchess were far more popular with the people of Paris than Louis and Marie Antoinette ever would be.

Much early revolutionary activity was funded from Philippe's deep pockets. It constellated around the Palais-Royal, which the duke turned into a sort of demagogue's shopping centre – Paris's most volatile public space, crammed with cafés and bookshops, a gathering place for the disaffected. In July 1789, three days of orchestrated violence began there, and culminated in the taking of the Bastille.

Philippe was an Anglomaniac. He admired English 'actresses', English racecourses, and English liberties. But he missed his chances to become a limited monarch on the English plan. The revolutionaries, a friend pointed out, squeezed him like a lemon and threw him away. His son – who later became King Louis Philippe – insisted

that Orléans was never personally ambitious; so was he truly an
idealist, or did he fund the revolution in a fit of pique? Was
Jacobinism a hobby to him, like his intrepid ballooning or his
pornography collection? After the death of the king, he became
politically isolated. He called himself 'the slave of faction'. France
was at war but, as Danton said, the National Convention was a more
dangerous place to be than the army. Philippe was guillotined in
November 1793, having dined that day on oysters and lamb cutlets.
His last words, to the executioner, were 'Get on with it.'

His astonishing career could stand a more sumptuous treatment
than this modest and workmanlike book affords. Philippe was often
outshone by the brilliant and beautiful people about him, so it is
not frivolous to wish that the usual dull engravings of severed heads
on sticks, available in any history of the times, had been replaced
by pictures of his tough, astute and glamorous mistresses. Ambrose
is adept at compressing complex events, but short on analysis. In
Philippe's case, it is vital to try to sift truth from rumour, as most
conspiracy theories about the French Revolution are routed via his
bluff person. Ambrose has made a brave case for Philippe's courage
and good intentions. Even before he became a regicide, his contemporaries were divided. His friend the Prince of Wales described him
as 'rather clever but a great beast'. It didn't take much brain to impress
a Hanoverian, and in truth, Philippe showed every sign of not
understanding his own story. He once admitted that, despite his
intensive education, he'd read no more than half a dozen books in
his life. Mirabeau, his fellow revolutionary, judged him in a single
sentence: 'I wouldn't have him as my valet.'

Remembering My Stepfather

It's fifteen years this spring since my stepfather died, and I'm remembering all over again the books he brought into the house when he arrived in our lives. I was seven or eight, the eldest child of three, and I already had a mother and a father, a family that seemed to need no supplementation, but my mother thought differently. First, Jack Mantel came as a visitor, then he moved in, and his possessions, books included, arrived by degrees from his mother's house. The books were tattered, brown-spotted. They did not seem cared for, or read, or to have anything to do with Jack in particular. But in gleaming repair were the steel bars and weights he used to exercise. They chimed like bells when he lifted them, and his breathing – a specialised system of grunts and gasps, which helped him bear the poundage – rolled through the house and out into the street. He had a stack of magazines banded together, with black-and-white photographs of other men with big muscles. The magazine was called *Health & Strength*. Both these things were in short supply in our house.

When Jack arrived, my father Henry did not move out. Jack was not tall but he was a solid and vehement individual and my father's body was about as thick as one of Jack's legs. Jack occupied my mother's bed and the back of our house, the kitchen and the glass lean-to, puffing and blowing, clanking the weights and trundling through from the street with the black, greasy parts of broken-down cars. Meanwhile, my father went meekly to his clerical job. He came home, occupied the front of the house, played his jazz records and read his library books. I read them too, whether they were suitable for me or not.

In these circumstances, a child cannot maintain loyalty unaided. It was only a matter of time before I peered into the boxes of Jack's books. Many of them were textbooks of electrical engineering, yellow

42

and impenetrable. Jack didn't go to the library. It would have been unlike him to have a ticket for anything, especially a public institution revered by right-thinking people. He hated the BBC, run as it was by snivelling establishment lackeys; I thought for years that 'Dimbleby' was a swear word. He contrived an indoor aerial so that we could receive ITV programmes, or rather a screen-filling snowstorm behind which we could hear a programme crackling. My mother paraded about the room with the aerial held aloft, like the Statue of Liberty holding up her torch, and flitting human shapes would appear. 'Stop! Stop there!' Jack would yell. We could have had an outdoor aerial – except that in some way we couldn't, because that was what other people had. Cutting off your nose to spite your face was one of Jack's areas of expertise. Over the years I grew to expect from him opinions that were ferociously contrarian, though he could always amaze me with a new one. When I was a teenager, I decided to learn first aid – I always felt we might need it, in a house like ours – and Jack's tirade against the Red Cross blew me across the room. He was a fountain of conspiracy theories. Every man's hand was against you. 'Why should I help any bugger?' he would howl, when famine appeals appeared on the TV. 'No bugger helps me!'

Of Jack's books, one in a faded cover, bleached to no colour, was called *Out With Romany*. My romantic mother had told me that Jack's mother was a gypsy, and I thought this was why he had the book. It contained nature tales, mildly instructive; Romany, I find now I come to look it up, had been a radio presenter for the BBC's *Children's Hour*, with a series that ran for many years from 1932. It is difficult for me to imagine Jack listening to *Children's Hour*, sitting cross-legged on the hearth rug with rapt and shining face. It is disillusioning, too, to learn that Romany was not a caravan dweller, but a Methodist minister.

A number of the books in Jack's boxes were Sunday school prizes, awarded to unknown persons. I had learnt about Sunday school from reading Tom Sawyer. Catholics didn't have it. I thought then, and still do, that there were nooks and crannies of the faith that the Pope didn't want explored, though if there had been an RC version, I'd have attended it faithfully till I was eighteen, just to get me out of the house at weekends. Jack, of course, belonged to no religion.

The Holy Trinity was nothing but another scheme to fleece the man in the street.

Some of Jack's books made it out of the boxes and on to a shelf. There was *Universal Knowledge*, a one-volume encyclopaedia published in the 1930s; the later parts of the alphabet had dropped out, so it was less than it claimed to be. Perhaps it was Jack who brought the disintegrating copy of *Enquire Within Upon Everything*, the domestic reference book published in many editions since 1856. I do not know the date of ours, but the advice had an Edwardian flavour. I dwelt for hours on the section called 'Etiquette' and the section called 'Poisons'. I liked best the advice on leaving visiting cards, which seemed to me mandarin-like and very particular, a distinguished thing to know; I also cherished those poisons that had no effective antidote, and inevitably led, after forty-eight hours of cruel and pointless suffering, to 'convulsions and death'.

When I was eleven, we moved away and changed our name, left my father behind and became, to outward view, a normal family. Jack even got a library ticket. He only took out science fiction, books often bound in the plain yellow covers of the Gollancz imprint. I looked into them and found the stories devoid of human interest. Unfair, I know. I have never given the genre a chance. It brings to my mind the chink of the weights and the smell of oil and grime. Jack was still a library-goer in his sixties, when a heart attack carried him off. In retirement – enforced on him early by a health crisis – he had taken to watercolour painting. His character had softened, although he became agitated and indignant when the library lady dared to recommend titles to him. His books were his private affair, and she should stamp them without intruding; that was his view.

Jack and I never had a conversation, about books or anything else, till a short time before his death. I think he read the first of my novels to be published, though none after that. It was characteristic of him that, once he started a book, he finished it, however much he despised it. He liked seeing my name in print, and I don't think it was just because it was his name too. I think it was, perversely, because he was proved wrong: the literary career, if no other, was open to talents, and in the airy world of Dimblebies I had cut loose and floated free.

Wicked Parents in Fairy Tales

2009

In Europe in the days when maternal mortality was high – that is, every age till very recently – a bereaved husband acted just like the father in the *Tale of the Juniper Tree*; he wept greatly, then he wept a bit less, then he rose and took a new wife. At some point, the child of the lost wife is sure to ask: 'What did my mother die of?' In the *Juniper Tree*, the mother died of 'joy'. It's a more acceptable answer than 'she died of you'. But not many children, in real life or in fairy tales, can have been fooled in this way. Generations have been born into blood-guilt and reared by wraiths, the dead mother hovering over the cradle, blighting the new marriage: souring the milk and cracking the bowls, starting fires in the thatch and unravelling the products of the loom. If the houses in fairy tales are ever orderly, neat and safe, it is a momentary illusion; you may be sure there is a nasty surprise lurking. Do you wonder what are those savoury aromas, wafting from the hearth? That is a human head boiling.

When we read fairy tales now, the tools of psychoanalysis jump to hand, like the animated dish and spoon in the nursery rhyme. But we mustn't forget the historical reality behind the stories. Step-parenting, with its grudges and feuds over right and inheritance, was a fact of life through the ages, and now, because of frequent divorce, has become a fact of life again. Modern families may not be quarrelling over inheritance, but they are still at loggerheads over who gets what share in the parent or child. We don't dismember the child for the cauldron, like the boy in the *Juniper Tree*, but we shred him by apportioning his time and love: weekdays with Mum, weekend with Dad. And in step-families, sexual tension is the great unspeakable. In the Brothers Grimm tale, Snow White is a child of seven. Her story makes more sense, of an unpalatable kind, in the versions where she is on the cusp of womanhood, a blossoming rival to her stepmother.

In life, as in the fairy stories, children will cling to even the most abusive parent. Hansel and Gretel make their way back to the couple who have tried to abandon them, and hope this time it will be different. We do not want to believe this happens in real life, but the news reports tell us it does. A casual boyfriend tortures and murders a baby while its mother stands by with, at best, glazed indifference. Normal parents cannot understand child-killers, but fairy tales hold up a distorting mirror that enhances our petty guilts. There can be few mothers who, trapped with a fractious, wailing, ungrateful baby, have not wished it momentarily removed, and then become afraid of the dark powers the wish might attract.

In the *Juniper Tree* a father devours his own son with relish. Juniper berries, of which this small boy is partly made, are a stimulant to the appetite, yet in excess they are poisonous. But then, the whole circumstances of this boy's existence are equivocal. A dream of juniper berries foretells a male child, but to eat too many can bring on uterine contractions. After the muddled father mistakes his son for his dinner, a saviour sibling comes to the rescue. As Marina Warner has pointed out, the little girl acts like a priestess in the ritual arrangement of her brother's bones. The boy comes back to life in smoke and flame; juniper berries produce a good deal of oily smoke and are favoured in rituals where an illusion must be produced, a forgotten face and form reconfigured. This story about ancient magic and folk medicine has somehow combined itself with a story about revenge on a wicked stepmother. But it is not surprising that a tree, with its resins, mists, perfumes and exhalations, is the central character.

The journey into the wood is part of the journey of the psyche from birth through death to rebirth. Hansel and Gretel, the woodcutter's children, are familiar with the wood's verges but not its heart. Snow White is abandoned in the forest. What happens to us in the depths of the wood? Civilisation and its discontents give way to the irrational and half-seen. Back in the village, with our soured relationships, we are neurotic, but the wood releases our full-blown madness. Birds and animals talk to us, departed souls speak. The tiny rushlight of the cottages is only a fading memory. Lost in the extinguishing darkness, we cannot see our hand before our face. We lose all sense of our body's boundaries. We melt into the trees, into the bark and the sap. From this green blood we draw new life, and are healed.

A Memoir of My Former Self

2010

Every so often, someone announces the demise of the memoir; the genre has had its day, we're told. But the bookshops are still stuffed with them: writers' self-explorations, sickbed journals, the confected 'life journeys' of celebrities, written by ghosts. I wonder about ghost-writing: what is it like to be so bad with words that you can't articulate the facts of your existence, and have to bring in someone else to do it? The ghost may do some fact-checking, but what are the chances of emotional truth, when a filtering sensibility intervenes, one that is trained to find shape and meaning in the shapeless mess of one damn thing after another? Shape is being crafted, we suspect, and meaning forced.

Readers seek emotional truth, as well as names and dates, but how it is generated is a puzzle. Everyone who has ever written a memoir (and emerged from the process with a scrap of dignity) must have put themselves through a fierce interrogation of their more operatic emotions. When we try to grasp the slippery realities of our early lives, we cannot help but think that highly charged emotion is validating in itself. If I am so upset about it, it must be true; I couldn't counterfeit such deep feeling. Or could I?

Susan Hill dealt with the subject cogently in her novel *The Beacon*. Brief and seethingly ambiguous, it tells how a family falls apart when one of the siblings, a journalist called Frank, publishes a memoir about a childhood in which his parents singled him out for punishment and often locked him in a cupboard under the stairs. Frank's memoir becomes a bestseller, then a film, but his brothers and sisters do not recognise his account of abuse and of their collusion in it. Their childhoods, they insist to each other, were ordinary, innocent; till Frank rewrote history.

The author is clever enough to leave our minds humming with
doubt. Her description of Frank at work on his memoir is striking.
When the book is still in his head he thinks of it as organic, 'like a
shrub in the earth'. The act of writing itself stirs up further memories. The book, he thinks later, arrived on the page 'like some effusion
he had not been able to suppress'. The simplicity of the process, the
easy flow, seems a guarantee of integrity. He is writing to repossess
his own life; he has no detailed sense of what, how and where he
has fabricated. The spirit of it is true, he convinces himself. He feels
sadness on behalf of the person he never was.

A few years ago I was writing a novel, *Beyond Black*, about a professional psychic, and I haunted platform 'demonstrations' by mediums
and Psychic Fayres where fortune tellers sat cheek by jowl in public
spaces, in 'function rooms' smelling of drains, sports centres smelling
of feet, and in the damp back rooms of pubs. Against a mounting roar
of prediction, rising and echoing in the rafters, money changed hands
for tarot reading, aura reading and once, in my case, for 'past-life
regression'. I didn't necessarily think I had a past life, but I wanted to
know how it would feel if I did. Regression is somewhat recherché and
there was no choice of practitioners that day, so I held hands with the
one available, who had a flabby, damp palm; I took an irritable dislike
to the man, whom in my mind I called Twerp, because no more up-to-
date term of abuse seemed to fit so well. Twerp began by boring me
into a stupor; I was spiralling up into the universe, he suggested, up
and up, round and round, until (after twenty minutes of this) I
descended into a field. What did I see? A wall, I said, mutinous. Why
didn't I rise up and look over the wall? I did, and my past life began.

What is hard to convey about the next hour is how my attention
was riven, split. One part of me was in the roaring room, despising
Twerp, annoyed with myself for producing a past life that was, in
the light of my background, predictable: born in the north to a
family of millworkers, I had produced a child of the early industrial
revolution, a miserable illegitimate infant called Sara, of an age to
clutch her mother's skirts. Go on to when she's twelve, Twerp
suggested; irritated by the interruption, my fantasy obeyed him. The
next moment, I was so shaken by sobs that I could hardly stay in
my chair. Crying hard, with a rending, tearing feeling inside my

chest, I told Twerp that my mother was dead and I was running away. On a hill above the town, I looked down on the sooty world I had known, turned my back on it and commenced a new chapter in my penny novelette.

I very much wanted to know how Sara got out of her plight – friendless, uneducated, destitute. But Twerp wanted her to be twenty-one now, and so she was: 'Are you courting, Sara?' Now it wasn't just me who was cross with Twerp; Sara was nettled too. As she crossed the Atlantic in an emigrant ship, as she set herself up as mistress of a small sewing workshop, as – enterprising even in her fifties – she set off to the west to found a new business, she had little time for courtship. Her one dalliance, with a small-town trader, foundered when he wouldn't show her his account books; she suspected a takeover rather than a marriage was in prospect, and guarded her assets fiercely. What became clear, as her life opened up, was how little her personality owed to mine. I could not predict her reactions, but I could certainly feel her emotions: I relished the quiet triumph of her later life when, a benefactor to her community, a stalwart of welfare committees, she lived in comfort in a house on a hill with the real love of her life, a white bull terrier called Billy. She wanted to tell Twerp about Billy, but all he cared about was the possibility of late-blooming romance.

If Sara had slapped him, what sort of a defence would I have had to a charge of assault? For part of a Saturday afternoon, she occupied my body space and had my voice at her disposal. Hypnotised, I was aware of everything around me, and especially the damp palm of Twerp, yet I was on board a ship, I was in a railway car, I was in an alien land. I was still inside Sara, or she inside me, when she reached her seventies and her heart failed. I was with her after her death; Twerp suggested she would meet her unknown father. From the afterlife, Sara was briskly dismissive. And I, having lived seventy-odd tumultuous years, and died on a stacking chair in a public hall, was a wreck. Did I believe in Sara? As a past self, no; but as a construct she had vitality, force, the steady heartbeat of reality; she was the most successful, convincing, rounded character I have ever made. What I felt, my hand lying in Twerp's, seemed utterly genuine.

Two things I learned. One: beware of 'effusions'. Two: if only I had applied myself, I could have been Catherine Cookson.

Dreaming of Pork and Porn

1990

Gulfman will be sweating and hoping now. He will be tuning in to the World Service, for the foreign newspapers are censored and the local ones tell lies. If there is an emergency, if he has to throw his life in a suitcase and quit, it will be only what he has dreamed of doing, thousands of times, when the mosquitoes bite and the bureaucrats need bribing. And there has always been the threat of *coup d'état* or sudden deportation. With part of his mind, he has always seen himself scrambling for a seat on the last plane out. But then there is the other part of his mind, which sincerely wants to be rich.

Wherever in the world they are, British expatriates will always tell you, 'It's not what it used to be.' There was always a golden age, when life was tougher but less complicated, and everyone knew his place and stayed in it, playing his allotted role in the long drama of the Englishman abroad. In Arabia and the Gulf they look back to the age before shopping malls, when provisions were obtained in the souq and the roads were rough tracks and Islam didn't get on the nerves so. Then in 1973 the oil price went up, the construction workers came. A concrete hell was born, with savage people in it. Salaries, fortunately, continued to go up too.

The first wave of 'Brits', as they describe themselves, were employed by the construction companies. These men with tattoos worked on short contracts, leaving their families behind. Bewildered, sunburnt and lonely, they got into trouble by smoking on the streets during Ramadan, or trying to chat up women. Often, one contract down and pockets full of money, they would jump ship. There were always more where they came from.

The second wave of expats were the professional experts – teachers, scientists, accountants, engineers. Their companies made an effort to retain them – housing them in what comfort was obtainable, paying them well and shielding them as far as possible from their hosts' strange religious and cultural susceptibilities. Families came out; a way of life was established, endurable but frail. It was dependent upon the successful functioning of air-conditioning units, and upon an ability to screen out many of the less pleasant features of Saudi life. In a land where people are stoned to death for adultery, it is dangerous to have a roving eye; in a land where the status quo is so precarious, it is dangerous to have an enquiring mind.

It is possible to make a photofit for Gulfman. He is thirty to thirty-five, lower middle class and embarrassingly aspirant. His education is redbrick/polytechnic. He believes himself to be shrewd, likes to say that he is a cynic. He reads Wilbur Smith and the free magazine that comes with his new Gold Card. Jewellery is worn – sometimes a Credit Suisse token on a chain. He despises the arts – he might go to the amateur Gilbert and Sullivan, if there is someone in it he knows. He likes to talk about camcorders, compact discs, kit-cars and tax shelters. His wife – very often his second wife – is deeply interested in nail polish. Her ambition is to open a nursery school.

Though it goes against his grain, Gulfman carries a sort of handbag for the many documents required to negotiate daily life in the Kingdom. Without these documents he is in peril; should he attract the attention of the police by, say, parking in the wrong place, he may be thrown into jail.

Gulfman curses his way early to the office, through traffic that knows no laws. The move towards 'saudi-isation' has been under way for many years, so he will work alongside his hosts, and find them friendly, up to a point, but resentful of any criticism, watchful. At noon, he curses his way to the Gents; the floor is awash, for it is prayer-time, and ritual ablutions are required, and once again his Saudi colleagues have been washing their feet in the sink. Religion embarrasses him, especially in its public manifestations. He takes obscure comfort from the blatant hypocrisies of Saudi life – the gambling and womanising outside the Kingdom. He is not equipped to understand moral systems. He is not paid to do it. At three o'clock he goes home to a dip in the compound pool, to a piece of Dutch veal and a censored video; he goes to bed early, the air-conditioners rattling, and dreams of *Men Only* and pork sausages.

Quick in and out is the idea now; a couple of years max, he will say. But soon Gulfman is securely bound by his golden handcuffs. He always needs to do another year . . . just for more security, then for a bit more. He may be paying off a mortgage and putting his children through a private school, or his parents through their hip replacements. He may be paying alimony, or saving up to have his tattoos removed. He might go to Australia, when he makes the break; for the UK is so cramped and cold and Mrs Thatcher is such a leftist.

In daily life, he has everything he needs. The shops are well stocked. Shopping keeps the family together; because of the laws that segregate the sexes, few other joint and public activities are on offer. Nothing is cheap but petrol and flat Arab bread, but when he is in the Kingdom he lives frugally. He lives on his expectations; he likes to plan his holidays. His outlook, though, has narrowed over the years. His family look forward to going to Hong Kong, and other places where they have heard the shopping is very good.

Gulfman seldom sees his Saudi colleagues outside work. (Contact is not desired on either part. Saudis see foreigners as contaminators; they are necessary evils, paid inferiors, servants.) Unlike the classic expat, Gulfman has no club; social life is conducted almost entirely in private houses, and is lubricated by home-made wine and a colourless spirit called Siddiqi. The authorities do not approve the viniculture but contrive to turn a blind eye. A familiar sight in any supermarket is a trolley groaning with grape juice, red and white, and stacked with bags of sugar; one room of his house stinks of yeast and rotting fruit, and murky brews bubble in plastic jerry-cans.

This double-think no longer bothers Gulfman. Daily life requires him to live by ill-defined rules which he does not understand, and which are always changing. In the Saudi system, which has to reconcile a medieval theology with the pleasures and horrors of the twentieth century, all inconvenient features of the world fall into a black hole. The Saudi newspapers do not report crimes, only punishments. The English-language press excoriates the Americans as corrupt, effete imperialists, yet for years something commonly called 'the American missile base' has stood in the middle of Jeddah, proud behind its ostentatious golden gates. It has anti-aircraft missiles, people assume; they do not speculate about what else. It does not hide itself; everyone, obeying the custom of the country, simply pretends it isn't there.

A Doctor's Diaries

2008

Do authorship and insomnia go hand in hand? I often wonder if for other writers, as for me, three in the morning is the time when a second self pursues an alternative agenda. Before dawn I jot down stranger versions of the book that I'm writing by day. I work through a less rational reading list. It's no time to pick up a new book, but the contents of an old one can appear startling. I try to follow the whims of my sleepwalking self. The book it leads me to usually has something to tell me.

This week I sleepwalked to *A Doctor's Life: The Diaries of Hugh Selbourne MD 1960–63*. This diary records, in the terse fashion of a man with little spare time, three driven, harassed years in the life of a hospital consultant. Hugh Selbourne was an inveterate journal keeper and this selection from his writing was edited by his son David, the writer and political commentator. We can't guess at the diarist's intentions; in his worst moments he thought his words would never be read, let alone published. So, constraints are off. Uncensored opinions are expressed and the writer himself, in all his irascible selfhood, takes us by the sleeve and furnishes us with an uncalculated account of his life and times.

Selbourne's background was unusual. Jewish, he was born in 1906 in Montmartre, and when the First World War broke out his parents moved to England and settled in the East End. They were not well off, but both sons became doctors. By the time of writing, he was practising in 'Lowry-land'; he acted as consultant to a group of hospitals in Hyde, Ashton and Glossop, those conurbations on the fringes of Manchester where moorland runs into grim terrace streets. It's fraught terrain, with an intricate and fascinating industrial history – yet famous, post-industrially, for nothing but the Moors murders and Harold Shipman. It's where I grew up, and this must be the reason I bought the book when Jonathan Cape published it in 1989. I have an inability to fully believe in the village where I was born, and when I was a child, if I found it on a map, I would stare and stare, squashing the name under my finger: there it is in print, so it must be real. In the days of Selbourne's diary, Pennine fogs rolled in to meet industrial smog; it seemed possible to me that one day the locale would simply dematerialise, the exit roads thinning into celestial ether.

The diarist was a hard-headed man with no doubt about the material stuff of his surroundings; this is a diary about fine cigars and bad food, blotchy medical reports badly typed by recalcitrant secretaries, and the contents, sometimes threatened by damp, of his 'lumber room'. His passion is for antiquarian books, and he owns them by the yard; we are not talking about first editions of Dickens, but first editions of Erasmus, 'printed Basle, 1517'. His regular beat takes him to his private consulting rooms at St John Street in the centre of Manchester, then to Shaw's, the book dealer, and then to Sherratt & Hughes bookshop, to pick up an armful of whatever is newly published. He comes home from a hard day to change into black tie and go to the theatre. The *Manchester Guardian* is the one constant in his busy days. He views television with the gravitas he brings to every activity, and records the weekly topics of *Panorama*. He is alert, insatiably curious, sardonic; in his diaries at least, he is not introspective. He is attuned always to the outside world, recording in his imperturbable way earthquakes in Chile, tidal waves in Japan, frequent air crashes with massive fatalities, as well as his spats with obstreperous motor mechanics and student nurses who fall asleep in his lectures. The moral he draws? 'June 5th 1960: The human species is degenerating.'

Most of his entries are about his patients. Those stiff little Lowry figures hide terrible secrets behind their mufflers: cancers, malignant hypertension, anaemia. They have inhaled asbestos fibres and been downwind of chemical escapes. They drink, smoke, cough blood. Bus conductors fall on them, and knock them 'cock-eyed' with their ticket machines. Bales of cotton tumble from lorries and bowl them over. Selbourne is a noted diagnostician; a GP diagnoses 'a sense of inadequacy' in a man he at once suspects has multiple sclerosis. GPs and the patients themselves often blame their illness on the weather, which does indeed seem to be the general, implacable enemy: 'slush and snow, frost and cold'. Midsummer day, 1962 brings 'severe gales', and August bank holiday of the same year 'rain, cloud, gloom and depression'. There is the odd ray of sunshine: 15 June 1961 'had mangoes with Indian doctors'.

By the time he wrote these diaries Selbourne was a grandfather. He loved his children and he wanted to control them. The editor has not censored out his old self; his father disinherited him at one point, and described him as 'bearded and devoid of ambition'. Selbourne was pessimistic about his profession, his patients and the NHS – which he saw as a necessary service for poor people, not as a force for equality. He keeps on working through ferocious angina attacks, gloomily jotting down his own medical facts and figures. The diaries find him on the cusp of two worlds. In these pages, Nye Bevan dies, and survivors of concentration camps visit his surgery, and in Wales there is a smallpox outbreak. But also, the diarist feeds his first parking meter, takes a drive down the M1, listens disbelieving to the news of Kennedy's assassination. His world was, I think, more cohesive than ours. He despaired of it, but he felt part of it – a citizen of a provincial city, with stern obligations to public work and to high culture. Around that culture, the net could be drawn tight, for in Manchester in those days the words 'Hallé Orchestra' were pronounced with the same reverence as 'Holy Ghost', and to describe someone as an elitist was to pay them a compliment.

When I first read the book, I thought it slight, an oddity. It had not acquired the patina of a period piece; nor had I. Now I sympathise with a diarist in his fifties – much done, much more to do. French-born he may have been, but by 1961 he was not just English but a perfect northerner. 'Jan 17th: At 5.20 a.m., extreme *angor animae* [fear of death]. Eased off after hot tea.'

Holy Disorders

2004

We are living in a great era of saint-making. Under John Paul II an industrial revolution has overtaken the Vatican. Saints are fast-tracked to the top, and there are beatifications by the bucketload.

Gemma Galgani became a saint in 1940, in the reign of Pius XII. It was a rapid promotion by the standard of those days. After a miserable life, Galgani died of TB in 1903, when she was twenty-five. Her life and writings, say Rudolph Bell and Cristina Mazzoni, authors of *The Voices of Gemma Galgani*, reveal her to be an old-fashioned saint – Italian, passive, repressed, yet given to displays of flamboyant suffering, to public and extreme fasting and self-denial, and the exhibition of torn and bleeding flesh.

Her behaviour recalled the gruesome penitential practices of her medieval foremothers, and resembled that of the 'hysterics' of her own day, whose case histories promoted the careers of Josef Breuer and Sigmund Freud. But we can't quite consign Galgani to history, to the dustbin of outmoded signs and symptoms, or the waste tip of an age of faith. When we think of young adults in the West, driven by secular demons of unknown provenance to starve and purge themselves, and to pierce and slash their flesh, we wonder uneasily if she is our sister under the skin.

Rudolph Bell's 1985 book *Holy Anorexia*, on Italian saints, is especially rewarding for connoisseurs of the spiritually lurid. St Maria Maddalena dei Pazzi lay naked on thorns. Catherine of Siena drank pus from a cancerous sore. One confessor ordered Veronica Giuliani to kneel while a novice of the order kicked her in the mouth. Another ordered her to clean the walls and floor of her cell with her tongue; but even he thought it was going too far when she swallowed the spiders and their webs.

Scourges, chains and hair-shirts were the must-have accessories in these women's lives. St Margaret of Cortona bought herself a razor and was narrowly dissuaded from slicing through her nostrils and upper lip. St Angela of Foligno drank water contaminated by the putrefying flesh of a leper. And what St Francesca Romana did, I find I am not able to write down.

Starvation was a constant for these women. It melted their flesh away, so that the beating of their hearts could be seen behind the racks of their ribs. It made them one with the poor and destitute, and united them with the image of Christ on the cross. What does this holy anorexia mean? Can we find any imaginative connection with a woman such as Galgani? Like her medieval predecessors, she received the stigmata, the mark of Christ's wounds. Like them, she was beaten up by devils. Like them, she performed miracles of healing after her death.

To talk about female masochism seems reductive and unhelpful. You have to look the saints in the face; say how the facts of their lives revolt and frighten you, but when you have got over being satirical and atheistical, and saying how silly it all is, the only productive way is the one the psychologist Pierre Janet recommended, early in the twentieth century: first, you must respect the beliefs that underlie the phenomena.

Galgani and her fellow female saints believed that suffering had an effect that was not limited in time or space. They could, just for a while, share the pain of crucifixion. Their suffering could be an expiation for the sins of others; it could be a restitution, a substitution. Margaret of Cortona said: 'I want to die of starvation to satiate the poor.'

Thérèse of Lisieux died of TB in 1897, just short of her twenty-fifth birthday. As she lay dying, bleeding from her intestines and unable to keep down water, she was tormented by the thought of banquets. Galgani, too, dreamed of food; would it be all right, she asked her confessor, to ask Jesus to take away her sense of taste? Permission was granted. She arranged with Jesus that she should begin to expiate, through her own suffering, all the sins committed by priests: after this bargain was struck, for the next sixty days she vomited whenever she tried to eat.

Within the church, pain can become productive, suffering can be put to work. But outside the church, suffering loses its meaning, degenerates into physical squalor. It has only the meaning we ascribe to it; but now we lack a context in which to understand the consent to suffering that the saints gave.

Anorexia nervosa is said to be a modern epidemic. If you skimmed the press in any one week it would be hard to see what is perceived as more threatening to society: the flabby, rolling mass of couch potato kids, or their teenage sisters with thighs like gnawed chicken bones, sunken cheeks and putrid breath. Are we threatened by flesh or its opposite? Though the temporarily thin find it easy to preach against the fat, we are much more interested in anorexia than in obesity. We all understand self-indulgence, but are afraid that self-denial might be beyond us.

Bell emphasises that what Thérèse experienced was 'holy anorexia', and that it is different from anorexia nervosa. But what may strike a secular reader is how similar they are. Starvation, as Bell shows, was not an extension of convent practice, but a defiance of it. A fast is a controlled penitential practice. Most nuns fasted to keep the rule: the anorexics fasted to break it. Most nuns fasted to conform to their community: the starvation artists aimed to be extraordinary, exemplary.

The secular slimming diet is also conformist and self-limiting. Dieting is culturally approved, associative behaviour, almost ritualistic. Restaurants adapt their menus to the Dr Atkins faddists; in a thousand church halls every week, less fashionable dieters discuss their 'points' and 'sins', their little liberties and their permitted lapses. Diets are prescriptive, like convent fasts – so much of this, so little of that. The anorexic, holy or otherwise, makes her own laws. Every normal diet ends when the dieter's will fails, or the 'target weight' is reached, at which point the dieter will celebrate, the deprived body will take its revenge, and the whole cycle will begin again – next Monday, or next Lent. Diets are meant to fail, fasts to end in a feast day.

Anorexia succeeds, and ends in death, more frequently than any other psychiatric disorder. Should we be comfortable regarding it as a psychiatric disorder? Is it not a social construct? If the fashion industry were responsible for modern anorexia, it would be true that we were dealing with a very different condition from holy anorexia. But the phenomenon of starving girls predates any kind of fashion industry. In *The Disease of Virgins: Green Sickness, Chlorosis and the Problems of Puberty*, Helen King has amassed a huge number of references to a disease entity that was recognised from classical times to the 1920s. Greensick virgins went about looking moony, and didn't menstruate, possibly because they didn't weigh enough; in all eras, food refusal was part of the condition.

Sometimes the starving saints broke their fasts, and were found at midnight raiding the convent larder. How did their communities accommodate this embarrassment? They simply said that, while Sister X snoozed celestially in her cell, the devil assumed her form and shape, tucked his tail under a habit, crept downstairs and ate all the pies.

The young women who survive anorexia do not like themselves. Their memoirs burn with self-hatred, expressed in terms that often seem anachronistic. In *My Hungry Hell*, Kate Chisholm says: 'Pride is the besetting sin of the anorexic: pride in her self-denial, in her thin body, in her superiority.'

Survivors are reluctant to admit that anorexia, which in the end leads to invalidity and death, is along the way a path of pleasure and power: it is the power that confers pleasure, however freakish and fragile the gratification may seem. When you are isolated, your back to the social wall, control over your own ingestion and excretion is all you have left; this is why professional torturers make sure to remove it.

Why do women still feel so hounded? The ideal body seems now attainable only by plastic surgery. The ideal woman has the earning powers of a chief executive, breasts like an inflatable doll, no hips at all and the tidy, hairless labia of an unviolated six-year-old. The world gets harder and harder. There's no pleasing it. No wonder some girls want out.

It is possible that there is a certain personality structure that has always been problematical for women, and which is as hard to live with today as it ever was – a type that is withdrawn, thoughtful, reserved, self-contained and judgemental, naturally more cerebral than emotional. Adolescence is difficult for such people; peer pressure and hormonal disruption whips them into forced emotion. Suddenly, self-containment becomes difficult. Emotions become labile.

Why do some children cut themselves, stud themselves and arrange for bodily modifications that turn passers-by sick in the streets, while others merely dwindle quietly? Is it a class issue? Is it to do with educational level? The subject is complex and intractable. The cutters have chosen a form of display that even the great secular hysterics of the nineteenth century would have found unsubtle, while the starvers defy all the ingenuities of modern medicine; the bulimics borrow the tricks of both, and are perhaps the true heirs of those spider-swallowers.

Anorexia itself seems like mad behaviour, but I don't think it is madness. It is a way of shrinking back, of reserving, preserving the self, fighting free of sexual and emotional entanglements. It says, like Christ, *noli me tangere*. Touch me not and take yourself off. For a year or two, it may be a valid strategy; to be greensick, to be out of the game; to die just a little; to nourish the inner being while starving the outer being; to buy time. Most anorexics do recover, after all. Anorexia can be an accommodation, a strategy for survival.

In *Holy Anorexia*, Bell remarks how often, once recovered, notorious starvers became leaders of their communities, serene young mothers superior, who were noticeably wise and moderate in setting the rules for their own convents. Such career opportunities are not available these days. I do not think holy anorexia is very different from secular anorexia. I wish it were. It ought to be possible to live and thrive, without conforming, complying, giving in, but also without imitating a man, even Christ.

Written on Our Bodies

2003

In 1972 I was nineteen, I was an undergraduate at a northern university, a small pale girl with inky fingers, high ambitions and a strange pain I couldn't account for. I took my pain to the student health service, and a doctor – male, middle-aged – looked at me in a way that suggested that he'd seen my sort before. In seconds he had consulted his inner encyclopaedia of aches, twinges and pangs. None, he said, corresponded to mine. It was all in my mind, perhaps? I had better have some anti-depressants.

In those days, if a young man said he had a pain, the doctors listened to his heart, took his blood pressure, examined the bit of him he was complaining about. But women patients – especially young women – were routinely suspected of casting mental distress into the form of physical symptoms. Doctors looked for anxiety and stress, for dissatisfaction and panic. What had we to panic about? We were hesitating, some of us, on the brink of a man's world. Conflict over our roles in life – career, marriage, children? – was believed to give us all sorts of pains. Would it be lipstick and lingerie, or a life with the boys in the line of fire? No one imagined it could be both, or neither.

When the anti-depressants didn't work, and Valium didn't either, the GP sent me to a psychiatrist. Look here, said the shrink, regarding me tweedily from inside his tweed jacket: wasn't all this a bit much for me, this business of studying law? If I were honest about what I really wanted in life, wouldn't I secretly prefer a job in my mother's dress shop?

My mother was a section head in a big-city department store, controlling twenty staff. The psychiatrist couldn't hear this: he could only hear 'dress shop'. He was invalidating, though he didn't know it, not just my hopes in life, but my mother's too. She'd never had a chance of a high school education. Her primary school had simply forgotten to enter her for the examinations at eleven. But what did it matter? She was only a girl. At fourteen, she was working in a cotton mill – the mill her own mother had entered at the age of twelve. At forty, she reinvented herself. She got a job on a fashion sales floor, dyed her greying hair blonde, and within months was promoted to management.

'Uneducated' doesn't mean 'unintelligent'; in my family, we knew that. But one of the most shaming moments of my mother's life, she confessed, was the moment when she faced the application form for the saleswoman's job. Educational qualifications? None. Zero, blank. This was why she was fiercely ambitious for me. In four generations, we'd come far. My great-grandmother couldn't read or write. She had ten children, and all of them stayed poor throughout their lives. But here I was, ready to tussle with anyone for a share in society. So why did I feel I was being punished – pushed down the ranks again, back into the woman's world? I was a feminist – insofar as I knew what one was. I was articulate; but somehow, every time I opened my mouth, I seemed to make my situation worse.

We're all familiar with the sad tale of the medicalisation of unhappiness: with the history of the brain-dampening wonder drugs prescribed by the million to soothe the condition of womanhood. My story fits within this larger history; even its personal, individual tributaries seem to flow into the common stream of women's experience. My generation prided itself on control of our own fertility. 'A woman's right to choose' was the slogan of the age: to choose, that is, whether and when we had children, and by implication to choose the shape of our lives. In part, our right to choose could be guaranteed by legislation. But in a larger way, it could only be guaranteed by a society that was changing around us, feeding our aspirations instead of punishing them. My own choices, as it turned out, were sharply curtailed. Biology has determined the way I've lived my life, just as it did for my great-grandmother.

For the descendant of the mother of ten is the mother of – none. I didn't, when I was nineteen, need a Valium, or a patronising lecture on limiting my ambitions. I needed a physical examination, and someone to ask the right questions; someone to listen to me, rather than to their own prejudices. The strange pain that was no known pain was the beginning of a disease process that left me infertile by the age of twenty-seven, and which leaves me, even today, an unwilling stranger in my own body.

The moment of choice came and went without my knowing about it. What happened to me was entirely preventable, and the why of it has little to do with me, much to do with the way young women were looked at thirty years ago. They were mad bitches one and all, out for men's jobs, wanting equality but whining for special treatment, always with some moan about the state of their insides: unreliable workers who'd be pregnant as soon as you'd trained them. When I went for job interviews, I'd be asked: 'Are you going to start a family?' If only I'd known, I could have put my hand on my heart and said no.

So where do we find ourselves? The huge advances women have made in education and career choice are still undermined by an expectation that she will, when all's said, mind the baby. And if she has no baby to mind, what is she? Is she one of those mad bitches, too mercenary to consult her female instincts? Is she a 'victim' of infertility, a pitiable statistic on a waiting list? If you want to know what feminism has achieved, a good measure is our attitude to the working mother. But you should also look at how the childless woman is regarded. The biological clock is often ticking most loudly in the ears of onlookers, critics. A woman who stays childless is still an object of curiosity, misunderstanding and dislike. People want to ask, but they can't find a tactful way. Sometimes they forget tact and ask anyway.

After my friends started to become grandmothers, I realised the time for shame was past. I am willing to talk about my life as a woman, knowing that I've hardly had one. Maybe doctors are better trained now, women's health isn't trashed so casually. I can hope that life would be better for my daughter, except, of course, that I don't have one. The women of any family have history written on their bodies. Mostly, it's a story of progress. But our story stops with me.

Every Part of My Body Hurts

2004

The weekend I first began to bleed, my family had just moved house. The furniture was shrouded, the mood was furious and purposive; we were redecorating, soaking and scraping off wallpaper, layer after layer of it: regency stripes, faded sepia vistas and blown roses.

My mother kept me up to the task, lugging buckets of water and pushing around a yard brush. Exercise was good for menstrual pain, she thought. As the paper dropped in curls to the floorboards, I would have liked to drop and curl up too; as I bled, sweated and shook, something was scraping and chiselling, urgently, inside my body. I felt – and I was right – that I was leaving normal life behind. The rest of the family were in a lively DIY commercial, while I had slid away from them into an after-midnight horror film.

To be fair, my mother had no idea anything was wrong. I was simply a fragile eleven-year-old confronted by the first shock of womanhood. It's probably still hard for a teenage girl to work out how her experiences compare to those of her friends. People talked – and still do – of a 'low-pain threshold'. I didn't want anyone to think I had that. I blamed my frequent gut ache on everything from constitutional nervousness to school dinners.

At eighteen, I went on the pill. My period pains eased. But soon nausea, vomiting, fatigue and aching legs took me to the doctor. These symptoms lasted though the month, and no one added them up. I was offered tranquillisers and anti-depressants, and the opportunity of a career as a psychiatric patient, which in the end I found the strength to decline.

Throughout my twenties I sought a diagnosis for increasing debility. Doctors read my notes and wrote me off. When I left off the pill, menstruation became agony; every part of my body seemed to hurt. When I was twenty-seven – a skinny, grey-faced scrap, bleeding continuously and hardly able to stand upright – my disease was named. But it was named on the operating table, and to make me viable I had to lose part of my bladder and my bowel, my womb and my ovaries. I woke up to a strange future – childlessness, a premature menopause, and a marriage, already tottering, that would soon fall apart.

It was 1980 when I had surgery for endometriosis, and my case was extreme. But figures collected by the charities set up by and for sufferers suggest it still takes an average of ten years or so for a woman to get a diagnosis. Endometriosis is a condition that is under-researched and poorly understood. We don't know for sure how or why it starts, but we understand something about its mechanism. The endometrium is the tissue that lines the womb, which is shed each month if there is no pregnancy. In endometriosis, these special cells are found elsewhere in the body – mainly in the pelvic area, though they can get just about anywhere. Each month, wherever they are, they obey their nature and bleed. The big three symptoms – of which all GPs should be aware – are painful menstruation, painful sex and infertility.

It is a peculiarity of endometriosis that the pain suffered isn't necessarily related to the visible extent of the disease. Many women are only diagnosed when they have difficulty conceiving. Early diagnosis is crucial. It must be treated and managed before permanent damage is done.

The incidence of endometriosis in the population is hard to work out. Some suggest an incidence of 1 woman in 10; I find that figure implausible, though I see that it would include women in whom 'silent' disease causes no trouble. For every such woman, case histories amassed by the charities suggest that there are dozens who are routinely given the brush-off by their doctors, who are told their pain is all in their minds, or who are dropped into the catch-all categories: ME, fibromyalgia, irritable bowel syndrome. All I can truly report is that the incidence of the disease is very high in the vicinity of me. Two of my sisters-in-law received a diagnosis of endometriosis in their forties – which goes far to explain their ill health of many years. The knowledge, though, is not much comfort now.

In the ideal world, a GP suspecting endometriosis would refer a patient to a gynaecologist who would arrange a laparoscopy, which can be done on a day patient basis. Any endometriosis can be photographed, and sometimes it can be treated at the same time with laser surgery.

Many women need a combination of surgery and drugs. In the early stages, the contraceptive pill can help damp down the symptoms; when the woman comes off the pill, she has a window of opportunity to become pregnant, and pregnancy itself retards the condition. But this is a risky strategy, and sometimes a baby isn't wanted, or practical; advice that pregnancy is a cure is objectionable and also wrong. Many women who have had children develop endometriosis, and some believe that endometriosis sufferers have a higher rate of miscarriage and ectopic pregnancy.

Some drugs aim to produce either a pseudo-pregnancy or a pseudo-menopause. Some find the side effects hard to endure, and the remission only temporary. The sad truth is that endometriosis can be a long battle, with many women undergoing repeated episodes of drug treatment and surgery. Even radical surgery did not end my own struggles. I was given hormone replacement – necessary, to stop osteoporosis – and within eighteen months I was again in severe pain, and again confronting disbelief and even ridicule. Doctors thought that, after a hysterectomy, the disease couldn't come back. Some still think that. But the disease has to be eradicated cell by cell; my surgery didn't do that. Subsequent drug treatment expanded me to twice my previous size; I went to live in a body I didn't recognise. Fatigue and intermittent pain are still my companions. My soul rattles around in its capacious house, and dwells on the life I might have had if, aged eleven, I'd thrown down my wallpaper scraper and yelled, 'I won't put up with this!'

But it's unlikely I'd have got much help. Myths about the condition had made their way into the textbooks. Endometriosis patients were 'anxious perfectionists', White, middle-class career women in their thirties. The truth was, it was these well-educated nags who were getting a correct diagnosis. Poor women and Black women – characterised as promiscuous – were likely to be told they had pelvic inflammatory disease.

We now know that endometriosis is an equal-opportunity disease. Girls can have it, grannies can have it. It is necessary for doctors not to prejudge, but to look at and listen to their patients: to exercise those old-fashioned lo-tech skills, and refrain – please – from the routine humiliations meted out to women with gynaecological disease. The injured self you take away from your consultation is the self you take home. Suffering may not be avoidable, but stigma is under social control.

Endometriosis is unpredictable, capricious, tenacious, a destroyer of careers, families and relationships, and it is worth more money and research effort – not only for what we would learn about the disease itself, but for the light that would be shed on infertility, immunology, and the connection between illness and psychological states. When I had surgery, I was given the impression that I would recover in the same way as I would recover from a broken wrist; there might be the odd twinge in wet weather. Nothing and no one prepared me for the profound derangement of my body that disease and efforts at cure would bring.

I now understand that, while the acute model dominates medical thinking, endometriosis can become a chronic condition, and sufferers may need long-term emotional and physical support. Doctors grow impatient; families are disappointed; half-baked advice is plentiful. Aren't you better yet? Aren't you pregnant yet? They can do wonders these days, people tell you.

What seems crucial is for the sufferer to become informed and active in her own treatment. No one will like me for saying this, but I've often noticed that it doesn't seem to matter whether a woman goes in for yoga or reiki or dancing on hot coals at the full moon – she starts to get better when she starts to take charge.

The mind–body link bears investigation; we need surer, swifter surgery and more targeted and tolerable drug therapy. Meanwhile it is urgent that doctors, nurses, teachers know about endometriosis and act on their knowledge, to spare young women years of pain, loss and emotional damage.

Once Upon a Life

2010

At five o'clock on the morning of 13 March 1986 I stood with my husband in the half-dark outside our house, listening. Nothing in this place was simple, so we thought: what if the car doesn't come? Beyond the contingent sprawl of buildings, the lunar landscape was silent: stars setting, and no birdsong in this parched place. The houses of our neighbours, unlit, seemed to have edged away from us, easing back into their little plots of dust. In the distance you could see the line of the highway: just the odd moving dot of a car, some early or nefarious commuter heading down to the snarled-up city. The grey light was indefinite; you wouldn't know, unless like us you repeatedly checked your watch, if this hour was dawn or dusk. We must have missed the call to prayers, blanked it. An Arab dawn comes, I had been told, when by the first glimmer you can distinguish a black thread from a white.

Then in the distance, hardly perceptible at first, the hum of a vehicle, coming uphill towards us, hidden at first by the curve of the road. When the car came into sight, the office car, we faced each other and smiled. My husband turned back to the house and locked the door. Our four years of Jeddah were over. We dropped the keys through the letterbox. I had hoped for a satisfying clatter: instead, a soundless tumble to the vinyl tiles.

It has an opulent image, Saudi Arabia, but the city was a building site in those days and everything around us had been provisional, odd or cheap. We had lived for two and a half years in city centre flats. The first was cavernous, bare and white, with acres of oatmeal carpet across which cockroaches sauntered in broad daylight, as if strolling in the park. It had vast double doors with many keys. To get out of the main door needed more keys. Then came the locked metal gate in the wall. When my husband returned from his office, with the *Saudi Gazette* and a brown bag of shopping, I could hear him approach, rattling like a jailer.

The apartment was on the first floor and the windows were made of frosted glass. The Saudis didn't much like windows. If you could see out, someone could see in; a giant, say, might be walking down the street, so better safe than sorry. After a few weeks the company moved us to another place, smaller, better for two. It was dark and the lights had to be kept on all day, as if it were the English winter. Each room had many doors, double doors made of dark wood, so it was like a coffin showroom. We took some of them off, but the impression of death persisted.

Our third move was to a small ramshackle 'family compound', which we shared with nine other households. All the men were employed by the mining company my husband worked for; the wives were not employed, and spent their days wistfully plotting the shopping trips they were going to undertake with all the money their husbands were making, walking in their imaginations through the streets of other cities where they were rich and free. Our dwellings were prefabs long past their use-by date, and rats bounced around in the roofs, but I liked my house because behind our bed there was a wide, bright window. Each morning the yellow dawn spilled in, and light, light, that's what I craved; my eye was starved for it, my bones ached for it, my soul had become in its absence a brittle piece of grit or gravel, something you might walk over the threshold on the sole of your shoe.

It was in the coffin-maker's flat that I had finished my first novel. There, I had received a letter from London to say that a publisher had accepted it. My husband brought it home from the office and put it into my hand. When I read its first line my mouth opened but my ribs had stuck fast with astonishment, so I couldn't utter, couldn't breathe in or out; and it seemed to me that in those suspended seconds an era went by, during which every cell in my body was exchanged for a new and better type.

In the house with the window behind the bed I wrote my second book. Then we were moved on again, to a blistering landscape outside the city, an expatriate settlement where you were unwatched, and so it was possible to step out without getting on your Islamic glad rags, your concealing drapes; except, of course, there was nowhere to step out to.

Since my first day in the Kingdom, I had kept diaries, and they were in my bags when we locked that fourth house behind us and stood in the dawn waiting for the car. I intended, as soon as I arrived in a safe place, to begin to write a novel about what I or a fictional representative of me had seen and learnt in Jeddah. But while I was in the city I couldn't do it and, after all, the story was not over; we might not get out, we weren't out yet. At the airport, the sun rose over the runways and burst through the glass walls, great fistfuls of light. It's too late now, I thought, for the sun to show me how it can shine. Our guts were boiling with agitation as we stood in line with our documents.

One heard of people turned back at this point, their exit visas not in order, some vital stamp or signature lacking; and then, who were they, where were they, with neither leave to go nor leave to remain? It was as hard to get out of the Kingdom as to get into it. In order to be discharged from the government ministry at which he was employed, my husband needed twenty-three separate signatures on a document; the twist was that they had to be acquired in a certain order. He had managed it with a certain sangfroid, but others had sweated for weeks over it, chasing senior ministry persons as their white thobes whisked into shiny black cars and they purred home to their palaces, their working day merely long enough to take coffee and visit ostentatiously the on-site mosque.

It was 7 a.m.; our papers were stamped. Yet even on board, perhaps we could be hauled off for some unexplained and minor infraction of an unknown regulation. We held hands surreptitiously (we were still in Saudi airspace) as the plane lifted into the sky. At Cairo airport they took our passports away. We didn't like that. In Saudi, to be without documents was to be without personhood and without any vestige of human rights you might possess. Not that you were human, really – you were just a bit of international flotsam with a temporary use and a short expiry date.

The passports came back, with a transit stamp. But look, there's our luggage, why is it going that way? My husband vaulted a barrier and firmly, wordlessly, removed the two cases from the fists of the man conveying them to perdition on some distant moving belt. It makes me smile when I look back, to think how lax airport security was in those days. Terrorism was a mere red blink in the collective eye, though in my gaze it loomed large. I had been thoroughly frightened by life in Jeddah, and my conversations with Muslim women, my neighbours in the city, had alerted me to the cavernous gap of understanding between the West and the Islamic world as one saw it in the Kingdom.

Feminism? A confidence trick, a trick that the men of the West had perpetrated on their womenfolk, to make them work both at home and outside. Freedom? A delusion. Democracy? An evil system, a defiance of the natural order. Obedience, deference to authority, reverence for tradition: these were the civic virtues paraded in the Kingdom. It was like travelling back in time. The Enlightenment? When was that?

At the same time, this society was fiercely modernising; technology was harnessed in the service of antique values. Self-appointed vigilantes patrolled the shopping malls, striking out with their sticks at human flesh or even inanimate objects if they saw some breach of the rules; it might be the flashing denim legs of a Filipina girl revealed for a second beneath an *abaya* gone adrift, or it might be the plate-glass shopfront of a business that, as the evening prayer call spiralled through the damp air-conditioned halls, had failed to slam down its metal shutters fast enough.

What were the rules? No one knew. What infringed them? A look or a smile could do it. Sometimes I would step out and know I'd got things wrong. Not even my Muslim women friends could explain how I could get it right. It's legs, one said, that are the objection; you should be covered to your ankles. No, no, said another, it's arms that are the problem; you should be covered to your wrists. I did both. I had no desire to show an unwonted inch of flesh. If you left your husband's side in the supermarket, some sad man followed you and tried to touch you up in the frozen fish. You were Western, and they knew you wouldn't scream: just a silent bug-eyed flinch, a squirm out of their reach. You were probably a prostitute anyway. Most European women were. Male desperation, loneliness and need, the misunderstandings they bred: these hung in the refrigerated air, permeating public spaces like dry ice.

I suspect that what I had wrong was the expression on my face. After my good news came from London, after I got changed in every cell, I met the days with a willing smile.

Cairo, then, was an intermediate space, a populous waiting room between phases, as if one were born, or half-born, into the clamour of a crowded maternity ward. 'Don't get trampled,' a colleague had warned us, 'when you get off the plane. All the Saudis stampede to the bar.' We sat on stacking chairs placed in a short row of five, above which some wit had taped a sign that said: VIP Lounge.

In time we were conveyed onwards into the padded blandness of a transit area. Now, we said, we have almost done it, almost. But our spines did not unstiffen until the plane rose into the air, out of Cairo, bound for Larnaca. It was now mid-morning. The stewardess gave me a glass of sherry and a newspaper. I folded it to the race-card for the course at Nicosia. 'On Sunday,' I said, 'we can go and bet on a horse.' I laughed. What strange shapes liberty takes: some bow-legged particoloured jockey, some stumpy pony lumbering towards the winning post, some dusty track measured in furlongs, some holiday crowd in a free state.

Cyprus was a breathing space for us, a short holiday. When we got back to England we knew my husband had to find a job and I – well, I had a job; I was a writer now; what I had to find was an income. The advance for my first novel had been £2,000, and even in 1986 it didn't go far. The first book had been a hit with the critics and the reading public had snapped up – oh, all of 500 copies, I supposed; nobody volunteered the exact figure, and I thought it would be tactful not to ask.

That first night, in a hotel in Limassol, I studied myself to assess my fitness for a future. I was ill and had been taking steroids. My face was puffy and, most ludicrously, since there were no hairdressers in Jeddah (or none I found), my hair, which was thin and frizzed by the drugs, had been uncut for nine months and hung in a tangle over my eyes. A telex to an efficient relative had secured me an appointment, one week on, at a salon in Windsor, where in those days we had a small flat; it was the place we were coming home to, with the castle looming in at our window.

I had decided when I was twelve that I would like to live in

Windsor, and bought the flat when I was twenty-seven, though the size of the deposit cheque unnerved me, and I scrambled the figures and had to write it twice. I had not always been lucky, had not always been blessed; but, illness aside, I had a savage and hidden faculty for managing my desires: for slapping and pounding fate, a rickety raw-faced amateur who should never have stepped into the ring with the hard-fisted likes of me.

In the interim, I rolled through the world like an unkempt pedigree dog. If you were a dog, someone had said to me recently, you'd be a golden retriever. That was me: lolloping towards April, waving my daft tail. My second book would be published a week or two after I arrived home. And that afternoon in Cyprus I had walked along the road by the beach, in the splashy sunshine, on my husband's arm, unmolested, no men shouting at me out of cars or trying to run me over – which procedures were quite usual in the Kingdom. I had walked along the rubbly seafront towards the town, heavy lorries grinding past, exhaust fumes wafting on the warm wind.

In Limassol there is, or there was then, a herb market in a hall like a vast glasshouse. The glass shimmered verdant and we inhaled green, the miasma of plant life, the world of chlorophyll as it shivered and dripped: scent of stem, of shoot, of sap, the air itself sighing with misty fragrance. On the way back we stopped at a tourist bar. We sat at a pavement table in the traffic fumes and drank cold beer.

It was such an easy, ordinary thing to do. In a moment, the constraint of four years eased, the extent of my inner impoverishment became plain and it almost shocked me how fiercely I had slapped my bet on the counter, staked my claim to the future. Now, now, I said – despite the steroids, the sickness, the embarrassing hairdo, despite the job search, the uncertainty, the displacement, now despite everything, despite the fact that I am thirty-four and just beginning, this is the happiest day of my life.

And it was. It is. Not many people have the good fortune to pinpoint it, to log it, to feel it while it's happening and skewer it down. We drained our glasses, brushed the crisp crumbs from our persons and strolled back to the hotel. 13 March, Limassol, 1986.

The Princess Myth

2017

Royal time should move slowly and by its own laws: creeping, like the flow of chrism from a jar. But twenty ordinary years have jog-trotted by, and it's possible to have a grown-up conversation with someone who wasn't born when Diana died. Her widower is long remarried. Her eldest son, once so like her, shows signs of developing the ponderous looks of Philip, his grandfather. Diana should be as passé as ostrich plumes: one of those royal or quasi-royal women, like Mary of Teck or Wallis Simpson or the last tsarina, whose images fade to sepia and whose bones are white as pearls. Instead, we gossip about her as if she had just left the room. We still debate how in 1981 a sweet-faced, puppy-eyed twenty-year-old came to marry into the royal house. Was it a set-up from the start? Did she know her fiancé loved another woman? Was she complicit, or was she an innocent, garlanded for the slab and the knife?

For some people, being dead is only a relative condition; they wreak more than the living do. After their first rigour, they reshape themselves, taking on a flexibility in public discourse. For the anniversary of her death, the princess's sons remember her for the TV cameras, and we learn that she was 'fun' and 'very caring' and 'a breath of fresh air'. They speak sincerely, but they have no news. Yet there is no bar on saying what you like about her, in defiance of the evidence. Private tapes she made with her voice coach have been shown in a TV documentary, *Diana: In Her Own Words*. They were trailed as revealing a princess who is 'candid' and 'uninhibited'. Yet never has she appeared so self-conscious and recalcitrant. Squirming, twitching, avoiding the camera's eye, she describes herself hopefully as 'a rebel', on the grounds that she liked to do the opposite of everyone else. You want to veil the lens and explain: that is reaction, not rebellion. Throwing a tantrum when thwarted doesn't make you a free spirit. Rolling your eyes and shrugging doesn't prove you are brave. And because people say 'trust me', it doesn't mean they'll keep your secrets.

Yet royal people exist in a place beyond fact correction, in a mystical realm with rules that, as individuals, they may not see; Diana consulted psychics to work out what was going on. The perennial demand for them to cut costs and be more 'down to earth' is futile. They are not people like us, but with better hats. They exist apart from utility, and by virtue of our unexamined and irrational needs. You can't write or speak about the princess without explicating and embellishing her myth. She no longer exists as herself, only as what we made of her. Her story is archaic and transpersonal. 'It is as if,' said the psychotherapist Warren Colman, 'Diana broadcast on an archetypal frequency.'

Though she was not born royal, her ancestors were ancient power-brokers, dug more deeply into these islands than the Windsors. She arrived on the scene in an era of gross self-interest, to distract the nation from the hardness of its own character. As she correctly discerned, 'the British people needed someone to give affection.' A soft-eyed, fertile blonde, she represented conjugal and maternal love, and what other source did we have? Until Tony Blair took office as a fresh-faced Prince Charming we had female leaders, but they were old and their cupboards were bare of food and love: a queen who, even at Diana's death, was reluctant to descend from the cold north, and a prime minister formerly known as Maggie Thatcher, Milk Snatcher.

The princess we invented to fill a vacancy had little to do with any actual person. Even at the beginning she was only loosely based on the young woman born Diana Spencer, and once she was engaged to the Prince of Wales she cut adrift from her modest CV. In the documentary *Diana, Our Mother*, her son Harry spoke of her as 'an ordinary twenty-year-old'; then checked himself, remembering she was an aristocrat. But in some ways his first thought was right. Like a farmer's daughter, Diana married the boy across the hedge – she grew up near the queen's estate at Sandringham. As the third daughter born to Viscount Althorp, she was perhaps a disappointment. The family's previous child, a son, had died within hours of birth, and Spencer and his wife Frances had to try again for an heir. The Jungian analyst Marion Woodman posits that unwanted or superfluous children have difficulty in becoming embodied; they remain airy, available to fate, as if no one has signed them out of the soul store. By Diana's cradle – where the witches and good fairies do battle – stood a friend of the Queen Mother, her maternal grandmother Ruth Fermoy. When Diana was six, Frances left her young family. Fermoy took sides against her daughter and helped Spencer get custody of his four desolate children. Later, promoted to his earldom, he remarried without telling them. Diana is said to have expressed her views by pushing her stepmother downstairs.

Diana's private education implanted few cultural interests and no sense of their lack. She passed no public exams. But she could write a civil letter in her rounded hand, and since she didn't have to earn a living, did it matter? In *Diana: In Her Own Words*, she speaks of her sense of destiny. 'I knew . . . something profound was coming my way . . . I knew I was different from my friends . . .' Like Cinderella in the kitchen, she served an apprenticeship in humility, working as an upper-class cleaner, and in a nursery mopping up after other people's babies. Then the prince came calling: a mature man, with a history of his own.

By her own account, Diana was not clever. Nor was she especially good, in the sense of having a dependable inclination to virtue; she was quixotically loving, not steadily charitable; mutable, not dependable; given to infatuation, prey to impulse. This is not a criticism. Myth does not reject any material. It only asks for a heart of wax. Then it works subtly to shape its subject, mould her to be fit for fate. When people described Diana as a 'fairy-tale princess', were they thinking of the cleaned-up versions? Fairy tales are not about gauzy frocks and ego gratification. They are about child murder, cannibalism, starvation, deformity, desperate human creatures cast into the form of beasts, or chained by spells, or immured alive in thorns. The caged child is milk-fed, finger felt for plumpness by the witch, and if there is a happy-ever-after, it is usually written on someone's skin.

In a TV interview before the marriage – the 'ghastly interview', as Diana called it – Charles wondered quizzically, 'whatever "in love" means'. He has been blamed ever since for destroying the simple faith of a simple maid. But off camera, Diana was preparing. Her choice of hymn makes the marriage a patriotic duty, like signing up for a war:

> The love that asks no question, the love that stands the test,
> That lays upon the altar the dearest and the best;
> The Love that never falters, the love that pays the price,
> The love that makes undaunted the final sacrifice.

By Diana's later account, the wedding day was 'the worst day of my life'. But at the time – July 1981 – she looked dazed with happiness. Even for republicans there was much to enjoy. A great city *en fête*. The oily reverence of the commentators with their peculiar word order: 'For the first time through the centre gateway of Admiralty Arch arrives Lady Diana . . .' Best of all, the outfits: Princess Anne dressed as an Easter egg, wearing a furious scowl. Diana's entrance into legend prompted a national gasp, as she tumbled from her coach like a bride in a bag. Her gown unfolded perfectly, like a paper flower. But some palace lackey had erred; the vehicle was too cramped for a tall flouncing lassie and her frock.

It takes a lot of know-how and behind-the-scenes sweat to transform Cinderella from dust-maid to belle. Fairy tales do not describe the day after the wedding, when the young wife lost in the corridors of the palace sees her reflection splinter, and turns in panicked circles looking for a mirror that recognises her. Prince Charles's attitude of anxious perplexity seems to have concealed an obtuseness about what the marriage meant to his bride. The usual young woman of the era had a job, sexual experience, friends who stayed within her circle – her wedding was simply a big party, and she probably didn't even move house. But Diana's experience as daughter of a landed family did not prepare her for Buckingham Palace, any more than Schönbrunn prepared the teenage Marie Antoinette for Versailles. It was Diana's complaint that no one helped her or saw her need. Fermoy had expressed doubts before the marriage. 'Darling, you must understand that their sense of humour and their lifestyle are different . . .' The bathos is superb. 'Mind how you go,' say the elders, as they tip off the dragon and chain the virgin to the mossy rock.

What would have happened to Diana if she had made the sort of marriage her friends made? You can picture her stabled in the shires with a husband untroubled by brains: furnishing a cold house with good pieces, skiing annually, hosting shoots, stuffing the children off to board, spending more on replenishing the ancestral linen cupboard than on her own back. With not too much face paint, jacket sleeves too short for her long arms, vital organs shielded by a stout bag bought at a country show, she would have ossified into convention; no one would have suspected her of being a beauty. Like many women in mid-life, she would have lived in a mist of discontent, struggling to define something owing, something that had eluded her. But in her case the 'something' would have been the throne.

Even in childhood photos Diana seems to pose, as if watching her own show. Her gaze flits sideways, as if to check everyone is looking at her. One 'friend' told a TV crew that as a teenager, 'whenever you saw her alone she would have picked up some trashy romantic novel'. Leave aside the casual denigration of women's taste: if Diana imagined herself – the least and youngest daughter – as magnificent, all-conquering, a queen, she had a means of turning her daydream into fact. Diana claimed that she and the prince met only thirteen times before their wedding. Did she keep a note? She lacked self-awareness, but had strong instincts. It must have been child's play – because she was anxious to please, or because she was crafty – to seem to share his visions and concerns. An earnest look, a shy silence, job done. Chaste maids were not too plentiful in the 1980s. The prince took advice: snap her up, sir.

Diana was no doubt really shy, and certainly unused and unformed: a hollow vessel, able to carry not just heirs but the projections of others. After marriage she had power that she had not sought or imagined. She had expected adulation, but of a private kind: to be adored by her prince, respected and revered by her subjects. She could not have imagined how insatiable the public would be, once demand for her had been ramped up by the media and her own tactics. In her circle there were no solid witnesses to the nature of reality – only those who, by virtue of their vocation, were fantasists, exalting sentiment, exploiting the nation's infantile needs, equating history with the history of a few titled families. She had a sense of her own fitness to be princess, and unfitness for any other role. But she had no sense of the true history in which she was now embedded, or the strength of the forces she would constellate. At first, she said, she was afraid of the crowds who gathered to adore her. Then she began to feed on them.

When Diana became the most famous woman in the world, it is not surprising that less popular members of the Firm were miffed. The queen herself had been a beauty, but may have thought it vulgar to be too interested in one's looks. Diana was allowed to interest herself in little else. Her dealings with the press and photographers were not innocent. The images had to be carefully curated – her good side, so to speak. There were unacceptable angles. And when an image is created by the lens it can fuzz and slip and blur. Unsure of her boundaries, the princess starved herself, as if her healthy frame could pare away to the elfin proportions of the models and dancers who fascinated her. She threw up her food, hacked at herself with a blade. In *Diana: In Her Own Words* she sneers at her young self – her tone contemptuous, punitive. She cannot forgive that girl, naive heroine of a gothic novel – whose fate is to be locked in a keep by a man of dubious intentions, and to be practised upon by older women who have secrets she needs to know.

In 1992 Charles and Diana separated. In 1996 the dead marriage was buried. This was not what had been negotiated, in the thirteen encounters. The prince resumed his old narrative, with the woman he should have married in the first place. Another story had begun to tell Diana. Cut loose, she opened the doors of her identity and all the dead princesses floated in, those deposed and exiled, beheaded and shot. With them came the screen idols and the spoiled glamour girls – Monroe naked and dead, Garbo who wanted to be alone. As we grow up, we aim to be 'self-possessed', not taken over by others. But as the novelist Ivy Compton-Burnett says, 'People have no chance to grow up. A lifetime is not long enough.'

Isolated by the pique and indifference of the other royals, neglected, crossed in love and bested by Mrs Parker Bowles, she found 'affinity', she said, with the rejected. To her credit, she had begun to work actively to lessen the amount of pain in the world. She visited the sick, and stopped just short of claiming the healing touch that custom bestows on the divinely anointed; had she become queen, she would surely have gone about raising the dead. Legend insists she showed the world that it was safe to shake hands with a person with Aids. Even in the unenlightened days of 1987, only the bigoted and ignorant thought casual contact would infect them, but any gesture from Diana was worth years of public education and millions in funding. She hung around with Mother Teresa, and did it while wearing couture; she moved towards suffering, rather than swerving from it. 'When people are dying,' she said, 'they're much more open, more vulnerable, much more real than other people, and I appreciate that.' Among the weak she recovered her strength – transformed from peely-wally puking maid to an Amazon heading to battle. She knew dread diseases would not kill her. Like Joan of Arc, protected by her own magic, she walked unscathed. Campaigning against landmines, she passed through explosive terrain. Her armoured vest was inscribed, 'the HALO Trust'. Her blonde head gleamed like a fell invitation, inviting a bolt from the blue.

The divorce was a sour one. It is difficult to extract sober truth from the bitching of the sycophants on either side. Diana won the War of the Waleses because she was ruthless, and had better legs. Her withdrawal from public life, dramatically announced, suggested that she would emerge as a new model. Possibly this transformation was under way, but it failed to complete, till death completed it. Instead, she behaved like a daffy celebrity, and her fans began to laugh at her attempts to hoover up a hero. What kind of mate fits the bill, if your first has been a future king? The chance of an ordinary life of trial and error was what she had rejected long ago – when, as her sisters put it, they printed her face on the souvenir tea towels. But though her sheen was smudged a little by her failures in love, the marks could be polished away. It was possible for the public to hold two views of her simultaneously, and perhaps they were not contradictory: goddesses are not known for propriety. It's no use saying to a super-being, 'Keep your hands off my husband.' She takes and consumes, and spits out the tough bits.

By the time of her *Panorama* interview, late in 1995, Diana had developed a habit of speaking of herself in the third person. Sphinx-like, unsmiling and with mater dolorosa make-up, she presented herself as both a victim and a person of great power, and though she spoke plainly enough, it was with the mysterious air of one forced to communicate in riddles.

When she referred to herself as a 'queen of hearts', the blood chilled. She seemed to be reading from her own obituary.

She was too much for the royal family, she said: wasted on them. She saw nothing good for Charles. 'Who knows what fate will produce?' It was not a question. In her polite duchessy way, she was cursing him.

But the end of royal status had stripped away Diana's protection, both practically and mystically. After the *Panorama* broadcast there was a buzz in the air: a doomy feeling, as if her options were running out. She still played games with the press, but they knew a dirtier game. They spat at her, insulted her to try to draw a reaction. She teased them, and they chased her down, not killing her yet. She is supposed to have feared sinister forces, anticipated that her end was prepared. As every fortune teller knows, such hints assume precision in retrospect.

A deathbed, once, was a location dense with meaning, a room packed with the invisible presences of angels, devils, ancestors. But now, as many of us don't believe in an afterlife, we envisage no final justice, no ultimate meaning, and have no support for our sense of loss when 'positivity' falters. Perhaps we are baffled by the process of extinction. In recent years, death narratives have attained a popularity they have not held for centuries. Those with a terminal illness scope it out in blogs. This summer the last days of baby Charlie Gard riveted worldwide attention. But what is the point of all this introspection? Even before the funeral, survivors are supposed to flip back to normal. 'Keeping busy' is the secret, Prince William has advised.

Grief is exhausting, as we all know. The bereaved are muddled and tense, they need allowances made. But who knows you are mourning, if there is nothing but a long face to set you apart? No one wants to go back to the elaborate conventions of the Victorians, but they had the merit of tagging the bereaved, marking them out for tenderness. And if your secret was that you felt no sorrow, your clothes did the right thing on your behalf. Now funeral notices specify 'colourful clothing'. The grief-stricken are described as 'depressed', as if sorrow were a pathology. We pour every effort into cheering ourselves up and releasing balloons. When someone dies, 'he wouldn't have wanted to see long faces', we assure ourselves – but we cross our fingers as we say it. What if he did? What if the dead person hoped for us to rend our garments and wail?

When Diana died, a crack appeared in a vial of grief, and released a salt ocean. A nation took to the boats. Vast crowds gathered to pool their dismay and sense of shock. As Diana was a collective creation, she was also a collective possession. The mass mourning offended the taste police. It was gaudy, it was kitsch – the rotting flowers in their shrouds, the padded hearts of crimson plastic, the teddy bears and dolls and broken-backed verses. But all these testified to the struggle for self-expression of individuals who were spiritually and imaginatively deprived, who released their own suppressed sorrow in grieving for a woman they did not know. The term 'mass hysteria' was a facile denigration of a phenomenon that eluded the commentators and their framework of analysis. They did not see the active work the crowds were doing. Mourning is work. It is not simply being sad. It is naming your pain. It is witnessing the sorrow of others, drawing out the shape of loss. It is natural and necessary and there is no healing without it.

It is irrelevant to object that Diana alive bore no resemblance to Diana dead. The crowds were not deluded about what they had lost. They were not mourning something perfect, but something that was unfinished. There was speculation that Diana might have been pregnant when she died. Was something of startling interest evolving beneath her skin – another way of living? The question was left hanging. Her death released subterranean doubts and fear. Even those who scorn conspiracy theories asked, what exactly is an accident? Why, on the last night of her life, did Diana go below ground to reach her destination? She need not have gone that way. But she didn't choose – she was driven. Her gods wanted her: she had been out too late.

From her first emergence in public, sun shining through her skirt, Diana was exploited, for money, for thrills, for laughs. She was not a saint, or a rebel who needs our posthumous assistance – she was a young woman of scant personal resources who believed she was basking with dolphins when she was foundering among sharks. But as a phenomenon, she was bigger than all of us: self-renewing as the seasons, always desired and never possessed. She was the White Goddess evoked by Robert Graves, the slender being with the hook nose and startling blue eyes; the being he describes as a shape-shifter, a virgin but also a vixen, a hag, mermaid, weasel. She was Thomas Wyatt's white deer, fleeing into the forest darkness. She was the creature 'painted and damned and young and fair', whom the poet Stevie Smith described:

> I wonder why I fear so much
> What surely has no modern touch?*

In a TV broadcast Prince William said, 'We won't be doing this again. We won't speak openly or publicly about her again . . .' When her broken body was laid to rest on a private island, it was a conscious and perhaps superfluous attempt to embed her in national myth. No commemorative scheme has proved equal or, you might think, necessary. She is like John Keats, but more photogenic: 'Here lies one whose name was writ in water.'† If Diana is present now, it is in what flows and is mutable, what waxes and wanes, what cannot be fixed, measured, confined, is not timebound and so renders anniversaries obsolete: and therefore, possibly, not dead at all, but slid into the Alma tunnel to re-emerge in the autumn of 1997, collar turned up, long feet like blades carving through the rain.

---

* Stevie Smith, 'Die Lorelei', *Collected Poems and Drawings of Stevie Smith* (Faber & Faber, 2015).
† These words are etched on the tombstone of John Keats in the Cimitero Acattolico, Rome.

On Grief

2014

'No one ever told me that grief felt so like fear.' With his first line, C. S. Lewis's *A Grief Observed* reacquaints his reader with the physiology of mourning; he brings into each mouth the common taste of private and personal loss. 'I know something of this,' you think. Even if you have not experienced a 'front line' bereavement, such as the loss of partner, parent or child, you have certainly lost something you value: a marriage or a job, an internal organ or some aspect of mind or body that defines who you are.

Perhaps you have just lost yourself on your way through life, lost your chances or your reputation or your integrity, or chosen to lose bad memories by pushing them into a personal and portable tomb. Perhaps you have merely wasted time, and seethe with frustration because you can't recall it. The pattern of all losses mirrors the pattern of the gravest losses. Disbelief is followed by numbness, numbness by distraction, despair, exhaustion. Your former life still seems to exist, but you can't get back to it; there is a glimpse in dreams of those peacock lawns and fountains, but you're fenced out, and each morning you wake up to the loss over again.

Grief is like fear in the way it gnaws the gut. Your mind is on a short tether, turning round and round. You fear to focus on your grief but cannot concentrate on anything else. You look with incredulity at those going about their ordinary lives. There is a gulf between you and them, as if you had been stranded on an island for lepers; indeed, Lewis wonders whether a grieving person should be put in isolation like a leper, to avoid the awkwardness of encounters with the unbereaved, who don't know what to say and, though they feel goodwill, exhibit something like shame.

Lewis, now most celebrated as a writer for children, was also one of the great Christian thinkers of the last century. His memoir *Surprised by Joy*, written before his marriage, is an absorbing account of childhood and a luminous description of his conversion experience. In 1956 he was lured out of his donnish bachelor state by Joy Davidman, an American poet. By his marriage he became stepfather to two boys. His life flowered. But four years later Joy died of cancer.

Born in 1898, educated at a public school, an officer in the First World War, an intellectual, a man who (by his own account) feared the collective and feared the feminine, Lewis found himself plunged into an experience against which intellect could not defend him, a process that is as common as the air we breathe, a process that involves a feminine dissolution into 'pathos and tears'.

In his memoir he recalls the death of his mother when he was a small boy. 'Grief was overwhelmed by terror' at the sight of her corpse, and he was not helped to mourn, his natural grief subsumed into the violent reactions of adults. The work of mourning, if not performed when it is due, seems to be stored up for us, often for many years. It compounds and complicates our later griefs. The loss of his wife plunged Lewis into a crisis of faith.

Why had she been taken away, when his marriage had made him a more complete human being? As a theologian he would come to credit God with some subtlety, but as a man he must have felt he had been thrown back into the classroom at his prep school, with its routinely hellish regime of arbitrary beatings. He soon saw that mourning kicks away the props we rely on. It confiscates our cognitive assets and undermines our rationality. It frequently undermines any religious faith we may have, and did so in this case. In his 1940 book *The Problem of Pain*, Lewis tackled what Muriel Spark, in the title of a novel, called The Only Problem: if God is good, why does he permit the innocent to suffer? Lewis had worked over the ground in theory. After his wife's death he had to do the work again, this time in raw dismay: dismay not only at the terrible event itself, but at his reaction to it. Unless his faith in the afterlife is childish and literal, the pain of loss is often intensified for a believer, because he feels angry with his god and feels shame and guilt about that anger; this being so, you wonder how the idea began, that religion is a consolation.

It is not that Lewis ceases to believe in God. It is that he is horrified at what he suspects about God's nature. How can one not rebel against such perceived cruelty? Conventional consolations are offered to him, and seem to miss the point. 'You tell me "she goes on". But my heart and body are crying out, come back, come back.' The Christian finds himself at heart a pagan, wishing to descend, like Orpheus, into the underworld, to lead the lost person back into the light.

Gradually the shape of loss emerges, but it is complex and ever-changing. Grief gives the whole of life 'a permanently provisional feeling'. Sorrow is 'a long valley, a winding valley where any bend may reveal a totally new landscape'. The dead person recedes, losing selfhood, losing integrity, becoming an artefact of memory. The process creates panic and guilt; are we remembering properly? Are we remembering enough? A year passes, but each day the loss strikes us as an absolute novelty. When Lewis wrote *A Grief Observed*, he did not objectify his grief in the language of psychology, but alternated between the terms available to, on the one hand, the spiritual seeker, and on the other hand the stricken child.

Nowadays, most of us have a humanist vocabulary at our command, but sometimes it seems no help at all. In 1969, in her influential book *On Death and Dying*, Elisabeth Kübler-Ross defined five stages of grief: denial, anger, bargaining, depression, acceptance. The model she created is apt to be misunderstood as a linear model, and can be used, by inept counsellors or half-informed friends, as a way of bullying the bereaved. What, are you stuck? Going round and round instead of forwards? Still mired in 'depression', two years on? Perhaps you need a psychiatrist.

Mechanical efficacy is attributed to the passage of time, but those in mourning know how time doubles and deceives. And though, in Britain, self-restraint is said to have vanished with Princess Diana, sometimes it seems the world still expects the bereaved person to 'move on' briskly, and meanwhile behave in a way that does not embarrass the rest of us. In *The Year of Magical Thinking*, Joan Didion's memoir of her husband's death, she writes of our dread of self-pity: Lewis too experienced this. We would rather be harsh to ourselves, harsher than a stranger would be, than be accused of 'wallowing', of 'dwelling on it'.

But where else can the bereft person dwell, except in his grief? He is like a vagrant, carrying with him the package of tribulation that is all he owns. As Lewis says, 'so many roads once; now so many culs de sac'. It is hard to spot signs of recovery, hard to evaluate them. Lewis asks: 'Am I going in circles, or dare I hope I am on a spiral?' The first acute agony cannot last, but the sufferer dreads what will replace it. For Lewis, a lightening of the heart produces, paradoxically, a more vivid impression of his dead wife than he could conjure when he was in a pit of despair. Recovery can seem like a betrayal. Passionately, you desire a way back to the lost object, but the only possible road, the road to life, leads away.

A Grief Observed is a lucid description of an obscure, muddled process, a process almost universal, one with no logic and no timetable. It is an honest attempt to write about aspects of the human and the divine which, he fears, 'won't go into language at all'. At the heart of the enterprise is his quarrel with God, and in the end God wins, first philosophically, then emotionally.

But there is a puzzle as to how to categorise the book: where should it be shelved? Lewis's reputation being what it is, it would be natural to place it under 'religion'. But many of the people who need it would not find it there because, like Lewis, they are angrily running away from God, hurtling to abandon a being who seems to have abandoned them. It is more a book about doubt than about faith; it does not warn, exhort or seek to convince. Anger finds a voice in this book, more anger than the faithful are usually able to acknowledge. But it doesn't belong in the 'self-help' section either: it has no bullet points, suggests no programme, offers no cheering anecdotes.

What it does do is to make the reader live more consciously. Testimony from a sensitive and eloquent witness, it should be placed on a shelf that doesn't exist, in the section called the 'Human Condition'. It offers an interrogation of experience and a glimmer of hard-won hope. It allows one bewildered mind to reach out to another. Death is no barrier to that.

PART II

Writing in the Dark

Outrage Merchant

Prick Up Your Ears

1987

There was an epoch – as remote now as the Roaring Twenties – when cheap rooms were to be had in Islington, London was Swinging, and gays were not terribly depressed. One of the types of the era is the provincial of talent, the outrage merchant who makes the Angry Young Men of a previous decade look merely tetchy. A bit of workaday iconoclasm, a fearless gob in the Establishment face, and off we stomp up the ladder of success, to the rhythm of the Mersey Beat. To evoke the sixties in this film it is sufficient to mention the Beatles: 'I'm about to get Brian Epstein on the phone . . . I've met Paul McCartney.' Playwright Joe Orton envies their greater fame. 'The lovable mop-heads,' he sneers; and suggests where he would like to shove his Remington. See . . . not even the Beatles are safe from the old scathing wit.

The film's version of Orton's life and violent death is taken from John Lahr's book of the same title. Lahr is played by the excellent Wallace Shawn, who has the face of a questing grub; it is a mischievous piece of casting, considering the necrophiliac nature of the proceedings. Alan Bennett's script is Ortonesque, but without the theatrical extravagance; it suits the cinema, in other words, and it is witty, acute and economical; the characters he deals in, and particularly Orton, with his casual attitude to the plainest facts of his biography, are busy inventing themselves, clawing their way to the creation of the ten-minute legend.

Orton grew up in Leicester, not 'in the gutter', as he says, but in a council house. Madam Lambert the elocution teacher gives him 'full marks for Dunkirk spirit'. At RADA he meets Kenneth Halliwell

(Alfred Molina), 'a cultivated person' who takes him up, educates him, and encourages his homosexuality. They try to write novels together, but it is Orton who has the real talent, and pupil soon outdoes teacher. Gary Oldham – fresh from his triumph as Mr Vicious in *Sid and Nancy* – plays Orton with a soft-voiced diffident charm, minimal proletarian features turning lustful under a John Lennon cap. Fame goes not to his head, but to more tender parts. Director Stephen Frears had such a success with *My Beautiful Laundrette* that he is now a great authority on homosexuality, and perhaps on any ambience which features plumbing; the state of the law and the urgency of his appetites mean that much of Orton's sex-life takes place in public lavatories. The scenes are quite tasteful – at least it's dark. 'The lavatories shocked me a bit,' says his sister, some years on.

Of course the film cannot cast much light on Orton's work. The cinema has one way with writers: they are pictured tip-tapping dementedly on a rackety portable, muttering curses and shredding first drafts. Presumably to show the real-life process of careful filing, recycling and self-congratulatory smirking would alert the paying public to the fact that the creative process is no more glamorous than a job with the Gas Board. But we do get a glimpse here of the cannibalistic fervour of the working writer; Halliwell complains of 'reading his manuscripts and finding that every single thing I have ever thought or said has been included'.

The point made is that their liaison is not deviant or grotesque, but ordinary. Halliwell is 'the first wife', someone says, who becomes a liability when his partner goes up in the world; gradually he appears more and more bloated and menopausal, downing Valium and standing on his dignity. The Islington rain streams down, the venetian blinds of the tiny room turn to prison bars, and Joe is out driving with Paul McCartney. There is a Moroccan interlude – filmed like an old Butlin's advert – and after that the cruelties and tensions never abate. The murder, when it comes – Halliwell hacked his lover to death – is very shocking, but not surprising at all.

Vanessa Redgrave, as Orton's agent, is her usual brittle self, wearing an antiseptic smile like a kindly school nurse; she has developed a tic of suddenly jerking one knee into the frame and massaging her calf, and as she does this only when men are around it must indicate concupiscence and not cramp. Julie Walters as Joe's mum grovels around in her Mrs Overall persona, with an outrageous accent and curvature of the spine; it is a little over-strained, and she is not the only one of the cast who thinks she is appearing in a pantomime. But the film succeeds; it was not easy to make. One producer said he would handle it if Orton could be made both American and heterosexual; other backers wanted 'an English *Cage aux Folles*'. Signs of the times. What would Orton have made of the eighties, and what would the eighties have made of Orton?

Mad, Bad and Dangerous

Fatal Attraction

1988

Adrian Lyne's film comes from the USA trailing a reputation for changing lives; for making people behave themselves by giving them a nasty fright. It is, though, a quite unremarkable film in most ways, with its B-movie conceits, cliché-strewn screenplay and derivative effects. If this changes lives, it can't take much: just roots that are deep in folk-phobia.

Instead of characters there are three potent symbols: Man, Wife, Other Woman. Dan (Michael Douglas) is a New York lawyer. In his apartment reigns a sweet, rich domestic disorder; a caramel-toffee light coats the tooled bindings of law reports, an overweight yellow Labrador basks on a well-stuffed sofa against a handmade quilt. Dan's wife Beth is played by Anne Archer: and is she fragrant? You bet she is. They have a chubby little daughter, Ellen, redolent of baby powder and innocence; unlike many lovable screen moppets, Ellen does not ruin her reputation by opening her mouth too much.

But then Mom and Ellen go away for the weekend, to find the family a new house in upstate Tweesville: to take them out of the fleshpots. Too late. Dan goes to a trendy book launch ('I hope you like sushi?') and meets Alex (Glenn Close).

Now, what more could Alex have done? She could have worn a T-shirt saying Beryl the Peril. She could have handed out cards stating that the nightmare life-in-death was she who thicks man's blood with cold. But her appearance should be enough to warn him. Her fashionable, photogenic face is made up of intersecting hatchet blades. She has a determined jaw. She has a head of immaculate pale-blonde corkscrew curls – the kind of head achieved only at some cost in money and physical pain – and when (later) she rises from bed after a night of passion, it does not resemble a white woolly mat, but is as cleverly corkscrewed as ever. It is clear that she has won the most important battle in life – that with her hairdresser – and that Mr Douglas should look out for himself.

Mr Douglas's face is based upon looser principles entirely. 'Meeting cute' with Alex on a windy street, he gets into trouble with his umbrella. Nothing is to be expected of a chap who has such poor control over his phallic symbols. (The film has, you see, lots of dubious subliminal ads for Dr Freud.) Soon they are back in Alex's apartment, getting down to it quite frantically. Curiously, their love-making is played for cheap laughs, and features the kitchen sink; I am sorry that I cannot be more explicit.

Alex's place is so obviously not the apartment of a little home-maker. Its rumpled sheets are a stark white, a brick wall is painted a cold grey; in the street outside, butchers carry joints of meat. *Madam Butterfly* is Alex's fave opera; the plot is expounded (for the drive-in market). She breaks it to her partner: 'I'd like to see you again.' Mr Douglas looks like a hamster threatened by a tomahawk. Later we hear him on the phone, lying to his wife.

When Dan tries to give Alex the brush-off – in a humane manner, because he is a nice guy, and her attempted suicide does detain him for some hours – she embarks on a campaign of persecution. Finding that she is pregnant, she rings his office, turns up at his home, threatens him with a knife – and worst of all, Ellen's pet rabbit is found, bubbling on the stove. Make no mistake: it is the Other Woman who has boiled the lovable lagomorph.

What is interesting is the way the audience's sympathies are manipulated. Alex is a siren, then she is sick and mad and dangerous; she has no human feelings that we need take into account, and when Glenn Close manifests them, with a haunted and poignant face, she is acting against the drift of the direction. But when – at an early date – Dan sets the law on the troublesome harpy, and when he suggests she abort her child, and when he half-strangles her, we must somehow sympathise with him. It is the casting that sets this up. A policemen tells Dan that he has made his bed, and must lie in it; but how should a hamster know?

The film's climax is bloody and, like the rest, derivative. The style is glossy and banal, with the air of an advertisement for some product which is never named; but we know what it is. The final sequence finds Dan and Beth safe in each other's arms, and the golden lighting gone up a notch; we are left with a family snapshot, basted in marmalade. The audience, who had tittered and shrieked throughout in a manner which would gratify the filmmakers, were unconvinced by this ending. They saw that Dan had got away with it. But 'do you know,' said one young girl on the way out, 'I don't think their relationship would ever be the same again.'

Good Clean Violence

RoboCop

1988

In the Detroit of Paul Verhoeven's black and gruesome comedy, the world news takes three minutes to read: it's all bad. South Africa has the neutron bomb. Some kind of civil war is going on in Mexico; in three minutes you can't get much detail, but who needs it? A Strategic Defence Peace Platform has accidentally wiped out Santa Barbara, and the casualties include two ex-US presidents who happen to be resident in the area. And now it's time for a commercial break.

The Family Heart Centre makes you an offer: 'You pick the heart – extended warranty – and remember, *We Care*.' Then there is 'Nuk'em – a quality game for all the family.' Omni-Consumer Products is flourishing in an 'economy ideal for corporate growth', but the quality of the city's privatised law enforcement is not what it might be.

Down at the police station, or the precinct HQ or whatever they are called, there unfolds a scene familiar to us from those repellent television series about tough cops: the scene where the officers shout, and bang their locker doors, and are given pep talks, and display their quirky urban humour, and exchange nauseating good-buddy sentiments over the closing titles. But something more than this is needed to combat Detroit's crime wave: 'a 24-hour-a-day officer, a cop who doesn't eat or sleep, a cop with superior fire-power' – and a cop who, of course, can't take industrial action.

The answer seems to be ED 209, a mechanical Rambo, a four-ton Enforcement Droid. But it is a faulty droid, and when it comes up for a boardroom demo it runs amok and wastes a junior executive. 'Just a glitch,' growls the company VP. Then Officer Murphy is shot into little pieces by the city's premier gang, and the board's whizz-kid comes up with an idea. Murphy is recreated as a 'product', a computer-assisted brain inside a titanium shell; he is now RoboCop, the ultimate law-and-order machine.

'F— me!' cry the criminals, as RoboCop blasts them into the hereafter. Rapists, robbers, terrorists are minced before our eyes. Villains are blown apart, defenestrated, melted down into pools of toxic waste. 'You have the right to an attorney,' the courteous robot voice reminds them, as he tosses them through plate glass. The pace is frenetic. The noise level is amazing. You absolutely cannot lose interest; every moment something explodes.

What to make of it? The film industry has never been sure about this director's work. His 1974 film *Turkish Delight* was nominated for an Oscar as best foreign-language film, but was marketed in the UK as soft porn. He has done well, in his own terms, to leave Holland for Hollywood: he says 'The whole cultural baggage of Europe is on our shoulders and it is pushing us down.' The ambiguity in his work remains. *RoboCop* is either a fascistic blood-ballet or clean satirical fun. Wimpish critics are muttering about the scene where Murphy – the human Murphy – is comprehensively shot; but you have seen worse in Vietnam films. Their violence is excused because of the directors' intentions, which are often impeccably liberal; but these intentions seldom cut much ice with the ordinary cinema audience, who drool – if drooling is their bent – just the same. No yobs will be spurred to imitate violence by this film. They lack the hardware.

RoboCop is a great success on the mean streets, but like all monsters he is poignant; and eventually he will turn on his corrupt masters, and they will turn on him. Memory traces of his violent death disturb his circuitry. He is a robot who can dream. He discovers from the police video records who he was before he died; he returns to his house to find it dust-sheeted, and his wife and child gone 'to start over'. There is a police strike, and the gangs tear apart the city in orgies of looting. RoboCop lives on a vacant lot by a brazier, morosely repairing himself with an electric drill, until the time comes for his revenge.

This film is energetic, visually brilliant and very funny, with a sharp script that is never allowed to hold up the carnage. Its violence is spectacular, totally unrealistic, and – who knows? – perhaps quite therapeutic. All in all, it provides a stimulating evening for those who can jettison the 'cultural baggage'; and a pure delight for those of us who have never had any culture at all.

Sixties Survivors

Withnail and I

1988

Digging up the 1960s is an industry now; it is heresy to say that perhaps the decade was not so special after all, that probably every generation feels that 'when we were young' was an age of tumult, hedonism and depravity unparalleled in the history of the world. But an especially self-conscious, self-regarding generation is now in middle age, endlessly speculating on the precise psychic turning point when cannabis gave way to coronary and the demo to the directorship; when exactly did we begin to wish our futures to be as they are, how did we get here from there?

Bruce Robinson's semi-autobiographical film is a dry, slight, small-scale comedy about one of these turning points. Withnail and Marwood are two out-of-work actors, living in operatic squalor in Camden Town; the year is 1969, and their shirt collars alone seem to embody the history of the decade. They are very poor, very cold, and cannot see how they will ever acquire the normal amenities of civilised life.

Withnail (Richard E. Grant) has a greenish Pre-Raphaelite pallor, caused by his habit of swigging lighter fuel. The energy that might have gone into public performance has gone into dramatising his own situation. He is one of those people who crop up in many of our lives at some time or other: an exhibitionist, a fantasist, destitute and unreliable, deeply embarrassing but wholly fascinating. Marwood (Paul McGann) is the 'I' of the title; he is younger, demurely pretty, and given to hypoglycaemic anxiety crises and sudden good ideas.

With one of these ideas, he breaks into Withnail's splenetic park-bench monologue: should they not get out of London, get some

country air? 'I'm in a park and I'm practically dead,' Withnail points
out nastily. 'What good's the countryside?' But there is nothing at
home except mildew and rats, and an elderly hippy called Danny
(Ralph Brown) who turns up from time to time and rolls joints
which he calls Camberwell Carrots. 'His mechanism's gone,' they
decide, looking at him hopelessly. Marwood believes 'We're making
an enemy of our own future.'

So they borrow a cottage in the Lake District from Withnail's
bizarre and rotund uncle Monty, drive up there in their terrifyingly
decrepit Jaguar, arrive in a howling gale, starve, freeze and are terror-
ised by a local poacher (Michael Elphick). In due course Monty
arrives in his Rolls, to bring light, order and claret into their lives,
and to claim his reward for such benevolence. Richard Griffiths is
beautifully cast as Monty, who is also an ex-actor of sorts, and a
man of sensitivity: 'As a youth I used to weep in butchers' shops'.
Pink and squashy, a foam-rubber hippo with priapic ambitions, he
pursues Marwood around the kitchen; Withnail, of course, has led
him to believe that Marwood will welcome his advances. Monty is
thwarted, and turns out to be a great romantic after all; and a telegram comes for Marwood. He has got a part.

That is all there is to the plot, but nothing more is needed; every
line is sharp, and the whole film finely judged and well paced. The
performances are quite out of the ordinary, Paul McGann's in
particular; and while the film is original and personal, there is
something in it that most people will recognise, however far they
have been from thespian leanings, dire poverty and Camden Town.
When Marwood gets back to London he finds that the part he has
got is a much better one than he expected. His future has arrived.
His life with Withnail is over, and they both know it. And of course
an era is over as well. 'We are ninety-one days from the end of this
decade,' Danny says, 'and there's going to be a lot of refugees. They're
going to go around the streets shouting, Bring out your dead . . .'

Not By Bread Alone

Babette's Feast and *Barfly*

1988

When Karen Blixen no longer had a farm in Africa and had returned to Denmark, she had a certain style to keep up; but she was in want of money. A friend advised her to try writing for American magazines: adding that their editors paid well and that their readers thought constantly of food. Gabriel Axel's film is a close interpretation of the story that resulted. *Babette's Feast* was turned down by the *Saturday Evening Post* and by *Good Housekeeping* but was published in 1950 by the *Ladies' Home Journal*: an unlikely first home for a piece later included in a collection called *Anecdotes of Destiny*.

In a place very gloomy and Nordic live two sisters, Filippa and Martine, named respectively after Melanchthon and Luther; one sings, the other doesn't. It is the middle of the last century. They live in a village full of bleak little boxes, like thatched site huts, and subsist on salt cod and bread-and-ale soup: a pious person's Lean Cuisine. Their father is the widowed pastor of an austere sect and does not wish them to marry and leave home; their suitors, a soldier and a French opera singer, retire hurt. They are transparently lovely girls: chillingly pure.

But a frail thread of connection persists, a wistful sense of what might have been. Time passes – to 1871, in fact – and there is another of those distant Parisian upsets. On a stormy night, they find on their doorstep a drenched, shivering female refugee, clutching a letter from the broken-hearted opera singer. 'Babette can cook,' it says.

They take her in, without much question; for the next fourteen years she serves them, unpaid, as a housekeeper. There is no money, but great generosity on both sides. Babette (Stéphane Audrane) has only one link with her past – a lottery ticket, which she renews each year.

By the time the community are due to celebrate the centennial of their pastor's birth, they are all ageing; and deaf, petty and tetchy. Babette wins 10,000 francs in the lottery, but to their surprise does not depart at once for Paris; instead she begs permission to stay and cook a celebratory meal. As the preparations for the feast get under way, the pious persons become uneasy; they see it will not be salt cod. There will be wine. A strange beast is unloaded from a boat: it is a turtle. Spectres of self-indulgence haunt the two sisters, as they dream in their starched linen nightgowns. The brethren resolve to eat but not to taste; their tongues are to be used only for praying.

This film is almost perfect. It could very easily have gone wrong; it could have made fun of the withdrawn, elderly innocents, or it could have been cynical about them. But its humour is gentle and observant, and its pace is calm and precisely calculated. The acting is a revelation; you will appreciate it, although it is done in Danish. The ironies are not obtrusive; some are sweet, others to be savoured. If there is a drawback, it is that the film exposes the crassness, pomposity and ineptitude of most of what is on the circuit. There may be some people who don't like it; but they will not be the sort of people you would like to dine with.

For it is gradually revealed that Babette is a culinary genius, once the famed chef of the Café Anglais: a woman whose 'caille en sarcophage' enraptured palates and made generals weep. The banquet is the centre of the film, the set piece. She begins with turtle soup; then blinis with caviar and sour cream. Then boned quail stuffed with foie gras (I think – Babette was rather too deft and rapid for a woman who for fourteen years had done nothing but boil fish) and certainly truffles, all in a pastry case, and a sauce of brandy, truffles and mushrooms. A merciful pause for a salad; then rum baba, and crystallised fruits. Amontillado sherry, and Veuve Clicquot: a whole set of new experiences for the flint-hearted sectaries, capable of melting their differences, rekindling their youth and sending them out warm and charitable into the keening wind.

Babette's whole 10,000 francs have been spent on the feast, but she does not mind that, because she is an artist and she has indulged her art; she has remembered her own nature, and introduced others to their real appetites. The pastor himself said, 'The only things we can take from this earthly life are the things we have given away.'

Barfly is a film starring Mickey Rourke as a drunken and predictable American poet: predictable as all drunks are predictable, and as all films about writers are predictable too. I wish I could recommend it as a *digestif*.

Fallen Angels

Wings of Desire

1988

Clouds drift over a black-and-white city; it is Berlin. Two angels
meet to compare notes. Their task in the city is to 'assemble, testify,
preserve'; their spirit nature is both a delight and a burden to them.
It is easier for them to commune with steeples, radio masts, birds
and aeroplanes than with the foreshortened humans at street level.

Their angelic vision flits from window to window, room to room.
They catch glimpses of the lives of passengers in speeding cars. The
city's heart is divided; and each inhabitant is enmeshed in his
mundane concerns, bound to the particularities of his situation. The
angels can touch human beings without being felt; lay an arm across
the shoulders of the inconsolable, lean their foreheads against the
brows of the distraught, and communicate comfort and hope.
Around them is the constant susurration of human voices, the bewilderment on human faces, fragments of trouble, pain and delight half
grasped, understood with a superior knowledge but never with a
human knowledge. They long for this knowledge, as children long
to exchange their own mental world for the brutal insights of
adulthood.

In this spectacular and romantic film, no theological complexities
surround the angels. They are simple superbeings, kindly and childlike: their perceptions are innocent. They are, in fact, aspects of
ourselves: our better nature. They have no pinions, no white robes;
they wear dark overcoats, and their only distinction is that each has
a little ponytail, like an ageing, semi-respectable hippy. Children can
see them. Like children, they ponder the mysteries of time and space,
of individual personality.

This film is quite unlike the director Wim Wenders's earlier natur-alistic work. There is a screenplay by Wenders himself and the playwright Peter Handke; the language is formal, incantatory. The cinematographer is Henri Alekan; he is seventy-nine years old, and the master of monochrome photography. The results of their collaboration are mysterious and distinctive, both powerful and insubstantial. It is difficult to come to a conclusion about this film; it speaks eloquently in its own cinematic tongue to those who wish to hear, and in 1987 it won for Wenders the director's prize at Cannes. He has (almost) eschewed his American influences; the film is European to a fault. At times – to judge it harshly – it seems a piece of mannered, indulgent emptiness. It has more surface than substance, more technique than theme; it feeds the eye and not the mind.

For most of its length there is nothing in the way of plot, but plenty to beguile the imagination. The angels oversee the city, and we are conscious always of the city's past, not because of the past's remains, but because of what time has destroyed. There are waste-lands, vacant lots, and the blighted territory of the Wall. An aged man, a Homeric figure ill-digested into the story, wanders through the city pointing out, as it were, its vanished landmarks, dreaming of the crowds, cafés, conversations of times gone by. 'Where are my heroes?' he asks, 'Where are you, my children?'

One of the angels, Damiel (Bruno Ganz), wants to become human. He longs to be bound to earth and eat earthly food. He dreams of coming home at the end of the working day to feed his cat; of getting his fingers blackened by newsprint. 'At last to guess,' he says, 'instead of always knowing.'

Then the angel sees a circus. It is set up on a patch of ground between high-rise blocks. Melancholy plumes of smoke issue from the chimneys of the caravans, and are sucked into the damp air. It is a poor circus, which cannot pay its bills. Damiel watches the trapeze artist Marion (Solveig Dommartin) and falls in love with her. This is the circus's last night. Winter is approaching; soon Marion will be forced to return to her earthbound life as a waitress.

When the angel becomes human, the film flowers into colour. Its airy, shadowy texture vanishes. At once the world looks more solid.

The ex-angel buys coffee from a roadside stall, and tastes it for the first time. He tastes his own blood. He has already encountered another former angel, who was able to sense his presence in the air; and now he meets him man-to-man.

This former angel is an actor, making a film in the city. He is the American actor Peter Falk, playing himself, crumpled and quizzical, joking about his identity as the screen detective Columbo. With the entry of this idiosyncratic, over-familiar character, the film becomes earthbound indeed. The love affair prospers. There is resolution without conflict, a facile, unexplained optimism. The film ends enigmatically: *To be continued* . . .

When Sex Began

Scandal

1989

When the advance publicity began, last year, I hoped that some disinterested person – if one could be found – would write a Young Person's Guide to the Profumo affair. The generation that forms the bulk of cinema audiences was not born then, and some of us who were did not register the tabloid furore, because we were only up to Enid Blyton. Until recently I knew three things about the business. One was that Mandy Rice-Davies said, 'He would, wouldn't he?', and that this was hysterically witty. It removed a useful phrase from common currency, and decorated it with permanent quotation marks.

The second thing was that Mr Profumo has Suffered Enough. This phrase would crop up early in any discussion, accompanied by pious sighs and judicious nods. One gathered that a revolution has taken place in Mr Profumo's life, comparable to that in St Augustine's; and that he is a chap of such tender, flinching sensibilities that his feelings are a sort of national treasure, the emotional equivalent of a listed building.

The third thing was about the early life of Christine Keeler, for a stray sentence sticks in my mind – 'She lived in Slough but moved to Staines.' It may of course be the other way about, but if intoned it has a fine, orotund ring to it, like the first line of a Victorian temperance ballad. I hope it is true.

Having seen *Scandal*, I don't know much more, but I do feel that, in a juvenile and irresponsible way, I've had a good time. In cinematic terms, director Michael Caton-Jones hardly puts a foot wrong. He focuses on an unconsummated romance between Keeler and Stephen

Ward, using the politics as a backdrop. The fifties – now universally known as the drab fifties, or the dreary fifties – is a decade thought to have outlasted its natural span; as Philip Larkin said, sexual intercourse began in 1963. The film tries to capture the transition, and conveys the flavour of the time by a mixture of the artful and the obvious. Quaint cute tones on the soundtrack give way to early Beatles. The nightclub floor shows have a kind of tacky bespangled innocence. Profumo's white Mini, parked outside Ward's mews house, becomes the symbol of an age.

As Keeler, Joanne Whalley-Kilmer suggests reserves of smouldering, secret intelligence; which is perhaps inappropriate. She sounds like – indeed she is – a nicely brought up girl trying, when she remembers, to sound vulgar; it should be the other way round. Mandy (Bridget Fonda) has an equally shaky accent, and in all the two of them are as decorous as embryonic duchesses; you could take them anywhere, even before Stephen Ward becomes their social secretary. There is an orgy scene that might have been contrived by Cynthia Payne; there is an absence of the sad and the sinister. But the film has pace, style, exuberance and wit, and writer Michael Thomas has come up with some marvellous deadpan lines: 'Oh, Dr Ward, I thought you ought to know, there's a Black man shooting at your front door.'

The casting of John Hurt as Ward is a declaration of intent. He is at the centre of the film, and it would be difficult for this actor to play an unsympathetic character. The sleazeball's philosophy Ward purveys – 'The trouble with this world is everyone's afraid to enjoy themselves' – is not attractive now, and there is a telling moment when, first approached by MI5, he smirks as if he has received a covetable stiffie for the mantelpiece. But the film places him firmly in the role of victim, with a couple of snarling policemen to gloat over his abandonment by his fashionable and well-connected friends. If his rise in the world is not adequately explained by the film, his fall is devastatingly recorded. It is as if the crowd, having enjoyed the circus, stood up and shot the ring-master.

Should *Scandal* have been made at all? Its subjects cannot really expect any deference or protection, since everything, however intimate or harrowing, is light entertainment now. People go out and scour the streets for TV crews to come in and film Granny dying; few couples, it seems, have sex without selling the serial rights. Only the Government has a passion for secrecy; everyone else is seized by the confessional urge. *Scandal* aims to kick the skeletons out of the cupboard and set them dancing in the streets. Ward broods alone with the Nembutal, Mandy basks in the flash-bulbs; it's meretricious, but what would you expect? The film has only 114 minutes to make its points. It makes them entertainingly, but it tells us as much about 1989 as about 1963.

Bittersweet Treat

When Harry Met Sally

1989

This amiable romantic comedy aims to strip away the complications from a complicated question: can a man and a woman really be friends, or does sex tend to get in the way? Harry (Billy Crystal) first meets Sally (Meg Ryan) when they are in their early twenties and have just graduated. They find themselves sharing an eighteen-hour car journey from Chicago to New York, where they are going to make their careers. Their conversation on the way marks them out as people with a very different approach to life. It is Harry who claims that sex ruins friendship; he goes on to tell Sally that he finds her attractive – 'empirically'. Sally takes a personal remark personally, and flounces about.

Harry reveals himself as a thorough-going pessimist; when he gets a new book he reads the last page first, in case he dies suddenly. Though he seems offensively sure of his own attractions, he has a certain dogged inclination towards romance. In his mouth, the simplest statement assumes the most fantastic complexity. Sally is a simpler, flatter creature. If she had been Ingrid Bergman, she would have lost no time in flying away from Bogart. 'I wouldn't want to spend the rest of my life in Casablanca, married to a man who runs a bar.' They part with a frosty handshake.

At various times over the next eleven years Harry and Sally meet again. Beautiful Meg Ryan does not manage to age much; Billy Crystal has a beard which appears and disappears, which I suppose may serve as an indication of the passage of time. We know that they will survive their various disaffections and divorces, come to appreciate each other and end up as lovers; but director Rob Reiner is not trying to surprise us, and has thrown in every ingredient necessary to keep us entertained.

The two leads have to carry the film, and it is hard to imagine them better cast. Crystal and Ryan offer us two believable, likeable and idiosyncratic individuals, and they are never heavy-handed with Nora Ephron's script. It's a very good script, with an unexpected wildness about it. 'You look like a human being,' Sally tells Harry, 'but actually you are the angel of death.' It's sharply observant, too, about American neuroses, urban fears: 'I'm definitely coming down with something,' Harry mutters. 'Maybe one of those 24-hour tumours that are going around.'

Talking on *Woman's Hour* recently, Nora Ephron explained how her most painful experiences have gone into her work. Her mother, who was also a screenwriter, used to tell her 'Everything's copy.' Given this, it is surprising that there is so little pain beneath the jokes. We understand that both the principal characters and their two best friends and confidantes find the business of sex and marriage lowering to their self-esteem and destructive of their hopes, and that as time passes it becomes harder and harder for them to take their fading charms to market. But their discomfiture never breaks the glossy surface, and this is what makes Reiner's film so different from similar material handled by Woody Allen. Its lightness of tone – it is a very cheering film – has probably bred its box-office success. It seems that people sometimes like to have their intimate dilemmas presented to them in terms that are slick and witty and bittersweet instead of just bitter.

You might, I suppose, object that Harry and Sally live in a vacuum; that they do no work, have no context, that their meetings in restaurants and public parks are heavy contrivances, and that the more the film tells us it represents real life the more plastic it appears. All this is beside the point. This film is your Christmas treat, and unless you die of a seasonal surfeit it will take you into the New Year laughing out loud.

Unsentimental Education

A Short Film About Love

1990

The word is out among film people that Krzysztof Kieślowski (I wish I knew what his friends call him) is the greatest ever Polish film director – which is tough on Andrzej Wajda. Further, he may be the greatest director currently working in Europe; further, he may be the greatest director in the entire history of the universe. Possibly Kieślowski himself finds all this embarrassing. If artists in the middle of a creative effort find praise pleasing, they may also find it beside the point; and it is belittling to genius suddenly to find itself in the forefront of fashion.

His new film is another part of his *Decalogue* sequence; the last released here was *A Short Film About Killing*, a powerful, almost unbearable account of a murder and an execution. *A Short Film About Love* looks quite different, and its subject matter, though handled in a highly distinctive manner, is more usual, palatable cinematic fare.

Like the earlier film, it takes us into the inner world of a lonely young man, a social misfit. Tomek (Olaf Lubaszenko) is a post office counter clerk. He is an orphan, and lives in a high-rise flat with the mother of a friend who is doing military service. He has no social life, and his one obsessive interest is spying through a telescope on the fascinating beauty in the opposite apartment.

He watches Magda (Grażyna Szapolowska) as, thinking herself alone, she hops unselfconsciously out of her underwear. He eats as he watches her eat; he observes her brisk encounters with various lovers. He sends her a notification of a non-existent money order, so that she will come to the post office. He gets a job as a milkman, so that he has a reason to go to her door each morning. He reports a gas leak at her apartment; the gas men search for it – by passing a lighted taper across the open oven door – and leave shrugging.

The laconic script and the telescope's framed, selected and partial images generate a sense of unease; we do not know precisely how peculiar Tomek is. Will he kill her, perhaps? No judgement or explanation is offered by the filmmaker. When Magda weeps, she turns her back to the camera, and hides her face in her long hair. Tomek functions in the world, he holds down his job, but like someone with a serious mental illness he makes objects of other people; it seems he cannot enter into any human feelings but his own. Or perhaps this is exactly what obsession is like: an intolerable, pathological narrowing of focus, to which any of us could fall victim in the course of our lives.

Inevitably, the obsessive and his object begin to collude. When his spying is discovered, Magda moves the bed so that he can get a better view. We begin to suspect that they have more in common emotionally than we first thought. Her self-esteem is low, his masochism is chilling. He tells her that he loves her. This statement does not seem in itself sufficient to her. 'And what do you want?' she says.

Magda is unfitted to give anyone a sentimental education. Love, she tells the boy, is nothing more than the desire to ejaculate. What she teaches almost kills him; and she herself does not like the brutal lesson. What marks Kieślowski out as a great director is that he allows the viewer's own perceptions space to develop. The situations he sets up seem alive with divergent possibilities. If the film has a flaw, though, it is that Magda's change of heart – for it seems she will start to believe in love after all – is not made entirely comprehensible. Would the boy's suicide attempt negate her whole life's sour experience? Or would it confirm her in her initial impression that Tomek is a creepy simpleton?

Natural Disaster

Sweetie

1990

Think of an Australian suburb. Think of *Neighbours*. Think of *Neighbours* on crack. Even then, you will have only a slight idea of what *Sweetie* is like.

Kay (Karen Colston) a pale, nun-like, narrow young girl, pays a visit to a medium. Irrational? A greater irrationality, the medium's idiot son, drools over the teacups. In the medium's house, every surface is emblazoned with multicoloured flowers, colours and textures clashing and rioting; it is as if nature in sinister abundance has conquered the world of artefacts. Prompted by the medium to discover her true love, Kay lays claim to Louis (Tom Lycos). He is reluctant at first, since he is engaged to one of Kay's friends, and has been for fifty-five minutes; but he and Kay are soon clasped in a passionate embrace in a multi-storey car park, rolling under a vehicle to escape detection by the jilted fiancée. What goes on underneath things is very important in this film. Sally Bongers's camerawork eschews conventional angles. One moment your attention is centred, the next it is being drawn as a fly to a sticky paper towards something in the corner of the screen. Heads disappear sometimes, and the cast act with their feet.

Thirteen months after their meeting, Kay and Louis are still together, living in a shabby rented house. Louis plants an 'anniversary tree', but trees of all kinds upset Kay. She worries that it will die and worries that it will live, that its roots will creep under the house, that its unrestrained strength will burst through concrete. For she has experience of natural disaster in the shape of her sister Dawn, known to the family as 'Sweetie'. 'She was just *born*,' Kay insists, 'she's nothing to do with me.' When her vast and terrible sister looms into view, Kay dwindles into a frigid melancholia.

Sweetie is director Jane Campion's first feature-length film, though her short films have attracted attention, and one won a prize three years ago at Cannes. It is mannered, droll and totally original; it walks the tightrope between tragedy and comedy in a most assured manner. On the visual level, its selective and eccentric decisions emphasise the art of seeing, not the art of film; and in its screenplay you will frequently hear the kind of thing that (unfortunately) people actually say. Campion and her co-writer Gerard Lee have an ear for the slightly skewed phrase, for the accents of gentility, for the periphrasis affected by those unsure of their ground. And yet the story is told, as it were, at an obtuse angle to naturalism; its characters cling to their symbols for dear life.

Sweetie (Genevieve Lemon) is perhaps one part simple to three parts malicious: a White, swollen figure with black nails, studded wristbands, an uncontrolled fantasy life and grotesque sexual appetites. She is repellent, destructive, maddening but somehow touching as well. After her trails her elderly boyfriend Bob, a greasy and narcoleptic creature whom she describes as 'my producer'. Sweetie has showbiz ambitions. 'The show world is full of unusual types,' says her gentle, ever-hopeful father. Her mother, more realistic, at one point runs away from home and takes a job as cook-chanteuse in an encampment of jackeroos.

It ends badly: a thwarted Sweetie, naked and howling, takes refuge in the tree house in the family garden. 'Gordon sends her meals up in a bucket . . . Kay says she saw the Pattersons watching over the fence.' When the collapsing, splintering climax comes, Sweetie's mother, bleeding profusely from a head wound, drapes the fallen monster's private parts with a decorous navy blue cardigan. Sweetie has been fatally mangled. It is a pity; I was greatly looking forward to her further adventures.

Taking the Mickey

Wild Orchid

1990

Once in a while we all need to see a spectacularly bad film, and it is a bonus that Zalman King's *Wild Orchid* features Mickey Rourke. These days the man's career has a gruesome fascination, like the site of an especially gory road accident.

Emily (Carré Otis) is a vacant-looking virgin from the boondocks. (I have looked this word up; it is derived most respectably from the Tagalog for 'mountain'.) In the first scene her tearful mother waves goodbye to her as she boards the bus for the big city. Mother would lie in the road and scream if she knew what was in store for her darling. But the first impression is that Emily will prosper, for she's being interviewed for a major post in a swish law firm. In addition to her dazzling legal qualifications she has six languages, 'including rudimentary Chinese'. (I am reminded of a sign in a shop window in Windsor – 'Scandinavian spoken here'.) Miss Otis, regrettably, does not manage English too well, but delivers her lines with the aplomb of someone sliding into a coma.

Suddenly, Emily is in Rio; cue the dancing girls, the carnival masks, the fevered rhythms, the heat of the night. She has been sent to negotiate a deal on a hotel complex, along with brisk business-woman Claudia (Jacqueline Bisset). Now, there was an innocent time, before JB, when a wet tee-shirt was just something you slopped out of a washing machine. These days, like other mature lovelies, JB asserts that beauty has been a burden – though you notice that these people never have plastic surgery in reverse. Her character speaks in a clipped English accent, as if interviewing the assorted sweaties and swarthies for a post at Cheltenham Ladies' College.

Except that these are her lines: 'So what's happening, boys – talk to me – what's the word on the streets?'

Enter Mickey. He has been dyed a strange yellow colour, and he plays Wheeler, a man of fabulous wealth. He is a property developer, who may mess up the deal for the girls; but the plot is secondary to the sex. Claudia is obsessed with Wheeler, but he won't touch her; she casts Emily in his path to see what will happen. Wheeler is impotent, though it's not put quite so brutally: 'I'm just not very good at being touched, Emily.' This does not mean we are short on action: the shuddering Emily is forced to witness sundry couples getting down to it, while Mickey salivates in the shadows. A curious thing is that clothes in this film almost self-destruct. You'll remember those chairs in old westerns, that used to snap with such ease over brawlers' heads. Here it's the same with garments. One tiny pull and there's a shocking rending of seams and boondocks are falling out all over the place. For much of the film Mickey affects a dusty black suit, like an old Irish priest. But there is no shirt underneath; presumably it unravelled while he was trying to put in his cufflinks. Oft-times, too, he broods astride a throbbing Harley Davidson, while the cries of the libidinous issue from beach and bush. 'My investors are flying across the world,' snaps Bisset, 'and planning a celebration . . . *dancing girls*.' Oh, shucks. You'd been hoping for a whist drive.

When she acquires a lover, Claudia keeps Emily on hand to translate. 'Tell him to take off his pants.' Since he is not Chinese, this does not tax Emily's skills. 'Ask him if he understands the tremendous pleasure women get looking at naked men.' We never do get to understand it, really; once we are acquainted with Mickey's life story, the writhing bodies are visible only through a blur of tears. 'He was an orphan on the streets of Philadelphia . . . stuttered so badly as a child he could hardly talk . . .' At times the whole enterprise seems to be slipping gently into aphasia.

It is unfair to categorise this film as soft porn. The sex is straight, dull and noisy, but the whole is far funnier than most of the comedies on the circuit. No connoisseur of the preposterous should miss it.

Happily Ever After

Romuald et Juliette*

1990

Charm is notoriously difficult to define, but this film has it; it is one of the summer's nicest surprises. Because of its charm, its inherent improbability hardly matters. It has the makings of a huge popular success, though this is unlikely to be perceived by its distributors. It might be perceived elsewhere: its director Coline Serreau's last film *Three Men and a Cradle* was remade as *Three Men and a Baby*, with Hollywood stars and none of those nasty subtitles. If the same thing happened to this film, I would not be optimistic. America has, as Chesterton said, 'a new delicacy, a coarse, rank refinement' which could sink this fragile enterprise under a ton of winsomeness.[†]

Romuald (Daniel Auteuil) is the president of a company which makes yoghurt. He lives in solid bourgeois comfort with his beautiful wife and two indulged children; he is ambitious, hard-driving and manipulative. Juliette (Firmine Richard) is a cleaning woman. She is Black, statuesque and clings tight to the fringes of respectability, despite her insufficient income. Into her shabby apartment are crowded her five children, product of five marriages. (To prevent confusion and jealousy, she has instituted a single official birthday for the five, an annual 'husbands' day', when her exes turn up with a present for each.) Juliette cleans the yoghurt company's offices when its high-fliers have gone home. Four days a week she finishes work at 4.30 a.m., on Fridays she has an easy time of it,

---

* The film was also released with the English title: *Mama, There's a Man In Your Bed*.
[†] G. K. Chesterton, *Charles Dickens*, Chapter 6 (Methuen, 1906).

and is through by 1 a.m. She goes home on the night bus, falls into bed and gets up again at 7 a.m. to see her children off to school.

Coline Serreau cuts nimbly between these two lives; Romuald addresses the board, Juliette trudges home with her shopping bags. In several short scenes she contrasts the cleaner's circumscribed and anxious existence with the glossy opportunities for pleasure and profit her boss's life affords. But social comment runs smoothly and unobtrusively under some excellent comedy; we are not preached at, nor asked to believe that poverty does not matter to a loving family. Nor is Juliette turned into a saint; she has her areas of ruthlessness.

Romuald's life is not as well ordered as it seems. His wife is having an affair with his most trusted colleague; his other workmates are plotting against him. They implicate him in insider trading, and contrive to poison the yoghurt production, so that fifteen consumers are carried off to hospital and the shares crash. It's complicated and it moves fast; the comedy is deadpan, swift and intelligent, yet amiable throughout.

It proves that the conspirators have underestimated Juliette. Though she has cleaned the offices for ten years, nobody knows her name. They hardly think she has eyes and ears, so are willing to make their dastardly telephone calls while she is emptying their wastepaper basket, or leave their treacherous notes on the desk she is about to dust. When Romuald finds himself sans wife, sans job, sans everything, Juliette turns out to be his only friend in the world. He hides from the Fraud Squad in her apartment – supremely indifferent to the difficulties he is causing for the family – and plots with Juliette's help to restore his fortunes.

Auteuil paints us a delicious portrait of an egotist capable of redemption; Richard's dignified performance is beautifully judged and controlled. The film is cleverly cast, with the right faces in all the minor roles, and proceeds with gusto to a happy ending. You do not have to believe in the ending, you simply have to hope that it could be so; this is a shrewd fairy tale, aware of the transforming power of money as well as the transforming power of love.

Don't Take the Vicar

Wild at Heart

1990

If you live on the margin, you meet other outcasts; if you are crazy, you belong to a secret consortium of all the other crazy people on the street. 'The whole world's wild at heart and weird on top,' says Lula, twenty-year-old heroine of David Lynch's violent and energetic new film. She should know. She has a cousin who used to put cockroaches in his underwear and who believed the world was controlled by aliens in black gloves. She has an Uncle Pooch, who raped her when she was thirteen. But like Lynch's other characters, Lula was never innocent, only inexperienced.

Lula's boyfriend Sailor is another who has never dipped a toe in the waters of ordinary life. When the film begins, he has just been released after serving time for manslaughter. We see the crime in blood-splashed detail; we also see how Lula's mother, before the crime took place, followed Sailor into a lavatory and suggested they have sex. By now you are beginning to get the picture. You cannot anticipate the steaminess of the sex scenes, or predict that you will see a man's severed head fly through the air, but already you feel that this is not a film you should recommend to the vicar.

Lynch's portrait of fifties America is savage, flamboyant and knowing. This is a culture that bares its heart; and what is a heart but another piece of offal? Sex is on offer, intimacy is not. Emotion is mediated through cheap music and free thrills. Violence is routine. Escape is the highest art; crossing the state line is life's essential act. The characters are not rebels, for there is no straight society for them to raise rebellion against. What lies in their past is vague but ghastly. You don't want or need to know.

When Lula and Sailor take to the road it is in flight from Lula's mother, an alcoholic fury who has the kind of fingernails you could use for a trepanation. Close behind the fugitives are Momma's hitmen; for various complicated reasons she has a contract on Sailor's life. Nicolas Cage plays Sailor with hunched shoulders and his familiar air of suppressed lunacy. Laura Dern's Lula is 'hotter than Georgia asphalt'. In various motel rooms they engage in desperate sex and conversation of staggering banality. Moving too close for comfort, the camera notes the liquid tackiness of Lula's nail polish, the sheen of Sailor's snakeskin jacket, the manic flicker of light in the white iris of a Black woman's eye.

The first hour has touches of brilliance and deft changes of pace and tone. It holds the viewer effortlessly. But this road movie is all style; as a portrait of quotidian psychopathy, it has neither the power nor coherence of Terrence Malick's *Badlands*. The scattergun nastiness is, after a while, profoundly unaffecting. The tone becomes uneasy. How does the director want us to respond? Is he quite sure himself?

The climax of the action comes in Texas, in the kind of hellish landscape that makes you wonder why they bothered, those chaps at the Alamo. You half-expect to see those other chaps, the ones with the chainsaws, out a-massacring; you would not be surprised if Lynch tossed in a cannibal, or had one of his characters change into a werewolf. At least part of his intention is parodic, and it seems unnecessary to put so much furious effort into parody. In the last half-hour, the structure falls apart. Lynch constantly, purposefully undermines his own best effects with macabre jokes and little pieces of whimsy. He does this, I think, to escape the charge of tenderness; for here and there we catch him softening towards his benighted creations. He supplies for them a happy ending of carefully calculated silliness, one which forbids identification with the characters and leaves the viewer feeling cynical. Perhaps that is precisely the effect he has been trying to achieve.

In the Company of Savages

Goodfellas

1990

In the pre-credit sequence of Martin Scorsese's excellent new film, three gangsters – that is, three 'wise guys', three 'goodfellas' – are driving along a highway at night. From the boot of the car comes a scraping and a knocking. They stop, get out, open the boot. Inside is a heaving bloody mass of humanity, barely alive. One goodfella draws a knife, one a gun. Give them the tools and they'll finish the job.

This scene takes place in 1970. We shall return to see it in context, and learn that the knife that Tommy Da Vito employs to lethal effect is his mother's kitchen knife. This small occurrence says much; Scorsese is interested less in the crimes his characters commit than in the world which nourishes them, the network of families which underpin the Family. But first we are taken back to 1955, to a Sicilian-Irish household in Brooklyn.

Henry Hill is thirteen years old and has dropped out of school to hang around the local cab rank, 'making deliveries' for a group of men for whom violence is the first resort. 'To me, being a gangster was better than being President of the United States,' he says in voice-over. He has a spurious sense of belonging, he has more money than any of the grown working-men of the neighbourhood, and soon he will meet Jimmy Conway (Robert De Niro), a big-time gangster who is 'already a legend'. His friends have the police in their pockets. Life is easy – if you want something, take it.

The morality is utterly alienating. So how will Scorsese persuade us to spend almost three hours in the company of these savages? No problem. He elicits fascinating performances: as Hill, Ray Liotta commands his scenes with no sign of inelegant effort. There is a strong screenplay, written by the director and by Nicholas Pileggi, on whose book the story is based. Scorsese has kept the chronology simple and approaches his narrative – which covers twenty-five years – with vigour and pace. He employs freeze-frames, sparingly; voice-overs, to generally good effect. Irony is present, but it is not heavy; the viewer is assumed to have powers of discernment. The comedy has the odd brush with nausea. There are no gimmicky excitements, for we know where the goodfellas are heading – not straight to jail, but to jail by a circuitous route, after a few good years. Or to a premature death, 'whacked' by associates after some blunder or misunderstanding, or simply after a card-game has got out of hand.

One memorable sequence indicates both the film's style and its makers' powers of observation. Hill takes his new girlfriend Karen to a nightclub. She's Jewish, from a respectable family in a neat suburb. He has to impress her. He takes her in through the kitchen, through the white tiles and bustle and forced smiles, glad-handing as he goes, dispensing wads of notes like a cash-machine run mad. The hand-held camera follows them into the plush dimness of the club; a special table is set up for them, under the stage. Then in the semi-darkness Hill acknowledges his friends. Faces peer from adjacent tables, nodding and leering, faces like a compendium of pathological types from a Victorian text on crime.

Hill and Conway are on the fringes of the Mafia; not being full-blooded Italians, they can never be 'made men'. They prosper, nonetheless: extortion, drug-dealing, murder. Hill and Karen marry. It is almost worth seeing the film for the single shot of their grotesque wedding-cake. But the dominant image of the wedding is that of money being slipped into the bride's palm. Then we see, in documentary detail rendered with a malicious pleasure, how murderers sustain the myth of themselves as kindly husbands and fathers, and how their wives collaborate, for cash.

I have never liked gangster films as a genre (and *Godfather III* will be upon us soon), but I found this one totally absorbing. For three hours Scorsese holds the viewer's interest without once soliciting his sympathy – that is a great feat of filmmaking.

Polite Young Things

Metropolitan

1990

I had a letter this week from a man who, when he was at Uppingham, had been forced to read *Emma* as a holiday task; he polished the book off in an afternoon, found it of 'incredible tedium' and has never touched Jane Austen since. This is quite different from the experience of the well-bred young Americans in *Metropolitan*; for them, Jane Austen's world provides a frame of reference and a touchstone for polite behaviour. Unfortunately the time is 'not so long ago', and the adult world is waiting to elbow their fictions aside.

This is a debut film, written, directed and produced by Whit Stillman, and made on a small budget. It is difficult to describe it without making it sound precious – but in fact it is fresh, funny and very appealing. Its young characters are the self-styled 'urban haute bourgeoisie' – UHBs for short – so they are not a class of people familiar to us from American films. I would not have thought they existed, these debs in long white dresses, these polite youths in tuxedos, who are anxious to reassure each other that there's 'very little social snobbery in the United States'. Indeed, they don't come over as snobs, but as fragile, vulnerable, filled with doubt about their own self-worth and social utility. Stillman seeks them out as Christmas approaches, in the opulent Park Avenue apartments of their (always absent) parents, and observes their rituals, secrets and games.

Tom Townsend (Edward Clements) is 'morally opposed to deb parties', yet is towed along almost by accident in the wake of the 'Sally Fowler Rat Pack'. Tom's parents are divorced, he lives with his mother in an unfashionable district, and has to hire his tuxedo; 'my resources are limited' is the genteel phrase he uses to describe his comparative poverty. However, he is taken up by the group because 'there is a real escort shortage', and so he gets to attend bridge evenings and balls and soirées that are not much livelier than an evening with Lady Catherine De Bourgh. He has endless opportunity to agonise about socialism and sex; and he meets Audrey (Carolyn Farina), a sweet young thing who puts the best construction on everyone's actions. Audrey's great heroine is Fanny Price, and Tom is ready with his opinion that *Mansfield Park* is 'a notoriously bad book'; later, though, he admits that he never reads novels, only criticism, as it saves time.

This is a tiny world, beautifully observed by the filmmaker, minutely dissected by its inhabitants in urbane and witty dialogue. Like most young people they are obsessed by their own emotions and can spend hours talking about themselves. This is not tiresome; Stillman is close enough to his characters to treat them with sympathy and gentleness, but far enough away to watch them with an ironic eye. We see them revise their childlike belief that sincerity is the only virtue to practise; they learn the value of concealment and the damage that candour can do. And we see the group split apart by an outsider, 'one of the worst guys of modern times', who is more ruthless, sexually and socially, than they.

Stillman suggests, without showing directly, the failures and disappointments snapping at their dancing heels. In the group, 'dead fathers are a common problem'. Divorce and step-parents are problems too; and Tom's father clears out his apartment and leaves town without telling the boy. There is a wistfulness about this understated, clever film; as one of the group says, 'few people's lives match their own expectations'.

I am glad to praise and not damn this week, as this is my last film column. It is not the advent of *Teenage Mutant Ninja Turtles* that has spurred me to retire, though the provocation is great; it's simply that I want to get on with writing fiction for the foreseeable future, and so am quitting journalism altogether. I have had a good time over the past four years, and have learnt to write in the dark. I have seen one perfect film – *Babette's Feast* – a great number of very good films, and bucketsful of the most wonderful trash. I have no tales of stars and directors to relate, as my natural reclusiveness and ill temper make me refuse all social invitations. I have had no misadventures, either: except that once when I was new to the job, and trying to find an obscure Wardour Street preview theatre, I mistook the street number and found myself in a dim grimy doorway, with a flight of stairs ahead, and a doorbell, and a notice pinned above it: 'Nice Blonde, Come Up'. I made a quick exit from there, and reviewed something else that week.

I should like to say thank you to the people who have written to me. Compliments have slightly outweighed abuse.

PART III
Turn the Page

Not 'Everybody's Dear Jane'

On Jane Austen

1998

At the beginning of Claire Tomalin's *Jane Austen: A Life* there is a pretty sketch map of Hampshire, showing the contours of the fields and woodland, and the great houses within reach of Steventon Rectory, where Jane grew up. There is Oakley Hall and Hackwood Park, Freefolk Priors, Laverstoke House, The Vyne. The imaginative reader cannot help looking into this map, rather than looking at it, visualising in three dimensions its impeccable greenness, order, propriety. As Jane Austen wrote, of a prospect she describes in *Emma*, 'It was a sweet view – sweet to the eye and the mind. English verdure, English culture, English comfort, seen under a sun bright without being oppressive.'

But in Austen's work, an idyll is always to be interrupted. Andrew Davies, who turned *Pride and Prejudice* into a wildly successful series for BBC TV [1995], began his story with just such a landscape, and the irruption into it of two galloping, masculine figures, who reined in their horses only to gaze down at a bijou mansion with the dewy-eyed pride of prospective ownership. It was a breathless, ebullient start, and many people puzzled over why he had preferred it to the book's famous opening lines: 'It is a truth universally acknowledged, that a single man in possession of a good fortune, must be in want of a wife.' Speaking to an audience at the Royal Society of Literature in 1996, Davies said simply that he had wanted to demonstrate this: 'It is a man's decision that sets the story going.'

It is hard to think that Jane Austen would have quarrelled with him. Within her stories, individual samples of masculinity may be bumbling, inept, malicious, or ridiculous. But biological status marks them out as the decision-makers, whereas women must struggle for social and moral agency. The men set the standards to which women must rise. It is the men who have economic power; they have command of the outside world, the post horses and the ships, the trading companies and the banks, the weaponry and the wars. Eliza Chute, a neighbour of Jane's, described her situation like this:

> Mr Chute . . . seemed to think it strange that I should absent myself for four & twenty hours when he is at home, tho' it appears in the natural order of things that he should quit me for business or pleasure, such is the difference between husbands & wives. The latter are sort of tame animals, whom the men always expect to find at home ready to receive them: the former are lords of the creation free to go where they please.

Women have dominion over their drawing rooms. They take a turn about the room, they progress sedately from the hearthside to the pianoforte. Unless men arrange a conveyance and an escort, their world is limited to the distance they can cover on foot. Jane Austen does not write about rich women who can order up a carriage, or about working women who must go out in all weathers and not mind about how they look. She writes about women of limited means who must mind about their appearance very much. Bad weather keeps them indoors, their little boots inadequate for the rutted lanes. They stay under the eyes of their families. If these families, through pride or plenty, free them from household tasks, they draw, make music, embroider, read sermons and hatch schemes for marrying off their acquaintances. If, like Jane herself, their circumstances are more pinched, they make light meals and darn stockings, and worry over the prospect of becoming a governess.

So must a biography of Jane Austen be confined to hearthside observations? A biography called *Jane Austen, Obstinate Heart* by Valerie Grosvenor Myer, rivets our attention to the matter of Jane's cut-price hair-dos and futile attempts to economise when buying a muslin veil. We attend at the myriad social humiliations of a young and pretty woman without a penny of her own, and see her wither into celibate spite, sneering at her married neighbours and their obstetric difficulties and cracking jokes about the deaths of newborn babies. A pleasant woman? Clearly not. But certainly one grounded in reality. Auden put it like this:

> You could not shock her more than she shocks me;
> Beside her Joyce seems innocent as grass.
> It makes me most uncomfortable to see
> An English spinster of the middle class
> Describe the amorous effects of 'brass',
> Reveal so frankly and with such sobriety
> The economic basis of society.*

Perhaps Jane did believe that the iron laws that govern nations govern the delicate negotiations of the heart. At any rate, all modern biographers want to pull her away from the context of the 'three or four families in a country village' that she recommended as a subject for fiction. It is interesting to see the different ways in which Tomalin and David Nokes in his similarly titled *Jane Austen: A Life* go about doing that, but it may be as well to look first at what an Austen biographer is up against.

Jane Austen came from a scribbling family, who loved theatricals and impromptu verses. They did not disapprove of her writing – they cheered her on. Her father tried to help her get a publisher, and her brother Henry actually did so. But after her death, they were anxious to guard her reputation, and this guardianship took the form of emphasising her conduct as a dutiful member of her family, rather than as an artist. If she kept a diary, it was destroyed. Her sister Cassandra preserved few of the letters she had received. A niece destroyed most of those that had been kept by a brother. A biographical note by Henry, written soon after her death, described Jane's life as 'not by any means a life of event'.

Men do not know what are the events of women's lives. A reader of Jane Austen's should have known that. But a memoir by Jane's nephew James Edward Austen-Leigh picked up the family theme: 'Of events her life was singularly barren: few changes and no great crises ever broke the smooth current of its course.' As both Nokes

---

* W. H. Auden, 'Letter to Lord Byron', *Letters from Iceland* (Faber & Faber, 1937).

and Tomalin show, this is quite untrue; besides, non-writers would not know exactly what, in a writer's life, a crisis looks like.

Jane's niece Caroline praised her satin stitch, but had nothing to say about her dialogue. James Edward, again, was sure she had behaved 'without any self-seeking or craving after applause'. What they willed to posterity was a bowdlerised life. Her great-nephew Lord Brabourne was sure that 'no malice' ever 'lurked beneath' Jane Austen's wit.

Later biographers conspired with the family censors. Nokes quotes Elizabeth Jenkins: 'Family disagreements, to say nothing of family quarrels, were unknown to them.' If that were true, what a very strange family they would have been. One can easily understand the process by which the writer became, as Henry James said, 'everybody's dear Jane'.* Her admirers snuggle up and pat her on the head. Because she dramatises the matter of female submission she was seen as herself submissive. Her work was appropriated for social conservatism. It indulged a long sentimentality about a more orderly world, a world of decorum, grace.

Jane's portrait has not helped her. There is only one authenticated likeness, a sketch by Cassandra of a woman with a tidy cap, full cheeks and a small mouth that might signal reserve, or self-control, or a repressed impulse to laugh or shout. It might, indeed, signal anything at all. Family members thought it was not a very good likeness. There is another watercolour by Cassandra, in which Jane has her back to the viewer.

So here are the roots of contradiction: in the absence of diaries, in the scarcity of letters, in the paucity of firsthand observation, in the anxiety of family and the glibness of commentators. Walter Scott praised her, but it was for naturalism; that is always a backhanded, self-limiting compliment for one author to pay to another. Henry James called her work 'instinctive and charming'; yet it is clear that the novels are the product of craft and artifice. Mid-century critics protest at her narrow focus, at her concentration on a narrow social band, and on the constant subject of marriage: how can one extrapolate from such littleness, and arrive at art?

---

* Henry James, 'The Lesson of Balzac' (1905).

Yet, though Austen sits comfortably within her social order, she is always testing out its assumptions. Her characters have to negotiate a course of social and moral obstacles. Success is not predetermined. It must arise from the exercise of private judgement, and that judgement must frequently be set against what seems safe or advisable. Jane Austen has a capacity for doubleness, for ambiguity, both in her writing and, it seems, in her life. Fay Weldon has cautioned: 'She is not a gentle writer. Do not be misled; she is not ignorant, merely discreet; not innocent, merely graceful.'*

Jane Austen belonged to a large family and to a large extended family. Any biography, within a few pages, leaves the reader floundering knee-deep in cousins. The starting point must, then, be well chosen. Tomalin and Nokes opt for very different beginnings: one frozen and vigilant, the other flamboyant and unexpected.

Tomalin begins in the winter of 1775, with Cassandra Austen awaiting the birth of her seventh child. By 11 November that year the leaves were off the trees, and by the end of the month it was dark at three in the afternoon. The expected child did not arrive. December came, and the ponds iced over. Edward Austen joked that he and his wife had 'in old age grown such bad reckoners'. Jane – 'She is to be Jenny,' her father wrote – appeared on 16 December, 'a present plaything for her sister Cassy and a future companion'.

Cassy was three. Her life would not be happy. She would become engaged to a young man who died before they could marry, and she would join her sister in spinsterhood. She survived Jane, whom she described as 'the sun of my life, the gilder of every pleasure'. The fortunes of Jane's brothers were various. One was a clergyman. Two made distinguished careers in the navy. Henry was a banker, and became a clergyman after that career failed. Edward was adopted by wealthy and childless relations, and became a landowner in Kent. George was mentally retarded, and was left with a local family who already cared for an unfortunate uncle. The family paid for him, but did not visit him.

It was Mrs Austen's policy to breastfeed her children for about

---

* Fay Weldon, *Letters to Alice: On First Reading Jane Austen* (Michael Joseph, 1984).

three months, then place them in a village household until they were three years old or thereabouts. Claire Tomalin wonders if this may be the worst possible recipe for a child's psychological health. A handover at birth might be preferable, before mother and child bond. To break the bond at three months, and then to break another . . . Today, we would foresee disaster. Unless George was a casualty, no disaster seems to have occurred. Physically, the regime seems to have been admirable. The little Austens fortified their immune systems with their mother's milk, and then grubbed around on the earth floors of the cottages, among the livestock, and grew hardy. None of them died in childhood, and it was unusual to rear so large a family without casualties. It doesn't become us to criticise Mrs Austen's regime, and Claire Tomalin does not. She wonders, though, at its effects on Jane's character. At seven, Jane was sent to a boarding school, where she almost died of a fever unreported to her parents until the last minute. A little later, she was not reluctant to go away again, to another school. From an early age she appears tough, self-sufficient, jaunty. She was not anxious, as long as she was with Cassy.

Jane's school days were short and irregular. Back at Steventon, her father kept a small school for boys. She was, Tomalin reminds us, brought up in an atmosphere of turbulent masculinity, of camaraderie and (controlled, clerical) wildness. Her earliest writings show a scathing sense of humour. Many of Jane Austen's readers want to identify her with the tomboyish Catherine Morland described in the early pages of *Northanger Abbey*. Claire Tomalin is one of these. She is in difficulties, then, when she comes to the first description of Jane, given by a female relation when Jane was twelve years old. Phila Walter said that Jane was 'not at all pretty', that she was 'whimsical and affected', that she was 'very like her brother Henry', and that she was 'very prim'.

Claire Tomalin has so firmly fixed in her mind her own version of Jane that this description brings about the book's only implausible passage. She declares that it means more or less the opposite of what it does. Phila must have found Jane unfeminine, she says, as she compared her to her brother; and she disliked Jane because she found her threatening. But to say that a sister and brother are alike is the small change of family conversation; it is not to impugn the masculinity of one or the femininity of the other. Tomalin, reacting against two centuries of mincing Janeites, cannot accept a Jane who was 'prim' – but it is not a strange thing for a twelve-year-old to be. And it may be that a little affectation is necessary, early in life, if you are to make a specialty of skewering it a few years on. 'Perhaps she made jokes Phila found disconcerting,' Tomalin suggests, 'or laughed in the wrong places . . .' Maybe. Or maybe she was just young and shy and acutely self-conscious. Shyness does not preclude strength of character.

Claire Tomalin's sensitive, intuitive reading of character is best employed when she comes to discuss Jane's early reading and what it may have meant for her development as a novelist. Her father did not censor her reading. Perhaps it did not occur to him to do so. She read female authors such as Fanny Burney and Maria Edgeworth. She admired Dr Johnson's *Rasselas*, and Cowper was her favourite poet. She was familiar with *Tristram Shandy*, and there are throwaway lines in her early writing that remind one of Sterne's casual surrealism. Most important of all, Tomalin claims, was Richardson's *Sir Charles Grandison*, which has a strong-minded heroine, much discussion of love and marriage, and, Tomalin says, 'gives detailed accounts of maternal drunkenness and paternal adultery, and lays out the correct attitude to adopt towards a father's mistress and illegitimate half-brothers'. Jane's memory was tenacious, her brother Henry said. But, Tomalin says, 'she appreciated, took what was useful to her, and kept her own voice and imaginative ground clear'. Jane Austen's early reading is no doubt the subject of a hundred theses, but that last half-sentence should be appended to all of them. She kept her ground clear; she was unlike other writers before or since.

Tomalin's commentary on the novels themselves is measured, deeply felt and full of insight. She traces in *Sense and Sensibility* the process by which the younger and giddier sister, Marianne, becomes briefly a tragic figure of real stature. The plot is schematic, but there are scenes – and Tomalin picks them out – which have 'the surprisingness of art that has lifted entirely away from pattern and precept'. She writes perceptively on *Mansfield Park*, and points out that Jane Austen herself may have been ambivalent about Fanny Price, whose moral certainties many readers have found easy to dislike. 'Pictures of perfection . . . make me sick and wicked . . .', Jane wrote. Tomalin's reading of *Pride and Prejudice* may be too cosy; this 'warm story' ripples with social insecurity, with class division and condescension. It is true that the Bennets' household runs on comfortable lines, but Austen makes explicit, again and again, that after Mr Bennet's death his wife and daughters will lose their home. Since none of them has the means of making a living, they will be poor relations, dependent for survival on Mrs Bennet's brother; it is not just desirable but essential that one of the sisters marry a rich man.

Lizzie does so, but we know it is a fairy tale. The reality is the dark bargain struck by Lizzie's friend Charlotte Lucas, her youth traded to the odious Mr Collins in return for an income and a roof. Tomalin decides that it is 'impossible to imagine Darcy inflicting a yearly baby on Lizzie', and Jane Austen, who was fond of finishing her plots off the page, seems to have decided that they would be very happy. But Mr Collins in the matrimonial bed is not an object we like to contemplate. Jane Austen is often pronounced 'anti-romantic', but a sharp turn of expression and scepticism about human motives is not quite enough to earn the label. Lizzie Bennet will never marry a man she cannot love, and for this attitude she is bounteously rewarded. Charlotte, who says, 'I am not romantic, you know. I never was', is punished by marriage to a man whose every utterance excites laughter or embarrassment.

Like Valerie Grosvenor Myer, Claire Tomalin has thought carefully about Jane's peculiar position in society. Jane's experience of the high life came when she visited her Kent connections, the wealthy family who had adopted her brother Edward and made him their heir. Claire Tomalin suggests that Jane's personal discomfort may have benefited her as a writer: 'No one observes the manner of a higher social class with more fascination than the person who feels [she does] not quite belong within the magic circle.' But Tomalin's social analysis does not stop at this level. She sees a deeper unease. We are accustomed to think of the society Jane describes as stable and cohesive, a society of stolid country gentlemen on their stolid mounts, of wives who are always 'breeding' – to employ the brutal term that women then used about each other. We think of them rooted in the landscape, year after unchanging year. Not so, Claire Tomalin says. She has looked at the antecedents of the Steventon neighbours, and finds them

> a fluid, arbitrary group, families who merely happened to be where they were at that particular time, some floating in on new money, others floating out on their failure to keep hold of old.

Jane was not, either, a stay-at-home. When she was twenty-five, her mother and father abruptly announced their decision to leave Steventon. They sold off everything – including Jane's piano and chest of drawers – and towed her off to Bath to live in lodgings. Once her unmarried status was agreed on, she was in demand as general nurse, caretaker, childminder, and all-around useful person. Travelling was unpredictable and exhausting, and she did plenty of it. She never had a home of her own, or even a room. Possibly she would have thought it strange to want one.

And yet, this was a world of settled complacency. William Chute, owner of the opulent and beautiful house called The Vyne, sat in Parliament for thirty years and never spoke once. Change and stasis . . . there is antagonism in the Austen landscape, a great, possibly explosive containment. This containment is not exciting enough for David Nokes. He chooses to begin his life of Jane perversely far from Steventon, with a male connection of hers:

> It is the rainy season in the Sunderbunds . . . The livid orange sun is striking over this dismal region of fetid salt-flats, swamp and jungle . . . It is three years since he last saw his wife . . . Toil and disease have wasted his body . . . He keeps her miniature portrait on the folding-table in front of him. It shows a slim, elegant woman with large dark eyes and flowing lustrous hair . . .

The woman in the portrait is Jane's aunt Philadelphia, who had gone out to India to catch a husband. She caught a respectable man called Tysoe Saul Hancock, but her daughter Eliza was alleged to be the daughter of Warren Hastings. Hastings settled £10,000 on her, and so she became Jane's rich Cousin Eliza. As a young girl, she went to France, and married a man she suspected of being a comte, and who suspected her of being a richer woman than she actually was. The bridegroom was not an aristocrat, just a landowner. Most of the land he owned was swamp. His life's work was to throw the peasants off and drain it. He never got far with this project. The Revolution caught up with him, and cut his head off. Eliza became a romantic exile, and after prolonged and sophisticated flirtation married one of Jane's brothers. Eliza was not only beautiful, mysterious and adventurous, she was also witty. She was novel in herself. David Nokes is excessively interested in her. It is hard not to be.

Indeed, he never shows much disposition to settle down with Jane. He is keen to demonstrate there was not much tranquility in her corner of England.

Hardship and illness, harsh weather and poor harvests, rural poverty and rural crime were as much a part of everyday life as the sound of the weathercock creaking in the wind. A typical charge list for the county assizes reveals cases of highway robbery near Wickham, attempted murder in Bedhampton, rape at Fareham, burglaries at Froyle, house-breaking at Alverstoke, sodomy in Winchester and bestiality on the Isle of Wight.

All true, surely. But if any of us were to make a study of a typical charge sheet for our locality, would we venture out of doors? Bestiality on the Isle of Wight probably did not affect Jane so closely.

David Nokes wants to write a different kind of biography; to clear some ground between himself and his predecessors. This is not easy, because early in 1997 Park Honan republished his *Jane Austen: Her Life*, first out ten years ago and now reissued with new material. It is, as Honan says in his foreword, 'acknowledged to be the most complete, realistic life of Jane Austen'. It is also a 'life and times' book, capacious, vivid and judicious. It is also a very conventional biography. David Nokes proposes less conventional terms.

> Often the most beguiling of literary forms, biography may also be the most complacent . . . In a sense, a biography is like a novel written backwards, taking as its starting point the well-known achievements of its subjects' maturity and tracing back the hints of inspiration which brought those great works into being. Blessed with the comfortable benefits of hindsight, a biographer may be tempted to describe the steady progress of genius from earliest childhood glimmerings to full adult brilliancy.

As if, in other words, the success were preordained, or at least foretold: not subject to accident, to chance. One sees the difficulty. Life, as Nokes says, is lived forwards. Jane at fifteen doesn't know what she will be at thirty-five. How does this perception help a writer? It helps a historical novelist a good deal, if he is writing about a real person before his or her days of fame. That person is in a way a 'pre-character', not yet seen by the world, and by an authorial sleight of hand which refuses hindsight a novelist can create a sense of possibility which corresponds to the possibilities of real life. But when a biographer tries the same trick, the result can be vaguely embarrassing. Nokes wishes to rescue Jane Austen from a frozen portrait in which she is 'saintly and serene'. But few discriminating readers of her work can ever have believed her to be so. The work he has set himself has been done, and his biography is accordingly strenuous, flamboyant and unnecessarily argumentative.

Nokes wants a Jane who is wild and satirical – which her juvenilia show her to be. Both biographers pay proper attention to early writings, especially 'Lady Susan', a narrative about a predatory woman which Tomalin suggests may owe something to what exciting Cousin Eliza had told her about *Les Liaisons dangereuses*. Tomalin and most other biographers date a seeming ten-year silence in Jane's writing to her family's departure for Bath: the disruption, the loss of her home and possessions. David Nokes prefers to believe that Jane – shabby and sharp-witted as she was – enjoyed Bath, as if she saw it through the eyes of the teenaged Catherine Morland, heroine of *Northanger Abbey*, and that is why she stopped writing. This seems unlikely, and yet he does well to run to earth the legend that Jane 'fainted' when her parents told her of their decision to leave Steventon. The first mention of such a severe reaction occurs in 1913, he says, in *Jane Austen: Her Life and Letters*, by William and Richard Arthur Austen-Leigh. From there, the story gets passed on from one commentator to another, till it becomes oh-poor-Jane gospel.

It's easy to understand Nokes's irritation. It's less easy to sympathise with his reading of some of Jane's letters between the news of the decision to go to Bath and the actual departure. 'There is something interesting in the bustle of going away . . .' The letters can be read as evidence of excitement and pleasure, or as the comments of someone who is making the best of what is inevitable. Jane often warns, in her novels, that communications which are true may not be the whole truth.

Besides, the question of the gap in her writings may be a non-question. We know very little of how she wrote, or how she revised, or what she destroyed. A ten-year silence on the page may not be a ten-year silence in the head.

David Nokes has a habit of losing Jane. He likes to describe the exciting things other members of her family are doing. And she isn't born until page 51. Then suddenly there is an intimacy: he knows what is in Jane's mind when she is writing. He describes her tussles with the manuscript of *Persuasion*. 'She lay awake in the darkness, searching in her mind for ways to improve those final chapters . . . Suddenly it all came to her.' The reader's objection is not that this is unrealistic. It is that it is presumptuous on the one hand and, on the other, not worth saying. 'Suddenly it all came to her' is not great insight for someone setting up to describe the creative process. It may, of course, be the best anyone can do.

Nokes's biography is stuffed with detail that blunts the edges of his arguments. Tomalin is more discriminating. She is not merely an attentive reader, she is a good listener. She can live with Jane's silences. These silences pose a problem,

> because it is hard to know how much they are real silences, how much the effect of Cassandra's scissors. Her silence about politics is famous . . . After her death, a niece, trying to recall what opinions she had expressed on public events, was unable to think of 'any word or expression' relating to them . . . Politics were of the masculine world, apart . . . Women's rights were another question on which she kept quiet . . . If she is not silent about religion, she is quiet . . . No one prays in her novels . . .

Tomalin listens to her silences and respects them. For many years of Jane's life, England was at war, but Jane's soldiers are for breaking hearts, not breaking heads. They are seen through the eyes of giddy little girls with no apprehension of death, and no idea of the reasoning behind the regimental mottoes. There is no reason to assume that

Jane, a member of a bustling and worldly family, was unconcerned or ill-informed about larger issues. But she limits herself to the women's story; her men, and the world they inhabit, are seen as if through a mirror. Their outlines are clear and their likeness is true, but the world behind the glass can only be observed; one cannot step through the glass. Another kind of silence was forced on her, a denial of self; in her lifetime, Jane Austen chose to write anonymously. To do otherwise would have been to attract the wrong kind of attention. A contemporary writer, Mary Brunton, said, 'I would sooner exhibit as a rope dancer'.

By reason of her silences, Jane Austen defies cheap psychology and trite formulation. The contradictions in her life and work are fertile, and when her biographers disagree – as they must do – the ordinary reader should applaud. Hearth and home may be her subject, but her method is never static. Lionel Trilling, in his essay 'Emma and the Legend of Jane Austen', quotes an anonymous critic from the *North British Review* of 1870:

> She contemplates virtues, not as fixed quantities, or as definable qualities, but as continual struggles and conquests, as progressive states of mind, advancing by repulsing their contraries, or losing ground by being overcome.

It is Claire Tomalin's biography, scholarly yet empathic, that best captures this sense of struggle, of flux, of striving against limitation, and its contrary: the struggle to subdue a nature to what society ordains it must be. She has listened hard enough to hear what may be Jane's first written words, inscribed in a tiny hand inside a story book: 'Mothers angry father's gone out'. She is the finest and most disinterested of biographers, because in her pages she has given Jane Austen her liberty and freed us, Jane's readers and hers, to enjoy the lie of the land and the cut of a uniform, and 'sopha conversations' and 'the glow worms in the lane'.

Killer Children

On Gitta Sereny

1999

It happened, once upon a time, that the Marquis de Sade was in a good humour. He wrote a novel *Aline and Valcour*, in which he created a utopia. In Tamoë there was no capital punishment. If society had to take measures against a murderer, it put him in a boat with a month's supplies, and launched him on the tide to meet his fate: to become, perhaps, someone else's problem. At any rate, the people of Tamoë did not have to think about him again, and were able to return to their sun-soaked, caring-and-sharing South Pacific lives.

When children kill other children, we come close to wishing for a Sadean solution. They come near to the top of the list of what society would prefer not to think about. We cannot kill them, but how can we bear for them to live among us? Under what circumstances can they do so? Without the dark dungeon and the lock, how can we withstand the assault on our own shreds of innocence? We would, if we could, launch them on dark waters of forgetfulness; simply rub them out, as monstrous blots. But since they cannot be made to disappear, we unite in moral panic. Their acts, their persons, provoke a hysterical vigilante reaction. The bereaved family's desire for revenge is vented again and again through the national media. Their private suffering becomes a public spectacle.

Outrage is mixed with bewilderment. Something in our language itself seems violated. 'Innocent' and 'victim' make a pair. The words are close-coupled. 'Innocent' and 'child' also make a pair. We are half accustomed to the idea of guilty victims; courts throughout the world have been trying women for years for the crime of being

146

raped. But 'innocent offender'? No system of justice can accommodate the idea, and no system of law or welfare is designed to deal
with crimes that are so rare.

Gitta Sereny has been involved with the case of Mary Bell from
its origin in 1968, when two young girls, aged eleven and thirteen,
were tried for the killing of two small boys, three and four years
old.* The girls were Mary and Norma Bell – they were neighbours,
but not related – and the dead children were Brian Howe and Martin
Brown. Both the victims were known to the girls, and to most of
the district. They were children who toddled from house to house
and played in the streets, in their working-class area of the north-
eastern city of Newcastle-upon-Tyne.

When Martin's body was found in the rubble of a derelict house,
it was unmarked, except for the blood and saliva that had run from
the mouth. Poisoning was considered and rejected, and it was
decided that the child had met with some strange accident. Nine
weeks later the body of Brian Howe was found on waste ground.
The pressure marks and scratches on his neck indicated that he had
been killed, but so little force had been used that the suspicion was
raised at once that the killer was a child. An officer on the case
made the connection with the earlier death, and it did not take long
for the police to find their way to the doors of Norma and Mary
Bell. Norma, at thirteen, was believed to have a mental age of eight
or nine. She was known for picking fights, especially with Black
children. She was one of eleven children in a chaotic but apparently
loving family, who would comfort and support her throughout the
ordeals to come. Mary, on the other hand, was shaping up as one
of the neighbourhood's bad girls. She was small and dazzlingly pretty,
her blue eyes alight with intelligence. Her character was histrionic,
impulsive and aggressive. She was – as the whole district would have
known – the daughter of a prostitute.

Because of the seriousness of the alleged offenses, Mary and
Norma were tried in an adult court. Norma, whose shyness and
fright made a great impression on everyone who witnessed them,

---

* Gitta Sereny, *Cries Unheard: Why Children Kill: The Story of Mary Bell* (Macmillan,
1998).

was acquitted. The more self-possessed Mary was found guilty, not of murder, but of manslaughter with diminished responsibility. The trial judge wished to make an order under the Mental Health Act, confining her to a hospital for treatment, but no suitable institution could be found. There was no choice but to sentence her to indefinite detention. She was sent to Red Bank in Lancashire, to a secure unit within a reform school; initially she was the only girl among a shifting population of some twenty boys. She remained the subject of media prurience, and tidbits of information were fed to the world by her mother, toward whom Mary was intensely ambivalent; she was not able to cut off from her, but maternal visits caused her evident distress.

At Red Bank, Mary was not given the psychiatric help that Gitta Sereny would have wished for her. All the same, she thrived under the care of a headmaster whom she liked and respected. One of the psychiatrists who had seen her at her trial suggested that she might be ready for release when she was eighteen. Unfortunately, at the age of sixteen, she was put into the adult prison system. She was released in 1980, a confused and helpless young woman of twenty-three. Her aftercare, as Gitta Sereny describes it, was insufficient and badly planned, but she did succeed in building up warm relationships with one or two people. Against all the odds, it seems, she has made a sustainable life for herself and her daughter, and now lives under an assumed name.

Back in 1968, Gitta Sereny attended the trial in Newcastle to report for the magazine section of the *Daily Telegraph*. She could not have known that she was about to begin half a lifetime's engagement with one of the accused children, but she was shocked by the newspaper reports that described Mary as 'evil' and 'a bad seed'. She was also disturbed by the process she saw unfolding over the nine days of the trial, which, she says, gave me

> serious misgivings about a judicial system that exposed young children to bewildering adult court proceedings and considered irrelevant their childhood and motivations for their crime. It seemed very obvious to me that there were elements of Mary Bell's story that were either unknown or hidden from the court.

She first aired her misgivings in *The Case of Mary Bell*, published in 1972. It was reissued in 1995 with a new preface and appendix, soon after two ten-year-old Liverpool boys had been convicted of the murder of the two-year-old James Bulger. This new case of killer children seemed to impart a fresh relevance to the questions Sereny had raised.

Gitta Sereny's ambition, which she achieved, was to talk to Mary Bell in adulthood, get a firsthand account of her childhood, and assess how her time in detention had affected her. Sereny's disposition is to presume that a child when it is born is intrinsically good, and that something done to the child by other human beings makes it capable of wicked acts. Her first question is: what are these things that are done? Her second question concerns the transformative, redemptive process. How can goodness be destroyed and then rebuilt, within a single personality? She stresses that her purpose in writing is not only to urge judicial reform. She wants to 'use' Mary and her story to make us look closely at how we rear our children, and to teach us to attend to the 'cries unheard' of their early years. She wants to help Mary answer her own question: 'How did I become such a child?'

Mary Bell was born in 1957, when her mother, Betty, was seventeen. Betty's first reported reaction to her child was 'Take the thing away from me!' Ten months later she was pregnant again and married Billy Bell, who was then registered as Mary's father. Later, when Mary asked the identity of her real father, her mother – portrayed by Sereny as hysterically obsessed with religious images and artefacts – would tell her 'You are the devil's spawn.' No candidate for fatherhood is produced by Sereny's book, and the reader will draw his or her own conclusion as to how close to home he might be found. It is safe to say, at any rate, that he lived somewhere closer than the infernal regions.

Throughout her childhood Mary was under threat, and her survival seems something of a miracle. At a year old she was found to have taken pills prescribed for her grandmother, which were kept in a place the baby could not have reached by herself. Next, her mother tried to give her away to friends. There was another alleged poisoning attempt when she was three, and a few months afterwards she narrowly escaped a fall from a third-floor window. Days later, Betty took her to the offices of an adoption agency and tried to give her away to a total stranger. Add into this picture the routine beatings, and Mary becomes no longer a demon but a victim. The demonisation is transferred to her mother, who refused to tell Gitta Sereny her side of the story. The rest of the family emerges from the account as blameless. The reader may be sceptical on this point.

The innermost secrets of Mary's childhood are yielded up slowly and with difficulty. She gave Gitta Sereny at least four versions of events, 'the last of which I have decided is probably as close to the truth as her memory could manage'. It appears that Mary had been subjected to extreme and prolonged sexual abuse. Betty was a prostitute who specialised in whipping her clients. At the age of four or five, Mary was present as her mother worked. She allowed her clients to sodomise Mary and introduce instruments into her body. She restrained her while clients ejaculated into her mouth. She allowed clients to whip her, to hood or gag her, and Mary was choked so that she briefly lost consciousness. The implication is that she had been picked up by the throat in a manner similar to the way in which she picked up or gripped the little boys she killed. She had survived; she thought the little boys would recover as she had. She describes her state of mind before the killings as 'beyond rage, beyond pain'.

There are, of course, people who think *Cries Unheard* should not have been published. At the end of her book the author describes how an outcry in the press followed the revelation that Mary had been paid for her collaboration. 'Disgust at Story of Mary Bell the Child Strangler', announced a story in the *Observer*, while the tabloids revived their 'evil monster' headlines. Mary and her daughter were traced and temporarily driven out of their home. They were taken to a place of safety by the police, their heads covered with blankets.

It is clear that the process of collaboration was long and difficult for both Sereny and Mary Bell, and that to revisit the memories of her crime, trial and detention was a fearful ordeal for Mary. If Sereny had made no payment to her, she would have been accused of making an unholy profit herself. If she believed, as she does, that we can learn from what happened to Mary, she was right to publish, and right to pay. It is true that, as she says, 'Not one word Mary Bell has ever said to me, not one word I have written, can be interpreted as an excuse for what she did.' The author's sincerity and compassion cannot be doubted. Nor, it seems at first sight, can her suitability for the task. She became a social worker during the Second World War and after the war cared for children in displaced persons' camps. She has written books about Albert Speer and about Franz Stangl, the commandant of the Treblinka extermination camp, so she has travelled further than most of us in the realms of moral squalor.

Yet she remains a sentimentalist – not about Mary herself, but about the world around us. Newcastle, she tells us on the first page of her preface, is a 'lovely' city. Sombre, grand, dignified are words that might apply: 'lovely', never. They are a 'friendly lot' in that city, with their 'virtually incomprehensible' dialect: presumably they were not very observant, in the days when Mary ran free in the streets, but Gitta Sereny attaches no blame to them for the little girl's plight. Rather, we are all guilty, because we have lost our spiritual values. Nostalgic for a lost Eden, Sereny writes of 'a fracture in the bulwark of security with which earlier generations protected children from growing up prematurely'. Not every reader will agree to join her in sighing for the good old days, when children were kept safely employed in mill and pit.

Again, whether she is writing about the court system, or the welfare system, or about the sad and damaged child at the centre of her narrative, her writing is of a maddening imprecision. Mary was not, as she states on the first page of her preface, found guilty of murder. She was, as Sereny states clearly on page 82, found guilty of manslaughter with diminished responsibility. Sereny knows the difference between these verdicts quite well, but continually uses 'murder' as a synonym for 'homicide' or 'killing'. She seems to confuse Mary's mental state at the time of the killing, which was certainly addressed by the court, with Mary's 'motive', which she thinks the court ought to have established – despite the fact that, after almost thirty years of work on the case, her own insights into Mary's 'motive' are shadowy and partial. 'The whole problem,' she says, 'of trying children in adult courts is that the entire judicial process is based solely on evidence . . . The only thing that should count is human evidence – the answer to the question "Why?"' By 'human evidence' she means the opinion of experts trained in therapeutic disciplines of which she approves.

Few people, in England anyway, are easy with the way children who commit serious crimes are dealt with by the courts. Some of the most pitiful pages in Gitta Sereny's account of the Bell trial are those in which Mary tells of her fear that, if convicted, she would be hanged, or if released, she would be beaten to death by her mother. No one communicated with her in a way that she could understand, and it is important that the insights Gitta Sereny has gained from talking to her be used by those who have temporary care of children during judicial proceedings. The Bulger trial has opened the way to public discussion, and in England reform is almost inevitable, since aspects of the trial and sentencing procedure have been judged to breach the European Convention on Human Rights.

It may be that reform will work along the lines Gitta Sereny suggests, with the age of criminal responsibility raised from the present ten years. She would like new procedures, so that children under fourteen who are accused of serious crimes are dealt with not in public but before a specially trained judicial panel. Children would be questioned only by the judge. There would be no jury, for juries are not trained, they are not experts. The court would be in charge of investigating the child's social and psychiatric background and throughout these investigations the child should be placed in a 'psychiatrically orientated children's facility'. Their eventual place of detention would have specially trained therapists; trained, that is, in the current orthodoxies. The parents of offenders – whether they like it or not, presumably – would be 'worked with simultaneously'.

And now we have arrived at what Gitta Sereny thinks is wrong with the world: not enough psychiatry. She discusses the intellectual climate of the late 1960s and suggests that one of the reasons Mary Bell's 'cries' went 'unheard' is that professionals had not taken on board the tenets of psychiatry and were not sufficiently aware of the importance of early childhood experiences in forming the personality. (Sereny thinks of the tenets of psychiatry as being like the laws of thermodynamics. She has lived for a long time in a world where they are the givens.)

The present writer would like to suggest that, in England, a different factor was at work during those years, and that a mindset prevailed which allowed damage and abuse to go unrecognised. They were the years of scrupulous professional regard for what was thought of as 'working-class culture'. In their numbing desire to be 'non-judgmental', educated people in the welfare trade did not 'talk down' to the economically disadvantaged nor teach them how to live their lives. This was admirable in theory, but in practice there was a drawback: these professionals had no idea how ordinary working-class families lived, because they only saw families who were in trouble. So the dysfunctional became a model, and their expectations for their clients – of stability and routine in childcare, for example – were low. They had every bit of jargon at their fingertips, and liberal clichés bubbled on their lips; it was just in practical observation that they were deficient.

When children are accused of serious crimes, Gitta Sereny would like the experts to go to work before the verdict, during the process of investigation and trial. This creates a difficulty. In a paper in the collection *Children Who Kill*, Dr Norman Tutt, a former director of social services, quotes a case in which three young men had been convicted of murder and arson. They admitted the arson but said that the body found in the burned house was already dead when they came upon the scene.

> One young man in particular denied murder, and I have on file report after report from psychiatrists who said 'We will not be able to treat this boy until he admits his offence.' In the end the Court of Appeal decided he had not committed the offence. Now you can see the dangers here. If the young person is pleading not guilty, it is very tempting to start talking to them about the offence and almost persuading them that they must be guilty, and that, if only they told you they were guilty, then you would be able to assist.

The collection of papers cited above, which includes an essay by Gitta Sereny, contains accounts of how accused children are dealt with in different European jurisdictions, though it does not deal with the US, where the process varies, of course, from state to state. Most European countries have set the age of criminal responsibility higher than England, and there is not much in common between the various systems. Norway has perhaps the most welfare-oriented approach; allegations against children under fifteen are investigated, but the accused do not appear in court. 'Once the police have decided that the child has committed an offence, there is no way of disproving the police's view . . . In Norway no one finds this very remarkable.'

Gitta Sereny does not propose a system quite so divorced from the reality of the complex, distrustful societies of the UK and the US. But she is more interested in the welfare of the individual child than in the cold abstract business of justice, and she takes it for granted that everyone will accede to her view of what welfare is – even though, in Mary Bell's case, it was not treatment by experts but the simple passage of time that made her learn to control her impulses and live within society. Libertarians will argue that, in our desire to protect and understand child offenders, we are in danger of creating systems which work to their disadvantage, systems in which they have fewer rights than adults. The problem seems almost intractable: it is certainly true that children do not know what is happening when they are being tried in an adult court, but anyone who has sat in a public gallery for a day will ask themselves whether adults understand what is happening in adult courts. There is no evidence, only a presumption, that children tried by special courts for young offenders find themselves any more comfortable or articulate there. If we were to decide, with Gitta Sereny, that an inquisitorial system is better for children than an adversarial system, what would be the justification for withholding its benefits from adults?

Again, there is a problem with the private nature of the hearings which Sereny proposes. We do not make trials public so that putative criminals can be cruelly exhibited, but so that justice can be seen to be done. We associate secret tribunals with totalitarian regimes. We would not accept that psychiatric treatment should be forced on adults, except in very rare circumstances, and where the need is proven. But it seems that Sereny is prepared for us to make assumptions about child offenders that would not be countenanced in the case of adults – assumptions that all of them are damaged in some way, that they are damaged in a way that psychiatry can repair, and that 'treatment' should therefore begin even before a case has been tried. She shows little appreciation of the intrusive nature of psychiatric treatment, or of the fact that it is subject to fads and fashions like other disciplines. It may be argued that psychiatric investigation cannot serve up 'truth'. It can only make an untestable version, a plausible story that fits together. It allows us to make metaphor, and myth. And that, if we are exact about the nature of the enterprise, is what Gitta Sereny has done in the case of Mary Bell.

To question how well she has made her story is not to question her empathy and compassion. The problem is her determination to use a unique case history as an 'example or symbol'. The problem is also the nature of memory, the passage of time and language itself, the language of the many versions, and the meaning that slides away between them. 'I must have done, I must have known, I must have thought . . .', says Mary, reporting on her state of mind as she killed Martin Brown. I must have . . . The eleven-year-old child speaks through the mouth of a woman of forty. It is hard not to think that Mary is a giant translation problem. If we could solve it, would we hear a language that means anything to us? Is Gitta Sereny correct to extrapolate what she has learnt about Mary and apply it elsewhere, to the 'countless thousands of children who are in prison in Europe and America'? Can we really draw lessons about childhood violence and social breakdown from the very rare instances of killing of children by children?

In England, the Bell case and the Bulger case (which are quite dissimilar) have acquired a grotesque, overblown metaphorical significance. It is the more routine adolescent malfeasances – bullying, vandalism, substance abuse, vehicle crime and petty theft – which degrade the fabric of communities. We feel threatened by these offences, and we use them to prove to ourselves that the world is getting worse; they tell us about the failures of social policy, of educational opportunity, of community supervision, and raise diffi-cult, divisive, political questions.

Yet our imaginative interest, to which Gitta Sereny caters, is in the singular, horrifying act of killing. An element within us craves the Sadean fix, or the oubliette: forget the murderous children, they are unnatural, they are nothing to do with us. But part of us wants more information – which again Sereny provides – to feed our fascination and fear. What is it that we fear? Not the loss to the victim, but the loss of innocence in ourselves; not Mary outside, but Mary inside; not her loss of control, but the fragility of it in ourselves. We can, as Gitta Sereny suggests, 'use' Mary, less to confirm our faith in society than to confirm the daily wonder that we believe in society at all. We can, with effort, see Mary not as alien, but Mary as kin, as a stained and transgressive being like us: with the malady of being human, and with no hope of a cure.

Figures in a Landscape

On Annie Proulx

2000

When writers of fiction go out to peddle their wares to the public, one of the favourite audience questions is 'How long did this book take to write?' It is a question which makes sense to readers, obviously, and to journalists, who like to sift authors into categories like 'late starters' and 'overnight successes'. But it seldom makes sense to practitioners. Maybe it's possible to pin down the moment when a particular plot line showed its colours against the undergrowth, or when a shift of the light threw up a detail once invisible against its background. You can say where an idea begins, but not where a sensibility has its root. Annie Proulx has emerged as a writer of classic stature, and profile writers are fond of remarking (quite incorrectly) that she didn't begin writing until she was in her fifties. They are confusing 'writing' with 'publishing', which is an elementary and condescending error. Everything in her work attests to long practice of keen observation, a hoarding of images and facts, and the painstaking perfection of a craft which allows her to address the most pungent and raw subject matter in a style remarkable not just for vigour but for delicacy and finesse. If you were to ask of the stories in *Close Range*,* 'How long did these take?' the answer would surely be 'A lifetime.'

Proulx's first novel, *Postcards*, was published in 1991; it was the story of a fugitive murderer called Loyal Blood, fleeing from Vermont across the West, successively a prospector, trapper and rancher; his

---

* *Close Range: Wyoming Stories* (Scribner, 1999), was shortlisted for the 2000 Pulitzer Prize for Fiction.

only contact with his disaster-struck family back home is the series of postcards that begin the chapters. Her second novel, *The Shipping News* (1993), which won a series of major prizes, introduced its chapters with illustrations from *The Ashley Book of Knots*. Here she chose the harsh environment of Newfoundland in which to let her main character, a hapless journalist from upstate New York, find an accommodation with himself and his forefathers. *Accordion Crimes* (1996) explored the American immigrant experience in a densely written novel of epic range and authority. Proulx understands people through the history and topography that shape them. Her battered protagonists have the quality of the landscapes through which they move. Her work comes from the cliff edges and rugged defiles of literature; it is risk-taking, rigorous and poised. She works language almost to exhaustion point, a ruthless poet hounding it for every nuance, each word whipped into line in paragraphs that build an astonishing stormy power. Like a poet, she sees ordinary things and defamiliarises them, universalises the parochial, brings local and specific detail into focus for every reader.

Close Range is her fifth book and her second collection of short fiction. In *Heart Songs*, published in 1988, her stories were set in rural New England, where she once lived. Here the location is her more recently adopted territory, of empty land, searing heat, bone-wrecking cold, air where one can see clearly and where it is difficult to sustain illusions about either man or nature: a territory in which, in the title of one story, it's '55 Miles to the Gas Pump'. The stories vary in length between a few wry paragraphs and what used to be called a novella. The best of them have a novel's worth of content, without clutter or digression. They are capacious stories, like soft leather bags, and they carry within them the present and the past of America, enfolded like twins in the womb.

The story that introduces the collection is 'The Half-Skinned Steer', a classic ordeal story, mordant, complex and gripping. It begins with a sentence that loops across the page and seems to snare a life in its tightening noose:

> In the long unfurling of his life, from tight-wound kid hustler in a
> wool suit riding the train out of Cheyenne to geriatric limper in this

spooled-out year, Mero had kicked down thoughts of the place where
he began, a so-called ranch on strange ground at the south hinge of
the Big Horns.

Mero left the so-called ranch in 1936, married and remarried,
made money, never went home. Why go home to the prospect of
bankruptcy and ruin?

It was impossible to run cows in such tough country where they fell
off cliffs, disappeared into sinkholes, gave up large numbers of calves
to marauding lions, where hay couldn't grow but leafy spurge and
Canada thistle throve, and the wind packed enough sand to scour
windshields opaque.

Now he is going home for his brother's funeral. Rollo, who had
been running the ranch with his son Tick and daughter-in-law
Louise, has met one of the bizarre fates to which Proulx, without
blinking, delivers her characters. The ranch's real owner is a wealthy
Australian businessman, who has turned it into Down Under
Wyoming. Among the theme-park animals are emus, flightless birds
related to the ostrich; they stand six feet tall, run at thirty miles per
hour, are omnivorous, and frequently aggressive:

Poor Rollo was helping Tick move the emus to another building
when one of them turned on a dime and come right for him with
its big razor claws. Emus is bad for claws . . . It laid him open from
belly to breakfast.

Mero doesn't like planes, intends to drive from Massachusetts.
'Had a damn fine car, Cadillac, always drove Cadillacs . . . never
had an accident in his life, knock on wood.' He expects the journey
to take four days. So what if he's eighty-three? 'He flexed his muscular
arms, bent his knees, thought he could dodge an emu.' As he begins
his drive, Proulx weaves in a second strand of story. It is a tale told
to Mero himself, before he left home, by his father's girlfriend. He
has forgotten her name, but not her peculiar allure, her bitten nails,
wiry veins, bulging eyes and arched neck. She's not a sexy package,
unless you like horses, and it is plunging, heated livestock that snorts
and dives through Mero's dreams, forcing him at last away from his
father's hearth, carrying with him the sinister tale of Tin Head, a

farmer with the worst of luck, a 'galvy plate eating at his brain', holding his skull together after a fall down cement steps. Tin Head's land is a poisoned realm, like the territory blighted by a radiation leak or an Indian spell, with three-legged calves and piebald children running on the range; and a careless day of bungled slaughtering leaves him haunted by the phantom of a steer he has stunned but not killed, stunned and partly skinned, left stumbling over its own stripped hide, silent because tongueless, choking on blood.

Events of the journey puncture Mero's geriatric complacency. A drama of cascading ill-luck brings him to a snowbound field, lost and freezing only a few miles from his old home, and we know this is where he will die, 'in the pearly apricot light from the risen moon', feeling the eyes of the half-skinned steer burning with hatred at his back. What is his crime? Perhaps his denial of his own nature, of his own responsibility, for he is 'a cattleman gone wrong', unable to face a bloody steak on a plate; perhaps it is his lean self-righteousness, his sanctimonious, self-serving refusal of family responsibilities, his arrogant conviction that the past can be thrust away. The reckoning is comprehensive, and we follow him through the breathless expedients of his last hours in the full knowledge of the curse that came down on Tin Head:

> He knows he is done for and all of his kids and their kids is done for, and that his wife is done for and that every one of her blue dishes has got to break, and the dog that licked the blood is done for, and the house where they lived has to blow away or burn up and every fly or mouse in it.

It is a chilling, comprehensive vision of disaster, made bearable only by the exquisite tenderness of Proulx's descriptive prose. What underpins it is fine judgement, for sometimes it seems that the urgent power of the foreground story will pull away and snap the mooring to folklore; the structure hangs together on the finest, strongest wire, almost invisible against the shivering landscape of human loss.

'The Blood Bay' also has its roots in a folktale, about a horse that (apparently) eats a man. It takes us back to the West of a hundred years ago; succinct, macabre, it produces a very different effect from the earlier story, making the reader slyly complicit in its central event: the sawing off of the legs of a frozen cowboy by a passer-by who covets his boots. Wyoming quickly reduces its people to objects, and the dead boy is 'blue as a whetstone' when Dirt Sheets spots him. As he hacks through flesh he admires the hearts and clubs in the tooled leather, and when later that night the feet thaw out, he throws them in a corner of the house where he and his workmates are sheltering.

Next morning Sheets is gone early, to 'telegraph a filial sentiment' to his mother on the occasion of her birthday.

> The Blood bay stamped and kicked at something that looked like a man's foot. Old man Grice took a closer look.
> 'That's a bad start to the day,' he said, 'it is a man's foot and there's the other.' He counted the sleeping guests. There were only two of them.

Pungent and droll, the story depends on the surreal understatement that is the hallmark of Proulx's largely inarticulate characters, and on the balance she keeps between the quaint formality of the narrative tone and the brutal aplomb of colloquial speech. In most, though not all, of the stories, the terrible and picturesque fates she deals out to her characters have a blackly comic undertow. At its best her comedy is laconic and muffled, like indecent mirth at a funeral. She doesn't play for laughs; a twisted smile merely arrives on the page. She is seldom close to whimsy, except perhaps in 'The Bunchgrass Edge of the World', a darkly fantastical tale in which an unloved fat girl forms a liaison with a talking tractor. '55 Miles to the Gas Pump' concerns Rancher Croom, a Wyoming version of Bluebeard, who keeps the corpses of his paramours stacked in the attic; it is a self-conscious shocker, and other authors could do it. Proulx is at her most impressive where she has scope to unleash her big rolling images, and in those stories where a sentence or two, perfectly placed, opens up the world-view of her characters.

They are people who are trying to make a living in a land that seems to want to kill them, and that is at best indifferent to human efforts. Animals die, debts eat up ranches, dirt roads serve only to connect one catastrophe with the next. Calving, branding, round-up punctuate the year, with its droughts and blizzards. The human products of this terrain are inbred and hot-tempered, fatalistic, predictable to others and mysteries to themselves; stubborn people, hard-drinking and violent, fitfully and inexpertly tender, battered by circumstances and by each other. Their brains are scrambled, their judgements are warped; their ropey scars are ornaments; they have hideous accidents, which they sometimes court as a way of establishing their self-worth. 'You rodeo, you're a rooster on Tuesday, feather duster on Wednesday' is the warning issued to Diamond Felts, high on the adrenaline of bull-riding and brisk sex with buckle bunnies. Diamond is not untypical: callous, mean, as unsocialised as a sasquatch. The women have a thin time and expect little from their relationships: 'There's something wrong with everybody and it's up to you to know what you can handle.' They hide their toughness under 'fuss-ruffle clothes with keyhole necklines', says Palma in 'A Lonely Coast', 'Listen, if it's got four wheels or a dick you're goin to have trouble with it, guaranteed.' Sometimes they settle their troubles with guns. If these are the themes of rural soap opera, Proulx's treatment of them is neither folksy nor cosy. This is country music played by the devil's orchestra.

Could they escape, these characters? Their very names are fetters, tying them to barely literate families, to dim garbled histories from other cultures. What would they do in the East, Dirt Sheets and Hondo Gunsch, Dunny Scotus and Jack Twist, Alladin and Diamond and Pearl? They could leave and be swallowed up in the vastness of the continent. Whether they are bigots or blunderers, whether they are damaged or the vehicles of damage, Proulx does not judge them. Nor are they interested in judging themselves, or protesting against what life has handed out. 'If you can't fix it you've got to stand it.'

Willa Cather wrote that 'in constructing a story as in building an airship the first problem is to get something that will lift its own weight'.* It is a maxim that Annie Proulx might endorse. The first impression is one of simplicity, but on closer inspection hers is an intricate craft, of shaping, paring and fitting together, nothing accidental, no effect without its exact calibration, no word without a job to do. Like Cather, she is attentive to the details of obscure lives,

---

* Willa Cather, book review, *Courier*, 4 November 1899.

and in her short fiction she has the gift of suggesting a great deal more than she says, populating the background with shifting shadows, while the foreground detail is specific and precise. She seldom allows her characters to introspect, or intervenes as an author to nudge us toward an interpretation of their actions. Instead, she watches as they move through their landscape. It is as if the terrain turns the people inside out.

Her imagery comes from the land and its history, pulling the people closer to the territory. Complex images cast their net wide into the culture that wove them, and it is because of their precise derivation that their elaboration can be sustained:

> Late August and hot as billy hell, getting on out of Miles City Pake's head of maps failed and they ended on rimrock south of the Wyo line, tremendous roll of rough country in front of them, a hundred-mile sightline with bands of antelope and cattle like tiny ink flecks that flew from hard-worked nib pens on old promissory notes.

Sometimes reviewers have complained that Proulx does not engage with her characters, but stays on the surface of her complex, fiery, twisting narratives. It is hard to make that charge stick when you read 'Brokeback Mountain', the account of a long love affair between two sheep herders, who do not describe themselves as homosexual and indeed do not describe themselves at all. Ennis and Jack are not yet twenty when they meet. After their dreamlike summer on the mountain, both marry, both struggle to conform, sustain their visceral need for each other by infrequent meetings. But from the moment we learn they have been observed in their camp through binoculars, our perception of the story is infused with a sense of dread: so much space, but no room for a secret. 'It don't happen in Wyomin.' The precedents are grim; Ennis remembers from his childhood how a man called Earl who ranched with his friend was mutilated and murdered with a tire iron. 'Dad made sure I seen it . . . Hell, for all I know he done the job.' When Jack's wife gives him a flat, cold account, over the telephone, of the 'accident' which kills Jack, Ennis is in no doubt that the tire iron has been employed again.

Proulx's subtle handling of their unlikely love story demonstrates how contained emotion banks up against the granite hardness of her narrative line. Her two herdsmen are as singular, and unfortunate, as those creatures in myth at whom the gods point a jealous finger; yet what destroys them is not some superhuman will but the cramped bigotry bred in hard country, the limited awareness of those whose constrained lives are spent nose to the grindstone. Proulx's concern with the economic conditions of these lives underpins her work. She is not a romantic, or given to the pathetic fallacy; these stories are never sentimental or elegiac. The characters are not doomed, they are harassed, disregarded and gnawed by chronic anxiety about the basics of existence. If the natural order is indifferent to them, so is the free market. They live in that kind of economic insecurity, without reserves, where the least piece of ill luck can break them. They are the victims of modish urban fads and fears of contamination: 'All over the country men who once ate blood-rare prime, women who once cooked pot-roast for Sunday dinner turned to soy curd and greens, warding off hardened arteries, E. coli-tainted hamburger, the cold shakes of undulant fever.' All the ranchers can come up with, to state their case, is a billboard which exhorts 'EAT BEEF'. But as one of them says, 'I suppose we should a put it on a blacktop highway where there's some traffic.'

In the future, survival in this territory may depend on fickle tourists and their appetite for a tamed wilderness and ersatz artefacts. Proulx views the prospect warily. You trash your own myths at your peril. Emus is bad for claws.

Conservative Rebel

On Rebecca West

2000

'Telling the truth is really a very difficult job indeed,' wrote Rebecca West. If, as she did, you live into your ninetieth year, your truth-telling is an enterprise likely to leave a trail of wounded in its wake. Born into the nineteenth century, she focused on the urgent concerns of the twentieth: murder and mass murder, treason and *trahison des clercs*. Her prodigious output included eleven witty novels, which offer a graceful and nuanced exploration of the emerging conscious-ness of twentieth-century women, and a short life of Saint Augustine, published in 1933.

She worked for five years on *Black Lamb and Grey Falcon*, sub-titled 'A Journey through Yugoslavia', which was published in 1941; part polemic, part poem, both monumental and idiosyncratic, it displays her unique blend of hard research, personal insight and descriptive felicity. Her reportage was both empathic and grandly opinionated; her illuminating, stern, deeply felt account of the Nuremberg hearings leaves in the mind pictures of the accused perhaps more vivid than anything in her fiction. *The Meaning of Treason*, first published in 1947, was an account of post-war trials, notably that of William Joyce, known as Lord Haw-Haw, who had broadcast Nazi propaganda to Britain; eloquent, personal and combative, it was a bestseller and the forerunner of the kind of documentary novel that would later make Truman Capote famous. No single form or genre was sufficient to contain her energy, and she lived as hard as she wrote. Rebecca West went everywhere, read everything, knew everyone. As Bonnie Kime Scott says in her editor's introduction to *Selected Letters of Rebecca West*, 'to read her letters in an informed way is to receive an education in the culture of the twentieth century'.

It is estimated that she wrote ten thousand letters in her lifetime, and some two hundred of them are reproduced here. She set a great deal of value on them; she designed them for the public realm and expected addressees to preserve them, though she insisted to Anaïs Nin that 'I loathe having the details of my private life published to the world.' Publication was Rebecca's business, and with it goes the artist's necessary self-exposure; but she found it difficult to accept that stories take on a life apart from their teller. Her life and work are fascinating because there were contradictions in her politics, in her sexuality, in everything she did and everything she was; in old age she spoke of the 'distressing multiplicity' of the human personality. She was a rebel whose instincts were profoundly conservative, a proud outcast who loved the status quo. She was a person of strongly expressed tastes and opinions: often wise, seldom benevolent. It is easy to be intimidated by West's mind, which is quick and digressive; in the digressions, she shows off her learning. Her fiction suggests she has the grace of empathy, and she takes herself to be perceptive in psychological terms and an acute social analyst. But you can also make the case that she is a class-bound snob, frequently as insensitive to the nuances of history as to the nuances of the heart; that she is aggressive, egotistical, a crusher of dissent, an intellectual bully. It is her vices, as much as her virtues, that make her letters so compelling.

Cicily Fairfield, who would later abandon her name and call herself after an Ibsen character, was born in 1892. Bonnie Kime Scott here supplies her with a ludicrous family tree, going back (with a few hundred years of ellipses) to 'Plantagenet kings'. It is only the generation immediately preceding Rebecca that matters very much. Her Anglo-Irish father was a clever and charming man whom she would later compare to Oscar Wilde, though 'we never had the satisfaction of seeing him go to prison'. He seems to have abandoned his family and died in 1906, leaving his widow poor, and with three daughters, of whom Rebecca was the youngest. Later, she would write to George Orwell, 'My childhood was spent in extreme poverty'. It was genteel poverty rather than the sordid kind, entailing cramped contrivance and self-denial, and she and her sisters were well educated with the aid of scholarships and grants. *The Fountain Overflows* (1957), which is perhaps the most winning of her novels, offers a reimagined version of her family life. Her eldest sister, Lettie, a clever and authoritative woman, was distressed by what she took to be a portrait of herself in the character of the humourless, talentless sister called Cordelia. Lettie and Rebecca would have a lifelong rivalry, the latter rebelling against what she saw as the dictatorship Lettie had exercised in her childhood.

At the point where the letters begin, Rebecca is fourteen, an evolving feminist under the influence of Emmeline Pankhurst, her daughter Christabel, and other leaders of the struggle for women's rights; 'a flapper dogsbody' was how she later described herself. Through the suffragists she met Fabian luminaries, and began to write for the *Freewoman* and a socialist paper called the *Clarion*. Her style was funny and disrespectful and hard-hitting. Shaw said: 'Rebecca West could handle a pen as brilliantly as I ever could, and much more savagely.' That hearty phrase, 'handle a pen' – as if a pen had parity with a chisel or spade – has the reek of seedy insecure masculinity about it, and tells us a good deal about the literary milieu in which she would make her name.

Meanwhile, at twenty, she held no reputations sacred. In her review of H. G. Wells's *Marriage*, she called the author 'the Old Maid among novelists': 'even the sex obsession that lay clotted on *Anne Veronica* and *The New Machiavelli* like cold white sauce was merely the Old Maid's mania: the reaction towards the flesh of a mind too long absorbed in airships and colloids.'

H. G. Wells was then in his mid-forties, and world-famous. Having been called an old maid, he was bound to want to alert Rebecca to the true state of affairs. He arranged a meeting. 'He talked straight on from 1.15 till 6.30 with immense vitality and a kind of hunger for ideas.' Mrs Wells, Rebecca noted, was 'charming but a little effaced'.

The effaced Jane Wells was to figure large in Rebecca's personal demonology in the years to come. More nanny than wife, she presided benignly over H. G.'s many love affairs, confident that he would not leave her for any woman who cared less than she did for his home comforts. Wells had already impregnated a beautiful and intelligent young girl called Amber Reeve, and the affair had caused many of his circle to drop him and Amber to be married off in haste to a suitable young Fabian. At the time he met Rebecca he was involved with the writer Elizabeth von Arnim. He flirted with Rebecca and dropped her. In the spring of 1913 she wrote a letter of extreme passion, not devoid of insight, accusing Wells of being 'unconsciously hostile' to her, and hinting at suicide. How unconscious was the hostility? Subsequent events would have ended the career of a less determined woman. The affair began; so did the letters. West and Wells called themselves 'Panther' and 'Jaguar', and the cumulative effect is as embarrassing as if they had styled each other Bunnykins. Can there be two sleek predators in one relationship? It was West who was left holding the baby.

Anthony was born on the day the Great War broke out.* Later Rebecca would write to him, 'You have one grievance against me, and one only: that I did not have an abortion and kill you.' Rebecca would later insist that Anthony's conception had not been intended, and for Wells he represented a failure of sexual technique; rather strangely, he blamed his failure to practice coitus interruptus on his fear he might be disturbed in the act by his valet. As an unmarried woman with a child, Rebecca was now outside polite society, and had to skulk out of sight, in provincial houses with sneering servants. The trials of the next few years were predictable: 'I never now can sleep till 1, and Anthony wakes me up several times in the night and finally starts singing comic songs and doing conjuring tricks and otherwise hymning the dawn at 6.30. The consequence is that when I put him to bed at 6 I cannot do anything except sit and stare at my work. I am dog-tired.'

Anthony grew up calling his mother 'Auntie Panther' and his father 'Wellsie'. The secret of his birth was kept from him and when he found out that he was Wells's illegitimate son he felt he had become 'a scandalous and disgraceful object'. Over the years Rebecca would make attempts to break off her relationship with Wells but was always drawn back by the idea that he might increase his provision for Anthony and that he might treat him equally in his will

---

* His middle name was Panther.

with his two sons by Jane. There were endless quarrels about the boy's upbringing. In 1929 Rebecca called Wells 'cruel and petulant and greedy', and later the same year, writing to Bertrand Russell, she said, 'His behaviour seems to me insane. I am aware from my knowledge of him that he has a violent anti-sex complex like Tolstoy's – You punish the female who evokes your lust . . . Anthony ought not to be left in the care of this lunatic'. Later she was to regret this letter, and when Wells died suddenly in 1946 she acknowledged how deeply they were bound together: 'Dear H. G., he was a devil, he ruined my life, he starved me, he was an inexhaustible source of love and friendship to me for thirty-four years, we should never have met, I was the one person he cared to see to the end, I feel desolate because he has gone.'

As Anthony grew up he was unable to accommodate himself to the versions of the world put out by his parents, and felt the need to make a version of his own. In 1955 he published a novel, *Heritage*, which could be read as a portrait of his mother, her husband, and Wells. West could not reconcile herself to what she described as the 'monstrous, clotted spite' of the novel. She who had protested about censorship wanted to censor her own son. 'God forbid that any book should be banned,' she had once written. 'The practice is as indefensible as infanticide.' The sentiment is intended to shock, and perhaps does shock, but only by its casual untruth; there are degrees of censorship, but not degrees of death. West seemed to act hypocritically in this affair, but she had found herself in a hard place; it is hard to make public virtues operate in the private sphere, hard to stick to your principles when they come and squat on your own doorstep. The truth seems to be that she did not think Anthony was entitled to his own story.

She got into her deepest tangles with him, and with others (like her sister Lettie), when she set herself to put the record straight, insisting that an exact account of what was said mattered more than a heartfelt account of what people heard. She prized the solid science of verification, and became enraged with those who inclined to veer away from the truth through fear of telling it. At worst, she had a mind that was closed and cold, like a small-town lawyer's: prizing facts but estranged from imaginative truth. It may have been the effort to mediate between two mindsets that led to the diversity of her work; neither novels nor reportage could satisfy a restless talent. Facts fuelled her imagination and her imagination bred the desire for more facts. Her standards for herself were impossibly high, and she never became complacent. In old age, she wrote,

> I am too good for the world of modern literature, and the way I come off so badly is that I know that I am not good enough for my world. I fall short and I fall short and only in parts of *The Birds Fall Down* have I ever felt that I was coming near what I wanted to do.

In 1930 Rebecca West married Henry Andrews, who was a banker and had business interests in Germany. She travelled with him and was able to assess the state of the country, which she found frightening. Already anti-German, and repelled by the Nazis, she asked in 1932, 'How can we have anything to do with these cannibals?' Eventually Henry lost his job with the Schroders banking firm because he protested against the replacement of a Jewish colleague by a Nazi. Before and during the war he and Rebecca helped German refugees to settle and find employment. Later she was at her most scathing in denouncing the ignorance of the portion of the public who had no idea why their country was fighting. 'I enclose a letter,' she wrote to Alexander Woolcott,

> which is, I think, a supreme achievement . . . The ghoul who wrote it is the wife of the Bishop of Lincoln . . . [who writes] complaining that the B.B.C. gave forth such alarming news bulletins, full of unpleasant stuff about the dictators, which might cause panic among the public and irritate these dictators, and prevented her from 'going happily to bed—' which I should have thought was a matter to be attended to by the Bishop of Lincoln rather than the B.B.C. I wept with rage . . .

At the time of this letter she was welcoming the 'bouquets' for *Black Lamb and Grey Falcon*. In the same letter to Woolcott she describes what the book had cost her:

> Why should I be moved in 1936 to devote the following 5 years of my life, at great financial sacrifice and to the utter exhaustion of my mind and body, to take an inventory of a country down to its last

vest-button, in a form insane from any ordinary artistic or commercial point of view – a country which ceases to exist?

Bonnie Kime Scott's selection of letters shows how West's interest
and sense of purpose evolved, from her first visit to the Balkans as
lecturer for the British Council ('a waste of your money and my
time', as she reported to head office in London), through two later
journeys, which created multiple personal entanglements and a deep
commitment to both the terrain and the people which would enmesh
her in controversy for most of her life.

After the Second World War she would feel that she was a pariah,
rejected by both the left and the right for her attacks on Tito, who
was admired by many in the West who were ignorant of his pre-war
Stalinist credentials. West did not trust an ideology that suppressed
nationalism or presumed to abolish it. For her, love of country could
not be superseded by internationalist ideals, and in 1947 she spoke
in a letter to Beaverbrook of 'the fact that treason is an attempt to
live without love of country, which humanity can't do – any more
than love of family'. She may not have reflected that stateless people
still live and are human, and find other passions to sustain them;
or that the same is true of the survivors of broken families. Perhaps
the point was too painful and too obvious. Anyone who follows
West's career, whatever his or her political views, will probably agree
that for Rebecca 'the meaning of treason' was personal and specific.

She often seemed to feel that those close to her were betraying
her and threatening her. She wrote in 1960 of 'the curious wish to
annihilate me and every trace of me' which she detected among her
acquaintances. Her post-war politics were distinguished by a flight
from socialism, her definition of herself as 'the last liberal', and a
progressively paranoid anti-Communist stance. At one time she
thought that her frequent digestive upsets might be caused by
poisoning, and when Anthony wrote *Heritage* she suggested that
Communists had got hold of him and inflamed his grievances.

She believed communism to be a serious internal threat to the
US, and got into trouble with fellow liberals by appearing to diminish
what they were suffering at the hands of McCarthy, though she
insisted that she had been misunderstood. She hit back at her critics

in a most haughty grande dame fashion, writing to Arthur Schlesinger in June 1953, 'My knowledge of you makes me quite certain that you are not experienced enough, or clever enough, or wise enough, to adopt the attitude towards me of a schoolmaster instructing a backward pupil . . .' In this letter she stresses her record as an anti-Communist, anti-fascist writer, and yet when she seeks a definition of liberalism she runs to get it in her own review of a book by Alistair Cooke; satisfied, it seems, to have quoted such an authority, she settles for an equation of liberalism with libertarianism.

It is easy to see why she might disgust her opponents and her supporters too; in discussion she is a little too fond of the '*on dit*', and of 'a friend of mine' who knows some trade unionists who know some Communists . . . At such times she is a kind of Jungian nightmare of the animus-ridden woman let loose into the world: you sense the base whispering rustle of collective prejudice, of gossips' poisoned partialities. Though she and her husband worked hard during the years before the war to help their Jewish contacts inside Germany, antisemitism leaks from her pores. In 1953 she can still write that Bernard Berenson, while a 'wonderful little creature', is '*nevertheless* [my italics] a Jew born in Wilna'. It is an antisemitism of a very English kind, bound up with a social snobbery which seems so natural to its possessors that it is never analysed or even noticed.

This prejudice comes as a package. She fears and flinches from homosexuality. She is anti-Catholic and anti-Irish – despite, or because of, her own Irish descent. Socially, she is so grand that in 1960 she condemns Richard Hoggart (of *The Uses of Literacy*) as 'very ordinary red-brick' – a provincial product, that is, not an Oxbridge man like the people one knows. There is more here than the usual disheartening story of youthful radicalism turning to elderly conservatism. It is as if West is enchanted with her own legend, believing that a youthful reputation for bohemianism guarantees good faith for the rest of one's life, and that to be forced out of respectable society is evidence of independence of mind. It seems a very modern mistake.

Bonnie Kime Scott, who is a professor of English at the University of Delaware, is not always the most reliable guide to the earthquake zones of West's political passions. One must offer respect to the magnitude of the task. Given the length and diversity of Rebecca West's career, the scope of her mind, the breadth of her range of reference and the cosmopolitan nature of her friendships, her editor needs sympathy, fine judgement and a wide general knowledge of the last century's trivia as well as its central events. Her task is complicated by the fact that some of the more intriguing and intimate documents are missing or destroyed. But it's hard to escape the feeling that she might have done better with the letters she has. The first task is to make a one-sided narrative rounded and comprehensible to the general reader, but her linking explanations are seldom enough to give a sense of the ebb and flow of her subject's fortunes. To fill in the gaps one needs biographies at hand: Victoria Glendinning's *Rebecca West* and Carl Rollyson's *Rebecca West: A Saga of the Century*.

Kime Scott does not correct West's mistakes: for example, about the title of Nancy Mitford's *Don't Tell Alfred*, or her spelling of the name of the South African leader, Verwoerd. Sometimes we get half a story. She publishes a letter telling of West's quarrel with Arnold Bennett over her hostile review of *The Strange Necessity* and her subsequent libel action, which is a serious matter for a writer; she does not tell us how the action was settled out of court, with West awarded costs and an apology. Sometimes she fails to annotate an interesting reference: a 1954 mention of 'Craig' and his past is unsourced, though it refers to a case then under judicial review, which is still controversial; Christopher Craig, at sixteen, was sentenced to ten years imprisonment for his part in a robbery in which he shot and killed a policeman, while his nineteen-year-old accomplice Derek Bentley was hanged. The evidence has recently been under review and the campaign for a full pardon continues. Sometimes the annotations are comically obtuse. When West retails a bit of gossip about the sex life of King Farouk, Kime Scott thwarts our curiosity by a pious recital of the King of Egypt's dates, his 'unpopular policies' and eventual downfall, which is not what we wanted to know. Sometimes she finds over-elaborate explanations: when in 1960 West is complaining about the state of the parliamentary Labour Party, she is much more likely to be talking about the MP Sydney Silverman than about Abraham Silverman, an 'economic adviser to the Analysis and Plans Section of the Air Force'. It looks very much as if Kime Scott reached for *Who's Who* and was happy with the first Silverman she found.

Rebecca West first visited the US in October 1923. She was treated as a celebrity, and despite her remarks in her letter to her sister Winifred, about the plainness of American women and the men's lack of virility, she was dazzled by what she saw and heard on her lecture tour, and the trip raised her self-esteem and her hopes for the future. In the years to come she found friends and lovers in America, as well as more targets for her wrath. West's judgements on fellow writers, whether they are English or American, are pithy and seldom charitable. When she writes that Evelyn Waugh is a 'filthy little creature' this is routine abuse, but she is more observant when she calls Shaw 'a eunuch perpetually inflamed by flirtation'. She is interesting about T. E. Lawrence: 'two men in one skin, and why had the one given the hospitality of his body to the other little horror'.

She is no less caustic about her own sex. Laura Riding 'writes quite atrociously, almost as badly as anybody I have ever come across, with the obvious exception of Middleton Murry'. Age does not mellow her. Reporting on a writer's conference at the Edinburgh Festival in 1962, she is astonished by Mary McCarthy: 'Who said she was beautiful? She has long greasy hair which she can't manage, and a behind built on the lines of a canal barge.' If this is more malicious that witty, she is sharp-eyed when she describes the deficiencies of Vanessa Redgrave's film performance as Isadora Duncan: 'Vanessa is made so awkwardly, she is the shape of an unskilled undertaker's apprentice's first attempt at making a coffin.' Writing in old age of her long-ago acquaintance with Virginia Woolf, she is almost benign: 'Any demented lady, even if a genius, is a difficult neighbour in the country.'

What might it have been like to get a letter from Rebecca West? She did not spare anyone's feelings, confident that her advice, even if unpalatable, would hold good in the long term. Her 1953 letter to Ingrid Bergman (about the lack of talent and prospects West discerned in her husband, Roberto Rossellini) must have left its recipient trembling with shock. But when she was her better self, she spoke out of her life's experience, with calm directness. Writing to her daughter-in-law, Kitty, about her threatened marriage, she says, almost humbly, 'I would like to put some things before you that might be useful.'

> Since you were both in your twenties when you married, one or other of you, and indeed both, were [bound] to fall in love again at some future date . . . I don't think . . . that you ought to think of this as an abnormal catastrophe – it is the necessary price you pay for early happiness. The only thing is that everyone should behave well, and that the later attack shouldn't prejudice what you've made of your marriage . . .

Over the years she had seen at first hand the histrionic behaviour of men, the stoicism of women; and yet she is not forcing a political point, but delicately pointing to a way of thinking that leads out of the fog of self-loathing and toward a reasonable future. She made many remarks to the effect that women must make the best of men, since no one was about to invent a third sex, but she herself seemed especially prone to misperceptions, especially liable to be deceived. The first five years of her marriage were among the happiest of her life. After she met Henry Andrews she wrote to her agent that he 'seems to be the nicest man I ever met . . . He says he's going to look after me and let me write, so it ought to be grand.' But not long after their marriage Henry suffered a small stroke, which was un-detected at the time but which led to progressive mental deterioration. Later, he became a figure of almost baffling diffidence. The poet Dachine Rainer, recalling her visit to West's country house, writes, 'When Henry met the train at High Wycombe I assumed from his manner and attire that he was the chauffeur. He began our drive . . . by saying "Miss West and I have been married for thirty-one years."'

Though Rebecca believed he loved her and always had her inter-ests at heart, he became more and more difficult to live with; in 1947 she wrote, 'Not a day but he does something completely imbecile which causes me a great deal of trouble, and often humiliation.' After his death, letters (which she destroyed) revealed that throughout the years of their marriage, he had been a persistent and ridiculous womaniser: 'If he was odd about money, he was odder about sex.'

Virginia Woolf, who did not entirely admire West, described her mind as 'tenacious and muscular'. She was often ill, but she was tough and resilient, mentally and physically. She struggled all her life under the burden of other people's expectations. She had become a successful, high-earning, critically esteemed author; but the world into which she was born did not necessarily value a woman for achievements like that. As a wife, a mother, she had been mostly a failure; her many love affairs had brought her both exquisite pleasure and the deepest humiliation. She was born equipped for happiness, with her share of personal beauty, an ear for music, a sharp visual sense, a lovely voice, a capacity for sexual pleasure. It was never enough, of course. In the late 1960s she wrote to Emanie Arling: 'It's been a bad life; and the only one I have.' There are occasional glimpses, in these letters, of the abyss that opened at her feet: the feeling that art has eaten up life. After Wells's death she says, 'I want to write nothing. I want to live and I have left it too long.'

Her life's work was not easy to classify, and she suspected that her failure to dominate a single genre, rather than spanning several, detracted from her reputation. In 1973 she wrote, 'I have forced my way into recognition of a sort, but I am treated as a witch, somebody to be shunned.' However inconvenient it might be, she did not deviate from her belief that prose should be 'a sharp instrument of truth', and tried her best to make it so. 'I do care above all for reality,' she wrote in 1973, and she did not spare herself in pursuit of it; she looked hard and saw clearly, and when circumstances proved her wrong she retained her moral poise.

Her life and letters press her claim that 'art is not a luxury, but a necessity'. They are a protest against emptiness, against superficiality, and against the sterility of the unexamined life.

A Past Recaptured

On Sybille Bedford

2001

In Oliver Sacks's book *An Anthropologist on Mars*, there is an essay on the artist's memory. He remarks that it is the discontinuities in life that fuel reminiscence and, through reminiscence, myth and art:

> One may be born with the potential for a prodigious memory, but one is not born with a disposition to recollect; this comes only with changes and separations in life – separations from people, from places, from events and situations, especially if they have been of great significance, have been deeply hated or loved . . . Discontinuity and nostalgia are most profound if, in growing up, we leave or lose the place where we were born and spent our childhood, if we become expatriates or exiles, if the place, or the life, we were brought up in is changed beyond recognition or destroyed.

Sybille Bedford is a distinguished and neglected writer whose life and work fits Sacks's observations perfectly. She was born in Berlin in 1911, and her parents' marriage ended soon afterwards. She was brought up in the German countryside by her father. When she was ten, her mother, a well-off Englishwoman, demanded custody, and Sybille was handed over at a railway station on the Dutch border. The years following were divided between France, Italy and England, where she received a patchy education. Fluent in several languages, she began writing in her teens, and it was the English language that gave her a focus, a sense of security. But her masterwork, *A Legacy*, concerned itself with her German self, with her earliest childhood and with events which took place before she was born. It is a fiction-alised reconstruction of life in Germany among the Catholic minor aristocracy and the *haute Juiverie* of Berlin, and its narrative spans almost fifty years, beginning in pre-unification Germany and ending with the Great War. Its child-narrator describes events she could not possibly have witnessed, but describes them with a sensuous precision that almost convinces the reader that her consciousness predates her birth.

This elegant and haunting novel, which appeared in Britain in 1956, was the first of Bedford's fiction to be published. Through her early career as a writer she seldom settled, moving between Rome, Paris, Provence, living the kind of scapegrace life that writers seemed to manage in those days, finding kind friends, patrons, hospitality – everything contingent and glamorous, perhaps better in the recall than the living: or at least the modern writer has to hope so. In 1958 she published *The Best We Can Do*, an account of the murder trial of Dr John Bodkin Adams, and she reported on a number of other major trials, including those of Jack Ruby and the guards of Auschwitz. In the early 1970s she produced a two-volume life of Aldous Huxley, whom she had known since she was a young woman. Settling at last in London, sitting on writers' committees, embracing writers' causes, she reported on her frequent European travels and wrote about food and wine.

There had been two other novels, *A Favourite of the Gods* and *A Compass Error*, published in 1963 and 1968 respectively; both were semi-autobiographical, drawing on summers spent in France as a young girl. Then in 1989 she published *Jigsaw*, which was shortlisted for the Booker Prize. A 'fictionalised autobiography', it continued the story of *A Legacy*'s narrator into her middle childhood, and provided an alternative history of her teenage years. Is it 'more true' than her novels? No one can say; almost certainly the author cannot. Taken together, the books are a close examination of the nature of confabulation by an author devoted to the pursuit of truth.

The first part of *Jigsaw* describes the village of Feldkirch in Baden, minutes from the French border, where she lived with her father, an impoverished minor aristocrat, in the chateau that her mother had bought for him. The two of them managed with one servant in a house of twenty bedrooms, with a collection of Renaissance furniture but no ready cash, with candles instead of electric light; the money had gone with her mother. She particularises the lives of the village people, their food and their clothes: their breakfast coffee made of roasted barley and chicory essence, their dark and shapeless work clothes. A pupil at the village school, she was taught that divorced people go to hell; this made her panic, since the company of the damned included her mother and father. When she picked up head lice, her father decided on home tutoring.

The end of this phase came for Sybille (known as Billi) when her mother claimed custody. The adult Bedford got stuck when she had to bring her mother into the story. She felt she could not be fair to her without including a complex sequence of tangled events, remote circumstances. Overnight, the problem was resolved: 'the writer had won over whatever we might call it; filial duty, decency . . .' A novel, after all, is not a court of law. It was necessary to accept that she would not make the reader warm to her mother, who seems to have possessed none of the usual maternal virtues. The writer is indebted to her for imprinting 'her unshakeable rejection of war, nationalism, social injustice . . . her passion for literature and art', but 'sadly, I was not often able to love her'.

When she is parted from her father, Billi is first told that she is to join her mother in Italy. Her mother is to marry a painter and they are to live near Florence. However, she writes, 'my mother's arrangements (as I had to learn) were often impulsive and reversible'. Another man comes along. His name is Alessandro; he is handsome, amiable. Her mother is now thirty-eight or thirty-nine, her new beau is fifteen years younger. There is an unsettled interlude for Billi. Her mother is prone to leaving her with comparative strangers while she pursues mysterious manoeuvres in another city or country. Who is responsible for Billi? Where will she live? Who will pay the bills? Her mother's money is evaporating and the German courts pursue her with letters to which are affixed vast, impressive seals. The project is to send Billi to England – but when she gets there she finds herself boarded out with acquaintances who have made no suitable arrangements for her schooling. Still, what is most dreary in English life is exotic to her. Tinned salmon and pineapple cubes, bloater paste and Marmite, she devours it all:

Food is as revealing as money and sex, and is revealed more often. People can't wait to tell you that they mustn't eat cabbage or have a craving for puddings; whereas how frequently do you hear, I've got ten thousand in my deposit account, or I can't bear parting with small change? As for the truth about sex . . .

Every time she visits her mother in Italy she notices alarming changes: more Black Shirts in the streets, more parades, wall posters, boasts and lies. Her mother sees the danger, her young stepfather shrugs it off: 'It won't stick . . . Musso's dream; playing lions, days without pasta, little boys carrying daggers, it's too silly, we're not cut out for regimentation'. All the same, by 1926 her mother and Alessandro find it wise to leave Italy. They migrate to Sanary-sur-Mer, a modest Provençal fishing port set among olive trees and vines.

At first her residence seemed just another transitional arrangement, but soon Billi would think of the small town as her home. In winter she studied in London with tutors, living in a bedsitting room, solitary, frugal, purposive: still delighted by the gushing profusion of London bathwater, a novelty to someone who had spent her girlhood bathing in scant rainwater heated on capricious wood-burning stoves. Returning to France each summer, she always had to intuit her mother's situation: financial or marital upset? Plans to move on?

By the time she was seventeen, a handful of writers, refugee politicians and painters had begun to arrive in Sanary, and Billi's relationships with them were to form the subject matter of two novels, *A Favourite of the Gods* and *A Compass Error*. With the first of these, published in 1963, Bedford set out to write 'a serious story written as a comedy of manners'. It is also perhaps one of those novels written to explain things to oneself. The emerging theme is the one Bedford has neglected – mother–daughter relationships – and here they are traced through three generations, beginning around the turn of the century. The first generation is represented by Anna Howland, a polished and beautiful New Englander. Travelling in Europe after the death of her revered father, she meets a prince by an Italian lake, and becomes the mistress of a Roman house, 'noble, shuttered, peeling . . . in a back-street in the papal quarter between the Tiber and the Farnese Square'. At first, the marriage seems a great success. Bedford neatly inverts the more usual story of the American heiress fallen among Europeans; Anna is adored by her husband's large family, and no one gambles away her dowry, or insults her moral values, or tells her how to behave. The family's Catholicism is of a relaxed and accommodating style, and the prince, Rico, is happy for her to pursue her cultural interests.

The first child of this marriage is Constanza, the 'favourite' of the title. She is beautiful, strong-minded and indulged. She loses her faith at thirteen, and takes lovers early and without ugly consequence – they only breed an increase in her benevolence toward the world. Her childhood ends with her parents' separation. When he married, Rico did not think of giving up his long-term mistress. Anna knows this, but does not admit to herself what she knows; she allows her knowledge to become conscious only when she wants to use it to break up the marriage. Later she regrets it – but she and the prince find themselves in a situation that neither of them knows how to negotiate. The forces that shape our behaviour, Bedford tells us, lie further back in the past than we know, back in a family and a culture we may have abandoned. Anna – herself coquettish but frigid – is compelled to play to type, and fling at the prince the New World insult 'you are all depraved'.

Forcibly separated from her father, transported to London to live in a hotel, Constanza can only guess at what has caused the break-up; she believes that her father has somehow embezzled her mother's money. In the years ahead, Anna becomes spoiled, precious, selfish. Constanza, however, becomes a society darling. The reader may be less enchanted with her, and even her creator describes her in distanced terms: 'People, even people whom she loved, were separate entities to her and she left them to their own convictions and decisions.' At the age of twenty-one, in 1914, she marries Simon Herbert, a bouncy egotist who sets a high value on himself; to the modern ear, he is a mass of affectations, camp in the most irritating way. Constanza, that sexual buccaneer, at first finds him only 'a comfort and a good companion'. But Simon and Anna make an unspoken pact to admire each other; Constanza's marriage is an attempt to heal her mother's fractured happiness. Later, a useful friend of the family called Mr James will tell her that 'the things one feels obliged to do against one's inclination are often the most harmful'. But Mr James with his caveats is never quite where he's needed.

In the second year of the Great War Constanza gives birth to a daughter, Flavia. Neither she nor Simon is very pleased. Simon has gone to war; invalided out to an administrative post, he develops political ambitions and starts an affair with a useful newspaper heiress. Constanza in turn has begun to have affairs. There is a messy divorce. Once again Constanza sacrifices her own interests. She is willing to play the guilty party, to keep Simon's good name clean for his political bosses. To give him grounds for an adultery suit she goes off to a hotel with a mysterious friend of Simon's called Captain Ware. The judge at the divorce hearing is not impressed by either parent, and awards custody of Flavia to her grandmother, Anna.

Ten years pass, years of growing discontent for Constanza:

> She had learnt to travel light. In her youth she had looked at fate as the bolt from the clear sky, now she recognized it in the iron rule of time on all human affairs . . . ; the second chance is not the first.

She still has looks, health, money and a large measure of freedom; but *carpe diem*, once the true gospel, is now a 'sad pagan creed'. In Italy, Mussolini consolidates his rule. Constanza is an anti-fascist 'by instinct and by reason' though the prevailing mood in her father's circle is of 'opportunism disinfected by a dash of cynicism'. She carries messages for the resistance, though the group she works for is 'professorial' and amateurish. Anna has taken her granddaughter, Flavia, back to Italy where, shut out from the last generation's secrets, she grows up fantasising about her grandfather and his family. 'Is the prince in Rome a hunch-back? . . . Does he stab his adversaries?'

Then the mysterious 'Captain Ware', so helpful at the time of her divorce, turns up in Constanza's life again. He now calls himself Lewis Crane, and claims to be an art dealer. The end of the story, chronologically speaking, is told in the opening pages. Constanza is en route to marry the art dealer in Belgium, with Flavia in tow. Their journey is interrupted, and they find themselves in a Provençal seaside town, looking over a villa which was meant for someone else. With swift illogicality, declining to explain herself, Constanza decides this is where they will stay. The closing pages are crowded with a melodrama over two versions of Anna's will, and show the child Flavia growing into a woman of decision. Once again, the invented character has drawn close to the reality of Bedford's own girlhood – the unreliable mother, the sojourn in a small Mediterranean town among friendly and curious strangers. In the final scenes the mother departs for Paris with a new lover, leaving Flavia behind. The stage is set for the next novel, *A Compass Error*.

A Favourite of the Gods is not Sybille Bedford's best book. It is a slow starter with a rushed denouement. Though the author works hard on behalf of her characters, the reader is struck by their pride, selfishness and lack of empathy. Faced by a problem, they usually feel that movement will improve matters. They pack a bag, take a boat, take a train – but all this self-assertion is confounded by fatalism, so that they allow accidents and coincidences to rule their lives. The casual pain inflicted by the characters on each other, and the corruption of communications between them, make the book a bitter farce in the chilling Waugh style; at its publication in the mid-sixties, it may have seemed out of tune with the mood of the times, and its rapid, glancing take on the rise of fascism may have meant little to readers bent on making over their memories and leaving the war years far behind. It may be that the book seemed a period piece that had not yet acquired a patina of charm.

Bedford's world is unashamedly elitist. Her most admired characters are aristocrats – sometimes aristocrats of beauty or wit rather than birth, but she prefers them if they are also the offspring of a distinguished family. The lower classes contribute much-prized servants, treated sympathetically by both characters and author. It is the middle classes who are not quite human; they are gossips, often malicious, and faintly ludicrous in their manners and morals. Her female protagonists are both beautiful and clever, with an economic freedom that allows them to escape the circumstances that generally constrict women's lives; but like Jane Austen heroines, they are looking for men who will instruct them as well as amuse them, men whom they can look up to. *A Favourite of the Gods* is, as designed, a comedy of manners: but of the manners of people for whom we don't care quite enough. Yet its sequel, *A Compass Error*, with its compacted dramatic action, is a powerful and merciless book – a classic coming-of-age novel which visits on its heroine a series of humiliations that cut to the quick.

The action occupies two months of summer. Seventeen-year-old Flavia has been left in Sanary: to prepare for her Oxford entrance examination, to lose her virginity and (quite separately) to fall in love. In her introduction to the new edition, Bedford is as cagey as ever; you must not think this happened to me, she tells us, but that something like it, if seen in a certain light, happened to a part of me, or to a person of whom I am a part. Her fictionalised self is a trainee gourmet, a trainee intellectual: a self-conscious child, earnest and vulnerable. She spends her days studying in a tower which is the home of a neighbour, and her evenings in the small town's cafés, exchanging pleasantries with the residents. One evening she joins the group that surrounds Therese, an artist's wife, whose show-off good looks and social ease immediately attract her. Therese takes her under her wing, and in a week or so takes her to bed. What Therese recommends is a life of compliance with one's instincts. It's fine to sleep with one's friends, she tells Flavia; one must be kind and generous, never possessive, never jealous; one must live in the present. To Flavia's innocent mind, this philosophy is powerfully attractive. It is easy to feel immune to jealousy when one has no experience of the pain of loss. She feels sure, also, that she will always like women, though she goes to bed with one of the local boys simply as a matter of getting it over with.

Meanwhile, what has happened to Mother? She has gone away with the man she hopes to marry. He is Michel, owner of the tower where Flavia spends her days studying. He is a politician who has withdrawn from Paris and the Chamber of Deputies on a matter of principle. He is 'the austere ideal' whom Flavia admires without reserve. Flavia knows that there are obstacles in the way of the new marriage. Michel is not yet divorced from his first wife, who is making difficulties over signing the papers. To cover the lovers' absence, Flavia has been told to say her mother is in Italy, visiting her family. The lie holds, until an enigmatic stranger called Andrée arrives in the district and throws Flavia's feelings into turmoil. She is Michel's wife, though Flavia contrives to miss all the clues that point her to this conclusion. She falls in love with Andrée, and after some days of hope and torment, and some tricky negotiations over an intimate dinner – consommé madrilène, sole florentine, and framboises naturel – takes her back to Michel's tower. Andrée, noting where the key is hidden, returns to the tower secretly to obtain Michel's address abroad. Flavia has ruined her mother's chance of marriage; for Andrée does not mean to let Michel go, and proceeds to send detectives to the lovers' hideout in Spain, to furnish evidence for a counterclaim and bring the divorce proceedings to a halt.

Andrée treats Flavia with a calculated cruelty, not simply abusing her naiveté, but mocking her for it. The scene in which she confronts Flavia with the knowledge of her gullibility is so pointed, so merciless, that the reader feels she has watched a stabbing in broad daylight. But worse is in store for Flavia. Her attempts to mend matters only make them worse. One false step is followed by another, and when she is truly enmired, snared in her own error, Andrée follows to sneer and berate her. Andrée destroys the benign Therese philosophy of easy friendship and easy sex: 'Physical passion . . . has little to do with friendship, moral worth, choice or will; it is not cosy, easy, reassuring, debonair.' Crushingly, she tells Flavia, 'You are as fit to live as the next person – if you lower your sights a little.'

Flavia's judgement has wobbled off course; she had not set out to do damage, but damage was done, and she was the agent of it. Is she guilty? She is guilty of knowing and not knowing, like her grandmother Anna; guilty of a failure of attention, of looking away at the critical moment. Bedford does not give the reader the consolation of believing that Flavia's error can be quickly retrieved, but tells us that she remained for many years in the wilderness of her own making. Her error is of the kind that is passed over, but not forgiven. As Ivy Compton-Burnett says, 'Time has too much credit . . . It is not a great healer. It is an indifferent and perfunctory one. Sometimes it does not heal at all'.

Something close to the originals of the characters of *A Compass Error* are found in the more autobiographical *Jigsaw*. The events that ensue are less compacted and less cruel than those of the fictionalised version, but still hard to stomach. In *Jigsaw* Billi falls in love with a woman called Oriane, 'a thwarted feline beast'. Oriane snubs the young girl in a cold-blooded fashion. Her infatuation becomes public knowledge, and Billi's mother, complaining of her immaturity – 'after all the trouble I've taken . . .' – packs her off back to England. In grimy London, the girl feels 'stony desolation'. The Christmas holidays come, and her kindly stepfather, Alessandro, pleads for her recall. Her mother receives her airily. 'He says I behaved badly to you. Perhaps so. One does.'

In the later part of *Jigsaw* Alessandro, whose philosophy is 'things just happen to people', falls in love with a younger woman, a friend of the family. He leaves – a trial separation. Billi's mother takes to morphine, in such doses that she is quickly dependent. These are harrowing, still-angry pages. The sense of being on the brink of disaster is still vivid, as Billi, shut in with her mother's physical pain and craving, humiliates herself to beg local doctors and pharmacists not to cut off her supply. Finally Billi sends a telegram recalling Alessandro, and a doctor in Nice proves willing to arrange treatment:

> Alessandro said, 'This cure? What will it do to her? Will it hurt her? Is it very bad?' . . .
> 'Very bad,' the consultant said. 'These cures always are.'

During this period her beloved Oriane treats the beleaguered girl 'as one might a clever and devoted stray dog who followed one about'. But it is Oriane who first, for her own studied amusement, treats her as a writer: 'mon jeune écrivain', a new kind of puppet, to be shut in a room with a supply of ruled paper and a tiptoeing maid. And when Alessandro finally leaves the catastrophic household, taking his departure at dawn, he turns back, and hands Billi his Remington portable typewriter. 'You had better have that. Use it.'

Bedford's stories are haunted by semi-selves. In the quasi-autobiographical form, every revelation is balanced by a concealment. No writer can produce except out of her own experience, however disguised, and for that reason the dull injunction to 'write what you know' is superfluous. But the essence of Bedford's achievement has been to stretch the boundaries of the little word 'I' while seldom actually using it. Working through the same elaborate story,

she allows chronology to slide beneath her reader's feet, shifts focus
and emphasis, sifts each event for all the meanings it will yield;
walks, in imagination, down roads not taken. Breeding a plurality
of artistic experience out of a single life, she has remained fastidiously
individual, and scrupulous in questioning her own motives. She
relies on a reader's close attention, emotional openness and tolerance
of ambiguity: 'It takes two to tell the truth . . . one to speak and one
to hear.' As her early life was marked by loss – of her father, her
country, the milieu and culture of a vanished era – it is natural to
catch in her work the accent of mourning. 'I did not see them again.
They are all dead now. Their houses are no more. Their few descendants must be dispersed over three continents.' The century she has
survived has perfected techniques of erasure. But art creates a past
that is constantly renewed, and these scenes, these pictures, will not
pass away.

Getting Through

On John McGahern

2002

That They May Face the Rising Sun is a novel about a private and particular world, which the reader enters as an eavesdropper. The writing is so calm that it seems the text is listening to itself. Its accent is a dying fall and its only tricks are tricks of the light. It is set in rural Ireland, in a country of mist, cloud and water. The daily events of the lakeside are the swans and dark cygnets gliding by, the rippling of perch beneath the surface of the water, the movement of the breeze through the leaves of the alders. The air is scented, wild strawberries glow in the banks, and the heron rises silently from the reeds. The dead are under the feet of the living, and it is their presence – the repressed, repressing generations – that makes the people whisper.

John McGahern is as attentive to their low voices as to the nuances of the shifting light. By the lake are the ruins of an ancient monastery – in traditional Irish poetry, an object of contemplation as fruitful and sombre as Gray's country churchyard; through the whole text, the spirit of the Irish language moves within English, like a ghost within a sheet.

Yet the tenor of the book is profoundly anti-nostalgic. In his novels and stories, McGahern has never provided Ireland with comfortable images of itself. The good old days, in this district, are days that never were. This is Leitrim, where the author lives, a country of many lakes, of deserted cottages on mountain slopes, and of small farmers; it is a poor and depopulated country, its western border formed by the River Shannon. McGahern tells the story of the lake dwellers through a whole year, from summer to summer. The time, roughly speaking, is the present day, though contemporary events seem as distant as the 'bad old bitter crowd' in the north. Though Ireland is a country of creeping suburbanisation, this place is still so remote that the people by the lake have no telephones till near the end of the story.

Extremes of poverty and ignorance have given way to modern prosperity, yet it is a place where a 'seventh son of a seventh son' still does good business as a healer. Most people have several trades as well as a little land, and inequalities of wealth are not confused with social distinctions. There are few Protestants and they 'have to keep their heads low'. Religious conformity keeps everyone comfortable. The older people don't like going away – they come back exhausted from a holiday or a visit to relatives, and Dublin is an alien place to them. 'Abroad' is where your grown, thriving children go during the summer holidays; one character, his wife mocks, doesn't know Italy from Mullingar. There is a sense of a dying community, soon to become a 'green wilderness'. It seems to be the last of the particular places, its character burning off like morning mist on a summer day.

Are the people by the lake happy? The evidence of McGahern's previous fiction suggests the question wouldn't have much meaning for them. *Getting Through* (the title of one of his short-story collections) is the best they can hope for. Born in Leitrim in 1934, the son of a police officer, McGahern took the bright boy's route to University College in Dublin, and went on to become a teacher. His first novel, *The Barracks*, was published in 1963, and reflects something of his own upbringing. It is the story of a policeman's wife, confined to the police barracks of the title as she dies slowly of cancer, consumed by the corrosive drip of her own thoughts. Elizabeth Reegan has no regrets, because she is too tired for them, and too tired to make any protest against what her life has become: the chopping of cabbage and the washing of dishes for her step-family and her restless, distant husband: the oppressive round of conversational interchange, the rain dripping into the silence when the interchange stops. For a first novel, it is a performance of an awesome grim confidence.

Two years later McGahern published *The Dark*. Its early pages contain a raw account of the physical and sexual abuse of the young boy at the centre of the narrative. Desperate to escape his home and his domineering father, the boy manages to negotiate the formidable obstacles of the examination system. He wins a scholarship, but his academic success is not enough to win him a new life. At university in Galway, he finds the violent transactions of family life have so scarred him that he cannot respond to a change of circumstances, and he settles for a safe government job that will not stretch his talents or nerves. His sister, meanwhile, has become a domestic drudge in the family of a 'respectable' shopkeeper in a nearby town, but has to flee back to her father's house because she can't fight off her boss's wandering hands.

The Dark is a harsh portrait of family violence and clerical hypocrisy, and of the cosy collusion between the Church and the kind of Catholic family able to fill the Sunday collection boxes. The novel was banned by the Censorship Board, and in 1966 McGahern was refused renewal of his contract as a teacher. He left Ireland for some four years, and then in the 1970s published *The Leavetaking* and *The Pornographer*. Meanwhile he refined his craft as a short-story writer – he has published three collections – and added to his gallery of characters, who are men and women beset by lifelong perplexity. It is the struggle to escape rural poverty that shapes (and deforms) many of them. Their own efforts are not enough; they believe you have to have influence, and connections, 'the pull', if you are to escape the land. In *The Dark* the father tells his struggling son, 'It's not what you want to be, it's what you'll be let be.' He prophesies his son's fate: 'He'll wear out his bones on the few acres round this house and be buried at the end of the road.'

This is a country where, as an old drunken schoolmaster says in the story 'High Ground', there are men digging ditches who might have been philosophers, only for want of opportunity. But however intelligent they are, these people believe they don't deserve much, and are reticent and timid in the face of the chances that do come their way. The brightest of them have been warned strenuously against intellectual pride. They have never learnt to inhabit their own lives; vaguely compromised by the choices they have made, they have sinned mostly by omission, failed to make relationships or never tried them, failed to reach out of their own self-absorbed uncertainties to grasp at some chance that might be passing. The young man in *The Dark* thinks of entering the priesthood – if he can force himself to say he has a vocation, the Church will offer him status, but he dreads the lifelong loneliness of celibacy. Religion is a habit and a duty; it preserves the social order. For some it is a protection against deeper thought. McGahern's people suffer from that old Catholic malady, accidie – emotional paralysis, spiritual sloth. They live most powerfully in anticipation and in memory. Experience is constantly giving them the slip; what they get is usually much less – for better or worse – than they anticipate.

The scholar gone wrong, the failed seminarian, the writer afraid of his material; these are disappointed men. They are joined in McGahern's fiction by the gunman disarmed: men like Reegan in *The Barracks* and Moran in the 1990 novel *Amongst Women*. These men fought for a free and independent Ireland and do not feel well rewarded; baffled, they feel that something has been stolen from them, filched from under their noses. They have the imperious nature of those who were men when they were only boys, and the restlessness of warriors in a waste of peace. They are formidable patriarchs; their houses and families, farms and parishes are their new battleground. The most meaningful things in their lives have happened already when McGahern takes up their story.

This is also true of the characters in *That They May Face the Rising Sun*. Many histories are digested into this simply constructed and gently paced book. It is a portrait of a community rather than a family, and most of its inhabitants are elderly, with the struggle of their lives behind them. Their task now is to come to terms with their memories and to find a place in a modern Ireland where 'with people living longer there's a whole new class who are neither in the world or the graveyard'. At the centre of the story are the Ruttledges, who have spent many years in London before buying twenty acres and settling by the lake. Their farm doesn't support them wholly and they still take freelance work from the London advertising agency that used to employ them. Kate is an Anglo-American, but Ruttledge is a native of the place. His uncle, 'the Shah', is a local businessman, the wealthiest man in those parts. Ruttledge himself had a good education. Opportunities have opened out for him, yet he has not been at ease with them. There is nothing wrong with his London life, nothing he could pinpoint, but 'it's not my country and I never feel it's real or that my life there is real'. And nowadays the flow from Ireland isn't all one way; exiles can return. Yet how do they fit in?

Ruttledge is an outsider by virtue of his professional status and his years away. His ambivalent status seems to hold him in a posture of diffidence. He is considerate and a good neighbour, well liked, sometimes condescended to in a friendly way. His neighbour Jamesie Murphy urges him to attend mass, because that's how you find out what's going on in the neighbourhood. To Ruttledge's protestation of unbelief, he says, 'None of us believes and we go.' But Ruttledge will not return to the Church, or settle for any shortcuts in human affairs. Cautious and guarded, it is he who holds the moral centre of the story, with his belief that 'happiness could not be sought or worried into being, or even fully grasped; it should be allowed its own slow pace so that it passes unnoticed, if it ever comes at all'.

Jamesie and his wife Mary have not spent a night away from the lake since the wedding of their son seventeen years ago. Their son has prospered and lives in Dublin, and they accept without resentment that they have little part in his world. Jamesie's main characteristic is his appetite for news. The neighbours say that a strange bird flying across the lake is enough to put him on the alert. 'I've never, never moved from here and I know the whole world,' he says. Jamesie has a brother, Johnny, who comes from England to visit him every year. His return gives a shape to the summer, like the annual rebirth of some small pagan god. His brother and sister-in-law whitewash and paint the house, air the unused bedroom, pick flowers to stand in the open window; as Jamesie sets off for the station to bring the exile home, Mary stands by with the sirloin, ready to sear it in the pan. Twenty years before, Johnny went to Dagenham to work on Ford's assembly line. Ireland's recent economic boom may have ended for ever her colonial status as supplier of cheap labour to English factories and building sites. But an older generation of McGahern's characters accepted emigration and the depersonalisation that followed, in a country where you were always a Paddy or a Mick, and the butt of jokes or outbursts of blue-collar rage.

Johnny's life in England has been solitary and monotonous, spent latterly in a small furnished room rented out by a Mr Singh, who accepts 'no marrieds, no women, no coloureds', though Kate Ruttledge points out in some exasperation that Mr Singh must be 'coloured' himself. English boarding houses used to put up signs saying 'No Coloureds, No Irish', and McGahern questions how far tolerance has increased. There was once a 'pufter' living at Mr Singh's house, Johnny reports, but he made the mistake of trying to get friendly with one of the Irish building workers and was 'taken away in an ambulance'. When Johnny loses his job at Ford he finds a new one as a janitor for his thriving Indian landlord. In the course of the story he thinks of returning to Ireland. But he is gently rebuffed by his relations; the place that can support Johnny's memory can no longer support his presence. For Johnny was one of the few not forced to emigrate. He had work, but went to England after a girl who later turned her back on him. In an act of violent severance still mourned in the neighbourhood, he shot his two gun dogs, Oscar and Bran. Jamesie says, 'He might as well have tied a stone round his neck and rowed out into the middle of the lake.'

It is not Johnny but Bill Evans, a broken labouring man, who is the figure of most pathos in the story. To watch him eat a bowl of potatoes or smoke a cigarette is to witness the greed born of deprivation. The details of his early life would be erased, if his will could do it; the people by the lake can fill in the gaps, because it is the familiar story of an unwanted, orphaned or outcast child, inducted early into hard labour, spending his life in a sort of semi-slavery on the land. By contrast, the lakeside's villain is John Quinn, a handsome man in late middle age, powerful, charming and universally distrusted. Quinn gives an account of his marital fortunes to Ruttledge: 'The first poor woman died under me after bringing eight children into the world . . . The second round of the course was not a success . . . What God intended men and women to do she had no taste for.' When the story begins he is looking for a live-in woman to replace his second wife, who has run away. He attempted to soothe her nerves one day, he claims, by rowing her out on to the lake, but the woman took fright and suspected that he was going to drown her.

The story of Quinn's first marriage is part of the community's mythology, a tale which still creates the kind of shudder that passes over people when a taboo is broken. Jamesie tells the Ruttledges how John Quinn drove his young bride back from the church to her parents' farmyard, at a pace which almost scattered the wedding guests and the waiting musicians. After a brief exchange of words he led the girl to a spot where 'the grass . . . turns red' by the lakeshore:

> They stood for a while in full view. Though the yard had turned quiet as a church what they were saying couldn't be heard. They were too far off. John Quinn put the blanket he had brought down on the rock. Margaret looked as if she was trying to break away but he could have held her with one hand. It was over before anybody rightly knew. He lifted the blue dress up over her head and put her down on the blanket. The screech she let out would put your heart cross-ways. John Quinn stood between her and the house while he was fixing his trousers and belt. He must have been afraid she'd try to break back on her own but she just lay there on the ground. In the end he had to lift her and straighten her dress and carry her in his arms. The mother and father stood there like a pair of ghosts. Not a word was spoken.

The wedding party dispersed with the food uneaten, not a note played, the musicians refusing their fee. Having wheedled his way into a happy family, taking possession in this brutal manner, Quinn established his own authority in the house over the girl's parents. He violated paradise, reducing a prosperous little farm, with its beehives and 'apple trees pruned into shapes like bowls or cups', into a quotidian domain of cabbages and turnips, their glum rows flanking a tin-roofed house stripped of its thatch.

There are two things that are shocking about John Quinn. One is his graphic enactment of his desires, in a place where men are in thrall to women and shy of them. The other is his intrusive, demanding style of speech, his habit of blatant self-promotion. The manners of the people in general are gentle, placatory; they speak 'a language that hadn't any simple way of saying no'. The Ireland they grew up in was not a place where contradiction or questioning was encouraged. Inner constraint was quite as effective as interdictions from the Censorship Board and the pulpit. To say nothing is

Hilary's great-grandmother, Catherine O'Shea, probably outside her house in Hadfield, Derbyshire. Though she was illiterate, a saying of hers inspired Hilary's first Reith Lecture: 'The day is for the living, and the night is for the dead.'

With her grandfather, George Foster.

Hilary's grandmother, Catherine Foster.

Hilary, aged about four, outside 56 Bankbottom, her grandparents' home in Hadfield.

Hilary (sitting on a chair, second from right), aged ten, at St Charles' Infant School, Hadfield. She was preparing for the eleven-plus exams and won a coveted place at convent school.

Hilary (left) in a production of *A School for Scandal* at Harrytown Convent School, Romiley. Her years there were not happy: she felt she was 'a trembling voyager in a sea of black ink, living in a permanent state of dread.'

At Ian Mantel's wedding, December 1976. From left to right: Jack Mantel's mother, Jack Mantel (stepfather), Margaret Mantel (mother), Ian Mantel (brother), Brian Mantel (brother), Hilary, Catherine Foster (grandmother).

In the garden of the house Hilary and her husband Gerald shared in Lobatse, Botswana, 1977. The couple lived there for five years.

At her mother's house in Compstall, Cheshire, in December 1979. Two weeks later Hilary underwent surgery to fight her endometriosis, an illness which left her 'an unwilling stranger in [her] own body'.

At Victoria Falls with Gerald during a holiday in Zimbabwe in 1978.

Jeddah, Saudia Arabia, 1983. Hilary spent four years there; it was a time in which she felt increasingly 'stifled, desperate for the open air'.

Round the corner from her apartment, on the street that inspired her third novel, *Eight Months on Ghazzah Street*.

At her apartment in Knaphill, Surrey, 2006. The building was converted from an asylum.

At Buckingham Palace, having received her CBE in 2015.

Holbein's portrait of Thomas More, 1527: 'Intellect burns through pale indoor skin, like a torch behind a paper screen. Concentration has furrowed your brow, the effort of containing multiple ironies.'

Hilary and actor Ben Miles playing with broadswords during rehearsals for *Wolf Hall* and *Bring Up the Bodies* at Hampton Court in 2014.

Curtain call on the opening night of *Wolf Hall* at the Winter Garden Theatre, New York, April 2015, with director Jeremy Herrin (left) and Nat Parker as Henry VIII (right).

Prior to the 2017 Reith Lectures at Gray's Inn, where Thomas Cromwell was a member and attended Twelfth Night revels.

safest, and speech must be disarmed by a ritual quality; so conversation proceeds by repetition, like Jamesie's frequent reassurance to Kate Ruttledge that 'you nearly have to be born into a place to know what's going on and what to do'.

Inference is superior to direct statement and avoidance to confrontation; two men, squared up to fight, suddenly begin to sing. To hold back information is to have power, and there is a 'silence and listening ... more useful than speech'. One of the book's strongest characters is also the most reserved and polite: Jimmy Joe McKiernan is a bar owner, auctioneer and a chief in the provisional IRA, and Ruttledge's one conversation with him finds him a man of civil, considered ruthlessness. His role and direction in life is plain, but his conversation does nothing to provoke.

McGahern concentrates on the proprieties and courtesies that obtain between the characters, leaving the reader to guess at what is unspoken. They are tireless in watching each other, and he is tireless in watching them. In his early books, his method was different; he was inclined to draw the moral and point the tale. He knew so much about his characters' inner lives that one felt he was their 'spiritual accountant', like Father Purdon in Joyce's story 'Grace'. In his last two novels, he has effaced not only authorial comment, but his characters' inner lives. Yet they don't seem unaccountable, either to writer or reader. McGahern shows what they do, and makes their actions speak. He seems to be saying, what you see is what you get; but you have to know how to look.

Yet until a late stage in the novel we feel he is holding something back. We want to know how this small place connects to Ireland's history. Who hid in these woods? Who was hunted through these fields? At last Jamesie tells Ruttledge of what he saw when he was a boy; how he continued planting potatoes with his father while the British paramilitaries ambushed a company of republican volunteers, tracking the survivors with bloodhounds and shooting them dead: while the massacre went on the man and boy continued their labour, ignored by the combatants as if they were standing stones, or some part of the natural world. Revenge was swift, and fell on a blameless small farmer of the district: 'They shot him because somebody had to be made to pay and poor Sinclair was a Protestant and the nearest to hand.' The whole sorry business is now commemorated in the district with a monument and an annual march at Easter.

How old is Jamesie, if he remembers this event, which surely took place around 1920? The reader revises upward his estimate of Jamesie's age, or slips the action back a few years; but it hardly seems to matter. It is in the nature of memory to be faulty. Jamesie remarks, 'the dead can be turned into anything'. At the end of the book Ruttledge gets his own chance to shape how the dead are remembered: Johnny dies suddenly, and Ruttledge lays him out, being qualified by dint of the job as a hospital porter he took to pay his way when he was a student. There is a grim humour in these pages, but the book's final note is elegiac: the dead man placed in the grave 'with his head in the west . . . so that when he wakes he may face the rising sun'.

In McGahern's work spiritual insight has to be earned, worked towards, achieved through experience; it's not going to be handed to you like the communion wafer. His characters hope for insight, and it is delivered in the fugitive moment. In *The Pornographer*, when the main character holds the beautiful young nurse in his arms, he reflects,

> This body was the shelter of the self. Like all walls and shelters it would break and age and let the enemy in. But holding it now was like holding glory, and having held it once was to hold it – no matter how broken and conquered – in glory still . . .

This insight is what is called grace; it is all McGahern allows his characters; perhaps it is all they need.

Even in *That They May Face the Rising Sun* – about ageing men and women whose individual quirks have become marked – he never condescends to his characters or treats them as 'eccentrics'. In the past he has written without compromise, he has set out to shock; in this book he writes with a tender propriety and reticence. He is respectfully curious about the lives of people for whom ordinary things are not easily gained. The nurse in *The Pornographer* wanted 'to have my own husband and child and home and garden and saucepans and pets'; with these humble ambitions, she could be one of the lakeside people, looking back over a life of hazard and hard work and forward to the qualified benefits of an internationalised and prosperous country where pieties have broken down and strangers order your affairs. The poor labourer Bill Evans is taken to town, given new clothes and a place in a housing scheme; he feels no nostalgia. John Quinn gets his comeuppance from his third wife, who proves to be no sacrificial virgin. And in one of the book's more surprising scenes, Jamesie sits gazing at a television, tuned into *Blind Date*, mesmerised by the sexual swagger of the participants and their vulgar raucous manners. The days of the lifelong bachelor in his untended cabin have drawn to a close. We are in the era of people who know what they want, name it, and demand it.

It may be, at first sight, difficult to see much in common between McGahern's Catholic Ireland and the Ireland of Elizabeth Bowen, whose 'Big House' novels charted the decay of the Protestant gentry. But both authors describe conservative and rural societies on the brink of destabilisation, and if you take thought you find that these Irelands are recognisably the same place. In *Bowen's Court*, her family memoir, Elizabeth Bowen writes that

> though one can be callous in Ireland one cannot be wholly opaque or material. An unearthly disturbance works in the spirit; reason can never reconcile one to life; nothing allays the wants one cannot explain. In whatever direction, the spirit is always steadily moving, or rather steadily being carried as though the country were a ship. The light, the light-consumed distances, that air of intense existence about the empty country . . . the great part played in society by the dead and by the idea of death and, above all, the recurring futilities of hope all work for eternal against temporal things.

This passage seems to catch, inadvertently, the essence of both McGahern's intentions and his methods. His art is shadowy and sly, his effects slow to take hold. He is a perfectionist, who discards most of what he writes. His novel *The Leavetaking* he rewrote entirely, and republished ten years after its first appearance; he says of the earlier version, published in 1974, that 'the work lacked that distance, that inner formality or calm, that all writing, no matter what it is attempting, must possess'. *That They May Face the Rising Sun* has the sense of grave integrity that is his aim. By virtue of its simplicity the novel accretes power. By its close, the barrier between exile and home, between the living and the dead, seems to become translucent. The generations blur. A person's story may be greater than he is, and last much longer. We are made of memories and we persist as long as our story is worth repeating. 'People we know come and go in our minds whether they are here or in England or alive or dead.'

The Right to Life

On Capital Punishment

2005

The trial of Dobie Williams lasted one week, from selection of jury to guilty verdict to death sentence. Dobie was a Louisiana man, poor and Black and with an IQ of sixty-five. He was convicted of the murder of a forty-three-year-old White woman who was stabbed to death in her bathroom. According to the prosecution, this lady called out helpfully, while being attacked, 'A Black man has killed me', and when her husband rushed into the bathroom, she indicated, while dying, that the Black man had gone out through a window so small and high up that the family had never bothered to put a lock on it. Betty Williams, the mother of the accused, commented, 'That sounds like somebody in a murder mystery book'.

Dobie was on weekend leave from a detention centre where he was serving a term for burglary. He seems to have been arrested because he was in the neighbourhood. No motive was alleged for the crime, other than that Dobie had been drinking that evening. None of the blood of the dead woman was found on his person or his clothes. To explain this, the police suggested that Dobie had stripped naked to commit the murder. Because the victim's clothes were pulled down – she was, after all, in the bathroom – it was insinuated that the accused had been attempting rape, though the victim had not in fact been raped and no such charge was brought. But the insinuation may have contributed to the jury's speedy verdict.

Dobie was said to have confessed on tape, but the recording was missing by the time the case came to court, and the police officers who had overheard this 'confession' gave conflicting evidence about it. Dobie was defended by an attorney later disbarred for unethical conduct, and, in *The Death of Innocents: An Eyewitness Account of Wrongful Executions*, as Sister Helen Prejean follows him on the long road to the execution chamber, she explains how the failures and blunders at the original trial made it impossible for his later defenders to recover the ground lost.

Dobie went to death row in 1985 and was executed in 1999, by which time he had been given eleven separate execution dates, sometimes receiving a stay just hours before he was due to die. Is this torture? It is, by most people's definition. In theory, the US Constitution does not permit it, but the Constitution is for human beings, and the system's acknowledgement of Dobie's humanity is scant. But he hangs on to a sense of his own dignity, refusing the grotesque ceremony of a last meal with prison staff: 'When they finish eating they're going to help kill me.' Sister Helen is horrified when she thinks of the cold-blooded ceremony to come:

> Dobie is not in a hospital dying of some disease, with his life energies and faculties fading. He's fully alive, has his full energy and emotions and consciousness. It makes his coming death impossible to comprehend.

In the room adjacent to the execution chamber, where he receives his final visits, there are murals showing Elijah ascending to heaven in his fiery chariot and Daniel in the lion's den.

Her task in the last hour with the prisoner is to try to keep him emotionally intact, so that he doesn't lose all dignity and is able to keep open the channels of grace which connect him to his God. Of course, if the prisoner remains emotionally contained, it makes the administration of the penalty easier. Faced with abject terror, staff might find it more difficult to deal with the task required of them. Faced with the protest and revolt of the powerless, they might feel their consciences touched and their notions of manhood afflicted (there are no women guards at executions). A prisoner reconciled to meeting his maker is easier for all concerned. 'Jesus is close to us here,' she urges. 'Jesus is helping you.' A thought arises, which seems almost too cruel to express: Sister Helen, in her heroic way, is helping to keep the machinery of death oiled.

In her book *Dead Man Walking*, published in 1993, Sister Helen explained how she first became involved with condemned prisoners, and she traces the cases of three men whom she accompanied, as their spiritual adviser, through their final days and hours. It was a bestselling and highly influential book, its arguments given wider currency by the film starring Susan Sarandon in the role of Sister Helen. This new book, *The Death of Innocents*, appears at a time when the death penalty system is in crisis. In 2000 James Liebman of Columbia University School of Law led a team which surveyed 4,500 death penalty cases and found 'reversible error' in 68 per cent of them. In his words – which seem the more true, five years on – the system is 'collapsing under the weight of its own mistakes'.

So far, the crisis is not a crisis of conscience; among a public largely uninformed about how death penalty cases are decided, support for the punishment still stands high. But the public now cannot ignore the fact that there is a category of irreversible errors, which send innocent people to their deaths. The 'innocence projects' run by law and journalism students have re-examined capital cases from the ground up; new DNA evidence has freed dozens of prisoners from death row. These instances are – or should be – profoundly shocking to a nation which has an often naive faith in its own standards of fair dealing. Sister Helen's book is designed to increase public unease about unsafe verdicts. 'Brace yourselves,' she says in her preface. 'These stories are going to break your heart.'

This ambition to stir up emotion may not suit all readers, but Sister Helen also excels in pressing her case through analysis and argument. Here many of the points so well made in *Dead Man Walking* are reinforced, with fresh instances and telling detail. Public support for the penalty is based on the idea that the death penalty deters, though there is ample evidence that it does not. It is also based on a simple notion of answering harm with harm, balancing each killing with an equivalent slaughter. Yet only 2 per cent of killers are actually killed in their turn; so why are they chosen? Overwhelmingly, those who get the death penalty are poor and Black. African-Americans are 12 per cent of the US population but account for 40 per cent of those condemned to death. People of colour are 50 per cent of homicide victims, but 85 per cent of the people on death row have killed White people.

The system values some lives more than others. And when we look at where the death penalty is most used, we find the southern states account for 80 per cent of executions; they are prisoners of a history in which Black people, especially, are to be feared, controlled and repressed. Throughout the nation, it is the right wing and the godly who support the death penalty, taking their authority from the Constitution – which they read as a document frozen in time – and from the Bible: from all those familiar Old Testament texts, read as direct instructions from a wrathful God.

Dead Man Walking is not just the story of the men whom Sister Helen accompanied to execution, but also a story about her own radicalisation. As a young nun, she thought her principal task was to save her own soul. Then in 1980, when, as she describes it, American 'rage for incarceration' was at its height, she woke up to the notion of social justice. As a social worker in a poor Black district of New Orleans, she began to understand why poor people remain poor, and to pick up on the fact that

> whenever White people were murdered it was always front-page news, but when Black people were killed the news evoked barely a five- or six-line article on the back pages.

The debate about capital punishment, she realised, is inseparable from the debate about race, and about poverty. You don't find wealthy people on death row. In her neighbourhood, they told her that 'capital punishment means them without the capital get the punishment'.

She admits to a certain ignorance about how her own country worked. 'When I first started visiting the condemned in 1982, I presumed the guilt of everyone on death row.' The death of an innocent person would be a fluke, she thought. In *Dead Man Walking* she examined cases where the executed men were guilty beyond doubt of the crimes for which they were killed by the state, but here she deals with two cases where she is sure the men on trial were innocent. They both believed that they had only to tell their story, and the truth would set them free. Her book is a detailed history of how wrong they were. When Sister Helen scrutinised the process of cases that interested her, and looked afresh at the initial trial process in each, she began to realise that 'the courts are a system of gates that shut like one-way turnstiles. Once you come out, you can't go back.'

It is vital to get effective legal representation at the earliest stages, and this is what poor people cannot get. The poor are defended by 'overworked, underfunded and inept attorneys', yet federal appeal courts routinely deny appeals based on 'ineffectiveness of counsel' – any lawyer not actually a corpse seems to be good enough. In the case of Dobie Williams, his counsel failed to conduct proper forensic tests, challenge the all-White jury, or properly frame pleas in mitigation of sentence. In addition, mistakes of fact made at the initial hearings can rarely be retrieved. The 'raw stuff' of the crime – police reports, eyewitness statements, physical evidence – is dealt with at first hearing. Even if the appeal courts can be persuaded to re-examine it, there are the practical difficulties of disappeared witnesses, and missing and deteriorated forensic specimens. The prosecution has first sight of the evidence, and prosecutors routinely, she believes, withhold from the defence what is not helpful to their case, walking a fine line between carelessness and misconduct.

The defects of the system are well illustrated by the second case she follows, which is that of Joseph O'Dell, a White man from Virginia. He was convicted of the rape and murder of a White secretary, who was bludgeoned to death after leaving a nightclub in February 1985. As in the case of Dobie Williams, the prosecution overlooked obvious suspects and wove a 'preposterous and convoluted' story to implicate the accused, who had been seen at the same nightclub on the evening in question. O'Dell's landlady, who was also his girlfriend, had found some bloody clothes in a bag in her garage the next day, led there by an 'intuition' after reading a report of the murder. The police found a blood type 'similar' to that of the victim and arrested O'Dell. They found semen 'consistent' with O'Dell's on the victim's body. The subsequent trial showed that if a prosecutor says 'consistent with' long enough and hard enough, a jury will begin to hear 'the same as'.

The first two public defenders assigned to O'Dell were unable to take the case. The third advised him to plead guilty; O'Dell believed he was collaborating with the prosecution. So he decided to defend himself. He was a veteran of the system – a child of rape, brought up in a violent family, he had a long criminal record. Yet he did feel, in this case, that if he could simply tell his story he would be believed. The prosecution had a different story and the will and means to make it stick. The physical evidence to link him to the crime was tenuous, and he had an alibi, though it was never properly investigated. But what sealed the verdict was a 'confession' to a notorious jailhouse snitch called Steve Watson. Watson later admitted that he had been lying, in order to get a deal on his own sentence, but he would not come to court and admit this, for the very good reason that he was threatened with a perjury charge. The prosecution relied on this supposed confession and asked the jury for the death penalty, saying that, as O'Dell had always managed to get out of jail before, he would do so again, and that only a death sentence would stop him committing further crime. They made this plea in full knowledge that the alternative to a capital sentence was life in prison without parole; but the jury did not know this.

In the next twelve years O'Dell was unable to get his story told or his evidence reviewed, and the testimony of an eminent forensic scientist who offered to take the case pro bono was disallowed; the one expert witness he did manage to produce was taunted and reduced to tears by the prosecution. Sister Helen follows the intricate and lengthy process of failed appeals, and describes how O'Dell's case became celebrated internationally. It was taken up by the Vatican and by the ordinary people of Italy, who made thousands of phone calls to the governor of Virginia and sent thousands of faxes to his office. The mayor of Palermo, a hero for his stand against the Mafia, made O'Dell an honourary citizen, and Mother Teresa called the governor to ask for clemency.

Sister Helen has complete faith that all this was helpful to O'Dell's case. But how far it hardened attitudes, we can never know. You can almost feel for the governor; if you were satisfied – and presumably he was – that the best efforts of the judicial system had been bent on the case, how far would you be responsive to the coaxing of some nun from Calcutta, or what you might very well see as the manufactured outrage of a bunch of distant papists?

After his death, Sister Helen took O'Dell's body to Italy for burial, and was granted an audience with John Paul II. This was the climax

of her campaign within the Catholic Church, and she credits the
O'Dell case with helping to change teaching which had stood since
the days of Saint Thomas Aquinas. When she began campaigning,
many individual priests and Catholic laypeople were abolitionists,
but the hierarchy was not, and in *Dead Man Walking* she tells of
her encounters with an obstructive prison chaplain who incarnated
the conservative, misogynist status quo. After her letters, and her
visit to the Vatican in the wake of the O'Dell case, Pope John Paul
spoke out unequivocally against the death penalty, and the Catholic
Catechism was altered. Unfortunately, it was altered by the removal
of words that specifically endorsed capital punishment, rather than
by the addition of words to exclude it. There is plenty here for
theologians and Catholic lawyers to argue over, so the change may
not be quite the lasting triumph that Sister Helen thought it.

Among the promoters of the death penalty, Sister Helen picks out
Justice Antonin Scalia of the US Supreme Court for special odium.
He is a prominent Catholic; how can he vote against the Church's
teaching? 'My morality and religious beliefs have nothing to do with
how I vote,' he says, and he aims to keep 'personal predilections,
biases, and moral and religious beliefs' out of the process of constitutional interpretation. Where does he leave them, the reader
wonders, when he goes to work? Is there a sort of depository or a
left-luggage office where you check in your personal experience and
judgement, while you shrink yourself to a cog or spring in the great
machinery of the law?

It is a sustaining myth of the law that it exists as an awesome
neutral force, a force beyond interpretation, beyond ideology, beyond
individual persons. Sister Helen shows, if demonstration is needed,
how the practice and effect of law arises out of culture. But Scalia,
with other conservative judges, is a believer in the Constitution as
a fixed text embodying the intentions of its framers, rather than as a
working document, evolving as it is read in the light of advances
in human sensibility. He realises that society's standards change,
but to feed that change through into penal policy is the duty, as he
sees it, of the legislative arm of government, not of the judiciary.

The conservative position is that because the Constitution refers
to and clearly envisages a death penalty, it is correct to maintain one

for all time – though the Constitution also says that no one shall be deprived of his life without due process of law. The whole purpose of Sister Helen's book is to show how that principle is violated frequently, violently and publicly:

> The crux of the constitutional debate is this: If, despite twenty-five years of attempted reform, the death penalty is still imposed randomly, the practice of the death penalty is unconstitutional as surely as if the Framers had explicitly forbidden its use.

There are really two arguments going on – one about the Constitution and what it means, and another about God and what He means. Justice Scalia leans on Saint Paul's Epistle to the Romans, Chapter 13: 'the powers that be are ordained of God', and so on. This text has been long used to sanction the actions of authoritarian government and to make rebellion illegitimate. (It can also be used to assert the divine right of kings, which should give any democrat cause to worry.) Sister Helen's reading of the epistle is more fluid and subtle than Justice Scalia's; she thinks Catholics ought to have a more sophisticated idea of how to interpret texts than fundamentalist Christians.

But why, the reader may ask, need we engage in this argument? In March 2005 the Colorado Supreme Court struck down the death sentence in the Robert Harlan case, where a juror took his Bible into the jury room and directed his colleagues' attention to his favourite texts in Exodus, rather than to the evidence. A Bible in a jury room, the court said, is an 'unauthorized extraneous text'. America is not a theocracy. But Sister Helen will sustain the argument with those who think it should be. If you want to sling texts at her she will sling some straight back. The humanist case against capital punishment was made in the eighteenth century, but she does not make it here. Secularist reasons for abolition are good enough for what Justice Scalia calls 'post-Christian Europe', but not for the godly US.

Justice Scalia's phrase is intended to stir controversy, no doubt, but is not far off the truth. Where Britain is concerned – we should probably leave the north of Ireland out of the debate – it is now seen as almost offensive to assert that we are a Christian country. There may still be an established church, but its congregations are slender and diminishing, and liberal pieties insist we are a multicultural, multifaith society; the heir to the throne is said to have pondered whether the royal title 'Defender of the Faith' could be altered to 'Defender of Faith.'* Sister Helen speaks of 'the fierce ambivalence' that 'almost everybody' experiences about the death penalty, but it is doubtful if you would find this ambivalence in the abolitionist countries of Europe; if it exists in individuals, it is more likely to be because of some personal ethical muddle than because the individual is searching for the answers in the Old or New Testaments.

There is a folk belief in the UK that if a referendum were held, capital punishment would be reinstated. But of course, this belief will never be tested. Capital punishment is off the agenda; no electable political party is offering to reinstate it, and in time there will be an electorate that cannot easily imagine it. Abolition is driven not simply by the fear of error or a sense of the inadequacy of the legal process, but by a knowledge of the penalty's corrupting power; the question becomes not simply 'Who can we justly execute?' but also 'Who can we justly call on to be an executioner?' From time to time, in this post-Christian society, the liberal consensus may be nibbled around the edges, and the mass-market press may whip up regressive panics about outsiders and social misfits; but there is no call for the return of the hangman. Once state killing has gone, it's gone. Not so in the US. The Supreme Court declared the death penalty unconstitutional in 1972, in the case of *Furman v Georgia*; four years later, *Gregg v Georgia* reinstated it. In 2000, as is well known, Governor George Ryan of Illinois placed a moratorium on the death penalty, and instituted a commission of inquiry into its workings. In 2003 he pardoned four men who were under sentence of death, and commuted to life imprisonment the sentences of 167 other offenders. But Governor Ryan did this as he left office; and the death penalty is still in force in Illinois.

How can a people's mind be changed? In his book *Ultimate Punishment*, Scott Turow refers to 'a struggle for the national soul'. In her acknowledgements, Sister Helen quotes the expressed hope of her publisher:

---

* In fact, the coronation oath in 2023 remained unchanged.

With the publication of *Dead Man Walking*, we opened the national conversation about the death penalty. With *The Death of Innocents*, we're going to catalyse public discourse that will end the death penalty.

In other jurisdictions, the legislature has led public opinion, but in the US a shift in public opinion is crucial to the debate; in a system where so many officials are elected, they are bound to follow rather than lead. Sister Helen calls for the public to 'assume ownership of our Constitution'. She frames her plea with an eye to the prejudices of those she needs to convince – not just the religious right with its old-style retributionists, but the suspicious and worried heartlands where liberal arguments are not going to appeal.

This lends her arguments a queasy tinge at times. She is keen to show that she is not soft on crime, and talks a great deal, and in heartfelt terms, about her work with victims' groups. Above all she is anxious that the public be well informed about the alternative to capital punishment. Support for the death penalty falls away, she remarks, when the voter is offered the alternative of imprisonment without parole. She makes this point in both her books, but never explores the difficulties of running a penal system which confines prisoners who are without hope of release, and hence without incentive for cooperation. Lifelong confinement may be the only way to protect the community in certain cases, but humanity suggests that whole-life sentences should be rare. A system aiming only at containment, with no interest in rehabilitation, is a debased system, which will find itself in charge of the aged and the dying, presiding over their physical and no doubt spiritual deterioration. Such prisoners may present, to Sister Helen or any other religious person, the toughest challenge of all; surely they would become the most intractable of human beings, the hardest souls to save.

The reader feels quite sure that as an intelligent and compassionate woman, she has thought about these questions, but they are not worked through on the page. She is out to win the argument, and sometimes it seems she is not too scrupulous about how she does it; perhaps she would say that if lives are at stake, there cannot be any scruples. She is ready to appease the public by offering them, in the shape of whole-life imprisonment, a sense of security and a limited retribution. She reaches out to those she feels may be instinctively (or unreflectively) in favour of capital punishment, by playing on their fears of government incompetence: 'Government bureaucrats can scarcely be trusted to get potholes in the streets filled, much less allowed to decide who should live and who should die.' This is a populist argument, a weapon apt to turn back on liberals who use it; when people are encouraged to distrust government, what is to stop them from taking the law into their own hands? She steers clear, too, of discussing how the murder rate, which naturally so frightens the public, could be brought down. The greatest single contribution Americans could make to public safety would be to introduce effective and stringent gun control, but Sister Helen doesn't address the issue, no doubt deeming it unwise to burst another bubble in the conservative version of the American dream.

Even if you cannot stand behind every argument the author makes, *The Death of Innocents* is a deeply convinced and deeply convincing book. Now we know what's wrong: racial bias, bias against the poor, inept counsel, over-zealous prosecutors trying to make a name, self-serving judges, missing witnesses, careless science, coerced confessions. Add in the use of jailhouse informants, the propensity of police officers to lie, and their evident inability to reason about the facts of a case, and you have a recipe for the continuing conviction and death of innocent people.

If you find Sister Helen's direct and emotional appeal not to your liking, you can read Bill Kurtis's *The Death Penalty on Trial*, an impressively brisk little book which takes the racial factor out of the argument by following the cases of two White men, one a respectable ex-army postal worker, one a misfit in his community, who found themselves condemned because of initial errors by the police – one an arrest in haste, the other an arrest which came out of the police's frustration at being unable to produce a suspect. Neither of these men was executed, but they spent respectively twelve and four years on death row before they were freed.

After a spell on death row, you wonder, what does the rest of your life look like? If at last the court process has vindicated such men, they are no longer, in all ways, innocent, but morally injured and compromised, having suffered an ejection from society that is beyond recompense. And yet, we must see these men as lucky. The weight of evidence seems overwhelming that, as Sister Helen says, the system 'virtually ensures that innocent people will be killed along with the guilty'. And for those who are not vindicated, it is surely little compensation, pace Justice Scalia ('How enviable a quiet death by lethal injection'), that he will be given the kind of euthanasia we give to our dogs when they are old and sick.

Where do we go from here? Possibly capital trials will become so expensive that they will break the budget in every state that wants to go in for them. A capital trial is – contrary to general belief – much more expensive than leaving someone to rot in jail for a lifetime. But the lengthy process of appeal and reappeal cannot be curtailed; defenders will fight on any grounds available to keep their clients alive, especially if they believe they may be able to beat the execution date by showing their client is innocent. Since the reinstatement of the death penalty in 1976, the courts have devoted themselves to a search for ways to limit the penalty and administer it equitably. One way to limit it is by excluding certain categories of offender. Dobie Williams would no longer be executed, since in 2002 the death penalty for convicts with learning difficulties was ended. A Supreme Court decision in March 2005 decreed that prisoners under eighteen would no longer be executed; Justice Anthony Kennedy, whose vote swung the 5–4 majority, mentioned the weight of international opinion, which had left the US the only country in the world officially to execute juveniles.

Another way to limit the penalty is to try to control what happens in court. There have been attempts by the Supreme Court to issue jury guidelines, to try to establish some objective criteria in working out who gets the death penalty. But justice makes two demands: one is for consistency, the other is that each case be dealt with on the basis of its peculiar facts. Checklists of aggravating circumstances and mitigating circumstances have proved hard to deploy because of the diverse nature of crimes and their victims, and because of the very slipperiness of the language in which we can discuss them. Recommendations that the death penalty be reserved for the 'worst of the worst' murders invite us to ask, which murders are lesser? Which murders are ordinary?

As Scott Turow points out, it is these 'worst' cases which are most emotive. It is in these cases that a community is most alarmed and the police are under great pressure to arrest someone, a someone whose guilt may almost be assumed in a huge communal sigh of relief. An atmosphere of terror is no climate in which to establish even the simplest facts. The increasing resources and precision of forensic science can help us toward simple facts, but it is important not to overstate what science can do. Science has to be paid for; there is no point in mandating early DNA testing unless the tests are properly funded and administered, and some states will not fund a post-conviction defence. There is a danger that the public will see forensic science as a pillow on which conscience can rest. But scientists disagree just as often as lawyers; expertise is variable; interpretation may be contentious; and in any event, science can only help a court when it is subject to the rules of evidence, and must depend on the understanding of judges and juries. Science may, in some cases, offer a final truth; but how do we get to it, and who will oversee the process?

As Sister Helen sees it, attempts to make the penalty more consistent have failed. Yet where defects are only procedural, they could be remedied; given political will and a bottomless public purse, possibly they could be fixed. If the bureaucrats were wise and the system fair – if the process met tightly defined legal criteria of objectivity – would it be all right to have a death penalty? Many would say yes. Sister Helen is clear in her view. 'I don't believe that the government should be put in charge of killing anybody, even those proven guilty of terrible crimes.' This is what the world would like to hear America say. You do not have to be a Christian, or have any faith at all, to support Sister Helen's basic position: 'Every human being is worth more than the worst act of his or her life.'

The death penalty is not wrong because it is inconsistently administered. If it were fairly administered, it would still be wrong. Finally, the issue is moral; a nation so God-besotted should be able to grasp that. When the government touches a corpse, it contaminates the private citizen. A modern nation that deals in state-sponsored death, becomes, in part, dead in itself; dead certainly, to the enlightened ideals from which America derives its existence as a nation.

Fashion Queen

On Marie Antoinette

2007

She arrived naked; on an island in the Rhine, on 7 May 1770, in a pavilion especially built for the purpose, the Austrian princess Antonia was stripped of her clothes under the cold and curious gaze of a party of aristocrats. She was fourteen years old, and she cried while this happened. A keen wind nipped between the Gobelins tapestries in which the pavilion was draped; a steady rain began to fall and run through the pavilion's roof.

The child had travelled from Vienna in a golden coach drawn by eight white horses. Now her new life was to begin, under a French name, Marie Antoinette. She was redressed, head to toe, as a Frenchwoman: whalebone stays and paniers to hold up her skirts, silk stockings embroidered with gold, and then the court robe, with its train, its flounces and frills, its beading and trim, gemstones and lace. Her feet crammed into high-heeled satin slippers, she was ready to go: blue eyes and Hapsburg lip, flat chest and pretty fair hair. Her teeth had recently been straightened; what pain and tedium that involved, we can only guess at. In her life so far she had been fond of dancing and playing with dolls. She had come from a musical, family-minded court, informal as courts go. But her formidable mother, the Empress Maria Theresa, sent her off with this warning: 'All eyes will be fixed on you.' And in that chilly, liminal space, so they were – taking in every inch of the white body on which history would inscribe itself, and on which we are writing still. She had only just quit the pavilion when the weight of rainwater brought the roof down.

She was being brought to France to marry the dauphin, Louis

Auguste, grandson of the reigning Louis XV. Acting always under scrutiny, under the public gaze, conforming to codes of which she was as yet ignorant, functioning within a system that confiscated personal emotions and replaced them with artificial sentiment, where codes of etiquette were more respected than the laws of the land or the dictates of the heart, she was expected to reconcile two nations with a long history of enmity, and she was expected to bear children to continue the Bourbon line.

In her numerous family she was one of the younger princesses, but death and the ravages of smallpox had taken older sisters off the marriage market. She had not been brought up for such a distinguished role; her education had been neglected, and if her personality was pleasant, her attention span was short. Bad omens clustered around the marriage. Black clouds hung over the wedding day at Versailles, and the wedding gown had been made too small, forcing her to stand at the altar with her bodice gaping, to show her shift and the lacing of her stays. At the public putting-to-bed ceremony, the new dauphine dived beneath the covers in shame and horror. What she saw there cannot have lifted a young girl's heart.

The dauphin Louis Auguste was a staid, corpulent young man, fifteen years old. The Austrian ambassador reported, 'Nature seems to have denied everything to Monsieur le Dauphin.' He had little sexual curiosity and no sexual appetite. Some historians think that his difficulties were psychological, others believe that a tight foreskin made the act painful. It was some years before the marriage could be consummated. Childless and pointless, the Queen had time on her hands; Caroline Weber's entertaining and thought-provoking book, *Queen of Fashion: What Marie Antoinette Wore to the Revolution*, explains how she filled it.

There is a delicate novel called *Farewell, My Queen*, by the historian Chantal Thomas, which tells us in great detail about the artificial life of the palace of Versailles, referred to by its inhabitants as *ce pays-ci*, as if it were a country by itself. The waste of ennui that was the Versailles day was strictly timetabled:

There was a Perfect Day; its program had been set more than a century earlier by Louis XIV: Prayers, Petty Levee, Grand Levee,

Mass, Dinner, Hunt, Vespers, Supper, Grand Couchee, Petty Couchee, Prayers, Petty Levee, Grand Levee . . . Every day since that time was supposed to reenact the Perfect Day . . . But reality never ceased to throw up obstacles. The reenactment was never completely successful . . . Tiny modifications became snags, reforms became upheavals, and so on, leading down to the days in July of 1789 that saw the King capitulate and the court disperse – the collapse, in less than a week, of a ritual system that I had assumed was fixed for all time.

At this distance we can see how well signalled that collapse was, how year by year the old regime spun its own metaphors of desuetude, like the cobwebs that would later drape its ballrooms. In summer the palace stank. Bedbugs, fleas, mice and rats outnumbered even its human parasites. The Austrian princess, with her insistence on washing her face before plastering it with make-up, was thought singular in this as in other matters. It fell to a revolutionary to be assassinated in the bath; you would never have found a courtier there.

To preserve self-respect without actually going to the trouble of washing, a great deal of perfume was required; and how it was supplied is the subject of Elisabeth de Feydeau's *A Scented Palace*, a biography of Jean-Louis Fargeon, the royal perfumer. The author is 'a professor of the Versailles School of Perfumers', and is against the Revolution, which she claims smelled 'of sweat, rotgut wine, urine and blood'. In her rhapsodic and often unintentionally funny book she supplies a great deal of solid information about how Antoinette's narcissism was serviced, and reminds us what old-fashioned royal worship sounds like. It seems the Queen had two ways of walking, one for public show at royal headquarters at Versailles, and one for her bijou private residence in the grounds:

> Marie Antoinette had a unique way of walking that made her literally and figuratively heads above any woman in France. She carried her head high, with a majesty that made her stand out as the sovereign in the midst of the entire Court, yet this regal air in no way spoiled her look of gentleness and kindness, her combination of grace and nobility. In the Trianon, however, her walk was different, more relaxed, but nonetheless inspiring no loss of respect.

Given that she had the usual complement of legs, how unique could her gait be? Please, the reader wants to say, let this poor woman, whom you insist on adoring, at least be human. She was not a goddess, and could not keep a deity's distance from events. Long before the Revolution, Antoinette (as her new subjects called her) was in a deeply vulnerable position. Figuratively speaking she may have moved, as Edmund Burke put it, 'just above the horizon, decorating and cheering the elevated sphere she just began to move in', but daily in her satin slippers she had to tread the same dirty floors as her jealous courtiers, and catch the acid comments of the disaffected and the disinvited.

In a court of factions, the princess was sure to upset some powerful body of gossips, whichever friends she chose and however she spent her time. From Vienna came a stream of advice and criticism: 'One day,' her mother wrote, 'you will agree with me, but it will be too late.' The princess was expected by her mother to exercise pro-Austrian influence in affairs of state; a powerful anti-Austrian lobby among the courtiers watched her to make sure she did no such thing. One faction constellated around Madame du Barry, official mistress of Louis XV, whose existence for a time Antoinette refused to acknowledge – a refusal that threatened diplomatic relations between the two countries. Another faction supported the King's elderly aunts; then she must consider the King's brothers, Provence and Artois, each with his followers and cliques.

In an atmosphere of vigilant malice, it was hard for the little princess to grow up. Dressing in the morning, she had to stand naked until she was handed a shift by the highest-ranking lady present; if, halfway through the ceremony, a lady of higher rank entered, Antoinette must shiver till the newcomer took her place in the line-up. She could do nothing for herself; if she wanted a glass of water, and the right person was not available to pass it to her, she had to go thirsty. Like a modern faddist, she made a pet of herself, and would drink only one kind of mineral water, which later, during the term of her imprisonment, the revolutionary Commune continued to supply.

After her husband's accession in 1774, she was not in his confidence, though to save face she pretended to be. French law did not allow a consort any formal status; though she had been crowned in a private ceremony, revolutionaries would later remind her of her unimportant role by pointedly referring to her as 'the King's wife'. As time went by with too little to fill it, Antoinette detached herself from the concept of her future: 'When one has passed the age of thirty, I don't know how one dares show oneself at [Versailles],' she said. She had not been encouraged to consider physical decay; when she had made her triumphal entry into France, and crowds turned out to see her, ugly people had been warned to stay away.

So how did she assert herself? Through dressing up, it appears; through the setting of trends, rapid changes of style, and highly conspicuous consumption. Caroline Weber says:

> I have scrutinized Marie Antoinette's fashion statements. And I have discovered that they were, in every sense, accessories to the campaign she waged against the oppressive cultural strictures and harsh political animosities that beset her throughout her twenty-three-year tenure in France.

Male biographers, Weber says, have not seen the importance of how the Queen dressed. Weber speaks of 'the startling consistency and force with which her costumes triggered severe sociopolitical disorder', knitting the Queen's fortunes, at each stage of her career, to what she was wearing. The Queen 'identified fashion as a key weapon in her struggle for personal prestige, authority, and sometimes mere survival'.

The metaphor of the body politic runs through the discourse of early modern Europe, a commonplace device for writers of all political tendencies. For some time now, contemporary feminist scholars have been looking at how the history of the Revolution was written on women's bodies: the bodies of the Amazons of street warfare, of the goddesses of Reason who replaced the Virgin in desecrated city churches, and of the Queen herself, pilloried by public opinion, then imprisoned, stripped of her grandeur, stripped of her womanly dignity, then executed. Antoinette was brought to France to perform the duty of a royal wife – to breed. Because at first she failed to do so, her intimate life became the focus of hostile attention. Scurrilous pamphlets chronicling her supposed infidelities and perversions were disseminated throughout Europe – not, initially, from revolutionary sources, but bankrolled by alienated courtiers who knew all the latest rumours. Provence was a culprit, as was the King's cousin the Duke of Orléans, who cultivated his popularity with the people of Paris, as times grew hard and hunger bit, by large-scale charitable works.

At the same time, in the years leading to the Revolution, criminal gangs in England conspired to produce defamatory material in the hope that the French crown would buy them off. Robert Darnton among others has studied the production and dissemination of these libelles, and Chantal Thomas in her book *The Wicked Queen* has pointed out that it is useless to scrutinise them for any correspondence to the Queen's real life or character; they are exercises in myth-making, in the creation of time-honoured extended metaphors by which the lechery and impotence of rulers are characterised as diseases in the body of the nation. But queens of France, by convention retiring and religious figures, had not usually been such high-profile targets. It is the strength of Caroline Weber's book that she spells out in detail how – and by how many inches, and dressed with what sort of feathers and plumes – Antoinette put her head above the parapet.

What was her style like? Weber says that she 'cultivated looks that were playful and coquettish, ephemeral and unpredictable, alluring and modern'. But a good deal of the pictorial evidence is against the author. The pouf, the tower of powdered hair worn by Antoinette and her imitators, is as modern and alluring as foot-binding. It didn't crush the bones, but what did it do to the brain? Like foot-binding, it was a mark of status; it said, I am an upper-class woman who need do nothing practical and nothing for myself, not even get through a doorway without inconvenience. Antoinette did not originate the style, but – as Weber admits – she adopted it early. One could multiply examples of the absurdities of this headgear, but Elisabeth de Feydeau gives us a pouf worth mentioning, one belonging to the Duchesse de Lauzun: it displayed

a churning sea with ducks swimming near the shore, a hunter lying in wait, and at the top of the hairdo a mill, with the miller's wife flirting with a priest. Beneath the ear, one could glimpse the unsuspecting miller, pulling a stubborn donkey by the halter.

Immobility would have been the best posture for the lady wearing her pouf and her paniers – and the caricaturists of the day found these fashions as ridiculous as we find them. High-born ladies at Versailles were ferociously corseted, even during pregnancy. They wore a thick paste of white make-up with rouge applied in unblended round spots. They walked with a peculiar shuffle, designed to stop them from treading on each other's trains, which was described by Henriette de La Tour du Pin in her lively memoir of Versailles – a book still unrivalled for conveying the social perils and absurdities of day-to-day court life under the old regime.

Did Antoinette rebel against the court's style? It seems she did, with limited persistence and limited success, and the help of Rose Bertin, an expensive, pug-faced arriviste who set about dressing and fleecing her aristocratic customers with guile, persistence and panache. The Queen's critics called Bertin 'the Minister of Fashion', with the implication, Weber believes, that women were mimicking male prerogatives. Bertin and M. Léonard, the Queen's hairdresser, were commoners who found themselves close to her, licensed to touch her skin. Their 'presumption' was disliked and feared in court circles; perhaps they were the forerunners of a greater presumption to come?

The years went by, one costly trend succeeded the next, national bankruptcy approached, and by 1788 there was talk of calling France's version of a parliament, which had never met in living memory. Bodices were loosened in pursuit of the simple look; they were tightened again in the name of propriety. Hemlines went up, ankles and embroidered slippers were exposed. Jewels were worn, then not worn, then worn again. Turning thirty, Antoinette had reverted to the conventional court gown, structured and rigid, and she eschewed the colour pink. As the years of revolution approached, she was no longer a glamorous woman – she had lost her figure, and her hair was falling out, but she retained, as she has for posterity, a sort of mystical body double in which her charms were intact. What can she have felt when she saw the simple white dresses she had pioneered become the everyday dress of women sympathetic to the Revolution? She cannot have felt her initiative had succeeded.

In the first year of the Revolution, Weber tells us, the Queen dressed as splendidly as she knew how, in a firm statement of her unassailable position. Within a few months, as a gesture to the nation, she adopted simpler dresses trimmed with the *bleu, blanc et rouge.* But when she and the royal family attempted to abscond, she not only ordered a lavish new wardrobe for the trip but took with her on the flight from Paris none other than M. Léonard, who contributed to the debacle that saw the family hauled back to the Tuileries and kept under guard. At this juncture – the time when the royals had lost most of their remaining friends among France's new rulers – the Queen, Weber writes, dressed in imperial purple, in a campaign planned in sessions with Rose Bertin. She had been a fan of pastels, but she thought that now was the time to show who was boss.

From the beginning of the Revolution, Antoinette had dressed up for the wrong party. In France when the Bastille fell, there were few republicans, and no one who imagined cutting off royal heads. There had been time, so much time, to negotiate, and so much goodwill squandered; Antoinette could never differentiate between mild constitutionalist reformers and those who became, after they had despaired of the monarchy's cooperation, its enemies. When France declared war on Austria in the spring of 1792, the monarchy still had a degree of formal power, and Antoinette used her position to feed her adopted country's war plans to her native land. She was, as her enemies had always suspected, sailing under false colours.

On 7 August 1792, Antoinette ordered her last pouf from Rose. Three days later the Tuileries was invaded, and women from the streets raided her apartments and took away her personal possessions. After the fall of the monarchy, her advisers tried to persuade her to wear stab-proof bodices, but she refused them. Perhaps she knew it was too late; clothes weren't going to save her. Caroline Weber makes the case for fashion as a statement of selfhood: 'Marie Antoinette's clothing had time and again conveyed insubordination, autonomy and strength.' But you could just as easily argue that her clothes had made her seem a greater fool than she was, and that it was through fashion that she unravelled herself. She had helped defeat her own mystique.

Before M. Léonard, whose arts she found so indispensible, ladies of rank had dressed the hair of queens of France; Léonard was the first commoner to touch the royal head. In the dark days of 1793, M. Sanson, the executioner, was waiting in line for the same privilege; but in between, only at the very end of her life was Antoinette reduced to doing her own hair. Imprisoned in the Temple with her husband and children, she continued to order from Rose; the Commune paid her (much-reduced) bills. Her last parcel consisted of black bonnets, black stockings and a black fan, mourning clothes for the death of her executed husband. It was at this point that the perfumer Fargeon – who, like Rose Bertin, had once been driven to bankruptcy by his clients' failure to pay their bills – decided to cut his losses and send the new regime his unpaid accounts for the last two years. It is one of the most piquant facts in de Feydeau's book: meticulous, the new Republic settled up.

Antoinette's last months, locked away without her children, were sad beyond bearing. Perhaps defeat was woven into her existence. It is Caroline Weber's great achievement to show how every thread was fought over during her years at Versailles. If court protocol made it hard for the Queen to get dressed in the morning at all, the way she chose to dress was often misread, or, one should perhaps say, read against her. When hunting she sometimes rode astride, rather than side-saddle, wearing riding breeches, a choice which caused a certain amount of psychic panic. With Louis impotent and clueless, were women taking the reins? The fact was that Antoinette was equally clueless, though capable of holding and expressing strong opinions. Her fitful pursuit of more comfortable clothing was equally doomed. The loose muslin dresses that she introduced for informal occasions – one is tempted to say for picnic-wear, picnicking being a solemn royal duty – signalled to critics her sexual availability. Her outerwear looked like underwear. She had ensnared herself in contradictions; an unused or underused wife was posing as a sexual toy.

No doubt, as Caroline Weber sees, her spending power and her ability to set the fashion were ways of asserting her personality. Early in the reign she held lavish costume balls twice weekly; she was fond of masks, and would sometimes go to the masked balls in Paris, but one cannot help feeling that superficial concealment was designed only to draw attention to the special status she both did and did not want. Always seeing the mask, unable to read what lay beneath the surface, she judged the people around her by their appearance.

At Versailles she was far from alone in superficiality and extravagance. The behaviour of other figures at court reinforced hers. The King considered himself thrifty but spared no expense on his table and his horses. In 1777 his brother Artois ordered 365 pairs of shoes, so that he would have one for every day of the year; Antoinette got by on four pairs a week. Though what she spent was a drop in the ocean of the nation's needs, her consumption was so conspicuous that she became known as Madame Déficit. She intended, her courtiers thought, to be 'the most *à la mode* woman alive'.

Was this a worthy pursuit for a queen? It was certainly a new ambition. Queens of France, Caroline Weber tells us, were expected to cost less than royal mistresses. Louis XVI had no mistresses; one woman was rather too much for him. So Antoinette took on both roles, and their dress allowances. At one of her regular costume balls, she persuaded the King to appear as Henry IV, while she dressed as his legendary mistress, Gabrielle d'Estrées. When her mother complained that, in a portrait sent to Vienna, she looked like an actress, she was saying in effect that she looked like a prostitute. Antoinette had a pretty singing voice and loved amateur theatricals. She seemed set on making royalty a branch of the entertainment industry, an ambition not revived until Grace Kelly married Prince Rainier, and Princess Margaret began to spend her time with show-business people and married a photographer. All roads lead to Diana – another mismatch, another fashion-plate, another doomed victim whose forms of self-assertion were puny and self-defeating.

Just before Diana's death her dresses were auctioned for charity at Christie's in New York. When they were turned inside out, they showed their secret structure, second dresses built inside the first; they were nothing like the dresses ordinary women wear, and with their elaborate frosting and beading they looked as if they might be stab-proof, if not bulletproof. The dresses stood up and almost walked; after her death, they alone retained the shape of the princess.

Antoinette's clothes also formed a sort of anticipated ghost. In the years before the Revolution, you could go to Versailles as a tourist and see the Queen's dress collection. Any respectably dressed person could turn up and take a look at the French monarchy in action. It seems odd, in one way: you would have thought that the monarchs would have cultivated their legend at a frozen distance from the populace. But if you actually visit Versailles you can see how it worked; the palace is so spectacular, so awe-inspiring, that proximity could create in the onlooker nothing but the conviction that the Bourbons were here and here to stay. In the medieval alleys of Paris revolution might have seemed possible, but at Versailles it hardly does, even now; the mind and will are benumbed by excess, the imagination is taken captive.

Antoinette had her own house, the Petit Trianon, a neo-classical château made over to reflect her exquisite taste. It was a stylistic break with the old-style opulence of Versailles, but the new style could not be mistaken for simplicity. The Queen did not break the codes of artificiality, but substituted a new code, which looked different, but was no more easy to achieve for outsiders. Vast expenditure and enormous contrivance produced what Caroline Weber calls the graceful, careless ambience of this retreat. The fashionable English garden had to be planned and landscaped just as carefully as the geometric gardens that Le Nôtre had contrived for the palace itself. Antoinette was not a great reader, and had probably never read Rousseau, but she had picked up the idea that what was natural was good, and to be imitated, at great expense if necessary. She turned Rousseauist thinking into a style statement and perverted it; the flowers you saw at the Petit Trianon were not just nature's flowers, but flowers of porcelain and enamel, gilded flowers, painted flowers. She sanitised nature and made it whimsical; at her toy farm, Le Hameau, she kept perfumed sheep. At the Petit Trianon and the toy farm, the Queen ruled, not the King: here, she said, 'I am me'.

A code of aesthetics, then, shielded the Petit Trianon from the dangers of strong emotion or the effort of hard thinking. A public figure, Antoinette wanted the one thing money couldn't buy her – a private life. For the Queen to be 'me' meant an effort of self-denial, in the true sense. In the musical comedies she was fond of staging in her private theatre, she liked to play the part of servant girls. They were cute, well-dressed little servants; it was an abdication, nevertheless, and a telling one. For how can the psychic space be filled between 'Queen' and 'me'? In Sofia Coppola's film *Marie Antoinette* – as in Stephen Frears's *The Queen*, about Elizabeth II – there are repeated scenes in which a rumpled royal person wakes up, dazed, and – yawning and rearranging herself – passes from the unreality of dreams to the unreality of a waking life as a queen. Coppola's film has a beautiful sleepwalker at its centre, and offers, for all its conscious absurdities and anachronisms, an emotional truth. The Queen is self-absorbed, but not self-possessed. It is the people who dress her who own her. The couturiers of the eighteenth century used to create dolls to show off their designs, and in the reign of Louis XV such a doll, dressed as his mistress Madame de Pompadour, had caused excitement as it travelled through Europe. These dolls were known as Pandoras. Rose Bertin made and dressed a life-sized doll to look like Antoinette, and so one wonders: was she ever 'me' or only a simulation of a person, a dressed doll wheeled along by other people, its outer surface decorated with mirrors to reflect her times?

Perhaps it is the concentration on surfaces that has bred oddities in Caroline Weber's treatment of the historical background to her story. Writing of events following the harsh winter of 1774/5, she tells us:

> That May, a scarcity of grain and misguided reforms by Louis XVI's Controller-General, Turgot, impelled starving people throughout the nation to stage riots known as the Flour Wars.

It is an odd locution; though there is an element of ritual behaviour in the events of that spring, in that the protesters petitioned for relief, as they usually did in time of famine, at the King's own gates, the riots were presumably not a theatrical performance to those who engaged in them; they were not 'staged'. She goes on to tell us that to quell the rioting both far and near, the historian Simon Schama has written, 'Turgot call[ed] out twenty-five thousand troops, and institute[d] summary tribunals and exemplary hangings'.

Could she not have checked the facts and given them direct, instead of quoting another historian? It is her anxious tactic, throughout the book, to ornament quite uncontentious assertions with frills and tassels of received opinion, as if we might not like them if she left them plain.

The year 1789 saw in a plainer age. In the time of Louis XIV – the Sun King – the splendour of his buildings, his court and his own costume were what proved to his people that he was a king. In those days, to seem it was to be it, but Louis XVI's court, powdered and reeking of Fargeon's chemical experiments, seems to exist in a different time frame from that of the sober black-clad deputies who met in Versailles in the spring of 1789 to represent the Third Estate, the common people of France. By 1789, the King's power to regulate his subjects' style and taste was in the past, though the King had not noticed. The deputies had been commanded into black, to contrast with the parakeet colours of their betters; but this was an age of commodification, where the illusion of caste could not be maintained. The *marchandes de modes* of Paris catered to the middle classes as well as the aristocracy.

As long ago as 1773, Rose Bertin had set up her shop on the rue Saint-Honoré, with lavish window displays. She tried to limit her clients to the nobility, but anyone could look and imitate. If anyone can dress up as a queen, anyone can, at a casual glance, seem a queen. In the complex pre-Revolution scam known as the Diamond Necklace Affair – which was a public relations disaster for Antoinette, although she was not at fault – she had been imitated by a prostitute who had been specially coached, to ape her style. The demimondaine had sent out all the right signals to the man who was to be conned. She moved in silence, in a floating white dress, a rose in her hand; at dusk in the grounds of the palace, she walked the walk.

Caroline Weber's book is absorbing, fascinating, a wonderful display of grace and expertise, full of telling details. She shows what she sets out to show: speaking of Antoinette's fashion choices, she says:

I will argue that these ensembles, too often dismissed as mere instances of the Queen's frivolity, identified her as a woman who could dress, spend, and do exactly as she pleased.

But what is new here? To posterity that is how she has always looked: a woman whose empty self-regard was at the centre of her world, and who employed considerable resources to salve her wounded vanity.

We can sympathise with the young exiled princess – isolated, homesick, not very bright. That she decided 'to play the game of fashion by her own, unconventional rules' cannot be doubted, but Weber comes close to representing Antoinette's fight against her personal circumstances as a proto-feminist campaign. But to reflect the great world only through what you wear is surely an acceptance, an accentuation of a subservient feminine role. The fashionable woman at Versailles marked the partition of Poland by adopting a new style of skirt, caught up in three separate hoops – one for Russia, one for Austria, one for Prussia. It's doubtful that Polish patriots were much cheered.

Antoinette is, as we say, having a moment. This is her season, because of the new film, and because 2005 was the 250th anniversary of her birth. The papers have been full of the news that she did not in fact say, of the starving populace, 'let them eat cake'; but in Paris, the Ladurée patisserie on the Left Bank has been filling its windows with tiers of pastel-coloured macaroons, inspired by her gowns. A rehabilitation movement is unneeded in English-speaking countries, where readers for generations have been sentimentally fixated on royalty and aristocracy, and there is always room for a new biography with a new version of the Queen's sufferings.

At the Bourbon restoration the French treated her as a martyr, an icon, but for many years seem not to have taken much notice of her – as a brand name, anyway – making do with their own set of sentimentalities and pieties about the Revolution. The palace of Versailles has presented itself to tourists as a grand and chilly spectacle, though one that is under-realised and under-explained. But over the last year, the Petit Trianon and the Hameau have been marketed as a major attraction. An expensive Marie Antoinette fragrance is on sale – which must please Elisabeth de Feydeau. The Queen's old bones have been dug up and redressed, providing a welcome distraction for a nation that hardly knows its role in the world, that has lost its sense of a civilising mission and is filling the hungry void with pastel froth.

The thinking of cultural historians for many years now has been that the revolutionary period embodied a crisis of patriarchy; the nation murdered its father, having found him wanting in fatherly care. It was her motherly credentials that were assailed when Antoinette stood trial. Her eight-year-old son had been induced to accuse her of teaching him to masturbate and of sexually abusing him as he lay in bed with her; the court was told that she did this to gain a physical and moral ascendancy over him, which she could assert if he ever became king. The accusation came from the peculiar mind of the prosecutor Jacques-René Hébert, who had long before turned current events into a perverse circus, with the royals as blood-bespattered mechanical dolls. Brought out in open court, this weird allegation brought cries of sympathy for the Queen from the public galleries. Caroline Weber quotes a contemporary report, to the effect that when Robespierre

> heard what a sensation the sublime manner in which the Queen had met the charge had made, and the effect it had on the audience, he, being then at dinner, broke his plate with rage.

Now, Weber is a respected commentator on the Revolution, having published a scholarly work called *Terror and Its Discontents: Suspect Words in Revolutionary France*. Presumably she knows that Robespierre was not the kind of man who smashed the crockery. It's more likely that, as Robespierre's latest biographer Ruth Scurr reports, he simply said that Hébert was a fool and risked making Antoinette an object of pity. It's hard not to think that, by bringing forward this picturesque version of events, the historian, like her subject, is playing to the gallery.

Antoinette's failure came early, as Weber describes: 'Her white blank slate of a body had failed to live up to its promise as a site of inscription for Bourbon custom.' It also came late – when the Revolution came, she turned her elegant back on the zeitgeist. It seemed, briefly, as if the Revolution itself might deliver to women a share of political power; this didn't happen. Set against this great disappointment, it doesn't seem to matter much whether pre-revolutionary nobles, finding their wives' bills mounting, feared that 'women were trampling sacred male authority beneath their dainty satin heels'. This form of female self-assertion had no pay-off, no consequences. The Revolution provided many occasions for dressing up, and many sartorial codes to be cracked: one can brood for a lifetime on Saint-Just's cravats and Robespierre's embroidered waistcoats.

Such speculations would be interesting, but would hardly have commercial appeal to readers. It appeals to us to look at the Revolution as a giant piece of theatre, and this year it is a girlie show. But the Revolution is more than this, and it cannot be understood by overstating, however entertainingly, the importance of its iconography. It is unfashionable to say this, in post-Marxist times, but it is true: if you want to understand what happened in the Revolution and why, it is better to keep your eye on fluctuating bread prices, rather than fluctuating hemlines. Antoinette did not know this, but it seems that we should know it, on her behalf. Antoinette was culturally retarded, a clumsy figure running to keep up with the times and tripping over her own skirts. Her private impulses were at odds with the general will, her caprices were at odds with republican *vertu*. After her death, the scraps of her clothing that remained were given to poor women in a hospital. But in the end, though the Queen did not foresee it, it was the bourgeoisie who triumphed: those who had the nerve to send in the bill. Monsieur Léonard, Rose Bertin, the perfumer Fargeon: all of them died in their beds.

Religion and the Decline of Magic

On Keith Thomas

2012

There never was a merry world since the fairies left off dancing
and the parson left conjuring.

John Selden (1584–1654)

The English historian Keith Thomas has revealed modes of thought
and ways of life deeply strange to us, and he illustrates them with
precise evidence. In his *Religion and the Decline of Magic* his subject
is early modern England, roughly between 1500 and 1700. To understand that world, we have to take ourselves back to the beginning
of the period, into the mindset of a pre-industrial society, when
most people were engaged in agriculture, most people could not
read, and the ritual year of Roman Catholicism shaped the experience of the ordinary man going about his ordinary days. To keep at
bay the misfortunes of the world, he followed the prayers framed
for him in Latin, a language he did not understand, attributing a
mechanical efficiency to their enunciation, heaping them up as if
he could build a staircase to a capricious God, whom he hoped, one
day, to see face to face.

Keith Thomas has made a special study of magic and magical
thinking. He sees that they were not quaint deviations from mainstream thought; they were not marginal to the early modern world,
but intrinsic to it. Closely allied to religious sentiment and ritual
expression, magic survived the Reformation, adapting its form.
Magic was not just the province of 'Hob, Dick and Hick', the simple
villagers, but also of the erudite and sophisticated; kings had their

astrologers to guide them, and the politically astute could manipulate popular belief in prophecies and miracles so that they had an impact on the affairs of nations. But our ancestors were not emptily credulous. They didn't believe in just anything. Their world view was diverse but coherent; it had its own pedigree, and left its own descendants. Their society, which seems to us static, traditional and hierarchical, proves on closer inspection to be constantly shifting, renewing itself.

When Thomas's *Religion and the Decline of Magic* was first published in 1971, it drew together two disciplines, history and anthropology, which early in the twentieth century had grown apart. But the author has no grand thesis to sell us. The joy of his dry and witty book is in its accumulation of fine detail, and also in its broad humanity. Emerging from most studies of the past, the reader feels a leaden ache, a sense of pity and waste and dread. From this book, the reader emerges exhilarated, provoked, amused, with an insight into the ingenuity and potential of human beings and a sense that the past was not a place of insensate ignorance and darkness, but a place we are privileged to revisit through the craft of such an original, painstaking and erudite historian.

It is important not to exaggerate the grimness of the early modern age. Our ancestors in Tudor and Stuart England may well have been healthier, happier and saner than those who toiled in the factories of the industrial revolution. Even though two centuries were marked by plague, civil war and religious turmoil, the English were spared some of the depredations of the long wars and cyclical famines that afflicted continental Europe. Even so, life expectancy was low and the levels of routine pain and misery were high. It was a world of thatch and bedstraw, where an unattended candle could burn down a town. One-third of infants died before the age of five, even among the aristocracy. The harvest failed about one year in six, and epidemics broke out in the wake of hunger.

Medical practitioners had built up an elaborate theoretical edifice, but it was of little use in practice, and even if it had been, poor people relied on the cheap and locally available services of herbalists and wise women. Every childbirth brought a woman to a liminal state, poised between this world and the next; the midwives who attended her were (alas for feminist sentimentality) often dirty, cruel and useless. There was nothing to buffer the individual from fatal or life-changing disaster. There was no insurance. There was no compensation. Sudden death could whisk you before God for his eternal judgment, without any chance of confession and forgiveness; hell gaped, its torments graphically illustrated for you, in colour, on the walls of your parish church.

As a dweller in this world, how did you combat quotidian misfortune and keep existential terror at bay? You could blank out the perils with strong drink. Or you could try to wrest control of the natural world, delimit the arbitrary, somehow fix God and the angels so they were on your side. You could pray, or you could cast spells, and Keith Thomas shows how the two latter activities often ran into each other: just as, later, magic and science would elide, the activities of alchemists beginning in one and ending in the other. Before the Reformation our ancestors lived in the hope of miracles, and their faith – with its saints and shrines and relics and pilgrimages – encouraged them to do so. Central to the mass was the rite of transubstantiation, which changed bread and wine to Christ's actual body and blood. As Thomas says, 'The mere pronunciation of words in a ritual manner could effect a change in the character of material objects.'

So, though the Church repeatedly condemned superstition, it is not hard to see why magical thinking asserted its grip. There was often a gap between what the Church taught and what the popular mind made of the teaching. Our forefathers desired eternal life but they also, Keith Thomas shows, sought 'supernatural remedies for daily problems'. Magic clung to religion, he tells us, as a 'corpus of parasitic beliefs', and there was a pronounced magical cast to many of the rituals of popular piety. Saints in heaven took an interest in affairs below, in the health of crops and animals. If they were not propitiated, they might turn nasty, blight the crops and spread disease. Pilgrimages and candles and offerings kept them sweet, and a sprinkling of holy water kept baser spirits away from cradle and marriage bed. The devil was shockingly proximate, not metaphorical but as real as your neighbour, as your spouse or child.

Keith Thomas does not induct us into this world through generalities, but by multiplying eloquent examples drawn from contemporary sources. We meet the master of Balliol who sold familiar spirits to gamblers and learn that in 1591 Christ's blood was on sale at twenty pounds a drop. We are introduced to witches and their victims, clergymen who double as conjurers, prophets and astrologers who get their predictions disastrously wrong. We meet the deeply confused Agnes Clerk, whose daughter was given a holly stick by fairies, and who took it to the priest to get it blessed, in the hope that she would be able to use it to find hidden treasure. We learn of the profits and perils of the travelling magician's life: in 1676 Joseph Heynes left Ware with 'five pounds . . . three maidenheads, and a broken shin'. We learn how the rituals of magic bridge the gap between the wish and the deed; how the thorn, the pin or the bristle, applied to an image, injures the living flesh.

What happens when a village witch meets a sceptical judge? What gives way when credulous Catholicism meets the demystifying tendencies of radical Protestantism? For centuries, strategies for self-help run alongside the hopes reposed in magic, and rationality and superstition mingle, the same head often accommodating both. Evidence may be partial, contradictory or baffling, but the author's capacious technique scoops it all in. Keith Thomas has given us a book of questions, rather than answers. It is an incitement to further investigation rather than an attempt to categorise, define or delimit the world we have lost.

Sir Keith Thomas was born in 1933 and has been shedding light on history, in a manner inimitable, since he began his career at Oxford in 1955. *Religion and the Decline of Magic* is one of the outstanding works of history of the last half-century, and will lead the reader to *Man and the Natural World*, published in 1983, as well as his 2009 work, *The Ends of Life: Roads to Fulfilment in Early Modern England*. How are such complex and wide-ranging works produced? In an insouciant, self-deprecating article in the *London Review of Books* Keith Thomas explained that historians like to keep their secrets to themselves: 'Just as the conjurer's magic disappears if the audience knows how the trick is done, so the credibility of scholars can be sharply diminished if readers learn everything about how exactly their books came to be written.' But he went on to unfold his thinking:

> I am a lumper, not a splitter. I admire those who write tightly focused micro-studies of episodes or individuals, and am impressed by the kind of quantitative history, usually on demographic or economic topics, which aspires to the purity of physics or mathematics. But I am content to be numbered among the many historians whose books remain literary constructions, shaped by their author's moral values and intellectual assumptions.

The modern researcher has a database, a digital camera, and a laptop, and without moving from his desk he can comb the catalogues of the world's great libraries. Formerly, scholarship was more exhausting. The raw materials of composition could fill a room, a house. Keith Thomas has performed his life's work with scissors and ink, staples, index books, old envelopes, cardboard boxes and a forest of slips of paper: 'some of them get loose and blow around the house, turning up months later under a carpet or a cushion'. He admits, 'The sad truth is that much of what it has taken me a lifetime to build up by painful accumulation can now be achieved by a moderately diligent student in the course of a morning.'

No advance in technique, however, replaces genius. Filing and sorting is a creative activity when a lively mind is directing the operation. Thomas's devoted and labour-intensive methods, allied to what must be an almost superhuman memory and power of organisation, have allowed him to create a dense network of cross-referenced and linked information, in a way that would be beyond the 'moderately diligent' or the narrowly schematic researcher. 'When I read, I am looking out for material relating to several hundred different topics . . . In G. M. Young's famous words, my aim is to go on reading till I can hear the people talking.'

What is most wonderful about Keith Thomas's book is that the reader can hear them too. There are many works of history that are revered, but few that are loved as *Religion and the Decline of Magic* is: for its generosity, for its humour, for the rewards on every page. It may be that in the light of later research, certain lines of argument in the book can be challenged or amplified. But its richness and freshness are undiminished, and as a source of insight it is unlikely to be superseded. It is a treasure house, stuffed from cellar to attic with the quotable and the remarkable: one of those books that seldom stays on the shelf for long, because it is always asking to be reread, always offering something fresh: a book always in transit, because its admirers are keen to press it on those who have yet to have the pleasure of discovering it. It is not just about magic, but also, in its mercurial agility, a magical work in itself.

A Book of the World

On V. S. Naipaul

2013

There are places on earth where, at certain moments in the cycle of day and night, the two are indistinguishable. It is impossible to know, without other referents, whether you are looking at dawn or dusk. And there are places at the margins of cities, or at the edges of the man-made sprawl of holiday islands, where at twilight growth and decay are indistinguishable; you can't tell, at first glance, whether you are looking at a building site or a ruin. Is that earth-coloured brick waiting for its glassy marble cladding, or is it crumbling back into the condition of soil? And that distant rumble, of traffic or marching feet: have the entrepreneurs arrived, or is it the barbarians? Is it possible that they are the same?

Instances of crepuscular insight, coupled with the qualms of self-doubt, are for the privileged but disinterested eye; they come more readily to the artist than to the politician or the aid worker or the hard-hatted man driving a digger into the jungle. You have to pick your place to stand, and work by the light of informed intellect, before you can judge whether social institutions or indeed whole societies are accreting meaning or leaking it away.

Over forty years of travelling and writing, V. S. Naipaul has made himself both a judge and an expert witness in the topography of 'half-made societies'. Visiting India in 1962, he saw 'towns which, even while they develop, have an air of decay'. Montevideo in 1973 is a 'ghost city' mimicking European glories. It is populated by statues and the figures of historical tableaux cast in bronze, but their inscriptions, with individual letters fallen away, are becoming indecipherable. The shops are empty but street vendors crowd the sidewalks. The restaurants have no meat. Public clocks have stopped.

As colonisers pack their bags and dream cities dissolve, the bush is always waiting to creep back. Tenderness toward the bush is an emotion only the secure can feel. Only those who are free to leave them can be sentimental about the wild places of the earth. The bush is a recurrent conceit in Naipaul's work. It has 'its own logical life', but it is a logic that leads nowhere, except into the self-serving thickets of irrationality. It is the place where the social contract breaks down; it represents not just the physical encroachment of nature but the proliferating undergrowth of the human psyche.

From the first, Naipaul's sardonic and fastidious approach distinguished him from those who write about the under-developed world in eggshell pieties. He has a sharp eye for the intellectually fraudulent, and is a scourge of self-delusion; he gives the underdog as bad a name as his master. Oppression, he notices, doesn't make people saintly, it makes them potential killers; all victims are dangerous. On the one hand he has been accused of contempt for peoples of the third world; less liberal readers have embraced him as a sort of projection of themselves, more derogatory about developing countries than they would ever dare to be, his colour and ethnic background excusing him from the obloquy they would attract if they expressed the same distaste and unease.

One reason to welcome the present volume (*The Writer and the World*) is that a gap has opened, over the years, between what Naipaul has written, what people think he has written, and what they feel he ought to have written. His asides are often more pessimistic than the body of his work, and his dogmatic pronouncements in interviews – 'Africa has no future' – contrast with the subtlety of thought and expression in his written pieces. He writes with delicacy and compassion about individual lives, and much of the work in this collection employs a calm perspective that his detractors often miss. And yet, there is no respite from the Naipaul personality, ferociously intelligent and permanently aggrieved.

As a travel writer he knows journeys are to be endured, not enjoyed. They look glamorous only in retrospect. Most people's journeys, in the course of history, have not been voluntary. Transportation, slavery and forced migration have taken more people away from their birth-place than has the desire for novelty. Naipaul is spiritually among them, as remote from the tourist mentality as he is from the mindset of those travellers who get into trouble only to feel smug on getting out of it. He is at all times anxious about his own person – the witness, after all, must be preserved – and his faculty of physical disgust is highly developed.

Given the chance, he heads straight for the nearest international hotel. He knows that the unfamiliar need not be sought, for it comes to find you; for the nervous man, familiarity can be destroyed by a walk into the next room. The real undiscovered country is other people, human beings in all their singularity. He lets them speak and shape his narrative for him, and his respect for their stories is far removed from the misanthropy with which he is sometimes taxed. It is true that he has a dread of the flamboyant and the wilfully eccentric: 'I recognized her as a "character",' he says, warily eyeing the manageress when checking into the only hotel in Anguilla that has electricity. 'Characters lie on my spirit like lead.'

Fastidious in his person as in his intellect, Naipaul is a puritan in matters of style. It is the spareness of his effects, his exactness, which transfixes the reader. Naipaul's contempt for 'fine writing' is clear. He cultivates plainness, so that his actual words are seldom remembered by the reader; what lingers is their authoritative rhythm, an impression of discrimination and scruple, of wit and restraint. 'I work with very strong emotions,' he has said, 'and one's writing is a refining of those emotions.' With Naipaul, style is substance. Each sentence pounces on its meaning, neat as a cat. Each paragraph has attack, dash, elan. There are no jokes, no whimsy; there is no descent to the demotic, no bravura display.

What has been important to Naipaul throughout his career is to make a relationship with language that is clean, unflawed, fit for a man who has had to write himself into being. It is a common experi-ence of expatriates and travellers that, when you meet someone from another culture, you begin to act out a part you feel you have been assigned in an earlier life. Your persona goes into action, and you deliver the lines provided by some mysterious central scripting unit. But there was no one to provide Naipaul with lines. He has had to write his own. He has represented no one but himself, spoken for no one but himself, and spoken in no one else's language. He seems impervious to the influence of systems, just as he is unaltered by changing fashions in writing. You sense that the curve of evolution in his own work comes from within himself and is something he alone fully understands.

Perhaps what we will say about Naipaul was that he was the self-made man who didn't stop at weaving the cloth for his own garments but clothed his own bones in prose. We will say he was the rational man who was afraid to see night fall, because it falls within himself. His shining belief in order and progress is stained by an area of internal darkness: by a natural apprehension – though not a certainty – that the power of reason will be defeated. 'The aim has always been to fill out my world picture, and the purpose comes from my childhood: to make me more at ease with myself.'

To our profit, this is the one aim he has missed. His readers may complain that they are trapped in an enactment of his own psycho-drama, but the point is that it is not simply his own; we are all afraid of the dark, and though Naipaul is an isolate, he is not a solipsist. The narrator of the novel *The Enigma of Arrival* writes, 'To see the possibility, the certainty, of ruin, even at the moment of creation; it was my temperament.' Naipaul's myth is that of the artist who has suffered more from his art than his life, more from his interpretations of reality than from reality itself. He is the person most haunted by what he has rejected, by the childhood he has cast off, by the private fear he has made into a universal condition. Wherever he goes, he is sailing the inland sea.

PART IV

The Reith Lectures, 2017

The Day Is for Leaving

St Augustine says, the dead are invisible, they are not absent. You needn't believe in ghosts to see that's true. We carry the genes and the culture of our ancestors, and what we think about them shapes what we think of ourselves, and how we make sense of our time and place. Are these good times, bad times, interesting times? We rely on history to tell us. History, and science too, help us put our small lives in context. But if we want to meet the dead looking alive, we turn to art.

There is a poem by W. H. Auden, called 'As I Walked Out One Evening':

> The glacier knocks in the cupboard,
> The desert sighs in the bed,
> And the crack in the teacup opens
> A lane to the land of the dead.

The purpose of my first lecture is to ask if this lane is a two-way street. In imagination, we chase the dead, shouting, 'Come back!' We may suspect that the voices we hear are an echo of our own, and the movement we see is our own shadow. But we sense the dead have a vital force still – they have something to tell us, something we need to understand. Using fiction and drama, we try to gain that understanding. In these talks, I hope to show there are techniques we can use. I don't claim we can hear the past or see it. But I say we can listen and look.

My concern as a writer is with memory, personal and collective: with the restless dead asserting their claims. My own family history is meagre. An audience member once said to me, 'I come from a long line of nobodies.' I agreed: me too. I have no names beyond my maternal great-grandmother – but let me introduce her, as an example, because she reached through time from the end of the nineteenth century to form my sense of who I am, at this point in the twenty-first: even nobodies can do this.

She was the daughter of a Patrick, the wife of a Patrick, the mother of a Patrick; her name was Catherine O'Shea, and she spent her early life in Portlaw, a mill village near Waterford in the south of Ireland. Portlaw was an artificial place, purpose-built by a Quaker family called Malcolmson, whose business was shipping, and corn, cotton and flax. The mill opened in 1826. At one time Portlaw was so busy that it imported labour from London. The Malcolmsons were moral capitalists and keen on social control. Their village was laid out on a plan ideal for surveillance, built so that one policeman stationed in the square could look down all five streets. The Malcolmsons founded a Thrift Society and a Temperance Society and paid their workers partly in cardboard tokens, exchangeable in the company shop. When a regional newspaper suggested this was a form of slavery, the Malcolmsons sued them, and won.

As the nineteenth century ended, textiles declined and the Malcolmsons lost their money. The mill closed in 1904, by which time my family, like many others, had begun a shuffling stage-by-stage emigration.

Two of Catherine's brothers went to America, and in time-honoured fashion were never heard from again. Catherine was a young married woman when she came to England – to another mill village, Hadfield, on the edge of the Peak District. Like Portlaw, it was green and wet and shadowed by hills. As far as I know, she never left it. She must have wondered, does the whole world look like this?

Her first home was in a street called Waterside, for many years the scene of ritual gang fights on Friday nights between the locals and the incomers. I know hardly anything about Catherine's life. I suppose that when a woman has ten children, she ceases to have a biography. One photograph of her survives. She is standing on the doorstep of a stone-built terraced house. Her skirt covers her waist to ankle, her torn shawl covers the rest. I can't read her face, or relate it to mine.

But I imagine I know where the picture was taken. There was a row of houses which fronted Waterside, their backs within the mill enclosure. In time the houses were knocked down, but the facades had to stand, because they were part of the mill wall. The windows and the doorways were infilled by blocks of stone. By the time I was alive to see it, this new stone was the same colour as the mill: black. But you could see where the doors and windows had been. When I was a child, these houses struck me as sinister: an image of deception and loss.

The door of a house should lead to a home. But behind this door was the public space of the mill yard. By studying history – let's say, the emigrant experience, or the textile trade – I could locate Catherine in the public sphere. But I have no access to her thoughts. My great-grandmother couldn't read or write. One saying of hers survives. 'The day is for the living, and the night is for the dead.'

I assume it was what she said to keep the ten children in order after lights-out. After her early years, as I understand it, Catherine no longer worked in the mill. But I am told she had a certain role in her community: she was the woman who laid out the dead.

Why do we do this, or employ someone to do it? Why do we wash their faces and dress them in familiar clothes? We do it for the sake of the living. Even if we have no religious belief, we still believe what has been human should be treated as human still; witness the indignation if a corpse is desecrated, and the agony of those who have no bodies to bury. It is almost the definition of being human: we are the animals who mourn. One of the horrors of genocide is the mass grave, the aggregation of the loving, living person into common, compound matter, stripped of a name.

Commemoration is an active process, and often a contentious one. When we memorialise the dead, we are sometimes desperate for the truth, and sometimes for a comforting illusion. We remember individually, out of grief and need. We remember as a society, with a political agenda – we reach into the past for foundation myths of our tribe, our nation, and found them on glory, or found them on grievance, but we seldom found them on cold facts.

Nations are built on wishful versions of their origins: stories in which our forefathers were giants, of one kind or another. This is how we live in the world: romancing. Once the romance was about aristocratic connections and secret status, the fantasy of being part of an elite. Now the romance is about deprivation, dislocation, about the distance covered between there and here: between, let's say, where my great-grandmother was and where I am today. The facts have less traction, less influence on what we are and what we do, than the self-built fictions.

As soon as we die, we enter into fiction. Just ask two different family members to tell you about someone recently gone, and you will see what I mean. Once we can no longer speak for ourselves, we are interpreted. When we remember – as psychologists so often tell us – we don't reproduce the past, we create it. Surely, you may say, some truths are non-negotiable, the facts of history guide us. And the records do indeed throw up some facts and figures that admit no dispute. But the historian Patrick Collinson wrote: 'It is possible for competent historians to come to radically different conclusions on the basis of the same evidence. Because, of course, 99 per cent of the evidence, above all unrecorded speech, is not available to us.'

Evidence is always partial. Facts are not truth, though they are part of it – information is not knowledge. And history is not the past – it is the method we have evolved of organising our ignorance of the past. It's the record of what's left on the record. It's the plan of the positions taken, when we stop the dance to note them down. It's what's left in the sieve when the centuries have run through it – a few stones, scraps of writing, scraps of cloth. It is no more 'the past' than a birth certificate is a birth, or a script is a performance, or a map is a journey. It is the multiplication of the evidence of fallible and biased witnesses, combined with incomplete accounts of actions not fully understood by the people who performed them. It's no more than the best we can do, and often it falls short of that.

Historians are sometimes scrupulous and self-aware, sometimes careless or biased. Yet in either case, and hardly knowing which is which, we cede them moral authority. They do not consciously fictionalise, and we believe they are trying to tell the truth. But historical novelists face – as they should – questions about whether their work is legitimate. No other sort of writer has to explain their trade so often. The reader asks, is this story true?

That sounds like a simple question, but we have to unwrap it. Often the reader is asking, can I check this out in a history book? Does it agree with other accounts? Would my old history teacher recognise it?

It may be that a novelist's driving idea is to take apart the received version. But readers are touchingly loyal to the first history they learn – and if you challenge it, it's as if you are taking away their childhoods. For a person who seeks safety and authority, history is the wrong place to look. Any worthwhile history is a constant state of self-questioning, just as any worthwhile fiction is. If the reader asks the writer, 'Have you evidence to back your story?' the answer should be, yes: but you hope your reader will be wise to the many kinds of evidence there are, and how they can be used.

It's not possible to lay down a rule or a standard of good practice, because there are so many types of historical fiction. Some have the feel of documentary, others are close to fantasy. Not every author concerns herself with real people and real events. In my cycle of Tudor novels, I track the historical record so I can report the outer world faithfully – though I also tell my reader the rumours, and suggest that sometimes the news is falsified.

But my chief concern is with the interior drama of my characters' lives. From history, I know what they do, but I can't with any certainty know what they think or feel. In any novel, once it's finished, you can't separate fact from fiction – it's like trying to return mayonnaise to oil and egg yolk. If you want to know how it was put together line by line, your only hope, I'm afraid, is to ask the author.

For this reason, some readers are deeply suspicious of historical fiction. They say that by its nature it's misleading. But I argue, a reader knows the nature of the contract. When you choose a novel to tell you about the past, you are putting in brackets the historical accounts – which may or may not agree with each other – and actively requesting a subjective interpretation. You are not buying a replica, or even a faithful photographic reproduction – you are buying a painting with the brushstrokes left in. To the historian, the reader says, 'Take this document, object, person – tell me what it means.' To the novelist, he says, 'Now tell me what else it means.'

The novelist knows her place. She works away at the point where what is enacted meets what is dreamed, where politics meets psychology, where private and public meet. I stand with my great-grandmother, on the doorstep. I break through the false wall. On the other side I connect my personal story with the collective story. I move through the domestic space and emerge into the buzzing economic space of the mill yard – the marketplace, the gossip shop, the street and the parliament house.

I began writing fiction in the 1970s, at the point, paradoxically, where I discovered I wanted to be a historian. I thought that because of my foolishness at the age of sixteen, not knowing what to put on my university applications, I had missed my chance, and so if I wanted to work with the past, I would have to become a novelist – which, of course, any fool can do.

For the first year or two, I was subject to a cultural cringe. I felt I was morally inferior to historians and artistically inferior to real novelists, who could do plots – whereas I had only to find out what happened.

In those days historical fiction wasn't respectable or respected. It meant historical romance. If you read a brilliant novel like *I, Claudius*, you didn't taint it with the genre label, you just thought of it as literature. So, I was shy about naming what I was doing. All the same, I began. I wanted to find a novel I liked, about the French Revolution. I couldn't, so I started making one.

I wasn't after quick results. I was prepared to look at all the material I could find, even though I knew it would take years, but what I wasn't prepared for were the gaps, the erasures, the silences where there should have been evidence.

These erasures and silences made me into a novelist, but at first I found them simply disconcerting. I didn't like making things up, which put me at a disadvantage. In the end I scrambled through to an interim position that satisfied me. I would make up a man's inner torments, but not, for instance, the colour of his drawing-room wallpaper.

Because his thoughts can only be conjectured. Even if he was a diarist or a confessional writer, he might be self-censoring. But the wallpaper – someone, somewhere, might know the pattern and colour, and if I kept on pursuing it, I might find out. Then, when my character comes home weary from a twenty-four-hour debate in the National Convention and hurls his dispatch case into a corner, I would be able to look around at the room, through his eyes. When my book eventually came out, after many years, one snide critic – who was putting me in my place, as a woman writing about men doing serious politics – complained there was a lot in it about wallpaper. Believe me, I thought, hand on heart, there was not nearly enough.

In time I understood one thing: that you don't become a novelist to become a spinner of entertaining lies, you become a novelist so you can tell the truth. I start to practice my trade at the point where the satisfactions of the official story break down. Some stories bear retelling. They compel retelling. Take the last days of the life of Anne Boleyn. You can tell that story and tell it. Put it through hundreds of iterations. But still, there seems to be a piece of the puzzle missing. You say, I am sure I can do better next time. You start again. You look at the result, and realise, once again, that while you were tethering part of the truth, another part of it has fled into the wild.

However, it took time for me to get to the Tudors. For most of my career I wrote about odd and marginal people. They were psychic. Or religious. Or institutionalised. Or social workers. Or French. My readers were a small and select band, until I decided to march on to the middle ground of English history and plant a flag.

To researchers, the Tudor era is still a focus of hot dispute, but to the public it's light entertainment. And there were shelves full of novels about Henry VIII and his wives. But a novelist can't resist an unexplored angle. Change the viewpoint, and the story is new. Among authors of literary fiction, no one was fighting me for this territory. Everyone was busy cultivating their outsider status.

For many years we have been concerned with decentring the grand narrative. We have become romantic about the rootless, the broken, those without a voice, and sceptical about great men, dismissive of heroes. That's how our enquiry into the human drama has evolved; first the gods go, and then the heroes, and then we are left with our grubby, compromised selves.

As you gain knowledge and technique as a writer – as you gain a necessary self-consciousness about your trade – you lose some of the intensity of your childhood relationship with the past. When I was a child, the past felt close and it felt personal. Beneath every history, there is another history; there is, at least, the life of the historian. That's why I invited my great-grandmother to this lecture; because I know my life inflects my work. You can regard all novels as psychological compensation for lives unlived. Historical fiction comes out of greed for experience. Violent curiosity drives us on, takes us far from our time, far from our shore, and often beyond our compass.

The pursuit of the past makes you aware, whether you are novelist or historian, of the dangers of your own fallibility and inbuilt bias. The writer of history is a walking anachronism, a displaced person, using today's techniques to try to know things about yesterday that yesterday didn't know itself. He must try to work authentically, hearing the words of the past, but communicating in a language the present understands. The historian, the biographer, the writer of fiction work within different constraints, but in a way that is complementary, not opposite. The novelist's trade is never just about making things up. The historian's trade is never simply about stockpiling facts. Even the driest, most data-driven research involves an element of interpretation. Deep research in the archives can be reported in tabular form and lists, by historians talking to each other. But to talk to their public, they use the same devices as all storytellers – selection, elision, artful arrangement. The nineteenth-century historian Lord Macauley said that 'History has to be burned into the imagination before it can be received by the reason.' So how do we teach history? Is it a set of stories, or a set of skills? Both, I think; we need to pass on the stories, but also impart the skills to hack the stories apart and make new ones.

To retrieve history we need rigour, integrity, unsparing devotion and an impulse to scepticism. To retrieve the past, we require all those virtues – and something more. If we want added value – to imagine not just how the past was, but what it felt like, from the inside – we pick up a novel. The historian and the biographer follow a trail of evidence, usually a paper trail. The novelist does that too, and then performs another act, puts the past back into process, into action, frees the people from the archive and lets them run about, ignorant of their fates, with all their mistakes unmade.

I am here because, as Grayson Perry said in an earlier Reith Lecture, I am one of the foot soldiers, one of the practitioners. We can't leave theory aside: it is impossible now to write an intelligent historical novel that is not also a historiographical novel, one which considers its own workings. But I have tried to find a way to talk about the past without, day by day, using terms like 'historiography'. I became a novelist to test the virtue in words that my great-grand-mother would recognise, from that journey she made, Ireland to England, from one damp green place to another: words like 'thread' and 'loom' and 'warp' and 'weft', words like 'dockside', and 'ship', and 'sea', and 'stone', and 'road', and 'home'.

The Iron Maiden

In my first lecture in this series, I talked about my great-grandmother Catherine O'Shea, and how she lived when she came to England. Catherine had ten children, and my grandmother, who was named after her, was almost the youngest. This second Catherine O'Shea married a man with the robust English name of George Foster. Some of his family lived in a small Derbyshire village called Derwent, which became a drowned village – it was one of the places that were flooded in the late 1930s, to make a reservoir. When I was a child, I used to think that the villagers had five minutes warning of the flood; that an alarm rang, and they grabbed their possessions and scrambled uphill, with the water swirling about their knees as they ran for their lives.

No one told me this; I just imagined it. But they did tell me that in dry years you could see the steeple of Derwent church standing above the waters. This was not a fact. It was something else. It was a myth. Derwent's church was blown up in 1947. People were seeing it ten years after it was gone.

I was an adult when I found this out. I wasn't pleased that I'd been misled. But I learned three things from the drowned village. First, how totally the past can vanish. Second, that you should check your dates. And third, that a myth is not a falsehood; it is a truth, cast into symbol and metaphor. Materially, Derwent was gone. Spiritually, it still existed.

In this lecture I should like to ask how our pictures of the past are formed. The process seems collective, mysterious, emotional as much as intellectual. Our mental pictures are soft-focus and yet curiously adhesive. We hear the facts, and our brains print the legend. Look, for example, at how we imagine the Tudor era – which, for the English, plays so central a part in their national story.

When the Royal Shakespeare Company began the process of adapting my Tudor novels into plays, I felt my job was to give the actors some sense of dignity. I needed to tell them this: despite what people say about the dirty past, when you live in the 1500s, you are not in fact squalid, you are not flea-ridden. And unless they have been knocked out, you probably have most of your teeth.

You are not, as one theory has it, exceptionally violent because you are driven mad by vitamin deficiency. You do eat up your vegetables, in season. And neither your king nor yourself throw your chicken bones on the floor; table manners are strict and they are more complex than they are today. You don't know how disease is transmitted, but you do know enough to associate sickness with dirt. It's true your elaborate clothes can only be brushed and aired, not washed – but they never touch your body; what you wear next to your skin is frequently washed linen. Life is precarious, it's true. Battle kills few in this era. But epidemics carry off golden lads and lasses. Young women die in childbirth. The months after you are born are the most perilous. If you survive your first five years, you are likely to live a span roughly comparable to modern people. You don't hit old age at thirty. So – I could tell my actors – wear your doublets with pride.

Of course, they were playing courtiers, the upper classes. But what about the poor, were they squalid? On screen, there's a sort of generic pauper who thrives from the ancient world to the Edwardian era – fitted out with multiple rents and patches, ragged beards or exposed bosoms, gap-toothed of course, hair stiff with dirt, generally plastered with grime. Where does all this dirt come from? It's hard for us, particularly in the overcrowded parts of the world, to imagine a pre-industrialised time. Those whose memories stretch back to the 1950s and 1960s are inclined to think the past was like that, but worse. But go back a couple of hundred years, and the smog clears.

Go back beyond tobacco, and even the domestic space smells sweeter. The by-products of heavy industry no longer cling to the hair and clog the lungs. Cities are fewer and smaller. Unless you are housed next door to some noxious trade like tanning, you can wake up and smell the flowers. As a Tudor you might not trust your local water supply, which is why you drank ale for breakfast, but the River

Thames out there was alive with salmon. Unless you were caught up in a war, the loudest sound you heard might be thunder, or church bells.

The past sees and hears differently. It measures differently, counts differently. In the medieval world, a thing doesn't happen in fifteen seconds, it happens in what they call 'the space of a Pater Noster', the time it takes to say a prayer. When we imagine a lost world, we must first rearrange our senses – listen and look, before judging. But we do rush to judgement, and our judgement swings about; at one moment we find the past frightening and alien, and the next moment we are giving way to nostalgia.

Each century speaks of the grotesque cruelties of the one that went before, as if cruelty were alien to the present, and we couldn't own or recognise it. It seems we are doomed to be hypocrites – repulsed by the cruelties of bear-baiting while polishing off our factory-farmed dinner. Often, we crave the style of the past while condemning its substance.

It's a relief to learn that some pre-modern nastiness is fabricated, for cash. The instruments of torture that you see in museums are usually nineteenth-century artefacts. If you take, for example, the Iron Maiden, a spiked metal coffin which impales its victim, it appears to have been created as entertainment by a Nuremberg antiquarian who put it on display in a used prison. And copies of this grim fantasy went on tour through Great Britain and America: and Bram Stoker, the author of *Dracula*, put it in a story. The Iron Maiden has been with us ever since – in a corner of our psyche where we keep the obscenities, under a veil of cobwebs.

What we are looking at is the commodification of the past. Suppose you have a cupboard and you want to make it pay? Why not call it a priest hole in the ancient houses of Europe. There are many more priest holes than there were ever renegade priests to go in them.

It's interesting that the Iron Maiden and similar artefacts were being created at a time when cruelty had gone behind doors. A point came, in the West, when executions were no longer public – but there were still executions. The nineteenth century also invented the executioner's mask. In fact, there hardly was such a thing. Why would a city's executioner wear a mask? Everyone knew who he was.

I don't deny the harshness of the past but we treat it like a horror film. It sickens us. It's safely distant and we pay to view. The heritage industry is built on confusion, a yearning for a past which is sordid and gorgeous, both together. Purer than our age, also more corrupt. There's a certain kind of historical fiction that feeds collective fantasy – witness the slavish, oily royalism of the genre, which I think taps into that common childhood daydream that we are not the children of our parents but of more distinguished strangers, who will turn up any day to collect us; to save us from our humiliating ordinariness and whisk us into fairy tale.

The historical novel in its modern, commercial form is usually said to begin with Walter Scott. It was he who turned the Scottish imagination tartan. Scott was a writer of great power. He saw the pathos of the small figure swept up in history's tide; he punctured myth, as well as creating it. But for his enchanted readers, a gold-tinted mist enveloped the poverty and hardship of Highland life. His books put an imagined past at the service of the present, creating a deep politicised Scottish identity that existed purely in the fictional realm, because it did not depend on class, income or religion. All other possible Scotlands lost out to Walter's and the English found it profoundly reassuring.

Driving around Loch Lomond in 1869, Queen Victoria rhapsodised about the landscape; it was exactly what she expected, as she said it was 'all described in Rob Roy'. There weren't many folk to blight the scene, and those she saw were poor in a picturesque way; they didn't seem to want anything, and she noted approvingly 'the absence of beggars and hotels'. When today you are standing in a Highland Heritage Centre, and have the chance to buy, let's say, a pottery figure of Bonnie Prince Charlie which is also a pepper mill – you can thank Sir Walter.

Scott was a shrewd manager of his own talent and he made a lot of money. For historical novelists, he is therefore both a source of encouragement and a warning to mind what you do. I don't think any of us escape unease about our trade. Historical fiction faces two ways – making its reader say, 'I'm glad it's not then', and at the same time, 'I wish it were then'. It has mostly been a conservative, nostalgic art form, prone to flatter the reader by embellishing the received version of events, and to sooth the reader, by taking the politics out of the past. The counterforce is real history – messy, dubious, an argument that never ends.

So, what can historical fiction bring to the table? It doesn't need to flatter. It can challenge and discomfort. If it's done honestly, it doesn't say 'believe this', it says 'consider this'. It can sit alongside the work of historians – not offering an alternative truth, or even a supplementary truth, but offering insight.

I remember a conference in the 1990s, discussing with a colleague what historians made of historical fiction. He said, 'It's like pornography to them – they think it's shameful, but they can't wait to get hold of it.'

We've moved on since then. Historical fiction doesn't just mean 'historical romance'. And writers of all kinds are aware of the potential deceptions of the smooth narrative. When the reader of a story asks, 'How do I know which bits of this are true?', he must ask that question of the historian, as well as the novelist.

If anxiety about historical fiction lingers, we must look at the impulse of paternalism that lies behind it. Readers are not victims who need protection. The novelist doesn't spoil history for others. She doesn't trash her sources once she's used them. The archive remains secure. The palaces and battlefields remain as if she had never passed through. Others can visit them, taking their own sensibility. She offers a version of the past; there can be others, and there will be. The novelist owns up to invention. It is the core of her art.

The historian's processes are more hidden. He's not a simple chronicler, piling event on event. He seeks out the meaning of the story he tells. But like the novelist, he is the product of his own biography. He brings his personality to his work. What he writes and how he writes may be swayed by academic fashion. He may be locked in a power struggle with some mighty historian of the last generation, trying to knock him off his pedestal. There are wars that are fought in footnotes, invisible to the general reader. They can become sharp and personal. It doesn't mean that the process is corrupt; it means it is human. The historian, ideally, struggles for neutrality. The novelist doesn't. She is allowed to be partisan. She must be. Her history comes from the point of view of her character; she is allowed to get behind him.

In my adventures with the Tudors, I have found that this is the point often misunderstood. I have been taken to task, for example, for my portrait of Thomas More – Lord Chancellor to Henry VIII, an astute politician who, four hundred years after his execution, was made a saint. While still hale and hearty, More wrote his epitaph, telling us what to think about him. I have taken his instructions, and my portrait is defensible. It's just unfamiliar to the general reader, but then that's not the point. It doesn't matter what I think of More. I am trying to get into the head of my main character – his rival Thomas Cromwell – and work out what Cromwell thinks of him.

Both men are artefacts – I am keen to point this out, by often referring to their portraits. Thomas More was a conscious creator of his own legend. Thomas Cromwell had entered into fiction less than twenty years after his death, when the Italian writer Matteo Bandello filled in his missing years in a way more entertaining than likely. At the Frick Museum in New York, Holbein's portraits of More and Cromwell hang either side of a fireplace. It is only a fireplace: it's easy to create a false polarity between the two men, who had so much to say to each other. Thomas More is looking fiercely, attentively at whatever passes before him, and Thomas Cromwell, it seems, is gazing into the next room.

He's not looking at us. He's giving us nothing. He's going to let us struggle. Historians and novelists are engaged in a common struggle with evidence; its subjective, partial, patchy, frequently encoded nature. Historians are trained in how to handle evidence, and novelists have to learn it. Engagement with the evidence is what raises your game. If you regard it as something that gets in the way, or as something for you to chew up and consume uncritically, your novel will be unhistorical and unconvincing. That may not stop it selling, of course, but it will stop it lasting.

When we offer historical fiction to the public, we do have responsibilities – to our readers, and to our subjects. We shouldn't condescend to the people of the past, nor distort them into versions of ourselves. We should be wary about the received version. We should not pass on error. We should seek out inconsistencies and gaps and see if we can make creative use of them.

The more history you know, the more you can enjoy good historical fiction. You may disagree with the writer's interpretation, but if the fiction is taking advantage of what the form can do, the propositions in it will not seem pure and simple: you will be alerted to the cracks and fissures.

A good novelist will have her characters operate within the ethical framework of their day, even if it shocks her readers. Generally – and nothing is true of all times and places – our ancestors had a respect for the past we lack, a devotion to authority, tradition, precedent, hierarchy. We find this difficult, and we also find it difficult to understand their religious experience. Their lives were lived in an exquisite tension between the claims of time and the claims of eternity. This life was short and hard. Its aim was salvation. The single aim of salvation permeated their thinking and governed their actions day by day. If we enter into their concerns, it helps us understand the history of the Christian West. But it does much more. It helps us see how in our own era, religious faith, globally, has the power to build or destroy.

And here I must make an apology. In these lectures, I am aware that my references are Eurocentric and my examples parochial. It's not that I think there is no other kind of history; it's just that we haven't got all night. And it seems most useful for me to work with what I know. But the first lesson in understanding the past is not to assume anything about ethics, values, tastes. You must ask whether there is such a thing as human nature. Many writers of historical fiction feel drawn to the untold tale. They want to give a voice to those who have been silenced. Fiction can do that, because it concentrates on what is not on the record. But we must be careful when we speak for others. Are we being colonialists? Are we parasites? If we write about the victims of history, are we reinforcing their status by detailing it? Or shall we rework history so victims are the winners? This is a persistent difficulty for women writers, who want to write about women in the past but can't resist retrospectively empowering them. Which is false. If you are squeamish – if you are affronted by difference – then you should try some other trade.

Above all, you shouldn't condescend to the past. We should not simply assume that 'later' means 'better'. Casually, we use the word 'medieval' to mean primitive; and 'modern' is a term laden with value judgements, mostly in our favour. We see ourselves as pre-enlightened and a past that's dark, constrained; we want to speed away from it.

But in early modern England, where I have located my fiction, the past was what we were fighting our way back to – a pristine world, unsullied, simple. We look forward, to the benefits of technology – they looked backwards, to the benefits of virtue. If you wanted to do something new, you were as well to present it as something old. But even then, you were chasing extinction. The golden age was always lost and gone, and the future offered more hazard than hope. Like us, the people of the sixteenth century had their prophets of doom. We have climate change and they had sin. We think we could avoid it, if we were less selfish – they thought it would end anyway. For them, time is not an arrow pointing forwards, but a candle burning down.

People who write fiction about the past are always asked for 'modern parallels', as if only the present validates the past, and as if historical fiction were an exceptionally tricky and labour-intensive way of doing journalism. But the past is not a rehearsal: it is the show itself. Our ancestors were not us, in an unevolved form. Often it seems that when we imagine the past, what we are recreating is the lost world of our infancy, when we were innocent. In our own personal olden days, we had no conscience, and knew no restraint. Like our imagined forebears, we were dirty, and we threw our dinners on the floor.

If we want to cast our ancestors as our shadows, as aspects of ourself unrestrained by shame, we should be aware of the psychological forces in play. Are we looking into the past, or looking into a mirror? Dead strangers are not our baby selves, nor our animal selves, nor our employees. They did not live and die so we could draw lessons from them. If I think back to the history I was first taught, it was distorted by all the wisdom of hindsight. We did not know history was a skill. We thought it was a branch of morality – all about issuing report cards. 'King Henry's conduct this term has been monstrous. Next term, he must stop taking wives, and concentrate on building up the navy.'

And worse, we thought history was out there somewhere, glowing like a planet, independent of human agency. Now I know that it is something we carry inside. Recently, a friend of mine visited Robben Island, where Nelson Mandela was imprisoned. The guide was a former inmate. At the door of each cell, he stopped: and knocked, and waited. The cells are empty: but he was listening for the unquiet dead. The island has held political prisoners since the end of the seventeenth century. Some still living, most dead, but all transformed: they have entered history – which means they work away, active among the living.

This prison guide was like the people of the drowned village of Derwent, who could see their church steeple ten years after it was demolished. He could see the spirits that lingered after the bodies had gone. I like his reverence and respect; I like his hesitation on the threshold, and his recognition that the space of the past belongs to those who have suffered in it. He brings me back to those words of St Augustine, with which I began my first talk: the dead are invisible, they are not absent.

Silence Grips the Town

Around the new year of 1928, a young Polish writer moved into a small room in the city of Danzig. It was a sort of outhouse attached to a school where her husband had been a teacher. He was dead now, and she was alone, and unable to afford the three rooms where they had lived together. All she owned was a typewriter and the contents of her head. The space into which she moved was meant only for temporary use, in the summertime. It measured seven feet by fifteen and it was furnished with a stove, a stool, a bed and a table. In this room, the young woman settled down to talk with the dead. In this third lecture, I want to tell you her strange story: how, as her commitment to the past turned to obsession, history chewed her up and spat her out.

Her name was Stanisława Przybyszewska; her contemporaries called her Stasia. Not that she spoke to anyone much, by this stage in her life. For seven years after she moved into the room, till her death at the age of thirty-four, she devoted herself obsessively to writing plays and novels about the French Revolution. She had little encouragement, little food, often no money, and a precarious supply of morphine, on which she was dependent. What she did have, to keep her warm through the Polish winters, was a burning conviction of her own genius.

Stasia was born in 1900. She was an illegitimate child, and her father was the writer Stanisław Przybyszewski: he was an associate of writers and artists like Strindberg and Munch, and he was famous in his day. He was best known as a playwright, and parodic in his self-importance: 'We artists know no laws.' By his own account, he was a Satanist. He had several illegitimate children by different women, and he neither nurtured them nor paid for it to be done;

he entered and left their lives when it amused him. Stasia's mother, Aniela Pajak, was a young artist, gentle and talented. Przybyszewski was married when they had an affair and there was no question of his leaving his wife. As a young single woman with a child, Aniela found Poland inhospitable. Mother and daughter became émigrés, living precariously in Vienna, then Paris, till Aniela died suddenly of pneumonia, leaving her daughter alone at the age of eleven.

Stasia was an intense, ferociously intelligent child, at home in several languages, but at home nowhere else. First, she lived in Zurich with friends of her mother's. Then she went back to Vienna to live with an aunt. In the middle of the Great War her aunt's family moved back to Poland, to Cracow.

Stasia enrolled as a trainee teacher. She had only seen her father twice, in her early childhood. Finally, he gave in to pressure from her guardians to acknowledge paternity, and when she was eighteen, he came back into her life. Her mother had always spoken well of him, never blamed him for abandoning her. So Stasia idolised him, saw him as a saviour, a twin soul, she didn't doubt his brilliance; though by this time his career was off the boil and he was working for the post office – which you would have thought offered limited opportunities for a Satanist.

But he got his fun elsewhere. He arranged meetings with Stasia at hotels. His wife of the moment was suspicious enough to set a private detective on him. He may have seduced his daughter. He almost certainly introduced her to morphine. He had used it to wean himself off alcohol, which was killing him. He was an addict, and soon, so was Stasia. She enrolled at a Polish university, but after the first term she had a breakdown. However, she was able to support herself by teaching, and in 1923 she married a young artist called Jan Panieński. With him she made her final move, to the city of Danzig, where she would spend the rest of her life.

The marriage seems to have been a strained companionship between shy introverts, who for a short time became dependent on each other, and who had both, separately, become dependent on drugs. Two years on, Jan went to Paris on an art scholarship, and died of an overdose. Stasia's letters contain no reaction to his death. Later she wrote, 'I was born for mental life, and had to dispense

with the sexual phase of my life very quickly in order to be free.'
Yet it's not so simple as that – alongside her passion for Revolution
runs a perplexed sexual awareness, an unruly force, half understood,
and channelled from her life into her work.

A turning point came when she read Georg Büchner's play,
Danton's Death, which deals with the last days of the Revolutionary
hero, the bold, vital, deeply compromised George-Jacques Danton.
This set the course of her future. She read the play eleven times,
and then she began to write. She had found her subject. It was not
Danton but his rival, Robespierre, the quiet and outwardly unremarkable man who was the most controversial as well as the most
unlikely of the Revolution's leaders. For what remained of Stasia's
life, her days and nights were an almost unvaried round, enslaved
to the typewriter while she attempted to capture on the page the
swirl of excitement and horror inside her head. She had a small
inheritance from her husband, and it kept her going for a year or
so. Then she moved to the room that I have described. A neighbour
sometimes brought her food. For a while she went out for cigarettes
and newspapers, and occasionally to see a film. And then she gave
up going out except to get her drugs.

Stasia was determined to rival her father as a playwright. By now,
she had seen his feet of clay – or his cloven hooves. His famous
talent had burnt out. His politics moved steadily to the right, and
he was received back into the Catholic Church. Stasia was able to
see that he was a mediocrity and a conman, yet her whole life was
shaped in reaction to him. She still hoped his name and contacts
would help her, so when she had finished a second play about the
Revolution, she sent it to him. The plot centres on a sickly girl who
attempts to have her father guillotined. Perhaps her own father read
too much into it. But anyway, he offered no help.

She sent out her work to publishers. Rejection made her physically
ill. In spring 1928 she started work on a new play. She had begun
to see Robespierre as a hero and one who needed her advocacy: a
single, lonely, burning flame of integrity in the chaos of five years
of revolution.

In order to preserve her solitude – to be alone with him – she
locked herself into a life of astonishing deprivation. December 1928:

It's difficult for me to write, my fingers are weak and numb from the cold. I can't hit the keys hard enough, and frequently miss them altogether . . . two years ago I was able to have a fire in the coal-burning stove almost every day . . . last year I could afford a fire only once a week. This year any fire at all is totally out of the question.

She seldom saw daylight. Often the cold was so intense that she could not think. 11 February 1929:

Yesterday it was minus 20 centigrade, today it is minus 25. From 9 p.m. deathly silence grips the town. From top to bottom the windows are overgrown with a thick white fur; it's better than curtains, but it gives the interior of my room the exact feeling of the most private dwelling, the grave.

Why do this? Because, she wrote, 'I can be a writer or nothing at all.' There's a tension in every artist between the outer and the inner lives. You want to be at your desk or in your studio, mining your resources, but you also want to be out there in the world, listening and looking to replenish your talent. There's no safe point, no stasis. It produces anxiety, even a kind of shame. Stasia found it easiest to lock the world out. Her only concern was that nothing and no one disturb her work.

After a year she had finished four major drafts of her play *The Danton Affair*. She was afraid to part from it. But she sent it out. Stasia had hardly ever seen a play, and even if she had known how to write one, she wouldn't sacrifice an exact retelling for the sake of the drama. So, the script threatened to become as long as life itself.

Yet even though it was the size of three or four normal plays, there was interest among the professional readers employed by the theatre companies. Not surprisingly, because her work is astonishing. It reads more like a vast transcript of the Revolution, verbatim, than like something invented. For three years there were tortuous nego-tiations. The National Theatre in Warsaw tried to beat out a version, and gave up. But in 1931 the play was staged – cut down from an estimated fourteen hours' playing time, but still five hours long. Stasia didn't go. She was disgusted with the cuts and it closed after five performances.

There was one other production, in 1933. It lasted twenty-four days, and this time she had reason for disgust, because the text had been manipulated to make it topical – it had become an anti-revolutionary play, a vehicle for the right wing. What she feared had happened: her work had gone out into the world and been misused and contaminated.

So, she decided, she would depend on herself. She turned to the novel, because there you have sole control. And she believed she had everything she needed inside her room.

The historian Edward Gibbon said solitude was the school for genius. Maybe. You will never be an artist if you can't endure your own company or define your own purposes and stick with them. But many artists set up a state of internal exile or, to put it more positively, a safe space inside: a place where you do your work, no matter what else is happening. Virginia Woolf said a woman writer needs a room of her own. She didn't stipulate 'a cell of her own'. Paradoxically, Stasia wasn't someone who rejected the world – she craved it. She sought connection – but on her own terms.

She wrote letters to famous writers – but mostly, she never sent them. Among her papers were the outlines of numerous prose works – novels, stories – and often the figure of Robespierre, disguised or occulted, appears in them, even if the setting is contemporary. Stasia always believed that if she chose she could walk out of her room, take up normal life, earn a living. But external realities – the lively and cosmopolitan city of Danzig, the world of the theatre and publishing – were fading. In the grip of her morphine addiction, and incubating tuberculosis, she became fixated on a bleak inner land-scape. She was 'living', she said, 'with people who died so long ago that there is not even a single vibration left in the air after them . . .'

She had no money for books or newspapers, hardly enough for pencils or carbon paper. She describes how she painted her scraps of food with disinfectant to preserve them. She was slowly starving, but it seemed that the frailer her body became, the more her thoughts raced, the more schemes she promulgated. She felt, she said, 'death cornering me'. But she would rally, and go back to her desk.

Her last letters were written to the novelist Thomas Mann. 'Every object in my room is laden with pain. And nowhere any love. I'm not pure enough. I've used myself up.'

And then the letters stopped. Presumably she was too weak to type or hold a pen. She died alone in her room on 15 August 1934.

Meeting her through the papers she left behind, you can be repelled by her untrammelled conviction of her own genius, by her rectitude. You can be bitterly amused – except that you know where it is leading. Was she a failure? She said not. In March 1929 she wrote:

> It has just dawned on me today that my life without entertainment, without friends, without sex, without the possibility of spending money on luxury items, is much much richer than the lives led by 99 per cent of the people . . . the joys, thrills and revelations that I experience in a single month are beyond the reach of most in the course of an entire lifetime.

And yet, she admitted, the writer needs a reader. Her work did have an afterlife of sorts. Her three Revolution plays were staged in Poland in the late 1960s, early 1970s, and then Andrej Wadja put on a version of the play about Danton in Warsaw in 1975. In 1983, Wadja released his famous film, *Danton*, the French–Polish production with Gérard Depardieu in the title role. He used Stasia's work as the basis for the script. This was the era of Solidarity, the populist social movement that preceded the downfall of the Communist state, and the film became a parable about current politics. Stasia loved the cinema, but I think she might have hated this reduction of her purpose. She had a story to tell but it was not the one the film was telling, and the Robespierre it presented was not her man.

Her name on the end of the credits brought her some attention. In 1986 there was a fine biographical study in English. The same year, Pam Gems reworked her scripts for the Royal Shakespeare Company. And then, in 2016, a book of her short stories came out in Poland. So, her name has survived. She is a truly European writer. Her work challenged clichés and entrenched pieties about the Revolution, so she is a good servant to history. She is also an awful warning. If anyone thinks writing is therapy – I beg them to look at this life.

What went wrong? Stasia worked and worked to get the truth, but she didn't find a way of serving the truth through narrative. She was crippled by perfectionism. She lost the distance that enabled her to judge her work, and she didn't have that pragmatic streak that says that compromise is not always dishonour. Detail matters. But there are other things that matter more: pace, grip, shape. An unperformable play or a half-finished novel is no use except as a stepping stone to a genuine communication.

But, if you pinpoint any moment in an artist's career, you will see the unfinished. Who is ready for completion? Who is ready for death? It takes us all by surprise – the pen poised, the potential unrealised, explanations wanting, an evaporation of effort into white space. With each line, each sentence, you succeed and fail, succeed and fail. And perhaps as a subject the Revolution sets us up for frustration – it eludes our analysis, simply because it isn't over yet.

Stasia was a hero worshipper. I think her exaltation of the individual was based on a romantic fallacy. But in fiction we end up writing about individuals, however hard we resist them. Novels and plays aren't primarily vehicles for ideas, though they are feeble if they leave the ideas out. I cannot say Stasia chose the wrong subject or the wrong focus. The great historian Michelet wrote, 'Robespierre strangles and stifles.' Yet when Michelet finished his great work on the Revolution, it was Robespierre he missed. 'My pale companion,' he called him, 'the man of great will, hard-working like me, poor like me.'

From the early days of the Revolution, when he was an obscure young deputy, Robespierre was drawn and painted. He seemed to attract the artist's eye and compel attention – so he exists in multiple versions. And through the sequence of his portraits, you see what revolution costs.

In five years, he ages twenty. In 1789 you see a dreamy, soft-featured young man who might be a poet. By 1794 the flesh falls away from a clenched jaw, the head becomes a skull. In revolution everything speeds up, every process is accelerated. This is true of politics and it is true of individuals. Authority gives way to liberty, but as soon as liberty is threatened it gives way to repression. Ideals are crushed by the weight and speed of events. The box is opened, the hopes fly out, the box is slammed shut and someone's head is caught in it.

And this is precisely why a writer is drawn to where all the human stories, and all the stories about power, are distilled. The makers of the Revolution knew they were actors. In Paris they could, in fact, leave their assemblies and revolutionary clubs, book a seat and see themselves on stage. They were caught up in a self-conscious spectacle, and they were aware of all the layers of meaning of the term 'representation'. What does it mean, to stand in for someone else? To embody the collective will? What happens when you step on to the stage of history? When your clothes become costumes, and your face a mask?

Sometimes our books write us. Stasia's version of Robespierre was a creation of her own need: she found her way to the loneliest of the Revolutionaries, and she clung to him. Her text itself is a riot of complication. She went to the Revolution, and forgot to take the reader. But if she goes wrong, she does it, like the Revolutionaries, on an epic scale.

A jealous rival of Robespierre's said, 'What a man this is, with his crowd of women about him!' In 1794, at his death, he was thirty-six – he was unmarried, supposedly engaged to the daughter of the carpenter with whom he lodged. The men of the Revolution were in general very young, so the widows, sisters, fiancées they left behind lived far into the nineteenth century, their lives spent in prolonged mourning for a time, place, events and men who must have seemed like hallucinations.

Stasia connects us to these women. She embodied the past until her body ceased to be. Towards the end of her life, she had begun to date her letters by the Revolutionary calendar. She had left us, chosen another time frame, which began again at the Year One. From her letters, there is an uncanny sense that she had passed through history. If historical fiction has a patron saint, it should be this woman, who slipped off mortality like one of those virgin martyrs who, allegedly, were devoured by wild beasts in the Roman arena.

Susan Sontag said, 'somewhere along the line, one has to choose between the Life and the Project'. Stasia chose the Project. It killed her. Multiple causes of death were recorded, but actually she died of Robespierre. You don't want to work like that, be like that. You hope your art will save you, not destroy you. But it's a sad fact that bad art and good art feel remarkably the same, while they're in process. As you work, you have to exercise self-scrutiny and fine discrimination, but in the end, the verdict is out of your hands.

Stasia couldn't see the difference between the truth and the whole truth: for her, to omit was to falsify, and because she was anxious never to mis-state, she over-determined her direction and her method. This is where her art failed. Artists are often asked to state their intention. They sometimes try. But really, this question is the wrong way round. Intention evolves as a result of capacity. You don't know what you're doing, till you try to do it. As capacity increases, so does ambition. But when it comes to getting the words on the page, you can only work breath by breath, line by line. And the line-by-line is what I will talk about in my fourth lecture.

Can These Bones Live?

A few years back, before I began writing novels about the Tudors, my partner and I bought a new-build house in Surrey. We bought it off-plan, and we watched it grow out of an open field. The site looked like a battlefield from the Great War. It was a churned-up wasteland filled with shattering noise, and if you visited it after working hours, you felt you had arrived in the middle of a temporary truce, and the ground beneath your feet was still shaking. There was a sea of mud in which stood pipes and half-built walls and shrouded piles of bricks, and abandoned diggers stood in ditches, their jaws encrusted with clay. The evenings were silent. There was no birdsong, because no trees: nature had been eradicated.

The outside of our house was to be plain: a modest tile-hung style. But one evening we came to check progress and realised that the plans had changed. The people around the corner were getting our facade. We were being Tudorised. Stacked on a truck were beams. They were not wood or plastic. They were in effect pictures of beams, on large sheets, ready to be stuck to the raw breeze block. And beside them, on similar sheets, pictures of pink herringbone brickwork, to be papered on the wall between the beams.

It went beyond bad taste. I felt shame. But we were too far along with the deal to pull out of it. Over the next few weeks, I talked myself around. The facade was not my problem. I would be inside the house. Someone else would have to look at it.

We only lived there for four years. It was like living inside a giant metaphor about the faking of the past. In those days, my thoughts were moving to the sixteenth century. I wondered how quickly I could learn to inhabit a new era. I thought, I don't want my walls to be paper-thin, my knowledge to be stuck on. I need a solid house for characters to live in. In fact, I should not call them 'characters', I should call them 'people' – they are real, even if they happen to be dead.

In the Old Testament, God asked the prophet Ezekiel, 'Can these bones live?' He answered yes: and so do I. The task of historical fiction is to take the past out of the archive and relocate it in a body. In this lecture, I would like to talk about the practical job of resurrection, and the process that gets historical fiction on to the page.

I've never believed that fiction set in the past, or the future, is an inferior form. It demands the same attention to style and form as a story with a modern setting, and places a greater demand on the skills of placing information, and of managing complexity. Every page in a novel is a result of hundreds of tiny choices, both linguistic and imaginative, made word by word, syllable by syllable. The historical novel requires an extra set of choices – what sources to consult, what shape to cut from the big picture, what to do when the evidence is missing or ambiguous or plain contradictory. Most of these choices are invisible to the reader. You must be able to justify your decisions to the well informed. But you won't satisfy everybody. The historian will always wonder why you left certain things out, while the literary critic will wonder why you put them in. 'Because I could' is not a good reason. You need to know ten times as much as you tell.

Debate about historical fiction often centres on research. Is it sound? Is it necessary? Some writers – not me – say it's what you do after your story is finished. That depends on the nature of your story. Are you using real characters and events? Or are you using the past as a backdrop? In either case, I think there is a misunderstanding about what research really is.

First, I hesitate to use the word. Writers shouldn't claim they are doing research when they mean they are skimming facts out of pre-existing texts. Unless they are also trained historians, novelists mostly don't have the skills for original research from primary sources. Typically, we first meet the material when it's been filtered – by historians, biographers. In the early stages, that's helpful. It helps you see shape, it stops you being distracted by irrelevant detail, and it keys you in to controversies. Your job at this stage is to stare hard at the pattern already picked out, and see if it shifts under your scrutiny.

Facts are strong, but they are not stable. Soon you find your sources are riddled with contradiction, and that even when the facts are agreed, their meaning often isn't. At this stage, you will want to seek out the earliest evidence you can get. If your story tracks real events, you will spend a lot of time sifting versions, checking discrepancies, assessing the status of evidence: always asking, who is telling me this, and why does he want me to believe it? The contradictions can be fertile. If you can locate the area of doubt, that's where you go to work. You may well consult original documents, and you will tramp over the ground, and visit the libraries, and allow your hand to hover over a document and imagine the hand that first wrote it.

At this stage, you are doing much the same job as an academic colleague. If you solve a puzzle, if you make a discovery, that's satisfying. We all want to chip in with a little contribution to the historical record. But your real job as a novelist is not to be an inferior sort of historian, but to recreate the texture of lived experience: to activate the senses, and to deepen the reader's engagement through feeling.

Research is not a separate phase from writing. There is no point where the writer can say, 'I know enough.' Writing a novel is not like building a wall. Your preparatory stage is about digging deep, understanding context, and evolving a total world picture. The activity is immersive. The novelist is after a type of knowledge that goes beyond the academic. She is entering into a dramatic process with her characters, and until she plunges into a particular scene, she hardly knows what she needs to know.

It takes time to locate yourself in a new age, a new geography. You have to expand your area of curiosity, away from political history and into every area of culture. Learn about art, trade, how things are made. Then lift your eyes from the page and learn to look.

At first you are a stranger in your chosen era. But a time comes when you can walk around in a room and touch the objects. When you not only know what your characters wore, but you can feel their clothes on your back: that rasp of homespun wool; that whisper of linen and weight of brocade; the way your riding coat settles when you mount your horse; the sway and chink of the items at your girdle or belt, the scissors and keys and rosary beads. You listen:

what sound do your feet make, on this floor of beaten earth? Or on these terracotta tiles? How do your boots feel as you pull your feet out of the mud? How old are your boots? What colour is the mud? When you can answer these questions, you are ready to begin.

But then, the next question: is the reader ready for your story? How will you give them the background information they need to make sense of it? Exposition is the trickiest bit of the trade. We all know how not to do it: 'Why masters, here comes the Lady Anne Boleyn, she who has supplanted the Spanish Queen Katherine in the fickle affections of our sovereign, King Henry VIII.'

You can't have your people telling their contemporaries what they would already know. Authors are always advised, 'show, don't tell', but sometimes dialogue just won't stretch to cover your points, and you must lay down the facts in a passage of narrative – quick as you can, tailored and succinct – remembering to privilege what matters to your characters, not just what has proved in hindsight to be important.

There's a lot of use in a stupid character, one who has to be told twice. There's more use in a stranger – some newcomer who can ask the questions the reader wants to ask. In every scene, the writer's opportunity comes at the point of change. A person doesn't notice the street he walks down every day. But when they knock down the house on the corner, and a new vista is revealed – that's when your character notices, and that's when you can describe. Landscapes, streetscapes, objects, are dead in themselves. They only come alive through the senses of your character, though his perceptions, his opinions, his point of view.

There are no special tricks to make exposition work. There are only different levels of skill, in the author. You need to be sure of the point you want to make, and then communicate it clearly. But you may have to decide at some point between competing evils – too much or too little information – the reader spoon-fed, or the reader needing more.

I'd prefer to leave the reader hungry. Your book can't do it all. If the reader is puzzled, there are other sources he can consult. But if you underestimate your reader's intelligence, he will put your novel down. You cannot give a complete account. A complete thing is an exhausted thing. You are looking for the one detail that lights up the page: one line, to perturb or challenge the reader, make him feel acknowledged, and yet estranged. The reader should be a welcome guest in your house of invention, but he shouldn't put his feet up on the furniture. Just when he's settling, you need to open the gap between them and us: just let in a flash of light, to show the gap is there.

I have one piece of advice: don't lie. Don't go against known facts. Mathematical truth may be pleasing, elegant, light. Historical truth is a rough beast – shapeless, blundering, hard to tame. It fights you every step. It cuts against storyteller's instinct. Your characters are never how or where you'd like them to be.

I wrote a novel set in revolutionary Paris, with three main characters – all young and strong and raring to go. Not one of them was at the fall of the Bastille. One of them intended to be, but turned up late. That's how reality plays out. George Orwell said that every life, seen from the inside, feels like a series of defeats. Glorious speeches often go unheard, except by posterity. The man who is fighting can't see over the hill, or out of the trench. If you describe a battle, you must ask yourself, at what point did it become possible to say that this side had won, and this side lost? Posterity gives out the prizes, sees who won the battle and who won the war. When you are situated in history, as we all are, you don't hear the great drumroll of fate, but penny whistles and the banging of dustbin lids. Every great shift in human history happens on just another day – a Tuesday in July, as it may be, the sun coming out after Monday's rain, the Paris streets filling up again, but a dozen things to delay you as you try to get across the river and, when you get there, the world-shaking event is over.

It's a relief, sometimes, to have a character turn up late. The big set piece is better left to the cinema. As an observer, I'd rather be in the tent the night before the battle with the generals than on the battlefield itself, or sweeping up the sodden bunting, after the big parade has passed. Not that you should evade the great moments, if you see a way of telling them. You should be ambitious: history helps you raise your game. If real events seem a pointless, shapeless muddle, you need to look for their inner nature, their private meaning for your character. His concerns will lead you through. Always, you should resist the temptation to tidy up the past.

You may remember the spectacular TV series *The Tudors*, in which Henry VIII was played by a very small Irishman. I watched this series keenly, because I was in the process of my first Tudor novel, and I knew that this version would be the public offering preceding mine – and so would condition expectation. Most historical fiction, I like to think, is in dialogue with the past. *The Tudors* was not holding a conversation – just stamping, whistling and making faces. It offered a strange blend of the ploddingly literal and the violently implausible. In trying to spare the viewer the effort of thought, the writers declared war on the laws of time and space.

I will give an example. In real life, Henry had two sisters. Margaret married the king of Scotland. Mary married the king of France. The writers rolled the two sisters into one, and called her Margaret.

This composite – who will she marry? The writers had overshot the date for Margaret's Scottish marriage, which took place when she was a child. And they had killed off the old French king, in order to get the glamorous Francis I on camera. So, they invented a bridegroom – a king of Portugal. They may have thought better of it, because very soon the bride murdered this fictional king. Margaret was free to marry again, a real person this time, with whom she had the wrong number of children.

One falsification trips another. Consequences cascade. The writers have eaten the future. James V of Scotland is mentioned in the series, but how was he born? With no Scottish marriage, he has no mother. Lady Jane Grey, though queen of England for a week, cannot be born – because her ancestor is cancelled. So is Mary, Queen of Scots: she can't be born either. So, all those historical romances about her must be reshelved, as fantasy. Suddenly Mary Stuart is no more real than a character in *Game of Thrones*.

Now you may say, what does it matter? No one ever thought *The Tudors* was accurate. When characters from the 1530s ride in eighteenth-century carriages, why not roll two sisters into one?

The problem, though, is the brilliant stories they missed. Look at the real women, Mary and Margaret – their lives are spectacular. They read like unlikely fables, but are soberly inscribed in the records.

The reason you must stick by the truth is that it is better, stranger, stronger, than anything you can make up. If its shape is awkward, then you must make your fictional technique so flexible that it can bend around the difficulty; because it is the shape of your narrative the reader will follow. You can select, elide, highlight, omit. Just don't cheat.

After all, you are the one who chooses where to focus. You have discretion in how you direct your reader's gaze, and your job is to select the scenes that deliver the most value – for information, for entertainment, for character definition, for the balance of the work as a whole.

An event you choose to tell may not be dramatic in itself. Your scene may be as simple as a woman writing a letter, when a man comes in and interrupts her. But when two people are talking in a room, they have a hinterland, and you must suggest it. To that one moment, you bring a sense of every moment that led us there, everything that has brought your woman to this hour, this room, this desk. The multitude of life choices. The motives, conscious or unconscious. The wishes, dreams and desires, all held invisibly within the body whose actions you describe. They hover over the text like guardian angels. The more you know, as a writer, the less you have to do on the page, because the reader trusts you and he's drawn into the effort of recreation – the reader becomes your ally in negotiating with reality.

You will not be error-free. Sometimes you have a straight choice of what to believe, with no evidence you can rely on. Here, the historian can state the problem to the reader, and back off. But sometimes a novelist must jump – guess if she needs to. If she grasps the context, her guess is valid. A historian aims to work from speculation to certainty, effect following cause. The novelist works in a world where choices are still open. Moving forward with her character, she hesitates with him at the fork in the road. His information is imperfect. His map is barely legible. In the novel, he is ignorant of the future, and free.

But you know the end, people say. So how do you maintain suspense? It's not a real problem. You succeed not despite the fact that your reader knows what will happen, but because of it. The

Greek tragedies, as the years go by, never turn out any better. Oedipus stays blind. Fate operates, and we watch it, hypnotised, and watch its victims struggle. It was only once that an audience went to see *Romeo and Juliet* and hoped they might live happily ever after. You can bet that the word soon got around the playhouses: they don't get out of that tomb alive. But every time it has been played – every night, every show – we stand with Romeo at the Capulet's monument. We know when he breaks into the tomb he will see Juliet asleep and believe she is dead. We know he will be dead himself, before he knows better. But every time, we are on the edge of our seats, holding out our knowledge, like a present we can't give him.

It's the same with the people in history. Our attention is transfixed, as we watch someone stride towards the edge of a cliff, when we can see the edge and the character can't. The reader becomes a small, con-flicted god, or a disbelieved prophet. He is in two places at once. He is at the foot of the cliff, wise after the event, and he is also on the path, he is before the event; he is the observer, and he is also the person who steps into air.

Only fiction can do this. It's the novelist's job: to put the reader in the moment, even if the moment is 500 years ago. There are techniques, but no tricks. You can only do it through honest nego-tiation with the facts and the power of the informed imagination.

Recently, I went to Windsor Castle, and I learned, to my delight, that the cooking for state banquets is still done in the medieval kitchens. Into the alcoves where open fires once burned, they have fitted gleaming stainless-steel ranges. Look up, and it's like a cath-edral. Great gothic arches span it, holding up the roof.

Except they don't. Early in the eighteenth century, restorers decided that the fifteenth-century roof looked insufficiently medi-eval. It was structurally sound, but it wasn't picturesque. So, they did a bit of faking. The gothic additions are hollow, made of pine planks, which were painted to look like old oak. They hold no weight, support nothing – except our under-powered imaginations. What I recommend to fellow writers is that, having found your story, you trust the men and trust the materials. The past will hold itself up.

Adaptation

In the stage play of my novel *Wolf Hall*, Thomas Cromwell wants the young nobleman Harry Percy to take an oath to declare that he is not now, and never has been, secretly married to Anne Boleyn. But Harry Percy thinks they are married. He protests, 'You can't change the past.'

'Oh,' says Cromwell, 'the past changes all the time, Harry. And I'm going to show you how easily it can be altered.'

He then grabs the young man and bangs his head on the table, as if to knock out his old memories and make space for new.

We all used to look forward to this scene, except the actor who played Harry Percy. Until this point, Cromwell had been an entirely reasonable man.

In the original novel, that scene is more complex. Cromwell persuades the earl that he must do as he's told, because Cromwell represents the force of the future – and Harry Percy is a member of an economically illiterate warrior class whose day is over. Swept away on a flood of words, concussed by metaphorical rocks, the young man gives way.

Why the difference? The theatre craves action – but it's not just that. The novel craves it too. But the hardest thing to put on the page is something that happens suddenly. The theatre is superb at surprise. It offers us thought condensed into action, just as the cinema does: it also takes an image and springs it open, so something powerful and unexpected jumps out. It puts the dead back into circulation, within touching distance.

When half-forgotten names are spoken – the names of real people, who happen to be dead – they shiver in the air of the auditorium, resonating in time and space. It makes me ask, is it enough to commemorate the dead by carving their names in stone? Or should we go into an arena and shout them out loud?

In these lectures I've argued that fiction, if well written, doesn't betray history, but opens up its essential nature to inspection. When fiction is turned into theatre, or into a film or TV, the same applies: there is no necessary treason. Each way of telling, each medium for telling, draws a different potential from the original. Adaptation, done well, is not a secondary process, a set of grudging compromises, but an act of creation in itself.

Indeed, the work of adaptation is happening every day; without it, we couldn't understand the past at all. An event occurs once: everything else is reiteration, a performance. When action is captured on film, it seems we have certainty about what happened. We can freeze the moment. Repeat it. But in fact, reality has already been framed. What's out of shot is lost to us. In the very act of observing and recording, a gap has opened between the event and its transcription. Every night as you watch the news, you can see a story forming up. The repetitious gabble of the reporter on the spot is soon smoothed to a studio version. The unmediated account is edited into coherence. Cause and effect are demonstrated by the way we order our account. It gathers a subjective human dimension as it is analysed, discussed. We shovel meaning into it. The raw event is now processed. It is adapted into history.

Most of us spend our lives in adaptation, aware we have a secret self, and aware that it won't do. We send out a persona to represent us, to deal for us in public; there are two of us, one home and one away, one original and one adapted.

Now technology has multiplied ways to play with our identities. In online games, we can choose an avatar. We can proliferate, untied from physical limitation. Reality TV sets up scenes in which people mimic their real lives – but trimmed to a tidier pattern, and with a neater script. Watching them fumble to imitate themselves, we say, 'Ah, but they're not real actors.' Television and the theatre pick up a fact-based story before it's cold, and dramatise it. The living being and her impersonator can share a space. In Shakespeare's day, they didn't put the current monarch on stage. But our present queen can view herself adapted into different bodies, on stage, on TV, in the cinema.

Meanwhile, her humble subjects must make do with faking themselves, photographing their own faces, then adapting the result till they have a self they like better. It's surprising novelists stay in the business, with so many keen amateurs in the lying game.

We writers console ourselves. We say, the media consume stories so fast that demand is always greater than supply. Everything starts with us, we say, sitting in a room: solitary, daydreaming, scratching away like a monk. We could adapt, we say, if the Middle Ages came back. A paper and pen will do to conjure a world. Our imagination, we say, needs no power supply.

But really, we wish we had a camera and a crew. In ten seconds, the screen can show nuances of character or plot developments that in a novel, or on stage, would be impossible to depict. The cinema has a wonderful easy power to tell us where to look: this is your hero, the man the camera is following.

There is a difficulty for a novelist who writes about what we used to call 'great men': we want to keep the greatness, while making them human. You don't want to cut them down to size in a spiteful modern way – even if you don't admire them, you have to recognise that an individual plus a reputation is more than just a private person, he or she is owned by everyone.

So, on stage, and on the page, there is a nervous moment, before you bring in the big character – as it might be, Henry VIII, or Marilyn Monroe. The expectation of the audience is vast – can the actor live up to it?

On film, there need be no make-or-break moment. The problematic body can swim out of the background, as if from a psychic veil, a mist; or the viewer can take it in bit by bit – a spur, or a stiletto heel. We don't need a look-alike. The cinema creates a mythic identity. We watch a film all together, in the dark. We engage in collective dreaming. And we eat – we eat with our fingers, cheap, gratifying, baby food – as if suspending adult life and adult judgement, sinking entirely into the story we are told. The image has taken reason prisoner.

And then we come out into the street and are angry with ourselves, for believing what we see. The cinema is excellent at verisimilitude but less good with the truth. Time's the enemy. There's a limit to how many complex events you can digest into the average length of a feature film. It is a rare gift, to be able to find images to carry facts. We have explanatory devices – voice-overs, captions; they can add creative value, or they can be desperate measures which regress to the text. I think that what the adaptor must do is set aside the source – whether it's a history book or a novel – put down the text, and dream it. If you dream it, you might get it right, the spirit if not the letter; but if you are literal, you will set yourself up for failure.

Mostly, as I take it, filmmakers don't set out to lie. Draft one may tell the truth: but a casual rewrite, in a series of rewrites by different hands, can shake out the truth and shake in a lie. As an audience, we recognise that film has the tools to do a really bad job. So, a whole industry has grown up, of resistance: an industry of carping and picking holes.

We need the pedants and the complainers, to drive us back to the sources, and to open debate about what people call 'real history', and how it is sold to us. But it's a mistake to focus on trivialities. The people who demand total accuracy usually do it from a position of ignorance. To satisfy them would mean too much destruction. It would be vandalism to dig up a twenty-first-century garden, so you only show sixteenth-century plants. You can make a literal reproduction of an eighteenth-century chair but it doesn't bring an eighteenth-century person to sit on it.

Not that accuracy is to be discouraged. A faithful representation is one that is stabilised by physical reality. In portraits of great women of the sixteenth century, they have a characteristic way of standing: head up, back straight, hands folded at the waist. Put a modern woman into a replica of that costume, properly weighted, and she can't stand any other way. Reality has a coercive force. The body adapts, and the body underneath matters as much as the clothes on top. It's the same with dialogue. Pastiche is not creative. We don't need our characters to mouth the words of another century, but to possess the common knowledge of their era – so they don't say what they could never think.

Compared to viewers thirty years ago, we are swift and sophisti-cated consumers of narrative. We have seen so many stories on the screen, and eaten them so fast with our gaze. Television can make our familiar world hyper-real, lying to us that no camera is present. But we wished to be undeceived – so we evolved the mock documentary, which makes fun of its own workings. The actors flick a furtive glance at the camera, mimicking the embarrassment of a real person, caught in the nefarious act of going about their day. It may be because we are used to this ironical mode – realism smirking at itself – that the dramatic reconstructions inserted into history programmes now look so earnest and clumsy. We can see its low-budget impersonation, and we refuse to suspend disbelief.

In the theatre we seldom refuse, as long as the events we're shown have emotional truth. Schiller's play *Maria Stuart*, first produced in 1800, sets up a meeting between Mary, Queen of Scots and Elizabeth I. In real life, these rival queens never met. But we recognise the dramatic need to put them in the same place: after all, they must have met in the space within their heads. They probably dreamed of each other, and the playwright joins us to the dream. The theatre allows us to be complicit in deception, without feeling guilt, because it doesn't disguise its artificiality. As with the cinema, we wait till the lights go down, then abdicate from our stubborn literal selves.

History is always trying to show itself to us. In the Western tradition, drama was a mature art when the novel was still young. We have built theatres for centuries – special buildings for the specific purpose of repeating human experience with small variations. In these buildings, day by day, everything is the same but not the same.

To adapt history for the stage you must make time and space, obey your laws. If you are working from a novel, that fiction becomes the canonical text, standing in for history. The novelist has some advantages. His stage sets are built out of black marks on white paper. On the page, a cast of a hundred is as cheap as a cast of two. For the stage, the adaptor must reduce the personnel, for practical as well as artistic reasons. Cut down the number of characters and you must adapt the story, reorganise events so that one person stands in for another.

It takes skill to manage that shift so you are still telling the truth – though not the literal truth. All we have is what Shakespeare calls, 'the two hours' traffic of our stage'. However gripping the action, it's a sad truth that an audience gets restless at ten o'clock. They might crave to see the wedding or the execution, then the curtain call. But they don't want to miss their train, or go home on the night bus with the drunks.

Each art form works when it plays to its strengths, or at least, understands its weaknesses. The screenwriter knows his director can populate a city, or whistle up a mob using computer-generated imagery. The playwright's mob is too meagre to be scary. His battle scene suffers because he only has four combatants and some clattery shields. It's tough if your story ends in a battle. But then, look at the climax of *Richard III*. No one forgets Richard yelling out his big offer: 'My kingdom for a horse!' But no one is going to bring him a horse, because the real and chilling end to his story has already happened in the tent on the eve of battle, when the souls of the dead gather to tell him that the game's up. 'The lights burn blue; it is now dead midnight.' Their intimate whisper is more final than the force of arms.

There is a way around the practical constraints – it is to use words as arrows that go straight to the heart of an audience. A stage play is a brilliant vehicle for the past, because it is a hazardous, unstable form, enacting history as it was made, breath by breath. The script sets parameters – this time, this place, this body. But the actor is not a repetition machine. Every show is different. History becomes interactive. Without speaking – by clapping, by sighing, by laughter, or by silence, and there are different kinds of silence – the audience directs the show, subtly adjusting the rhythm and nuance of what they see. The barrier that protects the actor is invisible, held in place only by the imagination of the onlookers. Reality can't be censored out. Sirens from the street cut through the mutter of Roman conspiracy, as if someone had anticipated Caesar's assassination and sent for an ambulance. In the Schiller drama I mentioned, *Maria Stuart*, there is an invented character who, towards the end of the play, stabs himself. In 2008, in Vienna, the play's audience were aghast at the rush of blood – it seemed so impressively real. It was. By some backstage muddle – by error, not malice – the stage knife had been replaced by a real knife.

Next day, the actor was back on stage, patched up. Living and dead in the theatre, we are not safe from each other. In *King Lear*, art brings a man to the edge of a cliff. Outcast, the blinded Duke of Gloucester comes, as he believes, to Dover, stumbling towards death. He thinks he has arrived at the edge of England. He launches himself into the empty air.

We, the audience, can see there is no cliff. The blind man is standing on solid ground. It's a trick adapted from low comedy, from farce – an old fool reacting to an imaginary peril. But then the truth comes home to us, in a pulse-beat: and not just the truth about the blind duke. The cliff is invisible, but real. That's where we all live, one inch, one heartbeat, from extinction. It's not a few seconds we spend there, it's our whole lives.

King Lear is not history, it's myth; but it tells profound truths about the workings of power and love. It does the artist's work of turning history inside out and telling us what's under the skin. Despite what Marx said, I don't believe history ever repeats itself, either as tragedy or farce. I think it's a live show and you get one chance. Blink and you miss it. Only through art can you live it again.

And without art, what have you, to inform you about the past? What lies beyond is the unedited flicker of closed-circuit TV. This technology offers to capture the world without bias, without inter-pretation. The pictures help us count heads in a crowd. They can help us nail a lie, or spot a wanted man. Yet the images from the mechanical eye have a peculiar chill, because they show us helpless against fate – parched automatons, occupying space without commanding it. Think of those pictures of Diana leaving the Paris Ritz through the service corridor – her retreating back, only minutes before her death. To these images you are history's lonely, appalled witness, the eternal bystander. No creative hand is at work – just life, mutely and stupidly recorded, shown to us when it's too late to act, too late to learn.

If we told our histories in that mode we would despair. Though the images of Diana are banal, artless, that still doesn't guarantee their perfect truth. The inquest heard that they came from five banks of cameras that were not quite synchronised: so, on that most unlucky night, there were five different time zones on offer in the Ritz Hotel.

Death is certain, the hour of death uncertain, and our precise position on our path towards it is not, even in retrospect, as easy to pinpoint as you would think.

If we crave truth unmediated by art, we are chasing a phantom. We need the commentator's craft, even to make sense of the news. We need historians, not to collect facts, but to help us pick a path through the facts, to meaning. We need fiction to remind us that the unknown and unknowable is real, and exerts its force.

Some writers and adaptors disclaim responsibility. They say the public wants escapism, so let's give them what they want. They cheat their audience as politicians cheat when they make uncosted pledges: the bill comes later, when we lose a grip on our own story, and fall into individual distress and political incoherence.

I have written a novel called *The Giant, O'Brien*, loosely based on the true story of a real-life giant who came to London in the 1780s, to exhibit himself for money. In my version, the giant is more than a freakishly tall man: he is the embodiment and carrier of myth, and he has a fund of stories about love and war and talking animals and saints. His followers join in, shouting with jokes and plot twists of their own. He tries to incorporate them and keep everybody happy.

So, his stories are interactive, democratic and popular – the only trouble is, they are corrupt. They get further and further from the story as he knows it to be. In the end, he realises the folly of telling people what they want to hear. He says, 'Stories cannot save us . . . Unless we plead on our knees with history we are done for, we are lost.'

History, of course, hears no plea: it is a human being who hears, the bearer of the tale. The giant's plea is for art and craft honestly deployed. Our audiences do not need to be protected from stories; they know when they enter the fictional space.

But we owe it to them to stretch our technique to offer the truth, in its multiple and layered forms – not to mislead because it is, on the face of it, the easier option. We should not avoid the complexities and contradictions of history any more than politicians should abandon debate and govern by slogans. We must try by all the means we command to do justice to the past in its nuance, intricacy, familiarity and strangeness. Historical fiction acts to make the past a shared imaginative resource. It is more than a project of preservation: it is a project against death. In the epigraph to my novel about the Irish giant, I quoted the poet George MacBeth, and I leave you with his thought about what we want from the past and how we get it:

> All crib from skulls and bones
> Who push the pen.
> Readers crave bodies:
> We're the resurrection men.*

---

* George MacBeth, *The Cleaver Garden* (Secker & Warburg, 1986).

PART V

The Moon Was a Tender Crescent

Bryant Park: A Memoir

2016

The day before Election Day, the weather in New York was more like May than November. In hot sun, gloved ice-skaters, obedient to the calendar, meandered across the rink in Bryant Park, which showed itself ready for winter with displays of snowflakes and stars. It was a great afternoon to be an alien, ticket in your pocket, checked in already at JFK, and leaving the country before it could elect Donald Trump. Breakfast television had begged viewers to call the number on-screen to vote on whether Mrs Clinton should be prosecuted as a criminal. Press 1 for yes, 2 for no. 'Should Hillary get special treatment?' the voiceover asked. There was no option for jailing Trump.

During his campaign, Trump threatened unspecified punishments for women who tried to abort a child. We watched him, in the second debate, prowling behind his opponent, back and forth with lowered head, belligerent and looming, while she moved within her legitimate space, returning to her lectern after each response: tightly smiling, trying to be reasonable, trying to be impervious. It was an indecent mimicry of what has happened at some point to almost every woman. She becomes aware of something brutal hovering, on the periphery of her vision: if she is alone in the street, what should she do? I willed Mrs Clinton to turn and give a name to what we could all see. I willed Mrs Clinton to raise an arm like a goddess, and point to the place her rival came from, and send him back there, into his own space, like a whimpering dog.

Not everything, of course, is apparent to the eye. The psyche has its hidden life and so do the streets. Midtown, the subway gratings puff out their hot breath, testament to a busy subterranean life; but you could not guess that millions of books are housed under Bryant

Park, and that beneath the ground runs a system of train tracks, like toys for a studious giant. Activated by a scholar's desire or whim, the volumes career on rails, in red wagons, toward the readers of the New York Public Library. Ignorant pedestrians jink and swerve, while below them the earth stirs. We are oblivious of information until we are ready for it. One day, we feel a resonance, from the soles of the feet to the cranium. Without mediation, without apology, we read ourselves, and know what we know.

There are some women who, the moment they have conceived a child, are aware of it – just as you sense if you're being watched or followed. I have never had a child, but once in my life, a long time back and for a single day, I thought I was pregnant. I was twenty-three years old, three years a wife. I had no plans at that stage for a child. But my predictable cycle had gone askew, and one morning I felt as if some activity had commenced behind my ribs. It wasn't breathing, or digestion, or the thudding of my heart.

I lived in the north of England then. My husband was a teacher, and it must have been half-term holiday, because we went into the city to meet a friend and spend the afternoon with his parents, who were visiting from rural Cornwall. They wondered why so many grand buildings were painted black, why even gravestones appeared to be streaked and smeared. That, we explained, was not paint; it was two centuries of working grime. They were startled, mortified by their ignorance. To them, heavy industry was something archaic, which you saw in a book. They didn't know that its residue fluffed the lungs like Satan's pillows, that it thickened walls and souped the air.

At lunchtime with my party of friends, I could not eat, or stay still, or find any way to be comfortable. I felt weak and light-headed. Heat swept over me, then chill. On our way home in early evening, we called on my mother-in-law, who was a nurse. 'I wonder if you might be expecting?' she said. In the kitchen, my husband put his arms around me. We didn't officially want a baby, but I saw that, at least for this moment, we did. None of us knew the next step. Were the chemist's tests reliable? Would it be better to go straight to the doctor? My mother-in-law said, 'I don't know what the right way is, but I'll find out first thing, as soon as I get into work.'

But by the time I left her house the space of possibility that had opened inside me was filling with pain. Soon I was shaking. As the evening wore on, the pain expanded to fill every cavity in my body. Even my bones felt hollow, as if something were growing inside and pushing them out. In the small hours, I began to bleed. The episode was over. No test would ever be needed. I never had that particular set of feelings again, that distinctive physiological derangement. But women are full of potential. Thwart them one way and they will find another. What never left me was the feeling that something was knocking inside my chest, asking to be let out. A sensory error, I presumed. Only recently did I have the thought that it might have been a real pregnancy – an unviable, ectopic conception. Such a mistake of nature can result in a surgical emergency, even sudden death. It is possible I had a lucky escape, from a peril that was barely there.

A few days after this thought occurred, I had, not a dream, but a shadowy waking vision. It seemed to me that a bubble floated some three feet from my body, attached to me by an almost invisible thread. In the bubble was a tiny child, which asked my forgiveness. In its semi-life, lived for a single day, it had caused nothing, known nothing, created nothing other than pain; so it wanted me to pardon it, before it could drift away.

I do not cede the child any reality. Nor do I think it was an illusion. I recognise it as some species of truth, light as metaphor. It had not occurred to me that there was anything to forgive – that anything was ensouled that could grieve, that could endure through the years. But there was a hairline connection to that day in my early life, and at last I could cut the tie and it could sail free.

It was imagination, no doubt. Imagination is not to be scorned. Fragile, fallible, it goes on working in the world. Since I cut that thread, I have been more sure than ever that it is wrong to come between a woman and a child that may or may not elect to be born. Campaigners talk about 'a woman's right to choose', as if she were picking a sweet from a box or a plum from a tree. It's not that sort of choice. It's often made for us. Something unrealised gives the slip to existence, before time can take a grip on it. Something we hoped for everts itself, turns back into the body, or disperses into the air.

But, whatever happens, it happens in a private space. Let the woman choose, if the choice is hers. The state should not stalk her. The priest should seal his lips. The law should not interfere.

That whole week leading up to the election, it was warm enough to bask on garden chairs. The market at Grand Central displayed American plenitude: transparent caskets of juicy berries, plump with a dusky purple bloom; pyramids of sushi; sheets of aged steak, lolling in its blood. By the flitting light of the concourse, I checked out the destination boards of another life I could have lived. Twenty years ago, my husband worked for IBM. It was projected that we would move to its offices in White Plains. For a week or two, we imagined it, and then the plan disintegrated. In that life, I would have taken the train and arrived amid Grand Central's sedate splendours, and walked about in my Manhattan shoes. Did the book stacks exist then? Surely I would have had foreknowledge, and felt the books stirring beneath 42nd Street, down where the worms turn.

As the polls were closing, I was somewhere over the Atlantic. As we flew into the light, one of the aircrew came with coffee and a bulletin, with a fallen face and news that shocked the rows around. 'They don't think', she said, 'that Hillary can catch him now.' I took off my watch to adjust it, unsure how many centuries to set it back. What would Donald Trump offer now? Salem witch trials? Public hangings? The lass who had prepared us for the news was gathering the blankets from the night's vigil. Crinkling her brow, she said, 'What I don't comprehend is, who voted for him?'

No one we know – that's the trouble. For decades, the nice and the good have been talking to each other, chitchat in every forum going, ignoring what stews beneath: envy, anger, lust. On both sides of the ocean, the *bien pensants* put their fingers in their ears and smiled and bowed at one another, like nodding dogs or painted puppets. They thought we had outgrown the deadly sins. They thought we were rational sophisticates who could defer gratification. They thought they had a majority, and they screened out the roaring from the cages outside their gates, or, if they heard it, they thought they could silence it with, as it may be, a little quantitative easing, a package of special measures. Primal dreads have gone unacknow-ledged. It is not only the crude blustering of the Trump campaign that has poisoned public discourse but the liberals' indulgence of the marginal and the whimsical, the habit of letting lies pass, of ignoring the living truth in favour of grovelling and meaningless apologies to the dead. So much has become unsayable, as if by not speaking of our grosser aspects we abolish them. It is a failure of the imagination. In this election as in any other, no candidate was shining white; politics is not a pursuit for angels. Yet it doesn't seem much to ask – a world where a woman can live without jumping at shadows, without the crawling apprehension of something nasty constellating over her shoulder. Mr Trump has promised a world where White men and rich men run the world their way, greed fuelled by undaunted ignorance. He must make good on his promises, for his supporters will soon be hungry. He, the ambulant id, must nurse his own offspring, and feel their teeth.

At Dublin airport by breakfast time, the sour jokes were flying over the plastic chairs: there'll be plenty of work for Irishmen now – if you want a wall built, the Paddies have not lost the skills. I wanted to see a woman lead the great nation, so my own spine could be straighter this blustery sunny morning. I fear the ship of state is sinking, and we are thrashing in saltwater, snared in our own ropes and nets. Someone must strike out for the surface and clear air. It is possible to cut free from some entanglements, some error and painful beginnings, whether you are a soul or a whole nation.

The weekend before the election, we were in rural Ohio. The moon was a tender crescent, the nights frosty, and the dawns glowed with the crimson and violet of the fall. On Sunday morning, in a cloudless sky, a bird was drifting on the currents, circling. My husband said, 'You know they have eagles in this part of the country?' We watched in silence as it cruised high above. 'I don't know if it is an eagle,' he said at last. 'But I know that bird is bigger than you think.'

Real Books in Imaginary Houses

2008

What do you read when you're not reading? I've reached that stage in the writing of my current novel when other people's fiction is wasted on me. It's not that it's so much worse than mine that I can patronise it, or so much better that it drives me to despair. It's not that I'm afraid of influence; after all, it might be influence for the better. It's just that I haven't the emotional stamina to enter and live inside someone else's imaginative reality. Even when I'm reading non-fiction, my mind wanders, between paragraphs, to the fact that I could be writing, not reading. Every word reminds me of another word, one I should be putting down myself.

Like many people, I am addicted to the physical act of reading. The worst withdrawal symptoms can be staved off by newspapers; but, as Charles Lamb said, no one ever put down a newspaper without a feeling of disappointment. Still, I'm not the worst print addict I've ever met.

There are some people who, when you take them to the country, look at the fields in astonishment because they haven't got writing on them, and your only hope is to find them a country churchyard where they can read the epitaphs – the more discursive the better.

But I am intrigued by the divide between those people who say 'I haven't time to read', and those for whom reading is like breathing and who, though they may be caught up with all sorts of texts, always have a novel on the go. For some people, the consumption of stories is a barely conscious function that runs parallel to eating, sleeping, having sex and earning a living. How do you live life without stories – live in just a single narrative, and that one your own? Show me a man – it's usually a man – who 'doesn't see the point of fiction', and I'll show you a pompous, inflexible, self-absorbed bore.

The people with no time to read play computer games and watch TV, but I can't think that the precisely calibrated set-ups and pay-offs of their chosen forms are comparable to the forfeits and rewards of fiction on the page. Fiction leaves us so much work to do, allows the individual so much input; you have to see, you have to hear, you have to taste the madeleine, and while you are seemingly passive in your chair, you have to travel.

But even within the group of daily readers, there are differences that are hard to reconcile. There are people who declare, 'I love reading', which is a lame-brain statement, like 'I love children'. When anyone refers – as papers and magazines do at holiday time – to the pleasures of 'escaping' into a good book, you can be sure the writer has no idea what books are for. They are not there to allow you to escape, but to give you information about the human condition, which is a thing you cannot escape. You find out the use of books when you are very young. History, biography, and novels in particular lend you experience that is not yet your own. They are an advance paid on life. They hand you different scripts to try. They rehearse you. If you want entertainment, roll dice; then you can maintain your happy-go-lucky innocence. Novels teach you that actions have consequences. They help you grow up.

But an experienced reader is also a self-aware and critical reader. I can't remember ever reading a story without judging it. If that sounds sad, it isn't. From an early age, the constant reader accepts a story as an artefact. Alive to the artificiality of texts, he finds it hard to understand the fundamentalist viewpoint, Christian or otherwise, which casts certain phrases as sacred. The constant reader is sceptical, irreverent and fickle. He doesn't make a god of any text, because he knows it is provisional and there'll be another one along in a minute. And even when he's reading a gravestone, he is aware that, as Dr Johnson said, 'In lapidary inscriptions a man is not upon oath.' The scholars who condemned *The Satanic Verses* didn't understand what a novel does; in a sense they took fiction too seriously, seeing it not as a rehearsal for a position, but as a position in itself: as a statement and not a conjecture. They made the naive mistake of identifying the writer with his book and supposing that he meant what his story said.

Sentimental people will try to convince you that stories, like the act of reading, are as natural as breathing. They say that we are narrative animals, but the broken stories of people who enter psycho-analysis suggest that if stories are natural to us, they are not easy to construct in a way that serves both our sense of personal continuity and our need for freedom. A story is always on the move, and from the author's point of view there is nothing natural about it. Constant readers become writers at the point in life when they acquire a fascination with a process of falsification: with imposing shape while simulating the evolution of character and event, making determin-ations while fostering an illusion that in the next chapter anything might happen. A novelist spends a lifetime in the business of pre-senting what's lifelike, but not like life. It's a sobering thought – life won't actually do. Verisimilitude and the truth are conjoined twins, one often flourishing at the expense of the other.

This is hard to understand when you're learning to write. Novices often turn up with some deeply unconvincing story with autobio-graphical roots, and when you suggest that it doesn't seem likely, they spring to its defence by insisting that 'it really happened that way'. It can be a thankless task, breaking people of their fidelity to the facts as they understand them, and the only way to do it is to send people back to pick apart the most convincing stories they know, and to provoke them to see where the author performs a conjuring trick. It seems harsh, to blow away the smoke and unveil the mirrors. But magic is a trade that can be learned.

Of course, there's a sorry subgroup of people who want to be writers, but don't actually like reading. More about them, maybe, another time.

A Life of Biggles

2009

Though I have never thought of myself as a book collector, there are shelves in our house browsed so often, on so many rainy winter nights, that the contents have seeped into me as if by osmosis. Biggles, properly known as James Bigglesworth DSO MC, is the subject of almost a hundred books by Capt. W. E. Johns, who published them over some forty years. My husband has eighty-five of these titles, and rules about his collection. He has to happen upon the books, not hunt them down. He won't pay silly money, and he'll have nothing to do with catalogues, internet searches or specialist networks. A day which to others is merely a dull day in a strange town is to him a Biggles opportunity; but as the number of second-hand bookshops seems to dwindle, I don't know whether he'll be able to collect the stories he's missing unless he breaks his self-imposed rules.

As a child I used to read Biggles myself in a mild way – enough to get a rough fix on his biography. He was born in India in 1899. I ask myself, why would any writer do that to his character? Why not a neat 1900? But he has to be just old enough to qualify for service in the First World War, and not so old that he can't fight in the Second. Biggles's invented career in the Royal Flying Corps was much more successful than the career of his creator, who was in himself dashing enough; Johns had been shot down after a bombing raid on Mannheim, escaped from a prisoner of war camp, was recaptured and survived till the armistice, and turned up on his family's doorstep long after they had presumed him dead. Johns was a many-sided and talented man: a patriot but not a jingoist, nimble, inventive and thoroughly professional as a writer – though his early, pre-military career was as a sanitary inspector. He adapted quickly to changing times, diversified his output, and turned his fiction to propagandist ends during the Second World War, when paper was in short supply. He dreamed up Worrals, Biggles's feminine counterpart, in the hope of encouraging girls into the WAAF. He wrote ten books about Gimlet, a commando, and six stories about Steeley, a hero for our time, a Robin Hood who steals from the rich and slips the proceeds to the impoverished families of former servicemen. Johns also produced science fiction for children, including a tale called *The Edge of Beyond*, which froze my blood when I was eight or nine.

Biggles's literary career began in 1932 when Johns created him for *Popular Flying* magazine. He 'could have been found', Johns wrote, 'in any RFC mess during those great days of 1917 and 1918 when . . . air duelling was a fine art'. Between the wars, Biggles was a charter pilot with a sideline in working for MI6. The scope of his adventures was worldwide – every Biggles book is a history and geography lesson. A squadron leader in the Second World War, he transferred to Scotland Yard in peacetime, and fought his own cold war as chief of the 'special Air Police Division'. There is, as you'd expect in books aimed at teenage boys, more concentration on hardware than on characterisation; but over so many years, Biggles and his comrades couldn't help develop as individuals. However malign the foe and urgent the enterprise, Biggles found time to lie in the grass and hear the larks singing. His adventures were profitable, judging by his Mayfair address. Spare, laconic and dryly humorous, he was by no means closed to finer feelings; there's no book called *Biggles Falls in Love*, but it did happen. Marie Janis was introduced in a short story in the unromantically named collection *The Camels Are Coming*; these were Sopwith Camels, not the kind with humps. Though posing as a Frenchwoman, Marie turned out to be a German spy, who trained in the same spy school as Biggles's lifelong enemy, Erich von Stalhein. On learning this, Biggles, 'burnt up with grief and rage', hit the bottle.

Erich was a worthy opponent, an honourable if wrong-headed product of the Prussian officer class. After 1945 he found himself serving Soviet masters who, because of his failure to entrap Biggles, exiled him to Sakhalin. He was rescued in *Biggles Buries a Hatchet*, and later he helped Biggles save Marie from a former Gestapo offi-cial who was holding her prisoner. A frail, grey-haired figure whom Biggles barely recognised, Marie ended her days domestically in Hampshire. 'Had you married,' Erich told Biggles, 'your loyalties would have been divided between your wife and aviation; and a man can't serve two mistresses honestly.' Fighting as a vocation, fighting as an art: it's an ideal almost medieval in its purity.

There was a time when Biggles used to smoke and drink with the best of them, and dine in Soho. But the world became strait-laced in the supposedly swinging 1960s, and bowdlerisation altered his character just as much as shifts in global politics. In *Biggles Flies North*, he and his co-pilot Ginger walk into a smoky saloon in the Yukon: 'Give it a name, stranger,' says the barman. 'I'll have some malted milk,' says Ginger. Biggles asks for Bovril. We don't own the 1939 original, so what they ordered originally we can only guess. It's the bowdlerisation that makes collecting Biggles such an intricate business. Ideally, you'd like to be able to place the versions side by side, and laugh at them.

Like every writer, I'm drawn by unlikely juxtapositions, precisely dated and once-only collisions between people from different worlds. In 1922, Johns was working in London as an RAF recruiter. Into his office walked an inferior physical specimen with a strange air of moral superiority. It was T. E. Lawrence, looking to enlist under an alias. The powers that be were meant to have sent the recruitment office a secret order telling them to sign up this fishy character; Johns later insisted he had seen no such instructions. He took the would-be recruit at face value, disbelieved everything he said, and booted him out. The man returned with a messenger from the air ministry, who handed over a letter; Johns looked at the official signature, shrugged, wrote 'special case' on the file and sent the fellow to the medical officer. Deeply unimpressed by the weedy person, the MO threw him out in turn. The affair escalated; Johns was told that if he didn't force the procedure through, his military career was over: 'You'll get your bowler hat.' So 'Aircraftsman Ross' was enlisted, and Johns picked up the phone to warn the training camp at Uxbridge 'Lawrence of Arabia is on his way.' Johns later said: 'Lawrence knew I knew . . .' They had a long talk before the imposter left, but Johns didn't say about what. What stayed with him, on parting, was the imprint of Lawrence's clammy handshake.

Of these characters, Aircraftsman Ross seems to me more of a fiction than Biggles. There's a story here, but I don't know what form it should take. Is it a stage play, perhaps? If so, someone had better get on with it. There will come a time when nobody knows who Biggles was, and maybe nobody will know who T. E. Lawrence was either. One hears of 'the waning of the common culture'. But perhaps it's just age creeping up.

Nostalgic for Disorder

2009

There was a time I couldn't walk past a bookshop without going in. I might try not to, but my feet (which look after my best interests) would just start turning of their own accord and walk me over the threshold. After all, you never know. There might be a life-changing book inside; by 'life-changing' I mean a book that contains the seed of another book, one I might spend four or five years living with and then writing.

These books are seldom found in a modern bookshop among the three-for-twos. Lost notions, forlorn phrases, time-worn ruminations, the received ideas and commonplaces of earlier times: these are what start new ideas growing. I am very happy in second-hand bookshops; would a gardener not be happy in a garden? Everyone laments that such shops are rarer than they were, but I can think of some I'll be relieved not to enter again: the ones where the owners sat dribbling on their cardigans and glowering at any intruder; where yellowing notices said 'MIND THE STEP'; where the air was seething with mould spores out to colonise your lungs; where the doorbell gives one tuneless ding, like the crack of doom. Those shops would feel as if they stocked archaic diseases as well as unwanted books: upstairs for Poetry and the Black Death, and a smallpox opportunity pullulating beneath those musty bundles of *The Cricketer*, with small monochrome photographs of brilliantined heroes who strolled between the wickets and who had never heard of the one-day game, let alone Twenty20 and other manifestations of the devil's work. Bound volumes of sermons in lead-coloured covers; missionaries' memoirs; toad-spotted topographical works on superseded shires; I was compelled to truffle through them all, if only to prove my contention that every second-hand bookshop in the world stocks a copy of Osbert Sitwell's *The Scarlet Tree*.

How nice, then, to go to Waterstones and not to have to disinfect yourself when you get home; yet sometimes as a reader I feel nostalgic for disorder, for the random and unpredictable. I find myself wanting to be free from categorisation, or to introduce another kind; I wish bookshops had a shelf called Really Interesting Books. We all know what a RIB is, I think. It's a book that is about more than you imagined when first you picked it up. RIBs are like treasure maps – the marks on the paper are only symbolic indications of the riches to be recovered. They tell you things you always somehow knew, but had never been able to articulate. A RIB is like going on your travels, but also somehow like arriving home.

As I largely gave up churchgoing when I was twelve, I am surprised that so many of my RIBs have 'religion' in the title. When I was sixteen, a RIB was R. H. Tawney's *Religion and the Rise of Capitalism*, first published 1926, reaching my hand around 1968. It is a humane and discursive book, and it stopped me thinking that history was just one damn thing after another, which is how it had been presented to me until then; it made me understand that you could actually think about history, rather than just memorise it. I don't have much from those years, but I do have my yellowed paperback copy, with marginal notes by me that turn out to be startlingly cogent; I wish I'd spent my youth less piously. A later RIB was Keith Thomas's *Religion and the Decline of Magic*, 700 enthralling pages, first published in 1971:

> Astrology, witchcraft, magical healing, divination, ancient prophecies, ghosts and fairies, are now all rightly disdained by intelligent persons. But they were taken seriously by equally intelligent persons in the past, and it is the historian's business to explain why this was so.

There it is again, the historian's business; I needed to be told what it was. I needed to be warned, also, that I should not condescend to the dead. That phrase in the introduction, 'equally intelligent persons in the past', is always whispering itself in my ear, and I hope it has opened my mind to the bewildering human strangeness of the pre-Enlightenment world; I have never been in danger of thinking that our ancestors were just like us but with different clothes. I have had half a dozen copies of Thomas's classic and given them away over the years, pressing them on people I thought would find it a

RIB. More recently, a RIB has been William James's 1902 book *The Varieties of Religious Experience*; being a very morbid person, I am drawn to the bad experiences, and have spent hours dwelling on the section called 'The Sick Soul', which ends with a stimulating footnote about a man being eaten by a tiger.

It is characteristic of RIBs that they contain stories, examples and illustrations; they are generous books, overflowing any category you fit them in to, constantly exceeding your expectations. To find one, you have to ignore the classifications shops and libraries create, and you have to get past the cover. It doesn't matter if the ideas in a RIB are contentious, exploded, disproved, unfashionable or unpalatable; it matters that they strike a chord with you at one moment of your life. Some years ago, I came across Daniel Corkery's book *The Hidden Ireland*, first published in Dublin in 1924. In my unblemished ignorance, I took it to be one of those sentimental fairy tale collections I disliked, but I carried it off anyway, and read on past the subtitle: 'A Study of Gaelic Munster in the Eighteenth Century'. What I found in the book nearly broke my heart; it is an account of poetry made by very poor men very long dead, in an Irish language almost lost and then revived, but revived by grammarians and politicians, and for purposes of scholarship and ideology rather than for purposes of beauty.

I have met many Irish people of my generation who learned the language at school and were bored by it and thought it futile, but for my part I felt a keen deprivation, and a dismay: if (in some 'Variety of Religious Experience') I were to meet one of my foremothers, then maybe she would speak that language, and I this, and – though I admit such a meeting is unlikely – it would be a kind of disgrace, a neglect. Though odd, my feelings were not sentimental; I simply became aware that all my life I had been living in a room with a door I'd ignored, while trying to climb out of a narrow window. My efforts to learn Irish didn't come to anything. I soon realised that knowing the language wasn't the point; the point was knowing what I didn't know, and listening for the music inside the silence.

No Passport Required

2002

Jean Baudrillard says we ask ourselves about our identity only when we have nothing better to do. It is, no doubt, a Western luxury, and an indulgence of the intellect. But it is precisely with Western luxuries that I would like to concern myself; I would like to dwell on the collective life of the European imagination, and ask whether and how, born in England at mid-century, writing as the new century begins, I can claim a part of that collective life.

We cannot take credit for our European identity. It stands outside the process of historical definition. It was created before history began, by the movements of shifting land masses, crumpling and folding into each other. The rise and fall of mountains precedes the rise and fall of cities. Europe had a rich inheritance of metals and minerals, so that the continent became supreme in the arts of working metal; and had unique topographical advantages, being blessed with natural harbours, with navigable rivers running deep into the interior of the continent.

So, what Europe mined could be transported; in time, the products of agriculture were also transported. Our early identity, then, is intimately linked to the natural world. As soon as we define man as apart from that natural world, the question of our identity, collective and individual, begins to arise. We begin to tell ourselves stories about who we are. We draw an imaginary line around ourselves and say, this is my space, my territory, this is where I belong. The attributes of that space decide the way we see ourselves. But our ancestors' space was also imaginary, and we are the children of the physical and mental journeys they undertook.

In our minds each one of us draws a line between homeland and exile. Our identity depends on how we locate ourselves, in time and space, along this line. When we stay at home – unless we are living through an ethnic war, or an intellectual crisis of self-definition – we are content just to be. When we travel abroad, our hosts ask us to account for ourselves, define ourselves. When I speak or read abroad, I am sometimes described as a British writer, sometimes as an English writer. To me, the first description is meaningless. 'Britain' can be used as a geographical term, but it has no definable cultural meaning.

As for calling me 'an English writer' – it is simply what I am not. I was born in England in 1952 into a post-war society that was both anxious and complacent. Anxious, because the struggle since 1939 had been so hard; complacent, because – as my elders would have put it – England had won again. We had not been invaded.

The gaunt old virgin Britannia had once again spat in the eye of the European rapist. The island status, the separateness of Britain, or England, was essential to her understanding of herself. For generations, our historians had proceeded as if 'Britain' and 'England' meant the same. Scottish children learned Scottish history, and English history. But English schoolchildren did not learn Scottish history. They learned English history alone – and they called it British history. Historically, the English have not bothered to define themselves. They just are. It is other people who, in their view, have the problem of definition.

English nationalism is not recognised to exist. The clashes between England and Ireland were not, in the past, seen as a battle between English nationalism and Irish nationalism. They were seen as a result of the Irish nation's stubborn refusal to recognise that it was, for all practical purposes, English. It would be amusing, if the results had not been so bloody.

I grew up in a village in the north of England, a descendant of Irish immigrants who had come over to work in the textile mills. My mother was a textile worker, as was her mother before her. As a small child, I grew up in what was essentially an Irish family, surrounded by Irish people who were old. By the time I was ten almost all of them were dead. My consciousness of being Irish seemed to die with them.

Where have they gone, those old people? There is a place in my head, where I sit down with them. But in what sense could I call myself English? I was born on the northern tip of the Peak District, a country of mountains and moorland, of few people and many sheep. It was not the town, so was it the country? I had seen the English countryside in picture books. There were trees, cottages of golden stone, cottage gardens bright with flowers. This bleak and treeless terrain where I lived was – obviously – some other place.

Very often, at our church, we sang a hymn called 'Faith of Our Fathers', which celebrated the Roman Catholic martyrs of the Reformation, and included the ambitious prediction that 'Mary's prayers / Shall bring our country back to thee'.

Even when I was quite young, I used to think how comical it would be if the police marched in and arrested us; for, whereas Protestants pray for the reigning monarch and the status quo, we appeared to sing along in hopes of the mass destruction of the House of Windsor.

After this event – and the mass re-conversion – after we were once more in communion with our European brethren, the hymn promised us this: 'England shall then indeed be free'. (Was it 'indeed', or 'at last'? By its nature, this seminal text of my youth is absent from dictionaries of quotations. I try to think who I could call, to sing it to me down the phone, but I don't know anyone who wouldn't be unreliable or embarrassed: like the mathematician of Browning's poem, 'I feel chilly and grown old'.) As I grew up, I came to see that Englishness was White, male, southern, Protestant and middle class. I was a woman, a Catholic, a northerner, of Irish descent. I spoke and speak now with a northern accent. And if I tell an Englishman my date of birth and my religion and ancestry, I am telling him, without needing more words, that my family are working people, probably with little education.

All these markers – descent, religion, region, accent – are quickly perceived and decoded by those who possess Englishness, and to this day they are used to exclude. You are forced off centre. You are a provincial. You are a spectator. If you want to belong to Englishness, you must sell off aspects of your identity.

Possibilities of self-redefinition were presented to me. I could become educated, go and live in the south if I liked, abandon my faith and change my accent. I did some of these things. The American novels I began to read had taught me that literature did not proceed entirely from the torture chambers of the imagination; having spent my teenage years with Dostoyevsky, I was more than happy to meet Updike and Lurie. But most of the US literature I encountered was, as it happened, East Coast and Waspish; and the Jewish novelists, in their moral sophistication and urban poise, seemed more central to the culture than the Wasps themselves.

So, if American novels entertained me, they hardly expanded my means of self-construction. Though I was grateful for a state-sponsored schooling that had lasted much longer than that of anyone else in my family, I had not really been educated, rather, brought up to pass exams.

My knowledge of Latin evaporated the minute I walked out of the exam room at fifteen, and I had never learnt Greek. My lack of knowledge of classical literature still embarrasses me. At no conscious level could I link myself to the ancient idea of Europe, to the defining myths, to the common culture that is shaped by our inheritance from Greece and Rome. And yet they must have been pervasive, I think: in the water or in the air; or let's say that the crumbs from that inheritance had fallen to me from the table of pan-European Romanticism. For when I began to write, at twenty-two, I defined myself from the first as a European writer.

The first book I wrote was *A Place of Greater Safety*, a novel about the French Revolution, set in Paris. It was not the first book of mine to be published; it occupied me for many years, and was not published until 1992. I had never been to Paris when I began to write. This did not matter. In my dreams of Europe, I had found the keys to the gate of an unknown city. For the constant and passionate imagination, no documents or passes are needed. It did not seem to me that I was writing of dead people or events that were distant and frozen. I was working at a transformative moment in the history of Europe.

I was then the least alienated of beings. I was at one with the work I did. By writing a novel one performs a revolutionary act. A novel is an act of hope. It allows us to imagine that things may be other than they are. The English are literal-minded about borders. For obvious reasons, they do not make a territorial identification with the continent of Europe. A stretch of water cuts them off. If you are in England, you can easily dismay your fellow citizens of Europe by a chance remark: by speaking of 'crossing to Europe'. You are speaking geographically, of course. You do not mean to imply that you are not 'in' Europe. Nevertheless, the unfortunate turn of phrase has some significance. It is difficult, from the point of view of a small offshore island, to develop a sense of the integrity of Europe.

I remember a few years ago visiting Passau, in Germany, and standing at the riverside at the point where one could take a boat either to Amsterdam or to Vienna. I felt, suddenly, a childlike moment of wonder: ah, Europe connects. I could have worked it out from the atlas. But it is a small thing to look at a map, and a greater thing to feel for yourself how a map relates to life.

Not every English-born person has been able to experience such a moment. My grandfather's generation left those British islands only to fight in wars, wars that redrew the map of continental states but left the returning islanders lonely and injured and confirmed in their separateness. But now, from England, it is possible to travel with your car through a tunnel or step on a train and be, in every sense, in Europe.

I do not think there can ever have been an item of government transport policy that reaches so far into the imagination as the Channel Tunnel. Our sense of ourself is altered, and for once, not by some great discontinuity, not by a fracture but by a process of linking up, of connection. There is no heroic sea voyage, no airport formalities, no moment of take-off, no traumatic parting from one's own solid earth: only the business of changing platforms at a London station.

It is a small miracle, a psychic transformation made possible by engineers. In the course of writing my novel, *The Giant, O'Brien*, I was led back to Ireland. My book was based on the true story of an Irish giant, a man called Charles Byrne, who was a little under eight feet tall: who journeyed to London, at the end of the eighteenth century, to exhibit himself as a monster, and who died there, and who was dissected by the Scottish surgeon John Hunter.

His bones are hanging up even today in a London museum: an

awful symbol to remind us of how the body of Ireland is cut apart.*
In the course of my writing, I felt a great sadness about the loss, for
me, of the Irish language. I was aware my mouth was empty, but I
was aware also that my brain was crammed with newly minted myth.

If you are a member of the Irish diaspora – and perhaps most of
all, if you are an American or Australian of Irish origin – you are a
victim of the Celtic Revival of the late nineteenth and early twentieth
centuries. This movement was an attempt of a type familiar to us
in Europe, an attempt to reach back to a mythical time and place,
where the world was perfect and whole, where the Celts were a pure
race, and the Irish language was a pure language. It was a sham, but
it was seductive.

It fed into the current of Irish nationalism – the chief language
of which, of course, is English. It was, however, a lasting, commer-
cially rewarding sham, and it has taken on a new energy in recent
years, with the rediscovery of a 'Celtic' brand of music that seems
to embrace many of Europe's outlying, forgotten, misty regions, and
give them a common identity, and at the same time set them defiantly apart from the mainstream. My own shelves, I should admit,
are stacked high with recordings of this music from Ireland and
Scotland, from Brittany and Galicia; in pursuit of the togetherness
offered by otherness, I too have made the cash registers ring.

The new-minted 'Celtic' culture offers the thing that is extremely
attractive to the exile: a spurious sense of belonging. To be Irish has,
recently, become suspiciously fashionable; though you are excluded
from fashion, I think, if you are a Northern Irish Protestant. But if
we ask 'Who are the Irish?' – and consult our history and not simply
our emotional need for self-definition – they are not only Celts but
Vikings, Normans, Anglo-Saxons, and Spanish and Scots.

When Mary Robinson became president of Ireland, she put a
candle in her window, perpetually burning, to light the exiles home.
I found myself thinking it must be a very high-tech candle, for you
could see it blazing on the sunniest day. It needed to be bright, for
there was a long way to guide us home.

---

* While the skeleton of Charles Byrne remains in the collection of the Hunterian
Museum, it is no longer on display.

About four years ago I visited Tromsø in Norway, one of the most northerly towns in the world. There, under the midnight sun, I felt instantly at home. Within its severe geometry, its black trees reflected in icy water, I felt more myself than I had felt anywhere before. It was a feeling I had not sought, that I had never expected, and that I have never lost.

On my next visit to Dublin, I bought from the National Museum a copy of a Viking armlet that had been excavated on a Dublin archaeological site. To my own satisfaction, I had come home in Ireland and in Europe. I had added another episode to my story of who I am; though it is powerful to me, I know it is a confabulation. And now I hardly ever go out without this symbol on my wrist, because at the beginning of the twenty-first century I am a primitive person, and not so secure as to leave my current place of residence without a marker to lead me 'home'.

In my lifetime Ireland has changed its idea of itself, perhaps even more than England has. Ireland finds itself, as a country within the European Union, in a state of unprecedented prosperity, and also fully recognising and celebrating the European dimension of its history. The year 1998 saw the bicentenary of the rising of the United Irishmen, an attempt by both Protestant and Catholic Irishmen to throw off British rule, with military aid from France.

The rising was a heartbreaking catastrophe. It led to mass slaughter of a helpless population, and is a source of continuing bitterness and misunderstanding. But to commemorate this dreadful event, modern Ireland has built a beautiful exhibition centre in Enniscorthy, and planted trees of liberty in the grounds.*

There, to my personal joy, the story of Ireland's struggle for freedom was set in a European context. The tragedy does not diminish, but collective memory is honoured, truth is served, and myth gains in force. Ireland's sense of connection to Europe is something the English are slow to acquire. Among novelists writing now, Michèle Roberts brings a polished Anglo-French sensibility to her work. Tim Parks, a long-time resident of Florence, wrote first with an expatriate's eye, but now infuses his unsettling narratives with a transnational jitteriness.

---

* The National 1798 Rebellion Centre, Enniscorthy, Co. Wexford.

Barry Unsworth, whose early themes were slavery and colonialism, has lived for many years in Italy. One of the most remarkable novels published in England recently has been his *Losing Nelson* (1999). It tells the story of a modern-day man, a writer, who is obsessed with the glorious deeds of Nelson, reckoned the greatest of England's sea commanders, and who is writing a glorifying biography of him. Yet he cannot get past one shameful episode in Nelson's early career: his betrayal of the revolutionaries of Naples, to whom he had offered safe conduct, but whom he betrayed back to the hangman.

Unsworth believes this episode is of great consequence in the history of southern Italy. But the critics largely ignored the central point of his book. Unsworth dared to displace the Anglocentric view, and sacrifice an English hero to our common European humanity. It is still such a frightening enterprise, for some, that they are almost literally unable to read what he has put on the page.

All the same, the country where I was born has changed enormously from that scared and insular post-war nation. The young are pro-European without having to think about it. The European Community is one of the givens of their world. The British parliament at Westminster has formally devolved a share of power to Scottish and Welsh assemblies. The English sense of identity is beginning to fracture. This is a healthy development. No one now would speak of an English writer, if he meant a Scottish writer.

Generations of emigration from the former empire have made Britain a pluralist, multi-ethnic, multi-faith society, and now, like the rest of western Europe, host to waves of refugees from disaster-stricken territories to the east. These migrant communities will have to reimagine themselves. We are all, as I have tried to show, members of imagined communities.

In the century ahead, shall we transcend nationalism, or accommodate it? There is a sense in which a postmodern world must be a post-nationalist world. But the idea of a nation will be with us for a long time yet, for historically, nationalist ideals have provided ideologies of resistance and emancipation, and in the present sorry state of Europe, I do not think we can reasonably ask thwarted and injured peoples to do without their nationalist ideals, or to ask them to bask in the light of a sunny cosmopolitanism – for them, the day has not yet dawned.

The greatest hope of minorities, I think, is that they can find a refuge in an imagined Europe of the regions: not in a superstate, a Europe created on the model of past nation states, but within a Europe of diversity in which plural identities can flourish: in which a man is free to define himself as a member of such a group or nation, but also to define himself as a European.

Meanwhile, I think it is the role of writers and artists to make sure that the idea of a nation is not regressive, not repressive, not injurious to the freedom of others. Can this be done? It is artists and writers who deal in symbol and myth, in the manipulation of our psychic realities. Myth is what can be collectively remembered, collectively imagined. I do not think you can separate what is remembered from what is imagined. Myth is a psychic resource that can energise us for better or worse. It is our way back into history, a substitute for lost languages and a mirror we hold to long-vanished faces: see, we say, they were just like us. Myth is a kind of sacred history.

It seems to incarnate a truth that goes beyond fact. It appeals to our origins among the gods, before we were merely human. It can offer symbolic consolations for the catastrophes that befall a people: in our heads, the wrongs of history are undone. Nations use their myths to affirm and reaffirm themselves. In times of war, occupation and diaspora, they provide at least an illusion of continuity. In times of prosperity they provide an assurance of a god-given right to thrive and to expand.

They can be a malign ideological mechanism: they can be used to exclude and excuse, or they can lead a whole people to adopt a lexicon of martyrdom and hopeless sacrifice. But myth can also be empowering and redemptive. The stories we tell ourselves, or which we appoint writers to tell us, can show us a better self, a self in potential.

Behind every nation or state there is the state-that-might-have-been. Myth expresses a need for rootedness and identity, but it also allows us to continue to exist when we are uprooted; it allows us to uproot ourselves and still live, to take a sea voyage from our own identity. Myth is in constant movement and change. It recreates itself through constant multiple reinterpretations, through countless acts of telling and reading and writing.

As writers, we have certain options, which we carry into the new century. We can, for example, like Samuel Beckett, repudiate the images of collectivity, seeing them as sentimental compensation for our individual isolation and misery. Beckett, notoriously, preferred to live in France at war rather than in Ireland at peace. But the émigré sensibility can become nothing more than affectation, an empty piece of provocation; you can choose to be an exile only because others stay at home.

More fruitful, perhaps, is the example of James Joyce, who shows that we can free ourselves from tribal constraints without abandoning ourselves to the despair of solitude. Joyce chose to blend Hellenic symbols with Irish symbols, to draw strength for his work both from a local culture and the culture of continental Europe.

Among twentieth-century novelists he is one of the greatest, most enriching examples of how a European identity may be imagined. At the beginning of the century, we want to carry our past with us, without being bowed under its weight. We want history to be our guardian angel, an airy companion who walks beside us into the new millennium. The creative imagination is a place of safety for the dead, where they can show their faces and be recognised. We have to conjure the people of the past, summon them back to life, so they can lead us to our future.

The god that artists must invoke is Janus, the double-faced god, the guardian of gates and doors. It is the duty and privilege of the novelist to look both outward and inward, to the past and the future, to the particular and the universal, to the parish and the world. My greatest wish for the writers of this century is that they will find a capacity to be both at home and on a journey; that they will find that Europe is our *Heimat*, and our home away from home.

'How I Became a Writer' Stories

2008

Every writer has a 'How I became a writer' story. It's what interviewers and audiences always ask for, and quite understandably; some explanation is needed for embarking on a course of conduct so egotistic, impoverishing and bizarre. Some authors reply sweetly: 'I was born a writer.' Most of us struggle to separate 'how' from 'why'. The initial impetus is lost in a murky swamp of happenstance. I sometimes say that I wrote my first book because it didn't exist, and I wanted to read it. That's true as far as it goes, but if I am asked about 'influences' I find it hard to give a slick answer. Some of us need a little push, before we recognise we have the right to pick up a pen. In my case it came from a book by the psychiatrists R. D. Laing and Aaron Esterson, *Sanity, Madness and the Family*.

Laing was the better-known partner in this collaboration. In the 1960s and 1970s, he was fashionable and famous. His cultural influence has lasted, though some wish otherwise; his work reinforced the scepticism many feel about the biological basis of mental and emotional distress. But he died in 1989, and if you mention him nowadays you are likely to be met with stories of his disorderly private life, or with a distorted version of his work. He didn't, as some claimed, accuse parents of making their children schizophrenic; he interrogated the whole idea of schizophrenia as a clinical entity. He was exceptionally alive to language and gesture, to the layers of meaning in every utterance; alive, also, to power play, to conscious and unconscious manipulations. He had seen the pain, terror and desolation of madness. He did not glamorise it or claim it didn't exist. He and his co-workers suggested that the way some families worked could generate psychotic behaviour in one member, who was selected, more or less unconsciously, to bear the brunt of family dysfunction.

I picked up his book one afternoon in 1973 and read it in one sitting. The people in it seemed close enough to touch. I had already read Laing's more famous work, *The Divided Self*, and I wasn't sure I entirely grasped it; its case histories made my heart sink, but I struggled with its abstractions. But *Sanity, Madness and the Family* is vivid, direct, gripping. It is a series of interviews with families, who each include one member who has spent time in psychiatric hospitals. Each interview is a novel or play in miniature. The material was gathered between 1958 and 1963, so the families described still live in the shadow of the Second World War. They are very different, on the surface, from families today, but I wonder if the dynamics have changed so much. The ploys, the shifts of sense, the secrets and the ambivalence still seem familiar.

In the hospitals where Laing had trained, it was axiomatic that doctors and nurses didn't 'talk to psychosis'. The patient was sick and generating nonsense, and you should not encourage it. Laing thought that, if you listened, the patient would tell you how her world worked; the language might be metaphorical, even surreal, but that was logical in a context where plain speech had been penalised and where children had been taught, as they grew, to distrust their own perception and memory, and give way to the memories and perceptions of others. In Laing's families, there is always a version behind the version. There are truths one member is allowed to air, that another member is forbidden to utter. The weakest finds him or herself in a lose-lose situation, unable to please, locked in a circuit of invalidation. Madness may, in some circumstances, seem a strategy for survival.

All this is played out in the pages of interviews, in trite little words that I cannot quote without the space to set the scene for each. So many of these family conversations seemed familiar to me: their swerves and evasions, their doubleness. All the patients profiled in the book are young women. I know their names are pseudonyms, but over the years I've wondered desperately what happened to them, and if there's anyone alive who knows, and whether any of them ever cut free from the choking knotweed of miscommunication and flourished on ground of their own: Ruth, who was thought odd because she wore coloured stockings; Jean, who wanted a baby though her whole family told her she didn't; and Sarah, whose breakdown, according to her family, was caused by too much thinking. In the course of the recorded conversations, their families trip and contradict them. The interviewer records their signals – winks, smirks, nods – and how, when the 'mad' member protests, they say: 'What, me? I didn't do anything.' Barefaced lies are countenanced, as being for the patient's own good. Left is right, up is down, and, often enough, your mother's your sister, and your father's not your father.

Laing asked his reader: 'Is it what you already knew, expected, suspected? Do these things go on in all sorts of families? Possibly.' I looked at my own home and drew some conclusions; after all, it is class and context that select some families, and not others, for 'interventions'. You didn't find social workers and mad-doctors knocking on suburban doors, and if my own friends were in trouble, they just stopped eating, bearing smiling and skeletal witness to long-running family tensions.

There is a right time to read every book, and 1973 was the time for me to read this one. I was a law student, and a placement with the Probation Service had put me on the alert for what is coldly described as multiple family dysfunction. On Manchester high-rise estates I had seen the sour human comedy enacted: dad pickled in alcohol, mum a nervy chain-smoking wreck, son a 'young offender' caught up in a spiral of petty crime, pregnant daughter banging on the doors of the nearest psychiatric unit. Ah, the seventies: what a golden age! I was struck by how the men acted and the women reacted, how sons fought and thieved but daughters fell ill. I needed to see my instincts systematised, and when I read Laing, the dynamics were suddenly clear. For most of my life I had been told that I didn't know how the world worked. That afternoon I decided I did know, after all. In the course of my twenty-one years, I'd noticed quite a lot. If I wanted to be a writer, I didn't have to worry about inventing material, I'd already got it. The next stage was just to find some words.

Female Role Novels

2009

Towards the end of last year, the *Guardian* published a touching letter from a reader recalling her childhood engagement with *Little Women*, Louisa M. Alcott's classic family story. Generations of girls, she said, have 'seared in their memory' the episode where Jo, the second of the genteelly impoverished March girls, sells her long hair to help fund her mother's visit to the bedside of her wounded father, who is an army chaplain. It's the time of the American Civil War, and Jo wishes she could enlist. That's all very well, I used to sneer; nobody's going to hand her a rifle and pack, and tell her 'Off you go, girl'. Jo is generally held to be a role model for the budding writer; why, then, did I hate her like poison? She's a tomboy, who outrages her sisters by whistling. She uses schoolboy slang, and says she wishes she'd been born male. So did I, once; but by the age of four I'd worked out that you weren't going to make the swap. Jo's fifteen when *Little Women* begins, and she hasn't worked it out yet. How I despised her, with her preposterous literary aspirations! She writes plays for the family to perform – toe-curling melodramas. And when she first presents a manuscript to an editor, she ties it up with a red ribbon. Somehow, even at the age of eight, I knew that was a ludicrous thing to do. And, given her general mindset, shouldn't she have been glad to get her head cropped? Mr March's misfortune is Jo's opportunity; that's what I thought, anyway, in my first acid efforts at literary criticism.

My preferred model for the life to come was *What Katy Did*. Katy is the eldest of a large family of brothers and sisters; her mother is dead, her kind papa is a family doctor. I don't know what, when I was eight, I wanted more – a benign masculine presence, or Katy's facility in making up stories, verses and riddles. I read Susan

Coolidge's book many times. She and the author of *Little Women* were rough contemporaries, born in 1835 and 1832 respectively. Neither married, and they both used their younger selves as models for their sparky heroines. *Little Women* has never lost popularity, but I was surprised to find Katy and her family on the shelves of a local bookshop. The cover of one recent edition pictures a young girl on a swing, foregrounding an episode in the story that, as a child, I didn't think was central. Rereading it, I have to admit it is. Katy, against adult advice, uses a swing that has not been properly secured. She falls, is paralysed, and becomes an invalid for many months. She plunges into depression till visited by her saintly cousin Helen, a longtime invalid, who teaches her how to be saintly too: not to complain, never to show her pain, to enact cheerfulness and make an asset of immobility.

It's sickening stuff, and for reasons of my own I wish now I had never read it. As a small Catholic child, I had already taken on board the recommended attitude to suffering. You didn't avoid it, but 'offered it up'. It seems likely I also internalised Cousin Helen's message. It went underground, and surfaced when I myself became ill in my early teens. At that time in my life, I didn't squeal and kick enough. If I had regarded pain as an insult and an outrage, I might have made such a nuisance of myself that I got help; my medical history and my life would have been different. You can control and censor a child's reading, but you can't control her interpretations; no one can guess how a message that to adults seems banal or ridiculous or outmoded will alter itself and evolve inside the darkness of a child's heart.

Perhaps if I'd had more books, newer books, they would have diluted the noxious message and made my own imagination less collusive. The portrait of the Carr family enthralled me; what was important was not the accident on the swing, but the shared imaginative life of these brothers and sisters. In *What Katy Did at School*, the Western girl (who has got back the use of her legs) goes to an eastern boarding school, sees other customs and manners, but finds another congenial society of witty young women who can all turn a verse. I didn't find out *What Katy Did Next* until I was grown up and bought a second-hand copy. What she does is go on a

European tour, and meet the dashing young naval lieutenant she will marry. It's a less amusing book than the earlier ones, a travelogue with a perfunctory storyline. But there is one heightened, hallucinogenic moment: while seeing the sights in London, Katy spots George Eliot getting out of a cab. 'She stood for a moment while she gave her fare to the cabman, and Katy looked as one who might not look again, and carried away a distinct picture of the un-beautiful, interesting, remarkable face.'

When I encountered this, I blinked and read it again. It was an intersection of two imaginary planes; as much a breach of the rules as if, nowadays, I woke up to find one of my own invented characters in the kitchen making tea. Who is more real, Katy or George Eliot? I vote for Katy. I am surprised, returning to them, to find Coolidge's books so relentless in their piety, though no more queasily moralising than *Little Women*. As a child I must have thought all books were like that: vehicles of moral improvement, edification; books talked like adults, served adult interests. It was not until I was ten, and began *Jane Eyre*, that I encountered a story which seemed designed not to improve me, but describe me: 'a tiresome, ill-conditioned child, who always looked as if she were watching everybody, and scheming plots underhand'. Jane is required by her guardian to simulate childlike qualities, but can't manage it. I understood that pressure. I recognised Jane's perpetual, fretful anxiety; the world around her is jostling with hostile forces, with mean and malign intentions that the March girls and Katy had never glimpsed. 'Let me be a little girl as long as I can,' wheedles Jo March. Oh, you double-dyed fool! I had never read a book that did not idealise childhood until Charlotte Brontë presented me with one. Jane Eyre will not thrive unless she grows up fast, and perhaps not even then. For the first time an author was trusting me with the truth; it was there, for me, that the writing life began.

On the Right Track

2008

I've finished my book, *Wolf Hall,* at last. At least, I like to say so. But then I find myself confronted with a question anxiously discussed in schools of creative writing: how do you know you've finished? A much-revered writer once told me that a certain novel of hers – a novel later shortlisted for the Booker Prize – was finished when her publisher sent a courier on a motorcycle to take it away. As my new one is a historical novel, I can claim that it's finished when I've dealt out the last few facts on to the page. We arrive at 6 July 1535. Thomas More is executed. The paperwork is done; the head is spiked on London Bridge; his prayer book is examined for blood splashes and disposed of. And Henry VIII goes on his holidays.

In an orderly world, I would have gone on my holidays too, but the closing stages of a book don't, in my experience, allow that. First there's the post-book mope: a feeling of leaden inconsequence, a doomy so-whatishness, a tendency to emit hollow groans and hide from the light. Then there's the post-book cold, three days of sneezing and eye-watering that is, pop psychology tells us, a substitute for weeping; it's a form of mourning the lost characters, though heaven knows I'm glad to see the back of Thomas More, I couldn't bundle him to the scaffold quick enough. And this is a book with a sequel, and most of these people I'll be returning to; imagine the cold I'm going to have when the whole project's finished, another two or three years from now.*

The next phase is the twitchy stage, where you realise you haven't finished at all. If you write on the screen, as I mostly do, you have a programme of rolling revision, so that there's never a moment

---

* The Wolf Hall Trilogy was finally finished twelve years later.

where you sit down before a complete draft to make a reappraisal. Some parts of the book have been picked over endlessly, and there is one paragraph in this particular novel that is a personal worst for me; I think I have rewritten it at least forty times. I remember how my first published book came together, back in the prehistoric type-writer age; I wrote it in longhand, typed it, then typed it again. This now seems both hideously laborious and pathetically inadequate. Now I pick away endlessly, balancing and rebalancing a paragraph, tuning and retuning it, trying to find some hidden note within it – and worry, a little, whether I'm privileging style over content, and all this tinkering is a substitute for fresh thought.

The received wisdom among writers is that it is essential to appraise your work on paper. I don't disagree, but my experience is that on paper you make one set of corrections, but when you go to input them, you make quite a different set – the paper version shows up the problems, but not necessarily the solutions. Then you print it again, find another set of problems . . . and so it goes on. In the days when authors still argued about whether writing done on the screen was inferior (because too easy) there was a theory that 'no one does proper revision these days – they just move text about'.

There were legends about writers who, finding their editor hard to satisfy, had bought a ream of coloured paper, changed their type size, changed their font, altered the pagination, and resubmitted the book without altering a word – to meet, a week on, with a beaming editor delighted by all the changes. I have never met an author who has actually done this. But we all know a man who knows a man who has a friend for whom it worked a treat.

In the haste of writing, carried along by the current of your own story, you make, I find, split-second decisions of huge consequence. Then when the whole thing has come together, you chew your metaphorical pencil over tiny points. With a historical novel you begin checking up on yourself, knowing that you can't be proof against error, that no one can, and that there is seldom a version that everyone will sign up to; the past isn't like that. There's a certain kind of reader (they pop up at readings and festivals) who worries about the ethics of historical fiction, feels vaguely guilty about reading it, and would like the author to make it clear just which bits are made up, perhaps by printing them in red ink. Some fine authors hardly care about accuracy. I heard Penelope Fitzgerald say that she did her research after a book, not before. Didn't she get angry letters, asked a shocked member of the audience? Oh yes, she said, smiling. They tell me about the birds in the trees, she said; in no way could the hero, in such a place, in such a year, have seen or heard a collared dove! She had a certain way of smiling, which suggested a mind above ornithology, an imagination licensed for its own flights.

I wish I could command such serenity. My most shaming moment as a writer came when a novel was about to go to press and I realised I had sent my characters on the wrong rail route between Norfolk and London. I caught the pages just in time. I think of the letters I would have got. Years later, they'd still have been streaming in. I'd have had to strike back and say, well, there you are, if you want a railway timetable, don't consult a novelist. But my heart wouldn't have been in it. I'd have known I was at fault. I'd still be waking up in the night, more than ten years on, and wondering what on earth possessed me to send them via Ely.

My mind is now on the next book and the next lot of mistakes I have the capacity to make; and I begin to think of the delights, too, of another plot, another chance, another shot at getting it right. I am bowling along in a cab, on my way to a clinic to have a blood test, and my mind starts moving towards the later Henry VIII, and his poor health, and I wonder what it was like for his advisers to roll in for the morning strategy meeting and find him surrounded by his doctors. I take out my notebook and write: 'Basin of blood. Urine flask. Holy Grail?' Then it comes to me that if the cab crashes, and I'm found dead in the wreckage, people will think it is my shopping list.

Elizabeth Jane Howard

2016

In recent years Elizabeth Jane Howard, who was always known as Jane, has become famous for a quartet of novels known as the Cazalet Chronicles, which draw on her own family story and were adapted for radio and television. Tracing the fortunes of an upper-middle-class family, the quartet begins in 1937 and covers a decade; a fifth novel, *All Change*, skips ahead to 1956. The novels are panoramic, expansive, intriguing as social history and generous in their storytelling. They are the product of a lifetime's experience, and come from a writer who knew her aim and had the stamina and technical skill to achieve it. It would be rewarding if the readers who enjoyed the series were drawn to the author's earlier work, when her talent seemed so effervescent, so unstoppable, that there was no predicting where it might take her. From the beginning she attracted superlatives, more for the gorgeousness of her prose than for the emotional extravagance of her characters. Their laughter was outrageous, their weeping contagious, their love affairs reckless. But there was nothing uncalculated about the author's effects. From the first, she was a craftswoman.

Howard's first novel, *The Beautiful Visit*, won the John Llewellyn Rhys memorial prize. It is daunting to think that *The Long View*, so accomplished, so technically adroit, was only her second book. It begins in 1950, and each part draws us backwards through the life of Antonia Fleming, till we arrive in 1926, when we find her as a young girl about to be tenderly deceived, baffled and bullied into wifehood.

Despite early praise and attention, it was hard for Howard to make a living. She came from a background where the necessity was not much considered. In *The Long View*, Mrs Fleming's passport states her occupation as 'Married Woman'. In this world, men are not obliged to explain or account for themselves. Creatures endlessly to be placated, they look to mould a woman into a satisfactory, if not perfect, wife. Conrad Fleming seeks to mould Antonia. He is a man of unblemished conceit, immaculate selfishness. Young female readers today may view him with incredulity. They should not. He is faithfully recorded. He is the voice of the day before yesterday, and also the voice of the ages past.

Howard was born in 1923 to a family who were affluent, well connected and miserable. Her father and his brother were the directors of the family timber firm. They didn't do much directing; 'They just had a jolly nice time,' she said. They had earned it. Her father had enlisted at seventeen, survived the Great War on the western front, brought home a Military Cross. He was a warm father, but duplicitous and unsafe. Her mingled fear and fascination fuelled the Cazalet novels, which are less cosy than they appear. Her parents' marriage and their subsequent relationships, together with her own, provided a model of instructive dysfunction for almost every story she wrote. 'There were only two kinds of people,' thinks Conrad in *The Long View*, 'those who live different lives with the same partner, and those who live the same life with different partners . . .' It is one of many such jaundiced observations – pithily expressed, painfully accurate.

Howard's mother, Kit, was a disappointed dancer. She had given up her professional career for marriage. The dancer's world is so brutally testing that it's hard to say, in any particular case, whether such a choice was coloured by a suspicion of being not quite good enough. Second-rate young men went abroad, their CVs condensed into the acronym FILTH: Failed in London, Try Hong Kong. Women in retreat from their potential could choose the internal exile of marriage, and the results were often dingy. Kit does not seem to have liked her daughter. Perhaps she was jealous of her. Howard was a young woman of spectacular looks. Repeatedly in the novels, mature adults gaze in mingled envy and delight at the person least to be envied, an adolescent who is a writhing mass of uncertainties. Howard had little formal education, but she was a reader. And her piano teacher imparted something of great value: 'how to learn: how to take the trouble and go on taking it'.

Briefly, she became an actor. The Second World War blighted her career hopes. Like Mrs Fleming, she saw 'the value of lives rocketing

up and down like shares on a crazy stock market'. In such an atmosphere, decisions were taken quickly – there was no long view. She
was nineteen when she married the naturalist Peter Scott, then a
naval officer, aged thirty-two. The night before the wedding, her
mother asked her if she knew anything about sex, describing it as
'the nasty side' of marriage. Howard's daughter Nicola was born
during an air raid. It was a horrific experience. She knew to save it
up and use it later. When the war was over, she abandoned husband
and infant daughter, something the world does not readily forgive.
She moved into a dirty flat off Baker Street: 'a bare bulb in the
ceiling, wooden floors full of malignant nails . . . the only thing I
was sure of was that I wanted to write'.

There was another marriage, a brief one, to a fellow writer. Then
she became the second wife of Kingsley Amis, an acclaimed and
fashionable novelist. Jane wanted love, sexual and every kind; she
said so all her life, and she was bold in saying so, because it is always
taken as a confession of weakness. The early years of the Amis
marriage were happy and companionable. There is a picture of the
couple working at adjacent typewriters. It belies the essential nature
of the trade. Howard was strung on the razor wire of a paradox. She
wanted intimacy, and writing is solitary. She wanted to be valued,
and writers often aren't. The household was busy and bohemian. She
kept house and cooked for guests, some of them demanding, some
of them long-stayers. She was a kind, inspiring stepmother to Amis's
three children. The marriage was, as Martin Amis has said, 'dynamic',
but the husband's work was privileged, whereas Jane's was seen as
incidental, to be fitted around a wife's natural domestic obligations.

During those years she wrote a number of witty novels, full of
the pleasures of life, while enduring periods of deep misery. Her
husband was making money and collecting applause, but she kept
faith with her talent. Well-bred people did not make a fuss or make
a noise, her mother had told her, even when having a baby. That is
a prescription for emotional deadness, not creative growth. But if
pain can be survived, it can perhaps be channelled and put to work.
In her novels Howard described delusion and self-delusion. She
totted up the price of lies and the price of truth. She saw damage
inflicted, damage reflected or absorbed. She had learnt more from

Austen than from her mother. Comedy is not generated by a writer who sails to her desk saying, 'Now I will be funny'. It comes from someone who crawls to her desk, leaking shame and despair, and begins to describe faithfully how things are. In that fidelity to the details of misery, one feels relish. The grimmer it is, the better it is: slowly, reluctantly, comedy seeps through.

The journalist Angela Lambert has asked why *The Long View* is not recognised as one of the great novels of the twentieth century. One might ask why Howard's whole body of work is not rated more highly. It's true her social settings are limited; so are Jane Austen's. As in Austen's novels, a busy underground stream of anxiety threatens to break the surface of leisured lives. The anxiety is about resources. Have I enough? Enough money in my purse? Enough credit with the world? In various stories, Howard's characters teeter on the verge of destitution. Elsewhere, money flows in from mysterious sources. But her characters do not command those sources, nor comprehend them. Emotionally, financially, her vulnerable heroines live from hand to mouth. Even if they have enough, they do not know enough.

Their unarmed state, their vulnerability, gives them a claim on the sternest sensibility. Why should I care, some readers ask, about the trials of the affluent? But readers who do not care about rich characters do not care about poor ones either. Howard's novels can be resisted by those who see the surface and find it bourgeois. They can be resisted by those who do not like food, or cats, or children, or ghosts, or the pleasures of pinpoint accuracy in observation of the natural or manufactured world: by those who turn a cold shoulder to the recent past. But they are valued by those open to their charm, their intelligence and their humour, who can listen to messages from a world with different values from ours.

But the real reason the books are underestimated – let's be blunt – is that they are by a woman. Until very recently there was a category of books 'by women, for women'. This category was unofficial, because indefensible. Alongside genre products with little chance of survival, it included works written with great skill but in a minor key, novels that dealt with private, not public, life. Such novels seldom try to startle or provoke the reader; on the contrary, though the narrative may unfold ingeniously, every art is employed to make the reader at ease within it. Understated, neat, they do not employ what Walter Scott called 'the Big Bow-wow strain'. Reviewing Austen, and admiring her, Scott saw the problem: how can such work be evaluated by criteria meant for noisier productions? From the eighteenth century onwards, these novels have been a guilty pleasure for many readers and critics – enjoyed, but disparaged. There is a hierarchy of subject matter. Warfare should get more space than childbirth, though both are bloody. Burning the bodies rates higher than burning the cakes. If a woman engages with 'masculine' subjects, it has not saved her from being trivialised; if a man descends to the domestic, writes fluently of love, marriage, children, he is praised for his empathy, his restraint; he is commended as intrepid, as if he had ventured among the savages to get secret knowledge. Sometimes, perfection itself invites contempt. She gets that polish because she takes no risks. Her work shines because it's so small. I work on two inches of ivory, Austen said, ironically: much labour, and small effect.

Time has sanctified Austen, though there are still those who don't see what the fuss is about. It helps that she was a good girl, with the tact to die young; with nothing to say about her private life and her heart guarded from examination, critics had to look at her text. Modern women have less tidy careers. When Howard died in 2014, aged ninety, the *Daily Telegraph*'s obituary described her as 'well-known for the turbulence of her personal life'. Other 'tributes' dwelled on her 'failed' love affairs. In male writers, affairs testify to irrepressible virility, but in women they are taken to indicate flawed judgement. Cecil Day-Lewis, Cyril Connolly, Arthur Koestler, Laurie Lee and Ken Tynan were among her conquests; though of course, the world thought they had conquered her. Divorces and break-ups may damage the male writer, but the marks are read as battle scars. His overt actions may signal stupidity and lust, but the assumption is that at some covert level he acts to serve his art. A woman, it is assumed, does rash things because she can't help it. She takes chances because she knows no better. She is judged and pitied, or judged and condemned. Judgements on her life contaminate judgements on her work.

Though authors such as Virginia Woolf and Katherine Mansfield opened up a new way of witnessing the world, good books by women still fell out of print and vanished into obscurity: not just because, as in the case of male writers, fashion might turn, but because they had never been properly valued in the first place. In the 1980s feminist publishing put them back on the shelves. Elizabeth Taylor, after a period of neglect, has come back into fashion. Barbara Pym was neglected, rediscovered, consigned again to being a curiosity. Sometimes a contemporary writer has to hold up a mirror for us; we have learnt to read Elizabeth Bowen through the prism of Sarah Waters's regard for her. Anita Brookner's critical fortunes show that it is possible to win a major prize, be widely read and still be under-valued. For all her late success, and perhaps because of it, Howard's work is misperceived. Her virtues are immaculate construction, impeccable observation, persuasive but inexorable technique. They may not make a noise in the world, but every writer can learn from them. In teaching writing myself, there is no author I have recom-mended more often, or more to the bewilderment of students. Read her, is my advice, and read the books that she herself read. In particular, deconstruct those little miracles, *The Long View* and *After Julius*. Take them apart and try to see how they are done.

I can't remember the exact date I met Jane. It was at the Royal Society of Literature, in the late 1980s, at one of their meetings at Hyde Park Gardens. The RSL is lively now and based elsewhere, but in those days the gaunt premises, their lease shortening, seemed left behind by the world. Knowing the dust and decrepitude of the upper floors, the empty chill of the basement beneath, I was not awed by the grand neglected rooms, nor the grand neglected Fellows who stood looking out on to the terrace. Sometimes when you admire a writer you are disinclined to find out much about them. I must have seen photographs of Jane, but ignored them. My mental picture was of a small sinuous creature, with a gamine haircut and wide eyes like a lynx; someone who spoke in a dry whisper, if she spoke at all. The reality was quite different. Jane was tall and stately, with a deep, old-fashioned, actressy voice. She had the feline quality I had imagined, but it was leonine, tawny, dominant, not slinking nor fugitive. If she had purred, the room might have shaken. She was an impressive and powerful woman.

But in conversation, I found, she was kind and unassuming. She never forgot, in her fiction, what it was like to be a young girl, and she carried an ingénue spirit inside a wise and experienced body. She seemed self-conscious about the impression she created, and anxious – not to efface it, but to check and modify it, so as to put others at their ease. If they were not at ease, they could not show themselves and there would be nothing for her to carry away. She was interested in people, but not simply in a beady-eyed writer's way. When she took the trouble to make a friend of me, she also made a friend of my husband, who is neither an artist nor a writer. She dedicated her last published book to us, jointly. It seemed too much. She had given me years of delight and instruction, and I felt I had not repaid her. In those years I was short of energy for friendship, though she must have seen I was not short of capacity. Our work did not make much of a fit, and we appeared together just once, at a small bookshop event. She read beautifully. Her professional training shone through, her voice strong and every pause judged to a microsecond. But she read unaffectedly, smiling, with pleasure in the audience's enjoyment. I was happy that the Cazalet novels brought her new fans. As much as her style, I admired her tenacity. She was still writing when she died: a book called *Human Error*. I wish I had asked her which of the selection available she had chosen as her focus.

No doubt the best conversations are those that never quite occur. I sensed that we both lived in hope, and had frequently lived on it. I always felt there was something I should ask her, or something she meant to ask me. The morning after she died, I was one interviewee among many, talking about her on the radio. I was working in Stratford-upon-Avon, so used the RSC's studio. It was a last-minute, short-notice arrangement and I had only just learnt of her death, so I may not have been eloquent. But I saw her face very clearly as I spoke. She had acted in Stratford as a girl, and she would have liked what the day offered: the dark wintry river, the swans gliding by, and behind rain-streaked windows, new dramas in formation: human shadows, shuffling and whispering in the dimness, hoping – by varying and repeating their errors – to edge closer to getting it right. In Jane's novels, the timid lose their scripts, the bold forget their lines, but a performance, somehow, is scrambled together; heads high, hearts sinking, her characters head out into the dazzle of circumstance. Every phrase is improvised and every breath a risk. The play concerns the pursuit of happiness, the pursuit of love. Standing ovations await the brave.

If the Glance of a Woman Can Sour Cream

1990

If you look at cricket writing – I don't mean ghosted memoirs or workaday match reports, but the considered literature of the game – you see at once that its prevailing note is elegiac. The reason for this is not difficult to grasp. Cricket is the most ephemeral of arts. Blink, and you have missed some unique moment. Even a great actor can hope to reproduce his effects, because at least he will arrive again at the same place in his script, with the same line to say. But a batsman plays his stroke only once before it becomes history. A catch is in the air only long enough for you to see it (or not) before the moment of contact (or not) with the palm. There is television, of course, to purvey a second-hand cricket, distorted in time and scale; but your favourite videos wipe themselves out, you find. Only the inner eye can be trusted, and the feeling of belonging to the crowd.

I think it is because of the transience of cricket, its central sad fact, that the cricket-lover grows attached to cricket grounds. On a dark day you can wake up and mutter their names, like a charm, to bring fine weather: Sabina Park, Eden Gardens. The grounds are not inviolate, of course. Sometimes they concrete them over and build hypermarkets. But they cannot, we think, do that to Lord's.

I came to this game lately, or too late anyway to know much about it: unathletic, with no eye for a ball, no head for statistics, and, worst of all, female. Hence my experience of cricket is the experience of a series of exclusions – and mainly the exclusion from proper understanding that playing the game would have brought. Lord's, of course, by barring women from the Pavilion, except under certain special circumstances, perpetrates a most famous exclusion. It is one I cannot bring myself to feel very strongly about, though I wonder about the reasons for it. It is true that applications for MCC membership stretch into the next century, but that is no reason to keep out the female members of Middlesex CCC. One suspects the reasons are not administrative, but atavistic. It cannot be that these days gentlemen fear their view will be blocked by bonnets, or their concentration broken by gusts of piercing chatter about the servant problem or the price of beef. But if, as anciently believed, the glance of a woman can sour cream, it can probably warp willow, crack the pitch, cause umpires' fingers to twitch. Such ancient prejudice must be respected. Lord's must be taken as it is. The Pavilion has its special and masculine atmosphere, its comfortable austerity, its other-worldly air. There is no harm in preserving it for those who can enjoy it.* Debarred from a convocation of bishops, one can still pray.

Outside the ambit of privilege, Lord's is an affair of wet plastic seats and the terror of wheel-clampers. Middlesex members have their own room now, made out of part of Q Stand, with great windows that entrap a liquid green light; members will feel, no doubt, a little nostalgia for the time when they had more to complain about. Life outside the Pavilion has its pleasures. You can observe the strange rainwear and even stranger sunwear of the British. You can eavesdrop on conversations, and grow wiser thereby. (Women are supposed not to know how men talk when they're alone. At Lord's they think they're alone.) You can read other people's low newspapers over their shoulders, and be pleasurably shocked by them. You can indulge in the fascinated, horrified inspection of other people's food. And, if I had been in the Pavilion, I would never have seen the small child who, one Sunday a couple of seasons ago, tottered down the steps towards the barrier, held out his arms as if to embrace the fielding side, the umpires and both batsmen, and cried with a beatific smile, 'Daddy!'

True, you can do these things at any cricket ground; though the infant might be a one-off. But Lord's is special: even those who hang about on the fringes of the game, hoping to come back in the next life as a leg-spinner, find themselves consoled by the sense of place, touched by its atmosphere, drawn into the game by its effect on the

---

* In 1998 the members voted to admit women.

imagination. As I am a novelist, I could write many semi-meaningful, perhaps not wholly original things about the correspondences between cricket and fiction. Cricket – or any complex, but circumscribed and self-limiting activity – is far more like a novel than life is like a novel. So I can at least persuade myself, when guilt gnaws, that by watching cricket I am actually working, absorbing principles of form and structure and bearing professional witness to the strange machinations of fate.

It is quite usual to think of the game in terms of dramatic spectacle, but in fact a year's cricket, or a Test series, is even more like a novel than it is like a play. The number of characters is large. Their fortunes rise, fall, interweave. People who seemed likely to occupy a line or two decide to stick around and arrogate pages to themselves, perhaps whole strands of the plot. There are climaxes, some of which prove to be illusory. Mere names flower out into human complexity; blind chance plays its part. Just as, in a novel, the fortunes of the protagonist may hang by a thread, or turn on an absurdity, so may the fortunes of a team; and behind the events from hour to hour a certain pattern emerges, which may be discernible only several years on. In a season, you can run through most of the emotions that life produces, and see most of fiction's standard plots work themselves out.

Now, Lord's is the place to entertain these notions. There is a concentrated quality about that arena, a special intensity, a quality of intimacy; this intimacy and intensity touch the non-participants. When you stand in the Pavilion and look at the gate through which the players go out on to the field, a slight intimation of dread flutters behind your ribs, a weak vicarious stage fright. Could that entrance ever, for anyone, become perfectly routine? Possibly. People grow used to anything. But for a moment you can put yourself into the boots of the player who walks out, you can feel *what it might be like* – and Lord's has performed its trick, it has served its purpose. It has triggered the act of imagination which links together all players, alive and dead, all spectators, every umpire, every groundsman, every bat maker and programme seller, tea-lady and passer-of-the-hat, and puts them at the service of the game.

So then you begin to talk of mystique, of magic, as if the bricks and the grass had something special, though you know cricket is made of people, techniques, time and weather. Again, that pervasive feeling of sadness creeps in, as if beyond the scattered applause you discern the roaring of bulldozers, the fall of a civilisation; and it is true that when you discover cricket – if you are one of those people for whom there is a moment of discovery – you are sometimes seized by an irrational fear that it is too good to last, that it will be abolished by some vile government, or that you will be sent away to a country where they don't have it. But there is no real reason, of course, why cricket should induce melancholy. It is best to get out of earshot of what Robertson-Glasgow called 'the strangling fugues of senile jeremiads' and avoid the company of those who ridicule the modern game and are for ever reminiscing, about Lord's or any other ground.* The best cricket season, in fact, is always the season to come.

For this reason, I like to go past Lord's in winter. I like to be driven past and to catch in the gaps between the grey walls – which might be prison walls – glimpses not of grass but of steel, of meshes and barriers and walkways, the exposed spiny architecture of the stands: so that I can imagine it as a fortress in which is placed, for our own protection, all our virtues, enthusiasms and strengths, and all the best parts of the summer to come.

---

* R. C. Robertson-Glasgow was a medium-fast bowler whose career-best performance was at Lord's in 1924 when he took 9 for 38 for Somerset against Middlesex. He later became an acclaimed cricket writer.

At First Sniff

2009

In any department store in January there is a reliably comic sight – buyers trying to choose discounted perfumes by sniffing the necks of the spray bottles. Scent makes sense on skin, and only on skin. Why are we such fools about fragrance? Led on by lush advertising, seduced by editorial gush in magazines dependent on their advertisers, we abandon natural discrimination and distrust our own noses. Scents are not so much objects as performances, processes, but we lack a process for appraising them. Book critics can be savagely partisan, opera critics sniffy, and film critics make you choose to stay at home. Could you review a scent as you review these art forms? Yes, I would argue. One word, for example, would sum up Beckham Signature: illiterate. Mitsouko would need a volume of essays.

Where do they lurk, the perfume critics? There are scent blogs on the internet, often well informed. But most bloggers write carelessly, and, in such a subjective matter, some precision is needed. Hope for the enthusiast arrived late last year with *Perfumes: The Guide* by Luca Turin and Tania Sanchez. The authors are in love with the subject, but they are sharp and funny. What women have always wanted to know is what scent drives men wild; researchers have the answer, say Turin and Sanchez, and it's bacon. Picking up the cue, Burger King recently launched Flame, a body spray that smells of 'flame-broiled meat'.

But it won't be the scent of Whopper that moves fastest off the shelves in the shopping frenzy of the early new year. Even before Christmas, celebrity scents such as Kate Moss's Velvet Hour could be found on sale at half price. Its name is reminiscent of what Guerlain long ago called *L'Heure Bleue* – that time of day, the *cinq à sept*, when cocktails are stirred and the discreet Frenchman would slip away to meet his mistress before going home to *dîner en famille*. Velvet Hour will do nicely for sex, but don't expect fidelity; ten thousand women smell like this. It's not really a twilight scent; you're more likely to spray it on before midnight, and lurch home at dawn in a dubious minicab with your shoes in your hand and panda eyes, so that its weary amber dry-down competes with the reek of spilled liquor. An initial sweetness of freesia gives way to incense, and throughout the evening it hits you with blasts of blatant patchouli, so by 3 a.m. you want to crawl out of your skin to get away. It's genius, in its way – the persona it layers over your own, the story it tells. Such a sad little tale, though. A medieval theologian, had he possessed one of Kate's tacky-looking blue flasks, could have used it to explain sin – so warm for the first half-hour, and afterwards so banal.

There are dull women, desperate for distinction, who wear the same fragrance all the time. They may be monogamous, but manufacturers have other ideas; they will change the formula and not admit it. Scent is bound in with snobbery; you may like some downmarket celeb fragrance, but what will you say if someone asks you what you're wearing? If this Christmas you were given Daisy by Marc Jacobs, you'll find it a pretty, amenable floral, the kind of scent that people describe as 'very nice'. But narrow your eyes and ask yourself this: why do they see you as the kind of woman who wants a bottle with three plasticky flowers on top? Do they think you're sweet but not very bright? Compare it with Stella McCartney's Stella Rose Absolute, which is, admittedly, more expensive. You could buy this scent for someone you don't know well; that's not faint praise. Its dark, chunky bottle could hold an expensive men's fragrance; it has a gentle citrus drift that cuts through sweetness, and a light amber note for balance; it's a lovely summery scent that doesn't layer a persona over your own, just makes you pleasant to be around. It's modern, fresh and natural; it gives rose enthusiasts enough to think about, but won't alienate less floral types.

I didn't much want to like it; what's Stella to me, I say, with the world-weary shrug of one who's nearer in age to her father. But that's why we buy scent, to meet our younger selves, or older selves, or the selves we could be. So, I can know I'm grown up at last, I want to like scents from houses who were making them when I was a girl and only had the personality and the cash for Apple Blossom. Estée Lauder's Sensuous startles me at first with dolly-mixture sugar, then a fleshy rush of premature intimacy. Thirty minutes, and woody notes creep through, bringing an enticing memory of peeping into the wardrobes of elegant ladies; and no, the note isn't mothballs. Perhaps it needs a bit of body heat to potentiate it – it has to work hard on a misty winter day – but three hours on, it shows surprising stamina, and it's spicy, interesting and adult, which is just what I want from Estée Lauder.

And if there's something here that still doesn't convince, perhaps my own skin is to blame? It's said that parfumers have stabilised their formulations so that they don't vary, except in their top notes, from skin to skin, but you may have every reason not to believe them. Comme des Garçons 888: do the designers mean to unleash this bully, that slaps you around the head with a big blast of coriander? With wear, its manners become milder. But still, this is what to give someone if you mean to be remembered and don't care how. The creators say they wanted to produce the olfactory equivalent of gold, but how they get from concept to the substance itself is a mystery. It will suit someone; I'm happy to meet her, after her Asbo is lifted. Perhaps I'm unfair. In eight hours of wear – which is what you really need to be sure – I might accommodate it. But equally, it might eat me.

Who's in charge here? It's a question scent raises often. Are you wearing it, or is it stalking you? Will it faithfully follow you everywhere? Unscrewing the surprisingly frail plastic cap of Prada No. 3 Cuir Ambre, I say to myself with a big happy smile, a dog is not just for Christmas, a dog is for life. You don't wear this, it pursues you; it's a gorgeous, insistent, leather scent with amber notes, smokily soft. It comes in a small nondescript bottle, its white label has small black type, it's plain as you like; it has no sprayer, because you're going to put this on drop by drop, learn it and learn to live up to it. You could perhaps mistake it for other leather scents, but what you couldn't mistake is its pedigree and its expense. If you can't afford it, just test it; you'll remember, and maybe add it to the ingredients of a better life. Perfumes like this reorient us when life is grey. The ideal scent keeps the wearer interested, evolves with him or her; you can't 'solve' it in one go like the plot of a bad detective novel. You need a perfect structure, like Chanel No. 5, to keep you safe; and then from time to time you need to subvert expectations, with something that cuts against your style and even your gender. Scent is a demanding art. It privileges what is subjective, skin-close. So, seek out what no one else is wearing. Keep a notebook. Scrub off your mistakes. New year is a time for experiment, redefinition, and perfume is a fine place to start.

The Joys of Stationery

2010

When narratives fracture, when words fail, I take consolation from the part of my life that always works: the stationery order. The mail-order stationery people supply every need from royal blue Quink to a dazzling variety of portable hard drives.

Their operation is error-free, sleek and timely. In fact, it's more than timely: it's eerie. I have only to call out to my spouse: 'Let's be devils and get bubble wrap,' and a man with a van is pulling up outside. Where I live – in the remote fastness of Woking – the morning post comes at three, my parcels go to the right number but another street, and on one occasion, when a hapless person tried to send me a present, Amazon denied that my address existed.

So this speedy stationery service looks spooky. Maybe they've implanted a chip in my brain, and soon I'll only need to think about my order, and coloured lights will flash at their HQ, and the laden vehicle will be screaming in my direction. I can sit and read the stationery catalogue for hours on end, marking its pages with the very Post-it notes it has previously sold me in twelve-pad packs. I often wish I could review it: it's crisp and perfectly achieved, and what it lacks in originality it makes up for in the graceful, coded compression of what it offers the dazzled reader.

If you think there's little on offer but paperclips, think again: you can buy biscuits, buckets and bayonet-fitting bulbs. Sometimes I fantasise that all my furniture has been destroyed in a cataclysm, and I have to start again with only the stationery catalogue. My entire house would become an office, which would be an overt recognition of the existing state of affairs. Sustained by a giant jar of Fairtrade instant coffee, I could spend whole days putting up Kwik-Rak shelving and assembling 'modular reception seating' into long, worm-shaped sofas. They don't sell beds – so much for office romance – but who would want to rest if you could spend the night printing out masterpieces at your ergonomic melamine workstation, and weighing them at dawn on a 'solar parcel scale', which takes up to twenty kilos and comes with a three-year warranty?

Writers displace their anxiety on to the tools of the trade. It's better to say that you haven't got the right pencil than to say you can't write, or to blame your computer for losing your chapter than face up to your feeling that it's better lost. It's not just writers who muddle up the tools with the job. The reading public also fetishises the kit.

We have all heard the tale of the author who is asked, 'How do you write?' and answers in an exquisitely modulated Nabokovian-Woolfian-Dostoevskian discourse, only to be floored by the flat supplementary: 'I meant, Mac or PC?' There is persistent confusion between writing and writing things down, a confusion between the workings of the writing mind and the weight of the paper scribbled over. 'How many words do you do per day?' people ask, as if the product unwinds in a flowing, ceaseless stream of uncriticised, unrevised narrative, and as if the difference between good and bad writers is that the good ones have no need to do it again. Almost the opposite is true; the better you are, the more ambitious and exploratory, the more often you will go astray on the way to getting it even approximately halfway right.

So while it's on its way to going right, you take comfort in buying new notebooks. Buying them in foreign cities is a good way of carrying away a souvenir. That said, *le vrai* Moleskine and its mythology irritate me. Chatwin, Hemingway: has the earth ever held two greater posers? The magic has surely gone out of the little black tablet now that you can buy it everywhere, and in pastel pink, and even get it from Amazon – if they believe your address exists. The trouble with the Moleskine is that you can't easily pick it apart. This may have its advantages for glamorous itinerants, who tend to be of careless habit and do not have my access to self-assembly beech-and maple-effect storage solutions – though, as some cabinets run on castors, I don't see what stopped them filing as they travelled. But surely the whole point of a notebook is to pull it apart, and distribute pieces among your various projects? There is a serious issue here. Perforation is vital – more vital than vodka, more essential to a novel's success than a spell checker and an agent.

I often sense the disappointment when trusting beginners ask me how to go about it, and I tell them it's all about ring binders. But I can only shake my head and say what I know: comrades, the hard-spined notebook is death to free thought. Pocket-size or desk-size, it drives the narrative in one direction, one only, and its relentless linearity oppresses you, so you seal off your narrative options early.

True, you can cross out. You can have a black page to show for your hour's work. Moleskine's website shows a page from a Sartre novel that is almost all crossing-out. But deletion implies you have gone wrong, whereas perhaps you are not going wrong, just generating material in an order the sense of which has yet to emerge. What you need is not to obliterate errors, but to swap them around a bit; then, often enough, they start to look less like errors than like the wellspring of new hope. For myself, the only way I know how to make a book is to construct it like a collage: a bit of dialogue here, a scrap of narrative, an isolated description of a common object, an elaborate running metaphor which threads between the sequences and holds different narrative lines together.

You must be able to loop back on yourself, and to be able to arrange the elements of which your story consists in an order that is entirely flexible. In the end you must make a decision, but why not postpone it till the last possible point? Because once you have made the commitment, what you have written starts to look right. It gains a brutal ascendancy over you. It's easy to revise sentence by sentence, but very difficult to recognise and accept, at some late stage, that the whole structure of a book went wrong because you let your stationery boss you about.

But these days, you'll say, doesn't everybody write on screen? True, but you can still, by premature decision-making about how you store your text, set up for yourself the equivalent of the hard-spined notebook. Files are not flexible unless their maker is. The good news about the computer is its endless scope for procrastinative fussing. Is this a nice font? Shall I rename all my files? Learn some new software?

At twilight, though, when the day's work is on pause, swivelling in my executive chair (variable seat height and *de luxe* lumbar support), I never reminisce about dear old WordStar 2000 back in the 1980s. I think instead about other trades I might have pursued, with different and privileged stationery: that pink tape, for instance, that barristers use to tie up their bundles.

Do they still, at the Treasury, use treasury tags? Could I use one? The shades of evening make me mourn lost paper sizes; when did you last see a ream of foolscap? The late author David Hughes once sent me a few sheets, and I'm keeping them carefully, for when I have a long, thin story to write.

The Books I Will Never Write

2008

Novels wear authors out, a clever man said to me recently. Writers get to a point where they're too weary to furnish another book, to start a new plot creaking forward on its course, to set up the characters and push them around the page. 'You seem to have plenty of energy,' he said. Was he pleased for me? He was an amiable man, so let's say he was, but he was also an academic, and what are authors to academics, except more work? It can be chilling to hear teachers of the novel talk about their subject. They may speak with intelligence and insight, but there is also something coldly businesslike in the way they sever product from producer. When you go to the hairdresser, bits of your person are snipped on to the floor, and a junior pushing a brush comes and sweeps them away. Those clippings are no longer owned by the living person who brushes herself down and slouches from the salon. In a similar way, your books can be alienated from yourself, become dead things; once they were part of you, but now they are just the messy and potentially irritating material for someone else's daily chore.

Yes, I have energy. But there is a shelf in my house, an invisible one, stacked with the books I'm never going to write. Every novel that goes to the printers has a dozen shadow selves. Vital decisions are taken before the first word goes down on paper. Sometimes they're brooded on, sometimes made in a split second, but the tone is set early, and the author gets a glimpse – it may be no more – of his or her intention. Then, on every page, further decisions are taken. This character comes to the fore, this one drops away. This piece of information is imparted, or held back. The story could be quite otherwise.

It is historical fiction, especially, that breeds variations on itself.

Which versions of the past to believe? Which sources to rely on? Then there are the people you meet by the way – incidental characters to you, but worth a whole novel. Recently I reviewed a biography of Philippe, the revolutionary Duke of Orléans, who had ambitions to take the French throne from his doomed cousin, Louis XVI, and set himself up as a constitutional king. What the book needed, I suggested, was more portraits of Philippe's glamorous mistresses. I wasn't being entirely silly. These women were power-players. Félicité de Genlis was a writer who shaped Philippe's political thinking, such as it was. Grace Elliot was mistress to the Prince of Wales before taking a short hop across the Channel; where did her loyalties lie? Agnès de Buffon was managed into her mistress-ship by Félicité, having been previously the mistress of Félicité's own husband, the Comte de Genlis. Grace Elliot, who wrote an entertaining but atrociously unreliable memoir, was the subject of Eric Rohmer's 2001 film, *The Lady and the Duke*; but Rohmer produced a soft-focus portrait of a Lady Bountiful who rescued distressed aristocrats from the guillotine. My Grace – the Grace in the novel I'm not going to write – is as cold as a knife blade and a spy for William Pitt.

Then there was the mysterious child Pamela, said to be a little English orphan, taken in and reared as if she were their own by Félicité and the Duke. Probably she was their own child; educated on an ideal plan devised by Félicité, she turned into a marketable beauty. She could easily have married a young revolutionary and ended up, within a couple of years, as a widow or a victim of the guillotine. Instead, she married Lord Edward Fitzgerald, who fell in love with her at first sight; Pamela closely resembled Elizabeth Linley, his dead mistress, who had been the wife of the playwright Sheridan, having eloped with him when she was twenty. Lord Edward became an Irish revolutionary, dying of his wounds in prison after the uprising of 1798; he left Pamela with three children, and the legacy of a traitor's wife. Such passionate people they were, so heartfelt, sincere; it's only in summary that they sound like characters from *Les Liaisons Dangereuses*. Have them, with my compliments, and the compliments of history; I'm not going to write their stories.

If so much aristocracy palls, take Margot Montansier. As a teenage girl, Margot was taken to Martinique by a lover, who is said to have abandoned her there; somehow, she got herself back to France, became an actress, then manager of a string of provincial theatres. From her base in Versailles, she became a close friend of Marie Antoinette, but when the Bastille fell, she was on the road to Paris to become a good revolutionary; then, in turn, a counter-revolutionary. A steely chancer with a penchant for men many years her junior, she married at sixty-nine, and lived to be ninety. As I write, the Théâtre Montansier, still prospering in Versailles, is staging *Le Mariage de Figaro* – that is to say, not the opera, but Beaumarchais's original play. Now, Beaumarchais, there's a story . . .

Some of these people have biographies to themselves, some are footnotes in those biographies. Any one of their threads, teased out, would weave a beautiful fiction. They're good ideas, each with a vast hinterland, and I can hardly keep my greedy hands off them. But I am fifty-six. Let's say four, five years to get from intention to finished product . . . like Margot, I shall have to live till I'm ninety and never retire.

There is a problem; as the clever man suggested, invention can exhaust itself, and yet some authors go on, their talent vitiated, dried out; a veneer of contemporary detail fails to disguise that they are living in the past. Can this be avoided by living in the past on purpose – by sticking to historical fiction? I doubt it, and I don't mean to try, despite the blandishments of the dead.

My notebook now is full of the people I've met in reading *Letters and Papers, Foreign and Domestic, of the Reign of Henry VIII*. I am enthralled by Pelygrene Sagbut, who at New Year 1531 gave the King a present valued at twenty shillings, a pair of perfumed velvet gloves. Who was Pelygrene, and did he have his memorable name embroidered across the knuckles? The same year brings a mention of 'Catalina, the Queen's slave and bedmaker. She married a Moor, cross-bow maker at Valdeyzcarria.' What can her story possibly be, and who has the energy and imagination to set Catalina free?

Women Over Fifty – The Invisible Generation

2009

On Sunday last I had a shock, waking up to find that my novel *Wolf Hall* was 2–1 favourite to win the Man Booker prize. It was almost as much of a shock to be described in the press (repeatedly) as 'the 57-year-old novelist from Glossop'. I've never been coy about my age, so I don't know why the truth should take me aback when set down in print. It made me laugh; I just couldn't think how I got to be fifty-seven. Do men ask themselves this question – how did I get to be thirty, to be fifty, to be ready for my bus pass? Or is it, as I suspect, just women who can't fit the puzzle together, who feel that a reference to their age is not neutral but a sort of accusation?

We've heard so much recently about the disappearance of older women from our TV screens, and about the difficulties, for older woman, of negotiating public life. Every media picture of the rare and glowing Joanna Lumley feels like a challenge; why can't you all be like that, why does she look like a princess and you look like a potato? Many women of a certain age, when a peer of ours is flashed up on screen, run an instant comparison: is it worse to have her jowls than my wrinkles?

Celebrities trade on their image; perhaps it's mean to snigger at their Botox, but their faces are their fortune and they set out their stalls to attract envy. Not so women politicians. We know we're being unforgivably shallow when we judge them on their looks, but we do it all the same. I have been known to say, regarding Ann Widdecombe, that you get the face you deserve. And my mother, who is the same age as Margaret Thatcher, could never see her in her heyday without remarking, 'I wish that woman would go home and look after her neck.'

When I was a child – in Glossop and district – no one supposed that women over fifty were invisible. On the contrary, they blacked out the sky. They stood shoulder to shoulder like penalty walls, solid inside corsets that encased them from neck to thigh, so there was no getting past them: if you'd rushed them and butted them with your head, you'd have careened off, sobbing. They stood in bus queues muttering dark threats against the driver. They stood in line in the butcher's shop, bloodied sawdust clogging their bootees, and amid the loops of sausages and the tripes they talked about My Operation – they boasted of their surgical crises, as Coriolanus boasted about the wounds he got for his mother country. Almost every one of these women was called Nellie, and the others were called Cissie. Why these names are synonymous with effeminate weakness I cannot imagine. They wore vast tweed coats or impermeable raincoats in glass-green, and their legs were wrapped round and round with elastic bandages, so they took up plenty of space in the world; to increase their area they stuck their elbows out. They had baskets and brown paper parcels. They said, 'that child wants feeding/slapping/its bonnet on', and younger women jumped to it. They'd been nowhere but they'd seen everything. They never laughed with you, they laughed at you. They did not use face powder but scouring powder. They could add up grocery prices at calculator speed, and they never took their eyes off the needle of the grocer's scale. Show them the ageing heroines of today, and they'd have snorted – they were frequent snorters. Helen Mirren, Joanna Lumley they'd have called picked wishbones. They'd have sneered 'bleached blonde' at Madonna, while grimly rating those sinewy arms; she looks as if she could scrub a step or mangle a bucket of wet sheets.

At fifty plus, these women ran the world and they knew it. When I was a child, I assumed that I would grow into one of them, and have a stubby umbrella which I'd use to point at the follies of the world. I never imagined I'd still be parting with money at make-up counters, or that I'd be racing off for a blow-dry when threatened with a photographer. I assumed I'd wear my hair in a round perm, the colour of steel and as tough. Think of the time I'd save; vanity is such a consumer of the hours. With the spirit of my foremothers inside me, I would write even bigger novels, fortified by pies, and any impertinent reviewers would get a clip around the ear. They

344

were tough as the soles of their shoes, these grannies, and they often lived to great ages; but when one of them died, her funeral stretched right down the main road, and a week later her daughter had stepped in to replace her, packed like an iron bolster inside her ancestral coat.

They were not, these women, peculiar to my birthplace; their geographical spread was the whole British isles. Except for their accents, they were interchangeable in their pride. They were un-yielding, undaunted and savagely unimpressed by anything the world could do to them. We could revive their dauntless spirit, instead of dwindling, apologising and shrinking from the camera lens; though one problem, I fear, is that you can't get the corsets these days.

The Other King

2009

Sometimes you buy a book, powerfully drawn to it, but then it just sits on the shelf. Maybe you flick through it, the ghost of your original purpose at your elbow, but it's not so much rereading as re-dusting. Then one day you pick it up, take notice of the contents; your inner life realigns. This is how I came to George Cavendish's book *Thomas Wolsey, Late Cardinal, His Life and Death*. It is one of the earliest of English biographies, but it reads as much like a novel as like a life story, though it was written before the novel was invented.* That's not to say it's made up; Cavendish, who was a gentleman usher in the great cardinal's entourage, was a first-hand witness and as accurate as he could be. What makes it startlingly modern is that events are conveyed through anecdote and dialogue, with turning points and dramatic highlights clicked into place; its language is direct and inventive; and the story it has to tell is fascinating, poignant and full of unexpected twists and turns. While attending on a political genius, the devoted attendant was nourishing a small writing genius within himself.

I bought my copy about ten years ago, second hand, a Folio Society edition with a faded grey cover. I hoped I might write a book about the Tudors, but this purchase was the first step towards a project I knew was distant. I had spent many years living in the eighteenth century. I had written about the French Revolution and about England and Ireland in the same era. I didn't know if I had the nerve or stamina to time-travel backwards. I knew whose career I would

---

* Cavendish's *Thomas Wolsey* was first printed in the early 1640s, having remained in manuscript for nearly a century, whereas Daniel Defoe's *Robinson Crusoe* (1719) is often considered to be the first novel.

like to follow – Henry VIII's minister Thomas Cromwell. I couldn't resist a man who was at the heart of the most dramatic events of Henry's reign, but appeared in fiction and drama – if he appeared at all – as a pantomime villain. What attracted me to Cromwell was that he came from nowhere. He was the son of a Putney brewer and blacksmith, a family not very poor but very obscure; how, in a stratified, hierarchal society, did he rise to be Earl of Essex?

I needed to know Wolsey to understand Cromwell. But what was Wolsey? A great scarlet beast, I thought, a pre-Reformation priest who belonged to the old world, not the fierce, striving, dislocated society I wanted to write about. I thought of him as a means to an end; I imagined I would dispose of him quickly to get to the meat of the plot. Then the day came when I opened Cavendish's *Life*; the author leaned out of the text and touched my arm, keen to impart the story of the man whose astonishing career he saw at first-hand: 'Truth it is, Cardinal Wolsey, sometimes Archbishop of York, was an honest poor man's son . . .'

Wolsey's father was a butcher – a fact which the cardinal's detractors never let him live down – but he was able to send his clever son to Oxford, where he was known as the boy bachelor because he took his BA at fifteen. This prodigy – and Cavendish's pride shines out of the page – rose quickly in the service of Henry VII, who sent him (a trial run for a promising young cleric) on a diplomatic mission to the court of the emperor, in Flanders. Three days afterwards, Wolsey appeared at morning mass. What, not gone yet? the king asked. Wolsey replied, 'Sir, if it may stand with Your Highness's pleasure, I have already been with the emperor, and dispatched your affairs . . .' Richmond Palace to London, barge to Gravesend, horseback to Dover, boat to Calais, horseback again, one night with the emperor, Calais by the time the gates opened at dawn, the Channel again, and back at Richmond in time to get a good night's sleep before handing over the emperor's letters: two and a half days, door to door. The old king was left in 'a great confuse and wonder'. He didn't realise that tides and post horses and border guards all bowed down to the whims of the future cardinal. This 'good speedy exploit' was nothing to what Wolsey would accomplish when the young Henry VIII came to the throne.

On 'a plain path to walk in towards promotion', Wolsey decided to 'disburden' his young, pleasure-loving king of affairs of state. 'He had a special gift,' Cavendish says, 'of natural eloquence . . . to persuade and allure all men to his purpose', and his head was 'full of subtle wit and policy'. He became Archbishop of York, Bishop of Winchester, papal legate, Lord Chancellor. The papacy eluded him, but in England he was *alter rex* – the other king – and Europe knew it: French diplomats blanched when he raised his voice. He was, as Cavendish admitted, 'haughty'; but he seems also – and this is what strikes the reader – a man of great warmth and personal kindness. He was a superb organiser of everything from wars to banquets, and he didn't do it wholly by charm; Cavendish was at his elbow one morning when Wolsey rose at four and 'continually wrote his letters with his own hands' till four in the afternoon, 'all which season my lord never rose once to piss, nor yet to eat any meat'. After this feat of concentration, the cardinal heard mass, ate dinner and supper together to save time, and went to bed early, ready for another lucrative and thoroughly gratifying day. Patron of artists, architects and poets, Wolsey lived 'in fortune's blissfulness'. Henry VIII's early years were, Cavendish says, 'a golden world', and the cardinal was its golden centre, with his household of 500 attending him around the clock, 'down-lying and up-rising': Cavendish knew them all, from the 'master cook who went daily in damask, satin or velvet', to the 'twelve singing children and sixteen singing men' to Master Cromwell, the ebullient, dry-witted and slightly mysterious lawyer with whom the cardinal spent long hours in secret talks. You imagine Cavendish, sweating slightly, ear glued to the keyhole.

Then suddenly, in the autumn of 1529, the golden world was finished. Wolsey stood by and watched the dukes of Norfolk and Suffolk ransack his London palace of York Place, and strangers swarm in to itemise his clothes, his silver, his linen. The king took everything. The cardinal was left with what he stood up in. Henry had no patience with failure, and Wolsey had failed to get him an annulment from his first marriage so that he could marry Anne Boleyn, whom Cavendish calls the 'gorgeous young lady'. Anne, 'having both a very good wit and also an inward desire to be revenged on the cardinal', joined forces with the noblemen who had hated

Wolsey for years because he 'kept them low'. On the dreadful day when York Place was taken apart, Cavendish travelled upriver with his master as he fled to his palace at Esher. Esher was a gentleman servant's nightmare: unaired, understaffed, ill-equipped. There, on All Hallows' Day, Cavendish saw 'Master Cromwell leaning in the great window', a prayer book in his hand. 'He prayed not more earnestly than the tears distilled from his eyes.' Now Cavendish understood how bad things were. He had never before seen Cromwell pray (or cry) – and he never saw him do either again. A moment, and the lawyer pulled himself together; he was going to London, he said grimly, 'to make or mar'.

The cardinal's people began fighting a rearguard action, encouraged by the king's double-dealing. Emotionally dependent on Wolsey, torn between minister and wife-to-be, Henry blew hot and cold, sending loving messages but standing by while bills were brought into Parliament accusing the cardinal of a long list of serious crimes. Was Cavendish superb in a crisis? We know, at least, that his writing was. Holding his readers in suspense, he diverts us with an anecdote: 'Now I will tell you a certain tale . . .' He talks to us directly, earnestly, as if looking into our eyes: 'You must understand this . . .' He leaves us poised and anxious at Esher, while flipping away to the action elsewhere: 'Now let us return again to Master Cromwell, to see how he has sped since his last departure from my lord . . .' Wolsey's enemies wanted him to go north, to his episcopal see in York. Every day he managed to stay near the court was a triumph; at any moment the king might change his mind, recall him. The Duke of Norfolk, boiling with panic, threatened Cromwell: 'show him that if he go not away shortly, I will, rather than he should tarry still, tear him with my teeth'. Cromwell conveyed the message to the cardinal: 'Marry, Thomas, quoth he, then it is time to be going . . .'

George Cavendish was with Wolsey in his uneasy exile and at his sudden arrest. The young earl of Northumberland arrived at the cardinal's lodging a day's ride from York: 'trembling . . . with a very faint and soft voice, laying his hand upon his arm', he said, '"My lord . . . I arrest you of high treason."' Cavendish followed the cardinal into his private room, barring the door to the invaders. Wolsey told him, 'Look at my face – I am not afraid of any man alive.' The journey south began, the cardinal under guard, towards the Tower. 'I know what is provided for me,' he said; he did not think he would evade his enemies again. Then he fell ill. Cavendish served the cardinal his last meal this side of heaven, a dish of baked pears. He was with him at Leicester Abbey, at his agonising death. Natural causes or poison? If poison, self-administered? Cavendish saw him laid to rest in a coffin of plain boards. He had washed his body for burial; beneath his 'very fine linen Holland cloth', this most vain, flamboyant and worldly of men was wearing a hair shirt. Ahead of Cavendish was a sticky interview with the king, who wanted to know what the cardinal had said in his last moments. He kept Cavendish on his knees for an hour while he questioned him. Whatever the cardinal's parting shot, Cavendish keeps it even from the reader. 'I have utterly denied that I ever heard any such words.'

Cromwell scrambled out of the wreckage of Wolsey's fortune. His enemies said the cardinal had given him a magic jewel which gave him power over Henry, but more likely Wolsey had given him a list of hints for dealing with a petulant, volatile and increasingly costly monarch. Henry soon regretted the hounding to death of his cardinal; he wanted him back, just as years later, after executing Cromwell, he wanted him back, too. The 'gorgeous young lady' had her head severed, wives came and went, some violently, Henry died swollen and monstrous and perhaps a little mad. Meanwhile George lived quietly in the country. He broke his silence only in 1554, when Henry's Catholic daughter Mary was on the throne. Shakespeare plundered Cavendish's manuscript for his play *Henry VIII*, and not just for that; when Cavendish refers to an ambitious man as 'hungry and lean', you can hear Will's brain whirring.

Cavendish's more famous brother, William, married Bess of Hardwick. For many years, oddly, it was supposed that William had written *Thomas Wolsey*. But it is all George's work: his beady eye for detail, his intimacy, his eye for emotional truth and his rolling, robust phrases. He functioned as a textbook for me: *Learn to Talk Tudor*. I reread him till the rhythm of his prose was natural to me. He made me love his cardinal as he did, so that when I came to write him, he wouldn't stop talking; I wanted Wolsey in every scene, and no more than Cavendish did I want to stand by, useless and wretched, at his miserable deathbed. The cardinal had planned a marble sarcophagus for himself, but now, I understand, it is at St Paul's, with the bones of Lord Nelson rattling inside it. Wolsey might have been amused. He was always seasick on his rapid Channel crossings. When Cromwell the blacksmith's son was granted a coat of arms, he adopted the cardinal's emblem, the Cornish chough; for ten years after Wolsey's death, the little black birds tweeted defiantly in the teeth of the Duke of Norfolk and all Wolsey's other begrudgers. But it was his servant Cavendish who gave him his lasting monument: 'And thus ended the life of my late lord and master, the rich and triumphant legate and cardinal of England, on whose soul Jesu have mercy! Amen.'

Anne Boleyn: Witch, Bitch, Temptress, Feminist

2012

As a small child I remember being told by a solemn nun that Anne Boleyn had six fingers on one hand. In the nun's eyes, it was the kind of deformity that Protestants were prone to; it was for Anne's sake, as everyone knew, that Henry VIII had broken away from Rome and plunged his entire nation into the darkness of apostasy. If it weren't for this depraved woman, England would be as holy as Ireland, and we'd all eat fish on Friday and come from families of twelve.

Anne Boleyn wasn't exactly a Protestant, but she was a reformer, an evangelical; and the sixth finger, which no one saw in her lifetime, was a fragment of black propaganda directed at her daughter, Elizabeth I. In Elizabeth's reign it was the duty of beleaguered papists to demonstrate that the queen's mother had been physically and spiritually deformed. Hence, not just the extra finger but the 'wen' on her throat, which supposedly she hid with jewellery: hence the deformed foetus to which she was said to have given birth. There is no evidence that this monster baby ever existed, yet some modern historians and novelists insist on prolonging its poor life, attracted to the most lurid version of events they can devise.

Anne Boleyn is one of the most controversial women in English history; we argue over her, we pity and admire and revile her, we reinvent her in every generation. She takes on the colour of our fantasies and is shaped by our preoccupations: witch, bitch, feminist, sexual temptress, cold opportunist. She is a real woman who has acquired an archetypal status and force, and one who patrols the nightmares of good wives; she is the guilt-free predator, the man-stealer, the woman who sets out her sexual wares and extorts a fantastic price. She is also the mistress who, by marrying her lover, creates a job vacancy. Her rise is glittering, her fall sordid. God pays her out. The dead take revenge on the living. The moral order is reasserted.

Much of what we think we know about Anne melts away on close inspection. We can't say for certain what year she was born, and there are many things we don't understand about how her violent death was contrived. Holbein created incisive portraits of Henry VIII and his courtiers, but there is no reliable contemporary likeness of Anne. The oval face, the golden 'B' with the pendant pearls: the familiar image and its many variants are reconstructions, more or less romantic, prettified. The fact that some antique hand has written her name on a portrait does not mean that we are looking at Henry's second queen. Her image, her reputation, her life history is nebulous, a drifting cloud, a mist with certain points of colour and definition. Her eyes, it was said, were 'black and beautiful'. On her coronation day she walked the length of Westminster Abbey on a cloth of heaven-blue. Twice in her life at least she wore a yellow dress: once at her debut at court in 1521, and again near the end of her life, on the frozen winter's day when, on learning of the death of Henry's first queen, she danced.

When she first appeared at court she was about twenty-one years old, lithe, ivory-skinned, not a conventional beauty but vital and polished, glowing. Her father Thomas Boleyn was an experienced diplomat, and Anne had spent her teenage years at the French court. Even now, Englishwomen envy the way a Frenchwoman presents herself: that chic self-possession that is so hard to define or imitate. Anne had brought home an alluring strangeness: we imagine her as sleek, knowing, self-controlled. There is no evidence of an immediate attraction between Henry and the new arrival. But if, when she danced in that first masque, she raised her eyes to the king, what did she see? Not the obese, diseased figure of later years, but a man six feet, three inches in height, trim-waisted, broad-chested, in his athletic prime: pious, learned, the pattern of courtesy, as accomplished a musician as he was a jouster. She saw all this but above all, she saw a married man.

Within weeks of his accession to the throne in 1509, the teenage Henry had married a pre-used bride. Katherine of Aragon had originally been brought to England to marry his elder brother. But some four months after the marriage, Arthur died. For seven years

Katherine lived neglected in London, her splendid title of Dowager Princess of Wales disguising her frugal housekeeping arrangements and dwindling hopes. Henry was her rescuer; he was in love with her, he told everyone, this was no cold political arrangement. Katherine was the daughter of two reigning monarchs: educated, gracious and regal, she had been trained for queenship and saw it as her vocation. She had been a tiny auburn-haired beauty when she came to England. Seven years older than Henry, she was shapeless and showing her age by the time Anne glided on to the scene. Katherine had many pregnancies, but her babies died before or soon after birth. Only one child survived, a daughter, Mary; but Henry needed a son. Private misfortune, by the mid-1520s, was beginning to look like public disaster. Henry wondered if he should marry again. Cardinal Wolsey, Henry's chief minister, began to survey the available French princesses.

It was only in theory, and for humble people, that marriage was for life. The rulers of Europe could and did obtain annulments, for a price, from sympathetic popes. Henry failed not because of papal high principles, but because a series of political and military events put Katherine's nephew, the Emperor Charles, in a position to thwart him. While his canon lawyers and courtiers cajoled and bribed, sweating blood to make Henry a free man, the king had already come up with an unlikely replacement for Katherine. We don't know exactly when he fell for Anne Boleyn. Her sister Mary had already been his mistress. Perhaps Henry simply didn't have much imagination. The court's erotic life seems knotted, intertwined, almost incestuous; the same faces, the same limbs and organs in different combinations. The king did not have many affairs, or many that we know about. He recognised only one illegitimate child. He valued discretion, deniability. His mistresses, whoever they were, faded back into private life.

But the pattern broke with Anne Boleyn. She would not go to bed with him, even though he wrote her love letters in his own effortful hand. He drew a heart and wrote his initials and hers, carving them into the paper like a moody adolescent. In time favours were granted. She allowed him to kiss her breasts. Her 'pretty duckies', he called them. She had made the man a fool.

This, at least, was the view of most of Europe. No one dreamed that Henry would put aside a princess of Spain for the daughter of a mere gentleman. Nor could the English aristocracy credit what was happening. Long after the break with Rome, they remained revolted by Boleyn pretensions and loyal to Katherine and the pope. Anne did have the backing of a powerful kinsman, the Duke of Norfolk; her father had been lucky enough to marry into the powerful Howard clan. But for some years, the situation was deadlocked. There were two queens, the official one and the unofficial one: the king was sleeping with neither. Wolsey had been fortune's favourite, but failure to obtain the divorce cost him his career. He was exiled from court; though he died a natural death, it was under the shadow of the axe. Anne moved into his London palace. Still, she kept Henry at a distance. She was, and is, credited with serpentine sexual wiles, as well as a vindictive streak that ruined anyone who crossed her. The truth may be more prosaic. Henry had decided at some point that Anne was the woman who would give him a healthy son. He wanted that son to be born in wedlock. It may have been he who insisted on self-control, and Anne who simmered and fretted.

The man who cut the knot and gave Henry his heart's desire was Thomas Cromwell, the pushy son of a Putney brewer. Cromwell had been in Wolsey's service and narrowly survived when the great man fell. In his forties, he was a bustling, jovial man with a plain face and a busy and ingenious mind. In a land in thrall to tradition, Cromwell was in love with innovation. One of his innovations was the Church of England. If Rome won't give you a divorce, why not grant your own? Since new things had to be disguised as old things, Henry stated he was, and always had been, lawful head of the English Church. Soon his subjects would be required to take an oath recognising this fact.

In the autumn of 1532 Henry and Anne crossed the Channel. They stayed in Calais, an English enclave, and held talks with the French king. The weather turned foul and the English fleet was trapped in port. Henry and Anne went to bed together, and married hurriedly in a private ceremony when they were back on English soil. Anne was six months pregnant when she was crowned queen. Henry was so sure that the child would be a boy that he had the proclamations written in advance, 'prince' proudly blazoned. When a daughter emerged, extra letters had to be squashed in. But Henry was not downhearted. 'If it is a girl this time, boys will follow.'

The psychology of the relationship between Henry and Anne is impenetrable at this distance, but contemporaries did not understand it either. The courtship lasted longer than the marriage. They quarrelled and made up, and if Anne thought Henry was looking at another woman she made jealous scenes. She was untrained in the iron self-control that Katherine had exercised. She thought, perhaps, that as Henry had married her out of passion and not out of duty, she would keep him enthralled until the arrival of a son made her status safe. But whereas duty is sustainable, passion seldom is. The discarded Katherine lived far from London, under house arrest, humiliated by her circumstances, unrelenting in her animosity to the woman who had displaced her and (as she thought) corrupted her good husband. Anne, for her part, was said to be plotting to poison both Katherine and her daughter Mary.

Aware of the reputation she trailed, Anne tried to limit the damage. She was a Bible reader, who told the women in her household to dress and behave soberly; cultured, she was a patron of scholars, and keenly interested in the reform doctrines that Henry himself would not embrace. But as Goodwife Anne, she didn't convince. Had there been lovers before the king? Gossip was rife. She surrounded herself with young men who vied for her favour. The conventions of courtly love mix with something very modern, very recognisable: a married woman's wish to test out how her powers of attraction are surviving the years. Henry was not a great lover, after all. Or so it emerged later, in a court of law. In the queen's private rooms, the young men and his wife were laughing at him: at the songs he wrote, at his clothes, and at his lack of sexual prowess and technique.

At some point in 1535 Anne had quarrelled with Thomas Cromwell. Later, in Elizabethan times, it would be suggested that the idealist Anne was in dispute with the money-grubbing minister over the fate of the monasteries. The dissolution was soon to begin, and the smaller institutions were now in the king's sights. Anne, the story goes, wanted to conserve the monasteries as educational facilities.

At best, this is only a partial reason for their split. Cromwell might well have retorted that the defence of the realm was more urgent. The outside world remained consistently hostile to Henry's romance and to his new title as Supreme Head of the Church in England. No regime in Europe accepted his actions, and Rome could not be reconciled. Even Martin Luther would not give the second marriage his blessing. A sentence of excommunication hung over Henry. If implemented, it would make England a pariah nation; any Catholic ruler would be authorised to step in and help himself to the kingdom.

Anne had not risen in the world as a solitary star; she trailed an ambitious family with her. By 1535 Cromwell was outshining them all, accumulating offices of state. Anne had been his patron, but he had outgrown her, and by the spring of 1536 she had lost her value to him. It was Katherine's death that changed everything. The old queen's end was lonely. Probably cancer killed her, though rumours of poison spread when the embalmer found a black growth clinging to her heart.

When the court heard that Katherine was dead, there was celebration. It was premature. On the day of the funeral Anne miscarried a male foetus. It was her second miscarriage at least. It seemed she was no good to Henry for breeding purposes. And in the eyes of those who did not recognise his second marriage, the king was now a widower, ready to make an advantageous European match. Katherine dead, Cromwell could patch the quarrel with the emperor. This would lift the threat of crippling trade embargos, and the threat of invasion. Anne was in Cromwell's way, but he could not have acted against her alone. He might have circumvented her, discredited her, sidelined her; but it was not his business to kill her. It was Henry who was disenchanted with the woman he had waited for so long. It was spring, and he was in love again.

What was it, this business of being 'in love'? It was still rather strange to the sixteenth-century gentleman, who married for solid dynastic or financial advantage. The love poetry of the era attests to skirmishing in the sexual undergrowth, to histories of frustration and faithlessness; Anne's group of friends was full of part-time versifiers and one of her circle, Thomas Wyatt, made an indelible impression on English literature. But Wyatt's tone is often cynical or disappointed. There was love and there was marriage and they seldom coincided. His own marriage was wretchedly unhappy. Anne's uncle, the Duke of Norfolk, allegedly beat his wife. But the king had higher expectations. In Katherine's time he had written a song which said: 'I love true where I did marry.' He expected to sing this song again, and this time to Jane Seymour.

One of Anne's ladies, Jane was the self-effacing daughter of a thrusting family. She was not especially young, nor beautiful, nor witty. What did Henry see in her? The Spanish ambassador sniggered that 'no doubt she has a very fine enigme'; it is an interesting way to refer to a woman's sexual organs. The ambassador did not think Jane could be a virgin after so long at Henry's court, but Henry did not doubt that this dull little woman had been waiting all her life for a prince's kiss. Anne has usually been characterised as clever and Jane as stupid, a compliant doll manipulated by her brothers and the papist faction at court. There is another interpretation possible; that Jane had observed, assessed and seized her chance, acting with calmness and skill. Whatever her true character, her exterior was soothing. Henry and Anne had worn their quarrels like jewels. But Henry was weary. His superb athlete's body was failing him. An accident in the spring of 1536 brought to an end the jousting career in which he had taken such pride. His temper was short. His weight was increasing. He had always worried about his health, and now he had reason. In a moment of despair, he had said: 'I see that God will not give me male children.' Jane cheered him up wonderfully; her family were numerous, and she was expected to breed.

If Cromwell devised the manner of Anne's downfall, the responsibility for it rests squarely with Henry. He was not a simple man who could be misled by his ministers. It is true he could be pushed and nudged and panicked; four years later, after Cromwell's execution, he would try to put the blame elsewhere, claiming that he had been misled. But the king was the man who gave the orders and as far as we know he never regretted Anne, or looked back, or mentioned her again after her death. The ruin of the Boleyns was sudden, compacted into a period of three weeks. Behind-the-scenes activity suggests that Henry explored the possibility of annulling his marriage and letting Anne retire, to the country or a convent; this was the way he would get rid of his unwanted fourth wife, Anne of Cleves.

But nothing in Anne's history or nature suggested she would agree to a quiet withdrawal. Like Katherine, she would go to war, and Henry did not have the patience to wait for Jane. When the arrests began, panic possessed the court. Anne's ladies, we can assume, rushed to denounce her in an effort to save themselves. Anne was not liked. On a personal level she was high-handed and difficult. She had alienated her powerful uncle, the Duke of Norfolk. Without the king's affection she was nothing. No one but her immediate family could be expected to help her. Her father did nothing, and her brother, George Boleyn, was soon locked up himself, accused of an incestuous affair with her.

Seven men were taken into custody. One of them, a nonentity, was quietly forgotten and quietly released. Another, the poet Wyatt, was Cromwell's friend. He may have saved himself by giving a statement against Anne, and no charges were made, though he was held for some time. Of the five men who would die, four had nuisance value to Cromwell; the other was collateral damage. They were personally close to the king, and this is what hurt Henry so much; the charge, which he appeared to believe, that Anne had been sleeping with his best friends.

When Anne was arrested and taken to the Tower she began to unravel; she talked wildly about her co-accused, repeated the words she had exchanged with them; desperate to make sense of her situation, she detailed public quarrels, the jealousies and infighting within her circle. Every word went back to Cromwell. He may not have had a case till Anne built it for him. Accustomed to brinksmanship, Cromwell had reached out to some unlikely allies in recent weeks: the papists, the old families who resented the Boleyns. They thought they were using him to bring Anne down, and that they could ditch him afterwards. He knew they were serving his purposes, and had every intention of ditching them.

Anne was not charged with witchcraft, as some people believe. She was charged with treasonable conspiracy to procure the king's death, a charge supported by details of adultery. It was alleged she had discussed which of her lovers she would marry after the king's death. The clear implication was that his death could be hastened. Only one of the men confessed: Mark Smeaton, a musician. In

Henry's England, gentlemen were not tortured. Mark was not a gentleman. But if he was physically ill-treated, no one saw the damage; Cromwell was frightening enough, even without a rack.

Anne's supporters hate anyone who says so, but it is possible that she did have affairs. The allegations seem wildly implausible to us, but clearly did not seem so at the time. It is said that the details of the indictments do not stand up to scrutiny, that Anne could not have been where she was alleged to be on this date or that. But this misses the point. If Anne was not where everybody thought she was, that did not count in her favour. If she had risen from childbed to meet a lover, that showed her a monster of lust. It is the incest allegation that seems lurid overkill. But the sixteenth century did not invest incest with especial loathing. It was one of a range of sinful sexual choices. In the days when brothers and sisters seldom grew up together, genetic attraction no doubt occurred more frequently than it does in the nuclear family. If the allegations were true, Anne's conduct was, contemporaries agreed, abominable. But they did not assume her innocence. Led by love or lust, people will do anything. Look what Henry had done.

The Duke of Norfolk presided over his niece's trial. Later Cromwell, who liked worthy opponents and had respected Katherine, would commend the intelligence and spirit with which Anne defended herself. But her 'lovers' had already been tried and convicted, and if they were guilty, Anne must be. Henry brought in the Calais executioner to behead his wife with a sword. He may have groaned as he disbursed the man's vast fee, but the expert was worth his price. Anne's death was instantaneous.

Her head and her body were placed in a discarded arrow chest and buried in the crypt of the chapel at the Tower. But her black eyes were open wide and fixed on the future, hypnotising later generations as they did Henry. Today, we are still scrapping over the how and the why of her rise and fall. The narrative of her destruction, though partial, is vivid and terrifying. 'I have only a little neck,' she told the Constable of the Tower. And, he reported, she put her hands around her throat. And laughed.

How I Came to Write *Wolf Hall*

2012

'Show up at the desk' is one of the first rules of writing, but for *Wolf Hall* I was about thirty years late. When I began writing, in the 1970s, I thought of myself simply as a historical novelist; I can't do plots, I thought, so I will let history do them for me. I had an idea that, after the French Revolution was done and dusted, Thomas Cromwell might be the next job. Blacksmith's boy to Earl of Essex – how did he do it? The story seemed irresistible. I thought someone else would write it.

The 500th anniversary of Henry VIII's accession fell in 2009. Dimly aware of this, but not yet focused, in 2005 I proposed to my publisher a novel – just one, mind – about his great minister. Still, no one had told the story. The Tudor scholar G. R. Elton had established Cromwell as a statesman of the first rank, but Elton's work had done nothing for his popular image. Holbein's portrait shows a man of undistinguished ugliness, with a hard, flat, sceptical eye. In *A Man for All Seasons*, he is the villain who casually holds another man's hand in a candle flame.

Biographies of him are cut up into topics: 'Finance', 'Religion' and so on. He seemed not to have a private life. It wasn't that I wanted to rehabilitate him. I do not run a Priory clinic for the dead. Rather, I was driven by powerful curiosity. If a villain, an interesting villain, yes? My first explorations challenged my easy prejudices. Some readers think I've been too easy on Cromwell. In fact, it's possible to write a version of his career in which he is, at worst, the loyal servant of a bad master.

The deaths of Thomas More and Anne Boleyn can be laid at the king's door. In the end, this was not the story I chose to write. In my interpretation, Cromwell is an arch-plotter, smarter than Henry though not meaner. He had plenty 'stomach', said his contemporaries: not a reference to his embonpoint, but to his appetite for whatever life threw at him. He was, as John Foxe said, 'given to enterprise great matters'. New wives, new laws, the split with Rome, the reformation of the Church, the filling of the exchequer: there seemed no limit to his massive, imperturbable competence.

When I sat down to write at last, it was with relish for his company. The title arrived before a word was written: Wolf Hall, besides being the home of the Seymour family, seemed an apt name for wherever Henry's court resided. But I had no idea what the book would be like, how it would sound. I could see it, rather than hear it: a slow swirling backdrop of jewelled black and gold, a dark glitter at the corner of my eye. I woke one morning with some words in my head: 'So now get up.' It took a while to work out that this was not an order to get the day under way. It was the first sentence of my novel.

Wolf Hall attempts to duplicate not the historian's chronology but the way memory works: in leaps, loops, flashes. The basic decision about the book was taken seconds before I began writing. 'So now get up': the person on the ground was Cromwell and the camera was behind his eyes.

The events were happening now, in the present tense, unfolding as I watched, and what followed would be filtered through the main character's sensibility. He seemed to be occupying the same physical space as me, with a slight ghostly overlap. It didn't make sense to call him 'Cromwell', as if he were somewhere across the room. I called him 'he'. This device, though hardly of Joycean complexity, was not universally popular. Most readers caught on quickly. Those who didn't, complained.

After I had written the first page I was flooded by exhilaration. I am usually protective of my work, not showing it to anyone until it has been redrafted and polished. But I would have liked to walk around with an idiot grin, saying to the world: 'Do you want to see my first page?' Soon the complexity of the material began to unfold. So many interpretations, so many choices, so much detail to be sifted, so much material: but then, suddenly, no material, only history's silences, erasures. Until a late stage, what would become a trilogy was still one book. It was only when I began to explore the contest between Thomas Cromwell and Thomas More that I realised I was writing the climax of a novel, not merely another chapter. The facts of history are plain enough, but the shape of the drama was late to emerge, and the triple structure later still. In my mind, the trilogy remains one long project, with its flickering patterns of light and dark, its mirrors and shadows. What I wanted to create is a story that reflects but never repeats, a sense of history listening and talking to itself.

Unfreezing Antique Feeling

2009

'You are the only woman alive,' claimed an irritated friend, 'who still uses cotton handkerchiefs. Everybody else makes do with Kleenex.' It's nice to be distinguished for something, even if only for the quantity of your laundry. I admit it, they all have to be washed and ironed and stacked in a box, and it's not a very twenty-first-century thing to be doing; if I wanted to be extra-provoking, I could dab them with lavender like a Victorian great-aunt. My excuse is this: I used to be a great weeper. And it's bad enough, in company, to be inexplicably lachrymose and blotchy, without strewing sodden tissues on the ground.

It was never personal setbacks that made me cry. It wasn't pain, or Hollywood weepies, or the misfortunes of my friends, or the television news, or cosmic despair; it was a view, a prospect, a picture in a museum, or some pinprick contact with the past – one of those moments when history dabs out a pointed fingertip and the nail sinks straight through your skin. I have cried in many art galleries, and aroused the suspicion of the curators. I once cried at Ullapool, because I was overwhelmed by the idea of 'north'. I cried the first time I visited Haworth, because I had suddenly glimpsed the narrow graveside nature of the Brontës' lives. I used to apologise and claim it was my hayfever, because it is terrible to be thought sensitive; people at once make plans to take advantage of you. And gradually, the friction of contact with the world thickened my skin and dried my eyes. I didn't cry much after I was thirty-five, but staggered stony-faced into middle age, a handkerchief still in my bag just in case.

A couple of weeks ago I visited a house in Hackney, looked after by the National Trust. I'd been thinking about it for some while but saved up the visit till I was ready to write it into my new novel. It was built in 1535 for Ralph Sadler, chief bag-carrier to the Tudor minister Thomas Cromwell. Ralph was about twenty-eight when he established himself in what was then a pleasant, healthy suburb. He would soon be promoted to Henry VIII's privy chamber, being (unlike Cromwell, his master) a gentleman born. The son of a minor official, Ralph had grown up in Cromwell's household. He was tough, cautious, clever and, surprisingly for his time, a man of some integrity. When the great ship Cromwell finally sank in the summer of 1540, Ralph was not one of the rats. He sustained his career without blackening the name of his former master. He served the ageing Henry, served his son Edward, retired from public life during Mary's reign and came back under Elizabeth. He was still in harness in 1587, at the trial of Mary, Queen of Scots.

In his house the National Trust has a treasure box that children can raid for dressing-up. There are puppets of Henry, and of Thomas Cromwell and Mary Stuart, though they don't have detachable heads. You can wear a hat like Ralph's, or put on Mistress Sadler's headdress and pretend you're the lady of the house, in charge of the great chamber and the parlour and the fine expanse of linenfold panelling, the best outside Hampton Court. Ralph must have been wealthy already when he built Bricke Place, as it was known then. His long career was sure-footed to an exemplary degree, and he only ever once did a foolish thing: turning his back on the advantageous marriages he could have made, he married a nobody for love. His wife was called Ellen or perhaps Helen, or possibly Margaret Barre; Tudor history is like that. She was, or possibly was not, an obscure relative of Cromwell's. Some sources – but they are suspect – said she was a laundress. She had married a man called Matthew Barre, who gave her two, three or maybe four children, before vanishing. A few years on, Ellen considered herself free, and when Ralph fell for her she didn't say no. They had nine children, seven of whom survived, and Ralph could never wait to get home to his family. He had to apologise to Henry, explain why his wife could not take up an appointment at court; she was 'most unmete', as she could never be a lady.

The inevitable happened; one day at the height of Ralph's success, Matthew Barre turned up, boasting around the London taverns that he was married to Sadler's wife. It took a private Act of Parliament to settle the matter, and save the seven children from being declared illegitimate. No one knows what happened to Barre; presumably he was paid off, and vanished for a second time. When Ralph Sadler died at the age of eighty, he was said to be the richest commoner in England. His monument is in the church at Standon in Hertfordshire, where he built an opulent country house; his papers are safe in the archives. What he owned and prized is now lost, except for inventories: his Turkey carpets, his ivory chessmen, his five hangings depicting the tale of 'Tobie and his dog'. The rooms at Hackney are furnished with miscellaneous goods from elsewhere, which illustrate the house's long afterlife as a merchant's house and as a school. It is interesting, in an impersonal way. It is the best we can do.

But down in the cellar are the real traces of the past, like the building's flesh and blood: Tudor bricks, small rosy bricks, made right on the building site from the earth near Hackney Brook. This is Ralph's house in process, in the spring of 1535, when the soft bricks were tipped from their wooden moulds on to straw and left to dry before firing in a kiln. The workmen have marked some bricks with an X, to show that they are the tenth, or maybe the hundredth. There are other marks, dots and whorls; they could be crude signatures, or good luck charms. In one of the bricks a blade of grass, blown on a spring breeze, is caught in outline like a fossil. Another brick, still wet, was trampled on by a dog.

Fond though I am of Sadler, I managed to get around his house without a sniffle, and with a certain sensible correctness; I have spent much time with historians this summer, and never seen one of them cry. But it was when I saw the grass stalk, the dog's pawprint, that I began to sense the spring of 1535, when Thomas More was still alive and pearls were still warm on the neck of Anne Boleyn. It was then that the shock of the past reached out and jabbed me in the ribs. They were as alive as I am; why can't I touch them? Grieved, I had to stuff my fingers in my mouth, fish out my handkerchief, and do what a novelist has to do: unfreeze antique feeling, unlock the emotion stored and packed tight in paper, brick and stone.

A Letter to Thomas More, Knight

2018

My dear More . . . but here's the first problem. How do I address you? Sir Thomas? St Thomas? Lord Chancellor? I can't just call you Thomas. Half the men in England are called that. Anyway, I don't feel that kind of easy warmth, though one of your modern biographers says that most people who work with you end up liking you. Liking you, disliking you, it shouldn't matter – not to sober historians. But when we see your portrait we respond to you as a man – sad, distinguished, ageing, fiercely clever. It gives us a privileged view, as if we are with you in your chapel or writing closet: a way of looking that pierces the fog of misrepresentation, but allows us to see you with respect and in the light of the mercy we all need. Face to face, we can't deny your flawed humanity. And if we admit to yours, why not ours?

Objectivity is impossible. The waters were muddied long since, by early accounts contrived with one eye on fast-track sainthood. When your son-in-law Will Roper wrote your story, it was routine to make a Life into what it ought to have been, and it's notable how some of your opinions firmed up, in the twenty years after your death. Fortunately, we don't have to rely on second-hand reports from another generation. You talk, you write, you sit and look at Hans Holbein: Hans Holbein looks at you.

He sees a vulpine genius. (I like foxes, I mean well.) You are engaged, vital, ready to smile or snap out an impatient remark. Intellect burns through pale indoor skin, like a torch behind a paper screen. Concentration has furrowed your brow, the effort of containing multiple ironies. When you practised as a lawyer, you used to let your gown trail off one shoulder; admirers copied you, making carelessness a cult. You've not shaved to meet the painter.

No time, and you'd like to be thought above such niceties; you're not vain, unless such nonchalance is a vanity in itself. Everything is in your lineaments – past and future – a whole eloquent biography.

As a little boy, you carried your books to St Anthony's School on Threadneedle Street. At six in the morning you sat down to chant your Latin, sharing a bench with other scholars from the City of London: the sons, like you, of lawyers and prosperous tradesmen. Then you joined Archbishop Morton's household, seeing close up how an astute and powerful churchman governed the realm. It's there, at Lambeth Palace, that you first emerged as a prodigy, a boy who will go far.

Oxford next; you're fourteen. Then back home to the City, to serve your apprenticeship to the law. Ahead of you, a seat in Parliament, and the friendship of our pleasant and energetic young king: promotion to the royal council, and finally – after you help pull Tom Wolsey down – to the post of Lord Chancellor. You always pretend to fight shy of honours. Nobody's fooled. Your heart may tell you that you crave homespun. But your hands were always ready to slide into those red velvet sleeves. Your humility is of the kind that bows the neck to receive a chain of office. The Tudor rose sits proudly on a puny chest. One never thinks of you as robust – just as a nimble man at his best fighting weight.

It's hard to be a politician and a saint. George Orwell (there's a man who might interest you) said that every life, viewed from the inside, is a series of defeats. I would amplify that, say it is a series of enforced compromises, slippages from our own standard: shabby little sins. In the hope of countering them, you contemplate a life radically different from the one you finally choose. You imagine you could turn away from the world, be a priest. You spend time with the monks of the Charterhouse, praying with them, watching their austere routines. Their lives are isolated, rough. They live in community but contrive hardly to meet. They stink like otters, people say, from their diet of fish. Almost alone among the orders, the Carthusians need no reformation; they have never derogated from their ideal of poverty, of solitude.

But you decide, your friend Erasmus tells us, that you cannot sustain that life. You must marry. You have studied enough theology to equip you to give a series of public lectures on St Augustine. You know you are drawn to what the saint calls 'stinging carnal pleasure'. You don't want to be a bad priest. You think you can be a good husband. Does guilt fret and scratch you, like the knots in your penitential jerkin of hair? Better to marry than to burn, as St Paul says. It's possible to do both.

Yours is not a face that suggests an easy temper. Holbein shows us contained tension, willed constraint, subdued passion about to break out. Perplexed, you ask yourself, what should I do? How can I serve flesh and spirit? The point about our human nature is that we must go to work on it. Why do we live? We live to die: that's what the Church tells us. You are a sharp, capable man of affairs, ready with an anecdote, a joke: worldly, urbane. But we must, as you write in your prayer book, 'set the world at nought'. We must be ready to leave the city for our inner desert. You write many books: polemics, histories, self-justifications. You make Utopia, an imaginary island; its chief town, London's shadow.

You marry twice. Proud of your family, you have Hans paint them, three generations clustered around you. You offer open house to wandering scholars. Friendship is one of your talents. You look like a man keen and merciless in argument, one who takes a deep and knowing pleasure in discomfiting his opponents. When Hans takes your likeness, in 1527, it's hard to see the 'lowliness and affability' a contemporary noticed seven years back. Is a dialogue always a contest that it is urgent to win? As letters from Europe bring news of splits and feuds among the faithful, you begin to think so. But when the portrait is made, you are still the 'man for all seasons'. Your friends must envy your domestic comfort: your music, your garden, your household pets. Do they know you whip yourself? Admittedly, the Church approves such practices. You're not alone in them. But is it a little extreme? Old-fashioned? Unnecessary? Your years of 'sad gravity' are coming. Life will afflict you soon enough.

I expect that when Hans came in to make his sketches, you knew what you wanted. You were a man attentive to your own image. Holbein is not the kind of painter who goes fishing for a man's soul. His eye is meticulous, his technique formidable, and his concentration fixes on the telling details of the surface his subject chooses to show the world. A painter knows the art of concealment, and why one might choose to practise it. If Thomas Cromwell, sitting across the fireplace from you, wishes to be shown as a thickset plebeian with the intellectual curiosity of a boiled pudding, then Hans will give him the satisfaction. Only later you will know, and the world will witness, the lethal speed at which that man can move.

Hans has placed a curtain behind you. It hints at what is still undisclosed. When I remember you – and I am sure I do – as our swift-talking host at our after-supper debates in the 1520s – you were the first to laugh, the first to be angry, about the absurdities and exactions of the clergy. We thought of you as reform-minded, even irreverent. But now you are growing frightened, even by your own past work, and fear corrupts and coarsens you. You attack your enemies – Martin Luther most especially – in the language of the gutter. You have admired intellectual daring, but chiefly in yourself; you fear other people's ideas are wild beasts, marauding in the streets and savaging the souls of simple people.

By 1530 – by which time you are ensconced as Lord Chancellor – the terms of the debate have hardened. You no longer rely on witty persuasions, but on more brutal methods. The king wants to cast off the queen. He says he is head of the Church in England – he, not the man in Rome. And the words of the Scriptures (in what you think are false translations) are debated not from pulpits but in alehouses, in the street. The Englishman wants to talk to his God directly. The honey of discourse has turned to the poison of heresy. Satan is under the supper table and he is about to kick it over.

Six people died, burned as heretics, during your two and a half years as chancellor. A modest death toll for such ferocious times? But you must also answer for the wider destruction: the dubiously legal detentions, the household raids. Suspects had their businesses ruined, their health wrecked, their families ripped apart. You were proud of your part in this. You thought you were saving Christendom. You thought diversity in opinion would lead to fatal weakness. You closed your eyes in prayer, and you heard the Turks and the heathens at the gate.

This causes posterity a problem. Something else is concealed by the curtain: your reputation. Sir Thomas, I advise not turning around: do not scoop that curtain aside, because you won't like what we have made of you. Your own partisans, after you were safely dead, made you more papalist than the Pope. They were using you, but at least they understood your world view. Your later admirers have made you a liberal icon, a martyr for freedom of conscience. They see in you certain secular virtues that you would have despised as vices. You were not tolerant and would have thought it shameful to be so. You did not believe that a man's own conscience should act as his chief moral guide. His guide should be the Church, her traditions, her practices, her authority: the consensus that holds Christian souls together. It is for this cause you die.

By and large, we do not understand this appeal to authority, to the majority opinion. We have to lie about you a little in order to like you, and some people treat any criticism of you as if it were heresy in itself. They are touchingly loyal to the simplifications of their schoolmasters, and they don't want their certainties disturbed. 'Burn heretics?' they say. 'More was not alone. Surely, that's just what they did in those days?'

But we can't simply say that the practices of your contemporaries absolve you. Thomas Cromwell has blood on his hands, but then he doesn't set himself up as a saint. And Henry does what rulers do: he kills to keep the state safe, to maintain his power. You were his good councillor once. When you resigned, he said he would be your good lord still. Two years on, he finds you have been ungrateful. That dangling rope in your portrait is a *memento mori*.

What the artist put behind the curtain – in 1527 we still can't see it – is what will destroy you, before a decade is out: circumstances and will. Your will, your slippery and subtle intellect, against Henry's will. Surely, from the inception, you know Henry will win? Not the moral game, perhaps. But you said it yourself, in your book on

Richard III – kings' games are 'for the most part played on scaffolds'. Henry wants you to swear an oath to say he is Supreme Head of the Church in England. Every public person must take it. It is a commitment to the new order, to a nation independent of Rome. Your old companions, your fellow councillors, advise you to swear. The clergy conform, the members of Parliament too. Why should you be the naysayer? The king is patient, but in the end your lodging is the Tower.

Your wife, Lady Alice, doesn't understand why you're destroying yourself. Come home to Chelsea, she urges you. To the warm house, the library, the orchard 'where you might in the company of me your wife, your children and household be merry'. Thomas Cromwell, the king's new right-hand man, wants you to be merry too. No advantage accrues to him from your death. Your change of mind would be a coup for him: it would make the king happy.

He wants you to sign a piece of paper, that's all. But he can't wear you down. You've been in the Tower for a year, and you're so lonely you might as well be a Carthusian. You tell your family to take the oath; do as I say, not as I do. The man of 'angel's wit and singular learning' is getting shabbier by the week. You are afraid they might hurt you, put pressure on you in that way. July 1535: the weather is closing in. So wet, typical of these cheerless summers. Thomas Cromwell somehow managed to arrange for the sun to come out for the coronation of Anne Boleyn, but two years have passed since then, the king still has no male heir, God is not looking England's way: the climate of opinion has darkened.

You will not die silent. That's another of posterity's misperceptions. In your months of detention you have been careful not to incriminate yourself, not to give your reasons for refusing the oath – at least, you will not give them in any official context. But after the court's verdict, you'll speak out. You'll say why you're dying: for what has always been believed, and always understood. For obedience to the Church, for self-surrender. If we don't follow the logic of your beliefs, we can see you were sincere in holding them. (To your discredit, you never conceded that to your opponents.) You have steeled yourself to face the worst the state can do. You don't know how you will die. Dishonourably, slowly, at the hangman's chosen

372

speed? Or the honourable, and allegedly quicker, death by the axe? You hope Henry will be merciful. He used to be merciful. You used to think you knew him. You counted on too much.

One more thing, and then we must part. In the days before your trial, you'll have visitors in your room at the Tower. Your fate is still not sure, and so they've come to take your books away; it's a last turn of the screw, a nasty, well-calculated piece of psychological pressure. But still, your heart leaps at the prospect of company. Admittedly, it's not the company you'd choose. The party is led by Richard Rich, the Solicitor General, a man about whom you're persistently rude. And with him is Richard Southwell, one of Cromwell's cronies, with his weak disdainful features. Still, as Hans would tell you, he can't entirely help his face.

Rich is polite, even friendly. He draws you into talk, to dispute. It's as if you were student debaters. You warm to it; Rich stands and takes it patiently, while you score points off him. But please note that Southwell is edging away. What doesn't he want to hear? When you're done, Rich will bustle off, and Southwell and the rest will follow more sedately with the books tied up in string. It doesn't seem as if much has happened. Except the books have gone: your first friends, your last. Silence falls. Only your persistent cough in the gathering twilight.

At your trial, Rich will perjure himself, some say. Southwell will claim he was too far off to hear the conversation, but Rich will allege certain treasonable statements. I look at the portrait, I see you looking alive – intent, about to speak. I want to lean into history, put my hand on your dusty sleeve and stop you – before Rich reaches for his pen, with the content of your conversation brimming and swilling in his brain.

Just write it down, Cromwell has told him, bring it to me. Write down anything he says, then we'll see. We can't be sure that Rich's evidence was crucial. There was never any chance that the king wouldn't get his verdict; you've defied him for too long. Still, it makes you angry, when you hear your words come buzzing back in the courtroom, stinging like demon flies. Richard Rich will die in his bed, wealthy, honoured, a serial betrayer. What he does to you, he'll do to Thomas Cromwell when his time comes, and more blame attaches to that: Cromwell was good to him. You're brought down, like most great men, by a man who is your inferior. No one wants it to end in that undignified way – you splashing to the scaffold, your heart's blood diluted by London rainwater.

History is always stranger than we imagine or can imagine. It's never black/white, it's never either/or, it's never 'if a, therefore b'. The chains of causation snap when you breathe on them. Some iron assumptions are cobweb-thin. History is never tidy or shapely. It doesn't have a dramatic arc. It's full of cul-de-sacs and anticlimaxes, cloudy mysteries reshaping themselves. The paper that Rich wrote for Cromwell is still extant. Thanks to Holbein we can see you clear as yesterday, your chain of office still bright, a gleam in your eye. But Richard Rich's paper is readable only under ultraviolet light. Spotted by damp and nibbled by rats, his words are passing away.

Touching Hands with the Lost

2007

This is the year of the return of Orpheus. It is 400 years ago that Monteverdi's opera *Orfeo* was staged in Mantua. It was not quite the first opera, not even the first to tell the story of the demigod musician – but it was the first opera to last. Monteverdi's contemporaries believed that actors in ancient Greece sang their parts, and so the new form was a conscious attempt to recapture what music meant to the ancient world: something that was not merely a skill, a display of virtuosity, but an enchantment, something that spoke to the soul, something deeply and sweetly natural. But when you choose to work with the Orpheus myth, you are even going beyond this: you are searching, in the dark, with your breath and your fingertips, for an art so powerful that, like the art of Orpheus himself, it can suspend or, as it may be, reverse the laws of nature.

The story of Orpheus was old when Ovid told it. In words, in music, in film, successive generations have worked it over, made it their own, every artist or would-be artist finding in it something personal and something new. When Eurydice, the bride of Orpheus, died of snake bite, Orpheus travelled to the underworld and used his skill in music to open the hearts of the gods, who allowed him to take back his beloved. One condition was made: that until they had left the underworld behind, Orpheus must not look at his wife's face. He led her towards the light, then, at the last second, his desire defeated him; he looked back, and with that glimpse Eurydice vanished for ever.

Earlier this year, Opera North's pacy and idiosyncratic anniversary production of *Orfeo* attracted the wrath of some critics, and boos from a few audience members who sought to establish their credentials by showing that Nottingham can be as churlish as Milan. But what did they want? Authenticity? Monteverdi's cast would have been all-male. Tender and funny by turns, the Opera North staging reminded us what a feat we undertake in suspending disbelief, as the furnishing of the court stood in for shady beeches; shepherds in song, overturning a sofa, suggested that Orfeo repose upon this grassy bank. In the underworld, Charon put down his newspaper – what else would death's boatman read? – to sing to Orfeo that he was unimpressed by his plea.

There was a scene in which the inhabitants of the underworld pinned Eurydice to the wall and fastened her there with duct tape, length upon snarling length of it, at first making nothing worse than a sinister ensnaring web. But as the ripping sound went on, minute after minute, into a theatre totally silent, I remembered the killer Fred West embalming the heads of young girls, wrapping them until they could barely breathe, and the sound of the tape tearing became the essence, the very sound of cruelty; and I thought, the dead girl is made a parcel, she is consigned, she is consigned to oblivion.

The Orpheus myth is a story about the power of art, but it is also a myth we play out in our daily lives. Often, when people have been bereaved, their friends warn them to let a year go by before they listen to music, knowing how it can break down the barrier we carefully erect between ourselves and the recently dead, and unleash a flood of pain and regret. But it is hard now to avoid music. In a way that Monteverdi could never have imagined, it is in the air around us, sometimes degraded into an annoying background jangle, sometimes blanked out and ignored, but always capable of catching us unawares, infiltrating our self-protection, and making the dead walk.

Sometimes miracles happen. Last summer a young girl called Natascha Kampusch, who had disappeared as a child of ten, re-emerged into the light as a young woman of eighteen. For eight years she had been held captive by a man called Wolfgang Priklopil. Having watched her for some time on her daily walk to school, he had snatched her from the street and kept her in a bunker that had probably been built as a shelter during the Cold War, a cellar under an ordinary-looking house that was near a busy road and less than fifteen kilometres from her original home in the district of Strasshof, north of Vienna. He had let her out from time to time, and even taken her to the mountains for a day. The neighbours saw her working in the garden, but they were incurious. They assumed she was his girlfriend, they said. You wonder how hard they looked – she was a teenager, he in his mid-forties; they didn't look hard enough to allow any uncomfortable thoughts to arise; they lived in a society defended by a requirement for privacy higher than any garden wall.

Priklopil had convinced Natascha that, if she tried to escape, he would kill her and then kill himself. As he was her only human contact, how could she afford to hate or defy him? When he put her underground, he controlled her light, air, water and food. On the day she escaped, she was cleaning his car and he was momentarily distracted by a phone call. She ran down the street and appealed for help to the first woman she met, but the woman didn't understand her: how would the dead speak? Natascha spoke like a radio announcer, imitating the only female voice she had heard in eight years. She was a waif, weighing less than six and a half stone; the policewoman who was the first official to see her described her as 'white as cheese', an unpoetic but no doubt perfectly exact expression of the effects of the underworld. On that day of her escape, Natascha kept running and took shelter in a house, this time making herself understood. A few hours later, Priklopil committed suicide by lying in the path of a train.

Natascha has been reticent about her ordeal. The story that emerges may be different from the version we have now. It may take her years to come fully back to life, and the story of how she does that will be as interesting as the story of her burial.* If she spoke from her heart, what would she say to her neighbours? Perhaps that they made the most basic error of all: they misidentified the living as the dead. She walked among them, solid and breathing, but they were unable to see her. No doubt they could not help their error. But if Natascha can come back, what else can come back? During

---

* She published the story of her ordeal in 2010: *3096 Days* (Penguin, 2010). Three years later the film version of the book was released.

the Second World War, 20,000 Hungarian Jews were held in a labour camp in Strasshof. No trace of it remains. It's thought that 200 people, who have been wiped out of the town's memory, died there. There are some ghosts who would not be welcome, even in thought form, and these ghosts include the past selves, the former selves of people who were alive in those years and who are alive today, but who have made great efforts to unremember.

When we talk about ghosts, we are speaking in layers of metaphor. We are not usually speaking about wispy bodies in rotting shrouds, but about family secrets, buried impulses, unsolved mysteries, anything that lingers and clings. We are speaking of the sense of loss that sometimes overtakes us, a nostalgia for something that we can't name. There is a way in which the question 'Do you believe in ghosts?' is unnecessary to ask: we all know a few, and they walk at all hours, if only through our memories. Our ancestors are encoded in our genes. Look at your face in the mirror, and one day you will see one of your parents, moving under your own skin; the next day it may be a grandparent who has come to visit. Within you, there are people you have never been able to mourn because you never knew them, people from the distant past; the traces of your animal ancestors still live in your instincts, in your physiology. As products of evolution, we carry all the past inside us; we are walking repositories of the lost.

I have written a memoir called *Giving Up the Ghost*, which is about my own childhood, but also about my ancestors and children who were never born, and about the ghosts we all have in our lives: the ghosts of possibility, the paths we didn't take, and the choices we didn't make, and expectations, which seemed perfectly valid at the time, but which somehow or other weren't fulfilled. I describe ghosts like this: 'They are the rags and tags of everyday life, information you acquire that you don't know what to do with, knowledge that you can't process; they're cards thrown out of your card index, blots on the page.'

As a historical novelist, I'm a great user of card indexes. I like to write about people who really lived, and try to wake them up from their long trance, and make them walk on the page. When you stand on the verge of a new narrative, when you have picked your character, you stretch out your hand in the dark and you don't know who or what will take it. You become profoundly involved in this effort to clothe old bones. The work of mourning is real work, like shovelling corpses, like sifting ashes for diamonds. When someone dies, we exist for years on a thin line, a wire, stretched tight between remembering and forgetting. When something touches that wire and makes it vibrate, that's a ghost. It's a disturbance in our consciousness, in that deep place where we carry the dead, like the unborn, sealed up inside us. You need not believe in life after death to believe in ghosts. The dead exist only because the living let them. They are what we make them.

Nothing illustrates this better than the afterlife of Diana. As the tenth anniversary of her death approaches, she keeps popping back to check on her own publicity campaign. When Diana Spencer married, she instinctively grasped that, even at the close of the twentieth century, a princess was not an ordinary person. Unformed, her early flesh soft and undefined, the princess nicknamed 'squidgy' moved on an archetypal plane: walking beside the virgin bride was the blurred outline of a shadow bride, a shadow princess, someone archaic, someone mythical. Her fabulous clothes and jewels elevated her into a great beauty, the most photographed, the most observed woman in the world, and because she was not an intellectual or analytical woman, she was able to present us with a blank slate and present fate with a blank cheque. To the public she was entirely a figure of fantasy, and she became a fantasy to herself, representing herself in the last years of her short life as someone with healing powers, like a medieval monarch – someone more royal than the family she had married into. If we think on some level that 'they killed her', perhaps this is why. Like a traitor, she tried to out-royal them; like a trainee goddess, elevated on her high heels, she teetered towards the abyss. She said to the whole world, look at the royal bride; then she found herself running, before the cold rapist's eye of a thousand cameras, trying to evade them by driving into the dark.

When Diana went into the underpass, she went there to be reborn. She came out with angel's wings. We should have been less surprised than we were by the public mass mourning. It is a commonplace that, in our society, we deal with death very badly. The Victorians knew how to do it. The black horses and plumes, the black-edged stationery, the jewellery made of jet, the black clothes of full mourning, the lilacs and greys of half-mourning – all these permitted you to give a public signal that you were bereaved, so that people around you treated you with consideration, with respect. But now it's a twenty-minute slot at the crematorium, a half-day off work, a funeral sparsely attended by gormless people standing around in anoraks, shuffling their feet in embarrassment and singing 'My Way'. There is a desire to steer away from what is called 'morbid', a dull sense of yearning towards the routine of a normal day: no sense of defiance in the face of death, no swelling organ chords and no hymn to ask, 'Where is death's sting? Where, grave, thy victory?' Death demands ceremony; at Diana's death, all the nation's bottled sorrow overflowed, all the omitted personal mourning translated into the transpersonal.

We mourned her in the only way we knew how, with teddy bears and doggerel verse and flowers rotting in cellophane; we mourned her with the crude, shared, generic language of the heart. And implicit in the way we have mourned her is the possibility that, like Orpheus, we could defy the laws of nature, that we could reverse time, we could stop it happening. No matter how little you care about royalty, it's impossible not to be agitated by those grainy CCTV images of Diana leaving the Ritz: so real, so close, so present, that you feel you could reach back, take her seat belt, pull it across her body, snap it shut, and rewrite the history of her final hour.

When I began to write, it was my first ambition to write a good historical novel and my second to write a good ghost story, and I didn't then see that these ambitions were allied. Technically, it's possible that the ghost story is the more difficult. If the author leaves events unexplained, the reader feels cheated. But if you explain too much, you explain away. A ghost story always exists on the brink between sense and nonsense, between order and chaos, between the rules of existence we know and the ones we don't know yet. When I was a child, I lived in a haunted house. I was brought up in a family that not only lived among ghosts but also manufactured its own. When I was ten, I lost my father. He didn't die, but went away, and very little but music remained of him. Forty years later, music helped bring him back.

First of all, I used prose. I dusted down a fictional version, in which the narrator says:

> We lived at the top of the village, in a house which I considered to be haunted. My father had disappeared. Perhaps it was his presence, long and pallid, which slid behind the door in sweeps of draught and raised the hackles on the terrier's neck. He had been a clerk; crosswords were his hobby and a little angling: simple card games and a cigarette card collection. He left at ten o'clock one blustery March morning, taking his albums and his tweed overcoat, and leaving all his underwear, which my mother washed and gave to a jumble sale. We didn't miss him much, only the little tunes which he used to play on the piano: over and over, 'Pineapple Rag'.

In real life it didn't happen quite so tidily. When I was about seven, my mother took up with an old lover of hers, and my father faded away, still living in the house but just flitting through, silent as a shadow except for increasingly rare hours when he sat down at the piano. The summer I was eleven, I went with my mother and my brothers and my stepfather to another town, and my name got changed, and I never saw my father again. In the years that followed I learned that any mention of him would cause more trouble than I was equipped to handle.

As I grew older, I was haunted by the thought that, if I passed him in the street, I probably wouldn't recognise him. Also, if he died, I thought my mother would get to hear, but I knew she wouldn't tell me. Perhaps it was after I knew that I wasn't going to have children myself that I thought more about him, but he always lived in some place I couldn't imagine; he inhabited in my mind a halfway house, neither living nor dead, and certainly lost to me. My memoir, published in 2003, was like a message in a bottle. It seemed a long shot that it would find him, but I hoped it might.

Soon after publication I wrote some short plays for Radio 4, for *Woman's Hour*, based on my story collection *Learning to Talk*: about someone like me, with a disappearing father like mine. I tried hard to get the music right. We couldn't use 'Pineapple Rag' – music so easily evokes a whole era that we were afraid that it would take the listener back to the 1920s, not to the 1950s where we wanted them to be. Instead, we opted for jazz and blues from the fifties and sixties, and the producer arranged for a piano in the studio – a suitably battered instrument – and for an actor who would be my father for three days of recording.

Sometime later, I had a letter from a stranger, which brought me news. It appeared that my father had married again; he never had any more children of his own, but became stepfather to a family of six, four of whom were daughters. It was the eldest daughter, a woman of my own age, who now wrote to me. He had died, I learned, in 1997. My new stepsister emailed me a photograph of him. A face not seen for forty years came swimming out of the darkness of the screen. I could see how he had altered, how he had aged, and how features of my brothers' faces, as they had aged, were mixed up in his. Later, when my new stepsister looked out for me the very few things he had left behind, she forwarded to me his army papers, and I saw how my personality was mixed up in his. She gave me a cassette tape, old and scratchy, which she said was a recording of some of his favourite music. It was labelled in the neat sloping capitals that I remember him using to fill in the crossword every evening in the *Manchester Evening News*. There were the song titles, full of loss and regret: 'Canal Street Blues', 'How Long Blues', 'I Don't Know Why', 'Walking Out My Door', and a song named 'Calling 'Em Home'.

I had called him home, I felt: not through telephone directories and tracing agencies, not by any rational means, but through the exercise of as much art as I had at my disposal. I'd used indirection to bring back the dead. For some years I lived in Africa, in Botswana, and people there used to say that to see ghosts you need to look out of the corners of your eyes. If you turn on them a direct gaze, then, like Eurydice, they vanish.

The whole process of creativity is like that. The writer often doesn't know, consciously, what gods she invokes or what myths she's retelling. Orpheus is a figure of all artists, and Eurydice is his inspiration. She is what he goes into the dark to seek. He is the conscious mind, with its mastery of skill and craft, its faculty of ordering, selecting, making rational and persuasive; she is the subconscious mind, driven by disorder, fuelled by obscure desires, brimming with promises that perhaps she won't keep, with promises of revelation, fantasies of empowerment and knowledge. What she offers is fleeting, tenuous, hard to hold. She makes us stand on the brink of the unknown with our hand stretched out into the dark. Mostly, we just touch her fingertips and she vanishes. She is the dream that seems charged with meaning, that vanishes as soon as we try to describe it. She is the unsayable thing we are always trying to say. She is the memory that slips away as you try to grasp it. Just when you've got it, you haven't got it. She won't bear the light of day. She gets to the threshold and she falters. You want her too much, and by wanting her you destroy her. As a writer, as an artist, your effects constantly elude you. You have a glimpse, an inspiration, you write a paragraph and you think it's there, but when you read back, it's not there. Every picture painted, every opera composed, every book that is written, is the ghost of the possibilities that were in the artist's head. Art brings back the dead, but it also makes perpetual mourners of us all. Nothing lasts: that's what Apollo, the father of Orpheus, sings to him in Monteverdi's opera. In Opera North's staging, the god took a handkerchief from his pocket, licked it, and tenderly cleaned his child's tear-stained face.

Though the climate of modern rationalism has a certain bracing and defiant appeal, we banish these old gods at our peril. In times of great happiness or great sorrow, in triumph or catastrophe, we are not governed by rationality, and it is honest to admit it. The gods' nature is curled up within our own, and if we deny them, they come out to torment us, with self-doubt and malignant sadness, and their breath is in the chilly wind we feel blowing out of the darkness. We see their bright faces in our love for our family and friends and country, and their dark faces in war and tribulation, in racism and hate crime. These gods are no role model for living. They have all the faults of the irrational. They are capricious, sometimes stupid, but if we deny and repress them it offers us no advantage; it's better to know their faces than not, and hope that, like Orpheus, we can move fate to pity. It is almost the definition of being human to want what is impossible. We want the child of twenty-two weeks' gestation to live and thrive. We want to live for ever, without infirmity and without the evidence of the destructive march of the years. We want to play games with time. We want to undo death; we love the idea of the soul, but we are incurably addicted to the body, and we want the dead back, or at least we want a ghost to walk.

But perhaps a ghost is not something dead, but something not yet born: not something hidden, but something that we hope is about to be seen. We want to go to the underworld, back into the darkness of our own nature, to bring back some object of impossible beauty: we know it probably won't work, but what matters is that we keep trying. The consolation lies in the attempt itself, the mercy that's granted to the hand that dares to stretch out into the dark: well, we say, I am only human, I've gone to the brink, I have done all that I can. As the last lines of the opera tell us: 'Those who sow in sorrow shall reap the harvest of grace.'

Acknowledgements

Part I

'Blot, Erase, Delete' published in *Index on Censorship*; 'Last Morning in Al Hamra' and 'Dreaming of Pork and Porn' published in *The Spectator*; 'On Grief' published in *A Grief Observed: Readers' Edition*, Faber & Faber. All other pieces published in the *Guardian*.

Part II

All published in *The Spectator*, May 1987–December 1990.

Part III

All published in the *New York Review of Books*, 1998–2013.

Part IV

The Reith Lectures broadcast on BBC Radio 4, June–July 2017. Extract from W. H. Auden, 'As I Walked Out One Evening', copyright © 1938 by W. H. Auden, renewed. Reprinted by permission of Curtis Brown, Ltd. All rights reserved.

Part V

'Bryant Park: A Memoir' published in the *New Yorker*; 'No Passport Required', published in the *Guardian*, is an edited version of the essay 'No Passports or Documents Are Needed: The Writer at Home in Europe', published in *On Modern British Fiction*, edited by Zachary Leader, Oxford University Press; 'Elizabeth Jane Howard', published in the *Guardian*, is an edited version of Hilary Mantel's introduction to *The Long View* by Elizabeth Jane Howard, Picador Classics; 'If the Glance of a Woman Can Sour Cream' published in *My Lord's: A Celebration of the World's Greatest Cricket Ground*, edited by Tim Heald, Collins Willow; 'At First Sniff' published in *Vogue*; 'A Letter to Thomas More, Knight' published in *Holbein's Sir Thomas More* by Hilary Mantel and Xavier F. Salomon, The Frick Collection, New York, in association with D. Giles Limited, London; 'Touching Hands with the Lost' commissioned by Opera North for their 2007 production of Monteverdi's *Orfeo*. All other pieces published in the *Guardian*.

Pictures

Alamy Stock Photo: pages 6 below/PA Images, 7 above left/GL Archive. © BBC Photo Archive/photo Richard Ansett: page 8. Courtesy of the Estate of Hilary Mantel: pages 1, 2, 3, 4, 5 below. Getty Images: page 7 below/ photo John Lamparski/Wireimage. www.johnhaynesphotography.com: page 6 above. © Jim Keenan: page 5 above. Courtesy of George Miles: page 7 centre right.